# WORLDS OF WRITING

# WORLDS OF WRITING
Teaching and Learning in Discourse Communities of Work

*Edited by*
*Carolyn B. Matalene*
University of South Carolina

*Random House/New York*

First Edition
987654321
Copyright © 1989 by Random House, Inc.

All rights reserved under International and Pan-American Copyright Conventions. No part of this book may be reproduced in any form or by any means, electronic or mechanical, including photocopying, without permission in writing from the publisher. All inquiries should be addressed to Random House, Inc., 201 East 50th Street, New York, N.Y. 10022. Published in the United States by Random House, Inc., and simultaneously in Canada by Random House of Canada Limited, Toronto.

**Library of Congress Cataloging-in-Publication Data**

Worlds of writing : teaching and learning in discourse communities of
    work / edited by Carolyn B. Matalene.
        p. cm.
    ISBN 0-394-38295-1
    1. English language—Rhetoric—Study and teaching.   2. English
language—Business English—Study and teaching.   3. English
language—Technical English—Study and teaching.   4. Business
writing—Study and teaching.   5. Technical writing—Study and
teaching.   I. Matalene, Carolyn B.
PE1404.W67   1989
808'.066'07—dc19                                              88-36977
                                                                  CIP

Manufactured in the United States of America
Cover design: Lisa Polenberg

# INTRODUCTION

For several centuries the printed word has been a central fact of our political and economic culture. But as this century, now labeled the information age, draws to a close, the printed word seems about to overwhelm us. Jobs in offices have increased as jobs in production have decreased; and, as the products of our economy have become more technologically complex, more and more writing is required to explain them. Yet, in her article "Toward an Ethnohistory of Writing in American Education," published in 1981, Shirley Brice Heath could reasonably conclude: "At the present time, in spite of heated discussions about the success of schools in teaching writing, there is almost no systematic description of the functions of writing in the society as a whole or in special groups and subcultures . . ." (44). This volume is intended to increase cultural awareness and to provide new information about the nature of writing in a number of the discourse communities central to our economic life.

As writing teachers are increasingly realizing, to be a white-collar worker today very likely means being a writer. The *Wall Street Journal* reports that office workers now spend up to 70 percent of their time dealing with written material. The documentation required to get a single new drug approved by the Federal Drug Administration, for example, runs to about 100,000 pages. And the paperwork required to run a medium-sized warship adds 20 tons to its weight. Thus—whether it be law, accounting, engineering, or management—again and again the actual profession we are preparing students to enter is the profession of writing.

Since Heath's call to action, researchers—among them Lee Odell and Dixie Goswami—have begun asking questions about writing outside the academy. The book they edited, *Writing in Nonacademic Settings*, presents new information about writers on the job, the quantity of writing they do, and the complexity of the tasks they face. The contributors to that volume—and other researchers in a variety of fields—have helped us get beyond exclusively text-based notions of writing.

Focusing primarily on the words on the page, a practice still common in school settings, cannot yield adequate explanations of the processes or the products of working writers. Nor can a text-based definition of writing provide an appropriate theoretical ground for preparing our students to become professionals. In fact, the more we study and learn about writing on the job, the more we realize that what finally appears on paper—as a memo, proposal, or report—is but the end result of a complex set of negotiations between the writer and the writer's real and imagined audiences; between the writer and the text's stated and unstated purposes; between the writer and the beliefs, practices, and constraints of the community.

In many professional contexts, however, the "writer" is not one person but a group. And when writers work together, the act of writing often serves important functions for the group well beyond that of producing a text. Working together to create a document may have more to do with reaching consensus, setting goals, inventing solutions, revising priorities, or establishing control than the finished pages reveal. But however a particular text is written, its readers bring to it a set of requirements and expectations about structure, intent, and language as complex as those the writer or writers negotiated. Thus, both writer and reader in any specific professional context belong to what Heath calls a special group or subculture, what composition specialists—borrowing from the linguists' notion of speech community—call a discourse community.

Our social world—a world of language—is made up of innumerable discourse communities. According to Patricia Bizzell's model, for example, the individual with innate capacities to learn language is born into a native discourse community and then enters the discourse community of school (219). Here, as Heath has shown in *Ways with Words*, the uses of language may be similar to or radically different from those of the child's native language community; and the children who cannot gain admission to this new community—who cannot master school literacy—fail.

Traditionally, English teachers from as early as the fifth grade—when the research paper is usually introduced—have focused their attention on the students who do not fail and have concentrated almost exclusively on preparing these students for the discourse community of intellectual life or at least of higher education: that is, academia. Students who succeed at school literacy and go on to college continue to be instructed in reading and writing according to the norms of academic discourse. Only journalism schools and business and technical writing courses have defined different or more specifically work-oriented discourse communities and tried to prepare students for them.

When students leave school or college, each enters a new discourse community, that of work. And each different "world of work" constitutes its own discourse community with its own purposes, audiences, and genres. The FDA, for example, produces documents vastly different from those of the Air Force; lawyers write in genres different from those of accountants. But discourse communities also overlap; the FDA and the Air Force, the lawyers and the accountants, may sometimes write to the same audience, and all writers must understand and depend upon conventions of discourse common to all readers.

Reports from many worlds of work, whether large or small, regularly complain that their new members do not understand these common conventions and cannot adapt to the specialized conventions of the discourse community they have entered. That is one reason writing teachers, especially those committed to reintroducing the rhetorical tradition to undergraduate education, have become more and more interested in the nature of writing on the job. Thus, in the last decade, a number of writing teachers have become writing consultants. The Association of Professional Writing Consultants, founded in 1982, meets annually at the Conference on College Composition and Communication to share ideas and practices; it has experienced dramatic increases in attendance and now has well over 200 members.

As writing teachers, some of our motives for teaching writing outside the academy are personal. Although we understand and sympathize with the problems freshmen encounter in writing research papers, we burn out offering the same solutions again and again. The problems of writers on the job, however, present us with fascinating complexity—new and complicated rhetorical exigencies. And they are real.

Some of our motives as consultants are intellectual. For teachers who have spent their working lives in colleges and universities, entering the world of goods and services is a journey to a new land, an experience as educational as a year abroad. Many of us began consulting because someone in the community called and asked for help. And as we tried to offer help, we realized how little we knew, how much we needed to learn, and, often, how irrelevant if not erroneous our in-school precepts sounded. Furthermore, when we returned to our classrooms, existentially aware of the myriad contexts of writing, we did so with new confidence and with immeasurably increased authority.

Moving between the classroom and the workplace has also heightened our awareness of the politics inherent in the curriculum. Thus, some of our motives are inevitably political. Many of us believe that if English departments are to continue to call themselves English departments (as opposed to literature departments), they must study all uses of language, not just literary uses, offering direction and insight to all users of English, not just to freshmen and poets and literary critics but also to underwriters, managers, and agency heads. Only if English departments genuinely dedicate themselves to literacy, responding to obvious social needs, providing language users with assistance as well as authority, will they continue to merit public support.

The connections writing teachers establish between English departments and the world of work are valuable to us as we teach our classes, and sometimes they even earn us extra money. But more importantly, they provide the bridge that enables the general public to understand and value the humanities through rhetoric. The rhetorical theories that writing teachers present to writers on the job—when they are relevant and effective—reveal to the educated public what the serious study of language involves and why it matters. Perhaps also, the work we do redresses the imbalance imposed by literary studies. For nearly a century, English departments have, as Robert Scholes puts it, "bracketed out" almost all nonliterary discourse from serious academic inquiry. That position is no longer tenable. Scholes says "By progressive reductions we sought a tidy corner in which to intepret and reinterpret our major works, and now we find the whole world of textuality invading our corner through a gap we are unable to close" (40). Of course, writing teachers have always believed that the texts produced in the world of practical affairs are worthy of both study and production; we invite the "invasion" of such texts—and wonder why contemporary literary theorists should be credited with discovering them.

The contributors to this volume, believing the time has come for English departments to "bracket in" some of the writing that accomplishes the world's work, offer here the results of their learning. They are all specialists in composition and most hold academic appointments in departments of English, but they also have extensive experience in helping professional writers on the job in a wide variety of discourse communities. Thus, they are in a unique position to help us become better at what we do, to provide information about writing in the world of work, and to help us design more effective writing programs.

Their articles are presented here in eight sections. Part One comprises comparative studies of academic and nonacademic writing, followed, in Part Two, by two articles arguing for the integration of these worlds in undergraduate writing instruction. Part Three presents research studies of the role of writing in different writing cultures: corporations, trade associations, and the military. Part Four focuses on writing constraints unique to discourse communities in business and industry. In Parts Five through Eight, consultants report on their work in four specific discourse communities: journalism, finance, computer technology, and the law.

In Part One, Kristin Woolever analyzes how very differently a literary academic and a technical writer structure the same information; what different goals they have, how differently they conceptualize their tasks. Stephen Doheny-Farina, in an ethnographic study of one writer in two very different settings, comes to important conclusions about the importance of the "institutional role" the writer must adopt in school or on the job. His analysis underscores a recurrent theme of *Worlds of Writing:* the role of writers in preserving institutional traditions and, conversely, in changing them. Mary Ann Eiler, whose research involves three very different discourse communities, explores the dramatic effects of genre on writers' processes. William E. Rivers presents survey research from writers who have moved from literary studies and academic discourse to technical writing and technical discourse; they reflect on what they had to learn and unlearn as well as on how they felt about adopting a new ethos.

Research in individual discourse communities—whether textual, ethnographic, or survey-based—may seem to suggest ever more numerous and more specialized writing courses for different career tracks. But in Part Two Janette Lewis and Theresa Enos, enunciating another recurrent theme of the articles in this volume, draw the opposite conclusion. Lewis argues that only writing courses rich in rhetorical theory based on the liberal arts can equip students with the adaptive capabilities required of them in the twentieth century. Enos presents a plan for a writing course that integrates theories of rhetoric and the literature of the humanities with the requirements, both human and formal, of technology.

The articles in Part Three analyze what happens when writers enter the discourse community of the corporation, the trade association, or the military. They soon learn, these researchers explain, that handbook standards of "correctness" are inadequate guides or judges for the texts they must produce. They have entered a new country and must learn a new culture and their role in it. Like immigrants, they need to master a new language and the rules for using it successfully. How writers are socialized into the culture of a corporation is the subject of Jean A. Lutz's research. Elisabeth M. Alford offers a case study of a trade association and analyzes its reliance on documents; she follows two new members as they learn how to produce appropriate texts and how to use these texts to achieve consensus among the conflicting aims of constituents. Both Alford and Lutz emphasize how writers effect change in organizations and associations. Lee Clark Johns, a full-time writing consultant, and Nancy G. Wilds, a writing teacher at the Army Staff College, examine the conservatism of large and complex discourse communities and the tenacious grip of established genres, however unwieldy and inefficient they might have become.

In contrast, the studies in Part Four reveal that the competition of the marketplace often inspires radical innovation. Muriel Zimmerman and Hugh Marsh present a case study of one industry's attempt to institutionalize a new process for proposal writing. Their account underscores the importance of writing in industry and confirms many of the findings of other researchers as well: the complexity of rhetorical tasks faced by writers on the job, the pressure to produce effective documents quickly, the practice of collaboration, the inappropriateness of pride of authorship. The conclusions they draw about the gap between academic writing instruction and the demands made on writers at work are especially pointed. They suggest radically new directions for undergraduate writing courses.

That writers in industrial contexts are always responding to a complex set of restraints—the nature of the industry, the location of the organization, the tradition of decision making—is the subject of J. C. Mathes's article. He brings together organization and communication theory to analyze the variables affecting written communication in some specific industries. Janis Forman's study of M.B.A. students learning to write strategic reports provides further evidence of the sophisticated knowledge required of writers if they would produce successful texts for the discourse community of management.

Some worlds of writing exist to meet the information needs of large audiences. These discourse communities, subject to unique constraints, naturally develop their own methods of production. In Part Five, Donald M. Murray introduces writing teachers to the world of print journalism—its aims and methods—and suggests ways in which their knowledge can help journalists. And in my own article I analyze the ethos of the newsroom and its effect on writers and writing. More communication as well as some mutual borrowing between these two discourse communities, I believe, might benefit both.

Another world of writing of central importance to our culture is the world of finance, examined in Part Six; it differs, writing consultants have discovered, not just by virtue of its emphasis on numbers. Dan Dieterich, a consultant to C.P.A.'s, explains how important it is to know one's audience when one is consulting in a specialized discourse community. Applying the Myers-Briggs indicator to work settings, George H. Jensen argues that we must acknowledge the reality of power in the functioning of discourse communities, and he traces its manifestations through personality types. Aletha Hendrickson analyzes the rhetoric of standard financial reports, explains how C.P.A.'s try to control the responses to their texts, and shows that even the most carefully constructed ethos can yield unexpected results.

A radically new discourse community, the world of computers, is the subject of articles by Edward Gold and Philip Rubens in Part Seven. Gold suggests ways in which writers can—and can't—bridge the gap between software developers and software users. And Rubens analyzes the multiple demands made on writers and readers by the new medium of electronic text.

The final group of articles, Part Eight, is devoted to writing in the world of law. Teresa Godwin Phelps emphasizes the centrality of texts—and their intertextuality—in the legal profession as she outlines the basic genres and functions of legal writing. Like other contributors, she concludes by urging us to pay greater attention to rhetorical instruction for our students. Both Phelps and John Warnock comment upon the inadequacy of writing as taught in law schools: the text-based formalism of law school writing as preparation for the rhetorical realities of writing in the practice of law. In considering the lawyer as writer, Warnock questions the whole notion of a discourse community—or at least superficial understandings of discourse conventions—and focuses instead on the role of the writer in making and in remaking culture. James C. Raymond, in the concluding essay, discusses the limits of theory and offers a useful metaphor for writing teachers and consultants, rhetoric as *bricolage*—the "fix-it technology"—or "the practice of simultaneously exploiting and resisting generalizations," lest we become too certain of our theories or too committed to our practices.

From these twenty-three articles, a number of common themes emerge. Perhaps the most important, the one that each writer seems to enunciate in concluding, is the call for writing instruction genuinely grounded in rhetorical theory. Such approaches might include rhetorical theory as a subject of study or rhetorical analysis as a practice, but, however conducted, would be directed toward making student writers fully aware of the complexities of the rhetorical situation, the political realities of exigencies and purposes, the tensions created by multiple audiences, the textual needs of readers, and the constraints imposed by cultural contexts. Only then will our graduates have what John Warnock calls "rhetorical imagination"; only then will they be adequately sensitive to time, place, audience, and purpose and thus capable of producing genuinely effective documents.

Because the functions of writing in our culture are not simple, writing instruction based on simple maxims and ossified formats cannot fulfill our students' needs. Asking them to fill up textbook forms—whether good news/bad news letters, inverted pyramids, or one-page memos—can only leave them unequipped for the complexities of the rhetorical tasks they will face. In fact, writing instruction that focuses on outmoded prescriptions condemns our students to being technicians, imitating the documents of the past, rather than scientists, analyzing, constructing, controlling, and shaping the future.

As these researchers reveal, writing in the world of work is not simple, for its

## Introduction · xi

function is seldom primarily or solely to convey information. Rather, writing in the world of work is a powerful medium—though often a transparent one—that fulfills a number of essential social functions. As a collaborative enterprise, for example, writing can provide a group with a way of discovering its purposes, a way of organizing thoughts and energies and directing them toward goals. To assign a writing task can mean assigning power; to complete the task can mean wielding power. Written documents are powerful instruments for conserving institutional traditions; they are also the medium of negotiation for effecting change. Organizations commonly use the processes of writing to hold themselves together; they use the products of writing to inspire the adherence of their audiences. The texts produced by writers in the world of work, then, are not only words and sentences, ideas and information, but also acts of discovery, negotiation, compromise, commitment, creation, persuasion, and control.

As writing teachers, few of us believe that we are conveying an adequate understanding of the difficult rhetorical tasks awaiting our student writers or that we are effectively preparing them to succeed as writers on the job. The courses we need, these teachers seem to be suggesting, are courses in what Elizabeth Tebeaux calls *pragmatic* writing—courses that emphasize common rhetorical principles but also analyze the applications of theory in specific discourse communities and test the adaptation of communication to varying audiences (423–425). Pragmatic writing courses are largely waiting to be designed, just as the textbooks to teach them are largely waiting to be written. Such courses and such texts will enable us to reclaim the rhetorical tradition for inclusion in the undergraduate curriculum. They will also require that we radically redefine what we mean by writing. No longer can writing be defined only—perhaps even primarily—as the action of one individual working privately to create a finished document; rather, it must also be understood as a collective, social activity by which texts are produced and transformed, knowledge is constructed and disseminated, communities are created and maintained, audiences are identified and persuaded.

This volume is part of a growing effort to pay serious attention to the vast amount of writing in our culture and to the rich variety of contexts from which it arises. We need to learn much more about that writing, about the different processes used to produce it, about the different standards used to judge it, about the different functions it fulfills. And most emphatically, we need to examine our own writing programs in light of what we learn.

Composition teachers, both in the academy and in the workplace, are known for their willingness to share their expertise; that spirit of collaboration, of course, made this volume possible. And I wish to thank all of my contributors for stopping their work and presenting their insights. I also wish to thank Steven Pensinger for his commitment to the field of composition and rhetoric and his willingness to commit resources to its development. David Morris and Fred Burns offered valuable editorial assistance.

Carolyn B. Matalene
*Columbia, South Carolina*

## Works Cited

Bizzell, Patricia. "Cognition, Convention and Certainty: What We Need to Know about Writing." *Pre/Text* 3(1982):213–243.

Heath, Shirley Brice. "Toward an Ethnohistory of Writing in American Education." *Writing: The Nature, Development, and Teaching of Written Communication.* Variation in Writing: Functional and Linguistic-Cultural Differences, vol. 1. Ed. Marcia Farr Whiteman. Hillsdale, N.J.: Lawrence Erlbaum, 1981.

———. *Ways with Words.* Cambridge, England: Cambridge University Press, 1983.

Odell, Lee, and Dixie Goswami, eds. *Writing in Nonacademic Settings.* New York: Guilford, 1985.

Scholes, Robert. "Some Problems in Current Graduate Programs in English." *Profession 87* MLA: 40–42.

Tebeaux, Elizabeth. "Redesigning Professional Writing Courses to Meet the Communication Needs of Writers in Business and Industry." *College Composition and Communication* 36(1985):419–428.

# CONTENTS

Introduction   v

PART ONE   COMPARING WORLDS: ACADEMIC AND
NONACADEMIC WRITERS AND WRITING   1

Coming to Terms with Different Standards of Excellence for Written
Communication   *Kristin R. Woolever*   3
A Case Study of One Adult Writing in Academic and Nonacademic
Discourse Communities   *Stephen Doheny-Farina*   17
Process and Genre   *Mary Ann Eiler*   43
From the Garret to the Fishbowl: Thoughts on the Transition
from Literary to Technical Writing   *William E. Rivers*
64

PART TWO   INTEGRATING WORLDS: ACADEMIC
INSTRUCTION FOR NONACADEMIC WORK
81

Adaptation: Business Writing as Catalyst in a Liberal Arts Curriculum
*Janette S. Lewis*   83
Rhetoric and the Discourse of Technology   *Theresa Enos*   93

PART THREE   UNDERSTANDING CULTURES: WRITERS AS
AGENTS OF CONSERVATION AND CHANGE
111

Writers in Organizations and How They Learn the Image: Theory,
Research, and Implications   *Jean Ann Lutz*   113
The Text and the Trade Association: A Story of Documents at Work
*Elisabeth M. Alford*   136
The File Cabinet Has a Sex Life: Insights of a Professional Writing
Consultant   *Lee Clark Johns*   153

Writing in the Military: A Different Mission   *Nancy G. Wilds*   188

## PART FOUR   WRITING IN THE WORLD OF INDUSTRY   201

Storyboarding an Industrial Proposal: A Case Study of Teaching and Producing Writing   *Muriel Zimmerman and Hugh Marsh*   203

Written Communication: The Industrial Context   *J. C. Mathes*   222

The Discourse Communities and Group Writing Practices of Management Students   *Janis Forman*   247

## PART FIVE   WRITING IN THE WORLD OF JOURNALISM   255

Don't Profess: Coach   *Donald M. Murray*   257

A Writing Teacher in the Newsroom   *Carolyn B. Matalene*   264

## PART SIX   WRITING IN THE WORLD OF FINANCE   281

Teaching Writing to C.P.A.'s—Or Anyone Else for That Matter   *Dan Dieterich*   283

Consulting with "Discursive Regimes": Using Personality Theory to Analyze and Intervene in Business Communities   *George H. Jensen*   291

How to Appear Reliable Without Being Liable: C.P.A. Writing in Its Rhetorical Context   *Aletha S. Hendrickson*   302

## PART SEVEN   WRITING IN THE WORLD OF COMPUTERS   333

Bridging the Gap: In Which the Author, an English Major, Recounts His Travels in the Land of the Techies   *Edward Gold*   335

Writing for an On Line Age: The Influence of Electronic Text on Writing   *Philip Rubens*   343

PART EIGHT  WRITING IN THE WORLD OF LAW  361

In the Law the Text Is King   *Teresa Godwin Phelps*   363
To English Professors: On What to Do with a Lawyer
    *John Warnock*   375
Rhetoric and Bricolage: Theory and Its Limits in Legal and Other
    Sorts of Discourse   *James C. Raymond*   388

# PART ONE

# COMPARING WORLDS: ACADEMIC AND NONACADEMIC WRITERS AND WRITING

# COMING TO TERMS WITH DIFFERENT STANDARDS OF EXCELLENCE FOR WRITTEN COMMUNICATION

*Kristin R. Woolever*
Northeastern University

*Kristin R. Woolever coordinates the graduate and undergraduate programs in technical and professional writing at Northeastern University in Boston. She also directs Northeastern's School of Law writing program. In 1987, Professor Woolever published a book on legal writing,* Untangling the Law: Strategies for Legal Writers *(Wadsworth), and she is putting the finishing touches on two new books,* Advanced Writing *(Wadsworth) and* Writing for the Computer Industry *(Prentice-Hall). In addition, she serves as a writing consultant for business, industry, and law firms throughout New England.*

Recent research into the communication process has created a new phrase that raises serious questions for anyone concerned with writing. With the publication of Dixie Goswami and Lee Odell's book *Writing in Nonacademic Settings*, it has become popular to label writing for the professions as "nonacademic," thus emphasizing the gap between academe and industry. While Goswami and Odell coined the term to describe the writing environment rather than the type of writing, their book ultimately suggests that the process of writing in the work world is different from the composing process used in freshman composition. The discourse community defines the writing process to a greater extent than many composition specialists have realized.

Further concerns about writing in varied contexts surface in Susan Peck MacDonald's recent article, "Problem Definition in Academic Writing," in *College English*. According to MacDonald, "discipline-specific features [of writing] have ramifications at all levels. . . . and success in understanding these internal axiomatics . . . is crucial to successful writing in any field"(315). MacDonald explores this principle within academic writing and finds, not surprisingly, that even in the academic community, different "rules" for writing apply in the sciences and social sciences than in the humanities. Writing-across-the-curriculum programs attempt to address this problem in many colleges and universities, but even these programs often fail to recognize that most of their students will move beyond the university to write in nonacademic settings.

What does all this mean for those of us who teach writing? It should make us reevaluate our methods in light of these central questions. If business and technical writing are "nonacademic," what characterizes "academic" writing? And if academe has its own discourse community, what ramifications does this have for college composition teachers whose classes are populated with preprofessional students?

Communicating well in any discourse community requires techniques appropriate for that specific context. Writing in the specialized world of academe is no exception—there are specific dos and don'ts for academic writers, just as there are special "rules" for legal writers, medical writers, business writers, and so forth. But too many recent graduates now working in industry suggest that their college writing classes missed the mark in teaching them how to write for the professional world, and some say that they have had to unlearn techniques they were praised for in undergraduate composition courses.

An immediate response to such complaints might be that the disgruntled writers did not learn how to apply the writing techniques they practiced in college. Perhaps these former undergraduates need to be spoon-fed the appropriate writing specifications for each new context. But the problem occurs too often. The gap between industry and academe is widening, especially in the area of writing instruction. Now that more and more writing specialists recognize the difference between academic and nonacademic writing, it is time to build some bridges.

Using specific examples from both academe and industry, this two-part article focuses on these central issues:

1. What are the major differences between college expository writing and nonacademic writing?
2. How can the university and the business world learn to respect the inherent differences in discourse communities and form a more productive partnership in teaching effective writing skills?

## ACADEMIC VERSUS NONACADEMIC WRITING

To focus the major differences between academic and nonacademic writing, this section begins with two examples. Both present the same information to the same audience, but one was written by a literature specialist and the other by a technical writer. In this first set of examples, note how the authors' ingrained writing techniques and basic assumptions about what the prose should do reflect their disciplines, even though the subject is exactly the same and even though this kind of writing is outside of the discourse each writer usually composes. The purpose of the writing assignment is to introduce to the faculty the new merit evaluation procedures recently determined by committee.

## Example 1

Despite its charge to revise and clarify the present document, the committee recommends the scrapping of that document and its replacement by a new one. We do this for a variety of reasons. The two most important ones are these: (1) any revision responding to criticisms of the present document by one or more department members tends to exacerbate problems raised by one or more other department members, and (2) the current system has evolved in such a way as to increasingly reward ordinary or normal faculty activity rather than extraordinary, that is, truly meritorious, activity. (This latter problem is best explained by the implicit inconsistency of the university's salary raise "system." We are told that all salary decisions are to be based on merit, yet "must" also find a way to reward normal activity as a way of providing deserved raises for all department members.)

In offering the following system we make four assumptions. Our first assumption is that we must use a single pool of money for two less than fully compatible purposes: one, to reward adequate performance of faculty duties with appropriate cost-of-living and/or longevity raises, and two, to reward meritorious achievement with significant salary increment. Our second assumption is that adequate performance of faculty duties involves three things: effective communication to students of the current state of knowledge in the field, contribution to the state of knowledge in the field through research and publication, and service: service to the university through participation in department, college, and/or university governance, and/or service to the profession through participation in scholarly organizations, in the organization of conferences, the work of editorial boards, and the like. Our third assumption is that only work beyond these normal activities should be considered meritorious (although for purposes of satisfying the university's demand that all salary increases be based on considerations of merit, we'll have to fudge the language here so that rewards for adequate performance of faculty duties are defined as merit, and rewards for exceptional performance of those duties are defined as special merit). Our fourth assumption is that the merit committee will have to take on the difficult task of making qualitative as well as quantitative evaluations.

Given these assumptions, we recommend the following document.

## Example 2

Among the options open to the Ad Hoc Merit Review Committee, these three were the most practical:

- Maintain the present document as it stands.
- Revise and clarify the present document.
- Construct a new, replacement document.

The Committee discussed each approach, ruling out the first two. Our decision was based on these main reasons. As the current system evolved through numerous changes, its application now rewards normal faculty activity rather than extraordinary, meritorious work. Also, we felt that revisions to the present document could only exacerbate the problems that now exist.

In constructing a new merit document, we made four assumptions:

- We must, as a practical matter, use one pool from the university to allocate both salary increases based on adequate performance, and to reward meritorious achievement.
- Adequate faculty performance, defined in the Faculty Handbook, involves teaching, scholarship, and service.
- Only work beyond normal activities should be considered meritorious.
- The Merit Committee's evaluations will be qualitative as well as quantitative.

For these reasons, and with these assumptions in mind, we suggest the following document.

As you can readily see, the two documents differ greatly. Some of the differences are obvious, but it is important to look beyond the obvious characteristics of each document to see the underlying "rules" that govern each. Consider first the obvious differences.

In the first version, the writer assumes that the audience will read the prose regardless of its design on the page. The paragraphs are long and densely packed with prose; few people would read it unless they had to, although the bulk of the prose gives it a visible substance. Further, the author has decided to establish a rapport with the readers by including in parentheses many of the behind-the-scenes strategies and opinions the committee used in preparing the final document. The overall organization of this version is deductive—in other words, the main point comes first, followed by the explanations. And these explanations follow in a logical pattern, from the two numbered reasons set out in the first paragraph to the four assumptions given in the second paragraph.

The technical writing specialist pays much more attention to the document's design on the page because he assumes that his audience will not read it otherwise. As in the other example, the organization here is also deductive, first establishing the context before presenting detailed information. The paragraphs are short and the important points appear in bulleted lists, drawing the reader's eye to that material. In this version, the writer purposely leaves out behind-the-scenes strategies because he has decided the audience does not really need to know that information and it only clutters the page. As a result, the prose is clear but has a sterile quality, despite the use of the friendly personal pronoun "we."

Behind these surface characteristics lie the real differences between the two examples. Both writers are following the unwritten rules of their discourse communities. The first version has a definite voice in the places where the writer takes the audience into confidence by using quotations around the words "system" and "must," as well as his use of the informal expressions "scrapping the document," "fudge the language," and the contraction "we'll." This collegial tone makes the reader respond as much to the writer's view of the information as to the information itself.

That is one of the key differences between these two versions: the first expresses as much about the writer as it does about the subject, while the second effaces the writer's personality almost entirely, focusing instead on the information. In this politically sensitive rhetorical situation, it is difficult to determine which example works best. There are flaws in both, as noted, and the ideal version is probably a document somewhere between the two. The former has a self-conscious voice intricately interwoven into the text, while the latter conveys basic information as efficiently as possible.

Note, too, the differences in structure between the two examples. The literary scholar is more comfortable writing in blocks of prose composed of sentences that structurally interweave through their use of conditional clauses and phrases. For instance, the sentence, "Our third assumption is that only work beyond these normal activities should be considered meritorious (although for purposes of satisfying the university's demand that all salary increases be based on considerations of merit, we'll have to fudge the language here so that rewards for adequate performance of faculty duties are defined as merit, and rewards for exceptional performance of those duties are defined as special merit)," contains numerous conditional clauses and phrases. Such a structure makes visible the writer's own interpretation processes, thus encouraging the reader to interpret as well. The explanatory phrases and the other uses of emotionally charged language ("truly meritorious activity," "implicit inconsistency," "two less than fully compatible purposes," and so forth) invite an emotional response. That makes sense from the point of view of a writer who writes primarily for a community of scholars holding interpretation of text as an essential right.

On the other hand, the technical writer goes to the other extreme. He is used to writing for people who do not want to spend any time interpreting the text but want to get the information necessary to take some sort of action. Usually, the audiences for technical documents have as priority the step beyond the written text, not the engagement with the prose itself. In this example, the structure reflects these priorities. There are virtually no emotionally charged words, no conditional or interpretive clauses, and no long blocks of text requiring the reader to put all else aside and concentrate on the document.

Even the opening lines of each example reflect these basic differences. "Despite its charge to revise and clarify, the committee recommends . . ." as opposed to "Among the options open to the Ad Hoc Merit Review Committee, these three were the most practical. . . ." The former obviously invites emotional engagement because it immediately suggests that the committee has taken an interpretive stance. The latter downplays the judgmental quality of the committee by simply stating as fact that three options were the most practical. In this last example, the judgment and interpretation have already been done; the reader bears no responsibility for it. In the first example, however, the reader is invited to take some responsibility.

In other words, example 1 depends more on the "personality" of the text. The writer, used to engaging in scholarly discourse, invites the readers' emotional and intellectual engagement with the facts, hoping that they will ultimately interpret the material as he does. On the other hand, the technical writer leaves no room for interpretation. "Just the facts, ma'am." As a reader, you have to work harder with the first example than you do with the second; you are more of a participant in example 1 because your invited response to the text affects its meaning. It is doubtful that example 2 can "mean" much more than the facts denote, nor are you invited to interpret them in any other way. Example 1 is discursive; example 2 descriptive.

But one set of examples is not sufficient evidence to support a case, especially since these illustrations are not true samples of either academic or nonacademic writing. Before drawing any conclusions pertinent to undergraduate writing instruction, consider a few more examples of nonfiction writing specifically from academic and nonacademic discourse. The same differences as noted in the previous set appear here, and even more differences surface. In fact, it is hard to compare the samples in any way except as they adhere to the standards of proper grammar and punctuation. Beyond basic grammar, the standards for the prose are totally different.

## Example 3

This memorandum, written by an engineer, details the problems his company has had with a subcontractor's work. The problems are so severe that the project has gone way over budget, and the matter is in litigation. Such a sensitive situation requires careful attention to precise language, but also language that makes its point forcefully. As you read this memo, pay special attention to the organization, page design, and wording.

> Three problems with the overhead door installation have prolonged the HOT-CELL chamber start-up period, resulting in exaggerated cost overruns. The delays are clearly the result of XYZ Company's inability to manufacture the door within their own specification, their inadequate seal design, and their slow response to our request for assistance. The three major problems are as follows:
>
> 1. The wall panels did not fit together at the joints.
> 2. The overhead door seals supplied by XYZ Company leaked.
> 3. The door motor wiring diagrams were incorrect.
>
> **POORLY FITTING WALL PANELS**
> Because the original wall panels on the overhead door did not fit together at the joints, XYZ suggested bowing the face panel as a quick field fix. The XYZ field representative dismissed this as a non-problem, but subsequent discussions with HOT-CELL revealed that the panel bowing was potentially serious. Consequently, the entire HOTCELL unit was disassembled and rebuilt.

#### LEAKING DOOR SEALS

XYZ Company supplied an extruded plastic bulb seal with a self-adhesive base. In addition to not being thick enough to fill the gap between the door and the bowed panels, the adhesive refused to stick to the door. Because XYZ delayed in responding to our urgent requests for assistance, we subcontracted ABC Company to install and test two alternate seals. Financial responsibility for replacing the seals has not been resolved.

#### INCORRECT WIRING DIAGRAMS

Poorly labeled electrical terminals, an incorrectly wired motor, and indecipherable wiring diagrams required our electrical contractor to trace the circuits before connecting the controls. The door limit switches and safety edges are still being debugged, forcing manual maintenance until XYZ provides a safe, reliable design.

XYZ Company failed to honor the assembly timetable, provided inadequate materials, and presently objects to paying ABC Company for the replacement seal. In our view, XYZ is financially liable to ABC. Despite XYZ Company's inability to provide any timely solution to the seal problem, we kept them fully informed of all progress, and they made no objection until we asked them to compensate ABC for the replacement seal.

As is clear, the engineer is angry at the shoddy workmanship and is not about to pay the overbudget expenses. Emotionalism is kept to a minimum because emotions encourage subjective responses, although some of the language used (for example, "forcing manual maintenance") shades the meaning just enough to create an impact while keeping the logical tone. Even in her anger, the writer follows the rules of technical discourse: (1) present the facts in deductive order; (2) write in a denotive fashion, reducing the opportunities for reader interpretation; (3) write in a decisive tone, so that the reader is not invited to help determine the end result; and (4) design the page to increase efficient readability and quick reference.

With few exceptions, these same rules apply to most technical writing. They are certainly apparent in example 2, given earlier, and are not applicable to academic discourse. Although academic writing is a form of problem solving, the rules for expressing the problem, as the next example illustrates, differ from nonacademic discourse, especially in literary interpretation. MacDonald makes an important point in her article on academic writing when she says, "For literary articles I had to go further into the articles themselves to understand the problems defined, and I was less able to construct a simple table to schematize the problems" (319). Because most basic composition is housed in English departments and many literature specialists teach writing, an understanding of the differences in discourse standards is crucial.

The following example from literary critic Northrop Frye's "The Argument of Comedy" illustrates some of the differences between academic—particularly literary—and nonacademic prose. Included here are the first few paragraphs of a long essay on Shakespeare's use of comedy.

## Example 4

> The Greeks produced two kinds of comedy, Old Comedy, represented by the eleven extant plays of Aristophanes, and New Comedy, of which the best known exponent is Menander. About two dozen New Comedies survive in the work of Plautus and Terence. Old Comedy, however, was out of date before Aristophanes himself was dead; and today, when we speak of comedy, we normally think of something that derives from the Menandrine tradition.
>
> New Comedy unfolds from what may be described as a comic Oedipus situation. Its main theme is the successful effort of a young man to outwit an opponent and possess the girl of his choice. The opponent is usually the father (senex), and the psychological descent of the heroine from the mother is also sometimes hinted at. The father frequently wants the same girl, and is cheated out of her by the son, the mother thus becoming the son's ally. The girl is usually a slave or courtesan, and the plot turns on a cognitio or discovery of birth which makes her marriageable. Thus it turns out that she is not under insuperable taboo after all but is an accessible object of desire, so that the plot follows the regular wish-fulfillment pattern. Often the central Oedipus situation is thinly concealed by surrogates or doubles of the main characters, as when the heroine is discovered to be the hero's sister, and has to be married off to his best friend. In Congreve's *Love for Love,* to take a modern instance well within the Menandrine tradition, there are two kinds of Oedipus themes in counterpoint: the hero cheats his father out of the heroine, and his best friend violates the wife of an impotent old man who is the heroine's guardian. Whether this analysis is sound or not, New Comedy is certainly concerned with the maneuvering of a young man towards a young woman, and marriage is the tonic chord on which it ends. The normal comic resolution is the surrender of the senex to the hero, never the reverse. Shakespeare tried to reverse the pattern in *All's Well That Ends Well,* where the king of France forces Bertram to marry Helena, and the critics have not yet stopped making faces over it. [58–59]

If you apply the four rules appropriate for technical writing to Frye's prose, you quickly discover they do not fit. Frye's work is not deductive in its presentation; in fact, his main point is still not apparent after the first two paragraphs. You need to read the whole essay to gradually understand its assertion that, as Frye puts it in his final paragraph,

> We have spoken of New Comedy as Aristotelian, Old Comedy as Platonic and Dante's commedia as Thomist, but it is difficult to suggest a philosophical spokesman for the form of Shakespeare's comedy. For Shakespeare, the subject matter of poetry is not life, or nature, or reality, or revelation, or anything else the philosopher builds on, but poetry itself, a verbal universe. That is one reason why he is both the most elusive and the most substantial of poets.

Frye takes the reader through the discovery process, alluding to his final point but never speaking it until the end when the reader has come to the same conclusion or is at least prepared to understand that conclusion. In that respect, even when the author announces the main point at the beginning of the prose, the development of the ideas is usually inductive in academic writing.

Certainly the second and third "rules" are governed by this lack of clearly deductive order. The writer invites the readers to participate actively in interpreting the material and encourages them to draw conclusions along with the author. It is almost a voyage together through the discovery process, with the author as guide. In the process of the journey, both reader and writer examine the text, the allusions to external texts, and other connotative scenery along the way. By the end of the prose, the readers know the conclusion in an almost personal sense because they have participated in formulating it. They are not objectively removed from it.

Finally, the page design supports this discovery process in that the readers must begin at the beginning and move carefully through the text to the end. It is difficult to jump ahead by way of headings or bulleted lists. It is even more difficult to refer to a specific point in the discussion and have that idea stand on its own as a unit for examination. Without the care of the author/guide, the readers can easily lose their way. But that encourages them to follow carefully and to digress only short distances in thought and pace, keeping to the planned course and arriving at the end with the author.

What does this mean for writers and for those who teach writing? If the rules change for each discourse community, how can we prepare students to write effectively in both academic and nonacademic settings? Based on the preceding discussion, the next section evaluates some of the assignments typical to freshman composition classes and suggests alternatives that better match undergraduate writing instruction and "real world" discourse.

## UNDERGRADUATE WRITING AND BEYOND

Over the last decade, composition theorists have turned their attention to the process rather than the product of writing. In other words, writing and thinking are integrally connected, making the act of writing a discovery process for the writer—a process of defining the ideas while engaging them in writing. Prose models as teaching tools no longer suffice because imitation breeds imitation, not creativity.

Clearly, attention to the composing process is a better way to teach introductory writing. The "Go thou and do likewise" mode of writing instruction should be outdated if writing is viewed as a static process different for everyone who writes. To succeed academically, undergraduates learning to develop critical thinking skills need to pay heed to their own composing processes and heuristics. In college, writing serves primarily as a method of problem solving. Most writing assignments in courses other than composition encourage the students to apply the principles learned in the class to a specific problem. The process of writing about the problem forces students to think critically about the issues and synthesize the material. Following prose models for such problem solving denies students the opportunity for critical thinking. On the other hand, the process approach used in freshman composition teaches students to examine their own thinking methods and enables them to succeed in other academic writing situations.

But we have gone too far in applying the process method to all forms of writing, thereby imposing one set of standards on all writing instruction. If the prose-models method does not work in the classroom because students should not copy others' structures, neither should writing as process be the standard method for teaching writing in all forms of discourse. Its basic premise—that writing is a form of discovery—serves the academic and creative writers well, but it falls short for many who write in the business and technical worlds. As the first part of this discussion illustrates, academic discourse depends on the discovery process and organizes the text to replicate the discovery for the reader. Success is measured by how well the writer draws the reader into the process and convinces the audience that the writer's discovery is valid. But the engineer or the corporate writer follows different rules. Undergraduate composition classes focus only on the composing side of the writing spectrum, leaving untouched the writing tasks for other purposes. As a result, professionals who learned writing in freshman composition classes have to refocus their skills when they sit down to write in the corporate world.

In most undergraduate writing classes, students write to learn about their own identity in the world. As discussed above, the composing process is one whereby writers learn how to express their views of the world around them. In this process, the world informs the writer and the writer informs the world. Understanding the nature of this cognitive process is the focus of most writing classes. Whether the class is based on student work or whether the instructor asks students to complete readings and respond in writing, the point of the class is to have the students explore their own relationships to the material and express those relationships in unique "voices." Common assignments include exercises in self-exploration, responses to external situations, creative "what if . . ." pieces, and the general narrative nonfiction essay. Each of these assignments, as well as others not included in this list, is inner-directed, focusing on the writer's thinking processes and ultimately on the creation of text that engages the reader with this process. In each instance, the writer's voice is paramount; the student's task is to discover that voice and share it with the reader.

As an example, consider this assignment from Walker Gibson's *Seeing and Writing* (36). Note how Gibson asks the students to focus only on thinking processes, not on how to present those thoughts once they are formulated:

> Look carefully at the ink blot [on the book's cover] for several minutes. What do you see there? Write out your interpretation so that your reader can see what you see.
>
> (Among the interpretations others have made of this ink blot are: two statues, two birds pecking food, a flower, a butterfly, two pelicans facing each other.)
>
> Now force yourself to make a different interpretation—a different "reading" of these shapes. Write out your new interpretation as before.

Of the several interpretations now before you—yours and those of the other observers—which one do you think is the best one? As you answer that question, what do you mean by "best"?

As you can see, the student must look at the material, interpret it, express that interpretation, and finally define the nature of the interpretive process. This assignment works wonders in a freshman composition class where students love to talk about themselves and discover their own voices. Although Gibson makes no explicit connection to the rules of academic discourse, the assignment definitely trains students to write in an academic fashion: they discover meaning by exploring relationships and defining value. The process transfers nicely to discourse about history, literature, social thought, and so on. But apply this method to technical and professional writing, and the result is paralysis. Why? Because the process method of writing instruction concentrates on cognition, while technical writing focuses on the next step: action.

The engineer, for example, is paid for her expertise in understanding and solving engineering problems. When she writes on the job, the problem solving is already completed; she needs no heuristic to help her understand the problem or to know what to write about. For her, the writing task is to report the results of what she has already discovered in the field. Further, as illustrated earlier, she must write the report in such a way that it is easy to read and to grasp the main points. She wants her reader to act on the basis of the information she presents, not to respond to her methods of inquiry or her process of evaluation. This is the other end of the writing spectrum—the end neglected in many undergraduate writing classes.

At this nonacademic end of the spectrum, the writer has a set of results and needs to report them to various audiences for various purposes. The basic problems for these writers are issues of organization for emphasis, choices of format for efficient readability, decisions about what to include and what to exclude, and considerations of appropriate tone. These issues are beyond the elementary problems of grammar and syntax, and the attention is on the reader's needs, not the writer's composing methods. In fact, the writer is almost effaced in most technical writing, whether the document is an engineering report or a computer manual. The main point is to get the information to the reader as efficiently as possible and to focus on that reader's response to the document. Will he understand how to work the machine? Will he accept the proposal? Will he revise the specifications?

For example, the following assignment puts into practice many of the skills a technical writer needs to explain a procedure. Unlike Gibson's assignment, this one directs attention to the expression of already formulated material. The relationships the student must think about are not those of writer to abstract ideas, but those of reader to specific procedures. Included is the original version given to the students, followed by one of the student's revisions of the document. Note how the student was able to make the instructions readable by concentrating on the the user's need for step-by-step organization, concise diction, effective page design, and consistent terminology.

## Example 5

### STARTUP PROCEDURE: <u>ORIGINAL</u>

ON CPU

1. Set load unit address 354. (A00119)
2. Press LOAD button.

   Operator will now be given the opportunity to insert or change the date and the time. If the time of the day is altered, remember to press the toggle switch TOD CLK.
   (ABOVE ENTRIES WILL BE DONE ON THE OPERATOR MACHINE (061))
   Completion of IPL can now be done by entering "IPL CMS" and press ENTER.
   Sometimes a normal IPL does not work. In these cases an IMPL should be attempted. Push the gray button on the CPU that is labeled Start Console File. This will load the IOCS onto 01f. Wait a couple of minutes until the message "IOC LOADED AND OPERATIONAL" appears on 01f. Then hit the load button on the CPU. The system should now come up normally. If it does not, then IBM may have to be called.
   When a display panel appears on the Operator Console with autostart options for selected CMS machines, choose machines you wish started and then press ENTER. The selected machines will automatically be logged on.
   From the Operator Console, enter the word "READYN" and press ENTER. The READYN exec will cause all network lines and local control unit addresses to be enabled.

## Example 6

### CPU STARTUP PROCEDURE: <u>REVISION</u>

On the Operator Machine (061):

1. Set load unit to address 354 (A00119).
2. Press LOAD button.
   Now you can insert or change the date and the time.
   Press the toggle switch TOD CLK to change the time.
3. Enter "IPL CMS" and press ENTER to complete the IPL.

---

IF the normal IPL does not work:

1. Implement IMPL by pressing the gray button labeled START CONSOLE FILE. (This loads the IOCS onto 01f.)
2. When the message "IOC LOADED AND OPERATIONAL" appears, press the LOAD button on the CPU.

---

IF the system still does not work, call IBM for help.

---

4. A display panel appears with autostart options. Press "Y" (yes) or "N" (no) for the USERIDS that you want to start. Then press ENTER. The selected machines will automatically be logged on.

5. Enter "READYN" and press ENTER. This causes all network lines and local control unit addresses to be enabled.

By focusing not on the writer's thoughts but on the reader's needs, the student has turned a disorganized unreadable piece of computer documentation into a clear set of instructions. It is obvious that freshman composition helped her to understand the difference between active and passive voice and to know how to revise the sentence structure correctly. But beyond that, few of the lessons learned there apply to this task.

Some might suggest that such a task is simple and that there is little need for instruction in how to write for the professions once students know basic writing. While this example is fairly simple, it illustrates the differences in discourse requirements and the variance in the nature of writers' goals. It takes as much study to learn how to focus on external needs as it does to turn inward and discover the inner voice or to share an interpretative journey through a literary text. The examples given earlier in the discussion indicate this clear split between academic and nonacademic writing. And many of the undergraduates—the majority, in fact—take jobs where they must write daily in nonacademic fashion. Undergraduate writing instruction does these people a disservice if it disinherits nonacademic discourse from its rightful place as part of the writing discipline. The writing community needs to recognize the difference and provide as much instruction in "writing for results" as it already does in "writing to discover."

To do so, we need to pay attention to both ends of the writing spectrum. Since the academic end is generally recognized and taught, it is more important here to focus on the nonacademic aspect of writing. What kinds of issues should writing classes address to meet the needs of the nonacademic writers? The following are five essential topics professional writing classes should address. This is by no means an exhaustive list, but it represents the major issues:

1. Determining the important ideas
2. Organizing for emphasis
3. Creating the appropriate tone
4. Guiding the reader through the prose
5. Designing the page to increase readability

Each of these topics focuses on the reader instead of the writer, thereby assuming that the writer's text must address readers' expectations and needs in varying settings. This means that the student of writing must move beyond the bounds of academic discourse to learn reader-specific techniques for communicating information.

What is needed, then, is a writing curriculum that speaks to the two aspects of our profession. In his first issue as editor of *College Composition and Communication,* Richard C. Gebhardt defines the two truisms in our profession as follows: (1) "writing helps people understand what they write about" and (2) "effective writing communicates to a variety of readers" (19). Over the last decade, specialists in rhetoric and composition have focused on the first of these principles in their attention to the writing process. Only now are we beginning to turn attention to the second goal of any good writer and of any good writing teacher: to move beyond writing as a means of knowing and to communicate what we have learned.

## Works Cited

Frye, Northrop. "The Argument of Comedy." *English Institute Essays* 1948. Ed. D.A. Robertson. New York: Columbia University Press, 1949, 58–73.

Gebhardt, Richard C. "Editor's Note." *College Composition and Communication* 38(1987):19–20.

Gibson, Walker. *Seeing and Writing: Fifteen Exercises in Composing Experience*, 2nd ed. New York: David McKay, 1974.

MacDonald, Susan Peck. "Problem Definition in Academic Writing." *College English* 49(1987):315–329.

# A CASE STUDY OF ONE ADULT WRITING IN ACADEMIC AND NONACADEMIC DISCOURSE COMMUNITIES

*Stephen Doheny-Farina*
Clarkson University

*Stephen Doheny-Farina is an assistant professor of technical communications at Clarkson University in Potsdam, N.Y. He edited the book* Effective Documentation: What We Have Learned from Research, *published by MIT Press. His articles have appeared in the journals* Written Communication, *the* Journal of Technical Writing and Communication, *the* Technical Writing Teacher *and the books* Writing in Nonacademic Settings *and* Text and the Professions. *He is an associate editor of the journal* Technical Communication. *His article "Writing in an Emerging Organization: An Ethnographic Study" won the 1987 NCTE Award for Scientific and Technical Communication as the best article reporting formal research. He received his doctorate in communication and rhetoric in 1984 from Rensselaer Polytechnic Institute.*

The differences between writing in academic and nonacademic discourse communities are being drawn very distinctly these days—and the distinctions are becoming ever clearer with increased research in writing in nonacademic settings (e.g., Odell & Goswami, 1982; Selzer, 1983; Paradis, Dobrin, & Miller, 1985; Odell, 1985; Doheny-Farina, 1986; Freed & Broadhead, 1987). With this growth in research have come useful debates regarding the rhetorical richness of one setting over another (e.g., see Odell, Goswami, & Quick, 1981, and a response by Herrington, 1985; see also Comley & Scholes, 1983, pp. 100–101). One reason for the flurry of activity surrounding writing in nonacademic settings may be that for many years, as Broadhead and Freed suggest, our only concern was the writing done in the academy. But that has clearly changed.

> The existence of a book such as Odell and Goswami's *Writing in Nonacademic Settings* suggests that the profession recognizes discourse communities both within and outside of the academy and that the discourse communities themselves variously condition the writing act in ways worth examining. [p. 156]

Our commitment to these distinctions has manifested itself in the rise of technical and professional writing as a subdiscipline. We have seen the growth of scholarly journals and professional organizations as forums for discussions of theory, research, and practice in nonacademic writing. In addition, we have seen a dramatic increase in the number of college courses and degree programs—from associates to doctorates—in technical and professional writing. Clearly, we have much invested in the distinction between academic and nonacademic discourse.

The title of this case study would seem to indicate that I am prepared to further this distinction—especially when you realize that this study describes and explains two very different types of discourse in two very different discourse communities. Even so, in my final analysis I will try to dispense with this distinction for this particular case. Of course, I suspect that some will read my analysis and conclude that, yes, this case reveals some fundamental characteristic that distinguishes academic from nonacademic discourse communities. I will not make that claim. Instead, I will assume that the two different types of discourse exemplified in this study can operate in either nonacademic or academic discourse communities.

I will assume that the academic and nonacademic discourse communities described in this study are what Perelman (1986) describes as "institutional" discourse communities. In institutions,

> both speaker and hearer exist largely as projections of institutional roles rather than as idiosyncratic individuals. True, an individual can personalize an institutional role, or institutional roles may be performed in quite different ways, but the extent to which a role can be personalized or the number of ways the role can be acted out are always limited by institutional rules and goals. [p. 474]

Thus, while my analysis focuses on a unique individual writing in unique discourse communities, I will argue that in both communities the writer is producing institutionally based prose. That is, I will ultimately argue that it is neither the academic nor nonacademic setting that distinguishes the types of discourse produced but rather the institutional role that the writer plays in each of those settings that fosters different types of discourse. In one role the writer serves to somehow change the discourse community and thus attempts to produce a radical discourse. In the other role, the writer attempts to preserve the discourse community and produces a conservative discourse. I will conclude by suggesting that academic and nonacademic institutions foster both roles.

## THE WRITER: ANNA

At the time of this study Anna was thirty-eight years old, married, and mother of a fourteen-year-old daughter.[1] She and her family lived in a small college town about twenty miles outside a large eastern city. Anna's husband taught philosophy at the private college in the small town where they lived. Anna was enrolled in the state university located twenty miles away in the city. When I began this study, Anna was beginning her final semester before graduating with a bachelor's degree in English. She was enrolled in only one English course: the senior seminar literature course. At the same time she was working part-time as a writer in the public relations department of a regional office of Responsible Childbirth, Inc., a health agency with offices nationwide, which offers birth control, abortion, and reproductive health services. After this study was completed, Anna graduated with honors, receiving an award given by the English department to the top graduating English majors of that year. The BA was her first college degree.

## RESEARCH METHODS

During the five-month-long semester, I collected data through the following methods (for a detailed discussion of the type of methodology employed, see Doheny-Farina & Odell, 1985):

1. *Observations/Field Notes.* At the university, I attended most of the senior seminar class sessions. In addition, I attended two conferences Anna had with the course professor. At Responsible Childbirth, I observed and took field notes during group meetings with Anna and her supervisors.

2. *Discourse-Based Interviews* (Odell, Goswami, Herrington, & Quick, 1983). At the university, I conducted two interviews that were based on Anna's literature course term paper: one with Anna and one with her professor. At Responsible Childbirth, I conducted two interviews that were based on a major report that Anna wrote. One interview was with Anna and one was with one of her supervisors.

3. *Open-Ended Interviews:* I conducted several formal interviews with Anna in which I would follow a line of questioning (e.g., "Tell me about your background. Where are you from originally?") I conducted many informal interviews with Anna, her professor, and her supervisors at Responsible Childbirth.

## LEARNING TO COMMUNICATE IN AN ACADEMIC DISCOURSE COMMUNITY: THE LITERATURE COURSE

Anna was enrolled in the senior seminar taught by Professor Skip Madison. This was the capstone course for the English department's undergraduate honors program. This particular semester the course focused on existentialist literature and the theater of the absurd. The course readings included John Barth's novel *The End of the Road* and plays such as Samuel Beckett's *Waiting for Godot,* Eugene

Ionesco's *Rhinoceros*, Jean-Paul Sartre's *No Exit*, and Harold Pinter's *The Dumbwaiter*. Class sessions were held twice a week in a conference room where eight students and Skip sat around a large table. During some classes Skip lectured. Other class sessions centered on discussions. The course required students to do all of the readings, participate in class sessions, and write a term paper. The term paper was the only writing assignment for the entire course. Early in the semester, Skip told students that the primary function of the course would be to place existentialism and existentialist literature in the context of the "history of ideas."

## RESEARCH QUESTIONS: THE LITERATURE COURSE

Besides announcing that the course paper should incorporate outside readings, Skip never delineated any specific, explicit guidelines for writing the course paper. Before Anna began working on it (midway through the course), I asked her about the requirements for this project. She could not identify anything other than a few perfunctory requirements: use outside readings, follow the MLA style guide, and produce text that is grammatically correct. She emphasized that the rest was up to her discretion. She repeatedly identified the writing of the paper as an act of personal expression.

At the center of this personal expression, Anna developed the concept of "psychological suicide," which would serve as the focus of her paper. In discourse-based interviews conducted after the course was completed, both Skip and Anna characterized the paper's central idea as hers. She owned it because it was her original idea. For example, when asked if a statement that defined psychological suicide could be deleted from the text of the paper, Skip replied that the definition was particularly important: "This is Anna's key definition. As far as I know, this is an original idea and there is no frame of reference for a reader, so it must be defined."

Thus, as I gathered this information during the semester, I developed the following questions:

1. Given the lack of explicitly articulated guidelines, how did Anna know how to write the paper? Specifically, how did she know how to develop and structure her argument?
2. How did she arrive at her "original" idea? How did her interaction with Skip and others enable her to arrive at her original idea?
3. In learning how to develop her paper's argument, how was she learning to play an acceptable institutional role?

The answers to these questions will provide some insight into the ways that Anna learned to communicate in this academic discourse community.

## ANALYSIS: THE LITERATURE COURSE

During the semester, Skip never explicitly discussed any rhetorical strategies that the students might use to produce a course paper. Thus, one answer to the first research question above is that Anna had been learning how to develop and structure literature term papers throughout her tenure as an English major at the university. In this research I cannot explore this possibility, since I cannot reconstruct enough of her previous academic experience. I can, however, explain how she was *implicitly* taught the required rhetorical strategies during Skip's course. In doing so, I will discuss some of the ways that Skip modeled the rhetorical goals and strategies that students needed to adopt in order to communicate within the discourse community. In addition, I will discuss some of the social elements that led to the construction of Anna's original idea. These discussions will show that Skip's senior seminar course was practice in participating in the rhetorical interchange of a community of academic scholars who shared a general interest in and knowledge of existentialist literature.

### *Modeling Rhetorical Goals and Strategies*

At various times during the semester Skip implicitly modeled the way a reasonable argument—an argument he would find acceptable for an academic discourse community—should be developed. When modeling an argument, Skip's apparent but unstated goal was to develop an "original" idea—an idea that furthered, countered, or somehow altered established interpretations.[2] By doing so, Skip could, in effect, lay claim to that idea. The following three examples illustrate some of the ways that a student could develop an argument and an original idea.

1. The original idea could represent an attempt to further an established theory or philosophy. He began by establishing two well-known opposites: the belief that human actions have fixed meanings, and that therefore human ethics are fixed, versus the absurdists' belief that human actions have no meaning, and that therefore it is impossible to judge the ethics of any actions. Given this framework, Skip then explained other theories of ethics and moral responsibility— such as Simone de Beauvoir's "ethics of ambiguity"—that could be explained in terms of the framework of the opposing poles. Finally, Skip used these latter perspectives as a point of departure to launch his own perspective.

2. An original idea could be a new interpretation of historical facts. For example, Skip employed a feminist perspective when interpreting the fact that the vast majority of absurdist drama has been written by men. During one class Skip briefly discussed an absurdist play that was written by a woman. He pointed out that absurdist and existentialist literature had been overwhelmingly dominated by men writers and the play in question was the only one he knew of that was written by a woman. He tried to explain this by proposing an idea that he admitted was undeveloped and speculative. First, he reiterated that absurdist literature evolved out of the notion that rational thought had failed and absurdism was the only

alternative. He then countered this idea by suggesting that women writers may not consider absurdism to be the only alternative to rational thought. "I don't think that womankind buys into the notion that rationality is the only reality."

At that point Anna noted that absurdist literature arose after the world witnessed the horrors of World War II. She speculated that women writers may not have responded to the war as did men writers because, as she said, "war is a man's game." Another female student contrasted an aggressive, territorial male reality with a nurturing female reality. Skip tried to put these speculations into context by citing the large amount of literature by women that focuses on healing, even when the characters are alienated. Skip discussed particular works by women and concluded by saying that "I don't think we will ever see a movement of women writers to produce a body of literature of nihilism." Later in the course this topic came up again and Skip suggested that it could serve as the basis for a paper topic.

3. An original idea could also be a new interpretation of characters and plots. For example, during one class Skip again used a feminist point of view—this time to reinterpret the actions of a literary character that had previously been interpreted from an absurdist or existentialist point of view.

Skip modeled this third way to develop an original idea by expanding upon a comment that Anna made during a class discussion of the actions of the female character of Rennie in John Barth's novel *The End of the Road*—a novel that several students thought exhibited overt sexism. At the end of the novel, Rennie dies from complications that occur while she is having an abortion. Anna suggested that the circumstances surrounding Rennie's abortion seem to indicate that the abortion was an act of suicide. Skip and the class discussed Rennie's actions in light of this suggestion. While he did not discourage the idea, Skip noted that it was probably an unestablished interpretation. He pointed this out by putting the idea in a context. "Our concerns (the abortion as suicide) may not have been the concerns of critics in the time the book was written."

Skip then asked Anna, "If Rennie committed suicide, why did she do so?" Anna replied, "It was an act of being herself—the first thing that she could do to escape being what Joe (Rennie's husband) wanted her to be." Considering this reply, Skip placed the idea in a context that could substantiate the idea: "There is a tradition—a line of thought—that in literature a woman can be liberated but she must pay the price." Skip then cited several works in which women learn, become aware, and then die. The women characters ultimately must suffer, paying the price that the men do not have to pay. Given this tradition, "if we accept Anna's interpretation, then we can place the book in a tradition." That is, Skip implicitly taught that a radically different interpretation could be valid if it could be somehow connected to an established line of thought. Making such connections was the way to structure a successful argument.

Overall, Skip implicitly communicated the following stages in any argument that developed a new idea:

- Examine an established idea or concept.
- Discuss what voices of authority say about that idea/concept.

- Propose and discuss manifestations and/or interpretations of the idea in literature.
- Use some device to extend, counter, or alter an already established idea, such as the three ways to develop an original idea that were discussed above.
- Exemplify the new idea through literature.
- Show connections back to the established idea.

If such a strategy was successful, a writer could claim to have developed an original idea. Thus, Skip communicated a framework that would enable students to develop speculative, possibly radical ideas but to express them in a structured manner—a manner that may be acceptable in a scholarly institution. Raymond (1986) points out that by encouraging radical ideas, literature teachers "risk the possibility that students would become passionately attached to eccentric opinion" (p. 5). But, as Raymond also points out, teachers who enable their students to be speculative within a framework will allow students "to raise questions as radical as those we see raised in the published scholarship we most admire" (p. 5).

In her paper Anna employed Skip's strategies to develop a speculative idea. She attempted to expand a theoretical conception of suicide established by Albert Camus. On the first page of the paper Anna defined the concept of psychological suicide which Skip, as noted earlier, believed was Anna's original idea. She wrote:

> Suicide, as defined by Camus, is either physical or philosophical. This paper examines a third interpretation of suicide—that of psychological suicide. Psychological suicide occurs when the individual suppresses his "authentic self" and replaces it with a person who relies on masks and role playing to give the individual meaning, direction, and purpose in life, thereby denying the absurd.

In separate discourse-based interviews, both Anna and Skip identified this passage as her key definition. When asked if Anna could have deleted that definition, Skip replied that because it was "as far as I know an original idea" the passage was needed because readers would otherwise have no frame of reference to understand her terms. Anna continued to build her frame of reference by distinguishing it from both philosophical suicide ("This is not the same as philosophical suicide, which occurs . . .") and from physical suicide ("Because psychological suicide has much in common with physical suicide, it is necessary to briefly examine the nature of physical suicide . . .").

The key element of Anna's rhetorical structure appears later in the paper when she again defines psychological suicide. In a discourse-based interview, I asked Skip if Anna could have deleted from her paper the bracketed definition at the end of the passage below:

> By expanding Baechler's definition of physical suicide to be "that which denotes all behavior that seeks and finds the solution to an existential problem by making an attempt on the life of the subject through the figurative use of masks and through role playing," we now have a working definition of psychological suicide.

> [Psychological suicide, as previously stated, is achieved when the authentic self is negated or suppressed in favor of a substitute persona.]

Skip replied that, while the entire passage could have been more concise, it was necessary to restate the definition here because it was at this point that Anna was "attaching" her concept to an authority's concept:

> That's the important link. . . . She is grafting onto his definition of physical suicide her definition of psychological suicide to show that what he is referring to as a physical state can also be maintained through a psychological state—which is what she is talking about.

In this way Anna's general rhetorical strategy mirrored the way that Skip presented new speculative ideas during class discussions.

By positing that Skip encouraged speculative, eccentric, or radical thinking, I imply that the origins of Anna's "original" idea were social in nature. The following attempts to make explicit the social construction of Anna's radical or eccentric interpretation of Rennie's death as well as the role that her interpretation played in the development of her paper's central argument.

## Social Origins of an "Original" Idea

Skip implicitly showed students how to develop an argument that defined a new idea. The key to this process was, as I stated above, to use some device to extend, counter, or alter an established idea. For Anna this device was a radical interpretation of one of the course texts: Barth's *The End of the Road*. The process of developing this radical interpretation involved a series of social interactions with Skip and others. By learning how Anna came to develop this radical interpretation, we can begin to understand the social origins of her original idea. The following will explain what led to Anna's reading of that text.

As Chabot (1985) explains, readers' interpretations depend on much beyond the text: ". . . at stake in any interpretive situation is far more than the understanding of the text at hand, but is in fact the reader's understanding of his entire experience to this point" (p. 28). How did Anna's "experience to this point" relate to her interpretation of Barth's novel? The answer can be described by looking at how Anna approached Barth's text as what Moran (1986) calls an "insider": "We all see differently if we know what we are seeing. . . . Inside knowledge alters the relationship to the things or events observed. I have written poetry. I am not a poet; I have written poems. The fact that I have written poetry makes me a different reader of poetry" (p. 8). Anna was not an insider to Barth's novel because she had written a novel. Anna was an insider because of some of the relationships she had with others—particularly those that involved her husband and her husband's academic world—gave her an insider's perspective on the actions of the character of Rennie in the novel.

Anna explicitly compared herself to Rennie in at least one way: both had some trouble asserting their own personalities. For example, in her copy of the novel, Anna underlined the following sentence that described Rennie: ". . . she always apologized to other people for not having their point of view" (p. 47). In the margin next to this sentence Anna wrote, "my problem, too."

Anna was continually concerned about the tentative way that she formed opinions. For example, early in the semester she noted her reliance on her fellow students in the class: "I rely heavily on other people's interpretations—not just the teacher's—of things in order to form my own opinion. It helps me firm up my opinion." Later in the semester, however, she was disappointed that her fellow students were not interacting enough to please her: "I've been distressed about class: the students are not participating. That's what it is supposed to be all about. It's a colloquium and we're not discussing. How do you find out what the book is about without discussion? I really depend on people's opinions to give me direction."

While Anna was uneasy about her ability to form her own opinions without hearing the opinions of peers, she was not completely passive. While Rennie was totally dominated by her husband's personality, Anna was wary of being consumed by her husband's presence. As a mother and housewife without a college education, Anna was sometimes frustrated when she interacted with others in her husband's academic world. "I got so damn sick and tired of people at parties asking me what school I graduated from," she said. So Anna made a concerted effort to establish a self distinct from her husband's. She enrolled as an undergraduate English major at the state university—not the school at which her husband taught: "I could have gone to [the college where her husband teaches], but I would have always been 'John's wife.' If I didn't get all A's, I'd be involved in a lot of self-flagellation. I wouldn't be me, even though me may not be all that great."

Although she was usually self-deprecating and tentative, Anna was clearly attempting to pull herself out of her husband's shadow. This effort extended to her work at the university. Again, she suffered some frustration as a result of her husband's influence on others. Several semesters before she was enrolled in the senior seminar, Anna felt that a paper she had written for a literature course was unfairly evaluated because the professor, who knew that her husband taught philosophy, expected her to demonstrate more philosophical training than she had. She faced this same issue early in Skip's senior seminar:

> I asked Skip what I should read as background. He said, "Oh, your husband will tell you what to read." I said, "no no." I wish I didn't tell Skip my husband teaches philosophy. I wish I said he's a garbage collector. Just because I live with him, I'm not a philosopher. I can remember students of his coming to me at a party and asking me about things in his class. I don't know anything. I'm separate from him. That's probably why I didn't take any philosophy courses. People assume I do and I don't like that. I'm lost in his accomplishments. I don't want that.

Given these attitudes and experiences, Anna brought to Rennie an insider's point of view that enabled her to interpret Rennie's death during abortion as a willful act of self-assertiveness. As noted above, Anna said, "It was an act of being herself—the first thing that she could do to escape being what Joe wanted her to be." Thus, an early stage of the process of developing her original idea was enabled by her perspective on her social life.

Another part of this process involved Anna's conscious ability to play different roles in different situations. She saw this as an ability that Rennie lacked. In contrast to Rennie, Anna worked on playing roles other than the role of wife. Anna described this ability with terminology from the course. For example, during one of Skip's lectures, Anna became interested in the notion of the "authentic self." "Authentic" individuals are acutely aware of their existential situation. At most times people deny the existential reality by playing roles or "wearing masks" in order to stay unaware. Anna saw herself wearing different masks in her different roles. As a student she wore one mask, as a worker at Responsible Childbirth she wore another. Ultimately, in her term paper she discussed some of the problems that can develop with this behavior. While she was simultaneously writing the paper and working at Responsible Childbirth, she compared her analysis of role playing and her own role playing: "I'm a different person here at Responsible Childbirth than I am at school. I wear different masks and I criticize that in my term paper. I criticize the inauthentic person and I find that I am inauthentic." And yet, when looking at Rennie, Anna recognized the importance of playing roles and wearing masks. When Skip asserted in class that Rennie, "through a majority of the book... is without self," Anna noted the significance of Rennie's inability to play other roles: "If Rennie could have switched masks, she could have survived Joe—but she couldn't do this." This idea of switching masks to survive rounded out her new interpretation of Rennie's death.

It was this new interpretation that eventually served as a catalyst for Anna as she developed a topic for her paper. With this interpretation, she took the next step by discussing the paper in a one-on-one conference with Skip several weeks after the class discussion about Rennie's death.

At the beginning of the conference, Anna offered a most general starting point: "I want your reactions to my ideas for a paper. It is something we touched upon: suicide as a viable alternative. I was surprised at my reaction to *The End of the Road*. I know that Camus and Genet rule it [suicide] out as a response."

In the process of helping her develop something, especially the reinterpretation of Rennie's death, Skip, as he would do during class discussions, attempted to find connections between established and new interpretations:

> Let me throw some ideas out for a moment: We have in *The End of the Road* what you want to interpret as a suicide. In many of these plays we have what could be suicides—symbolic or otherwise.... There is not a literal suicide in any of the literature. There's no proof anywhere that any one person set out to commit suicide. ... You could discuss metaphorical suicide.... You may end up with a situation in which you redefine suicide because Rennie's death could not be ruled suicide.

Anna took notes as Skip spoke. Ultimately, he told her that he thought that this idea could work. Before they finished, Anna raised the idea of the "authentic self" and asked a few questions about it. During this conference she did not relate that idea to her speculative thoughts on the theme of suicide.

After that first conference, as Anna continued to develop her paper further, she chose to write a literature-based paper to serve as the medium to illustrate her ideas. By recalling her past experience with the professor who thought she should write a philosophically based paper for his literature course, Anna explicitly ruled out the possibility of doing that for this course:

> In another class I did a paper for a professor who knew I was the wife of a philosophy professor and I was penalized for not writing a philosophy-based paper. I don't want to address philosophical issues in [this paper)—other than with Camus, who writes literature. . . . [This will be a paper] in my field, which is literature. It is not a sociological or philosophical paper because those are not my fields. I'm tentative and I don't want to go out of my field of expertise. I've been criticized by professors before because I haven't promoted a thesis strongly enough. I see this paper as a challenge to present a strong case—a strong thesis and back that up with literature.

To develop a strong case she decided to focus not on Rennie, who Anna argued committed physical suicide, but on the character of Jake Horner, who, in direct contrast to Rennie, wore many masks in order to survive. She discussed this with Skip during another conference.

> ANNA: I don't want to get into a philosophical paper on suicide. But I want to deal in terms of literature because that is where I have the most experience. I want to focus on psychological suicide—like what Jake Horner does in *The End of the Road*—escape mechanisms mean not facing reality. If Camus says you have two choices: suicide or not, then I think suicide need not be physical. Does this sound good?
>
> SKIP: Yes. . . . So in other words you are taking the Camusian choice and changing it from a "life or death" choice to a "life or . . . [Skip paused and searched for a word] a deadlife" choice. I like that.

Again, Skip emphasizes the established base upon which she can develop her argument—an argument that contains an element so new that Skip has to coin a new term for it.

Accordingly, her paper centered on this new definition of suicide, as illustrated below by the paper's abstract:

> Once the individual confronts the absurdity of his existence he must choose one of two courses of action. He can live with what he knows, or he can commit suicide because he cannot live with what he knows. Albert Camus offers two types of suicide: physical and philosophical. This paper attempts to establish a third type of suicide—that of psychological suicide. Psychological suicide occurs when the "authentic" self is negated or suppressed in favor of a substitutive persona. The person who commits psychological suicide sees his life as a drama in which he plays many roles and wears many masks. He believes that "life as drama" gives unity, order and direction to an otherwise meaningless existence.

Does psychological suicide have benefits that make it the suicide of choice? Does it really provide order in a disordered world? The word suicide does imply death. If this is so, what is the nature of death in the context of psychological suicide? These questions are addressed within the realms of literature, not philosophy. John Barth's *The End of the Road,* Leo Tolstoy's "The Death of Ivan Ilych," and Saul Bellow's *Seize the Day* all provide insight into individuals who chose psychological death or deny it as an acceptable alternative.

Although my analysis certainly cannot explain all of Anna's rhetorical choices, it does reveal the social construction of her central thesis and the structure of her argument. One way to interpret the social construction of Anna's term paper is to look at it as practice to enter a discourse community of scholars (Bizzell, 1986; Bruffee, 1984). From Anna's perspective, we can assume that one of her central tasks was to make sense of her experiences (which include reading course texts) in a way that would seemingly contribute something to the discourse community established in the course.

From Skip's perspective, we could assume that he, consciously or unconsciously, attempted to teach students some strategies that they would need to learn in order to eventually become members of that discourse community. By helping students learn how to find and structure an argument for these communities, a professor teaching an advanced literature course is, in effect, teaching students to play an acceptable institutional role and thus furthering that discourse community. In this case, Skip embodied the demands of the discourse community and, as Bruffee (1984) describes, played a role in the process of sustaining that community:

> Teachers are defined in this instance as those members of a knowledge community who accept the responsibility for inducting new members into the community. Without successful teachers the community will die when its current members die, and knowledge as assented to by that community will cease to exist. [p. 650]

For Anna, writing in this particular course was practice for assuming a role in a larger academic discourse community.

Yet her experience in this academic community also influenced her experience at Responsible Childbirth—the nonacademic community. While we cannot separate her interpretations of Barth's novel (and the other course texts) from her social life, neither can we separate her experiences at Responsible Childbirth from her interpretations of those course texts. As the second half of this chapter will show, we can begin to understand the nonacademic discourse community and Anna's role in it by examining the sources of her ambivalent attitudes toward the concept of "wearing masks and playing roles" that arose in the literature course. As discussed earlier, Anna argued that Rennie could have survived if she had been able to switch masks successfully and had played roles other than that of Joe's wife. Anna recognized the necessity to be inauthentic in order to function in different situations. And yet she criticized the role playing and inauthenticity of the central characters of the three novels she analyzed in her paper. Most importantly, as the quote cited earlier indicates, she, too, exhibited this type of behavior while at Responsible Childbirth—and she was very uneasy about it. "I'm a different person here at Responsible Childbirth than I am at school. I wear different masks and I criticize that in my term paper. I criticize the inauthentic person and I find that I am inauthentic." The source of this ambivalence—which will be explained below—reveals the nature of Anna's experience in the nonacademic discourse community.

## LEARNING TO COMMUNICATE IN A NONACADEMIC DISCOURSE COMMUNITY: THE JOB

Anna's experience at Responsible Childbirth, and most likely the experience of nearly all Responsible Childbirth employees, had been heavily influenced by a series of events that had occurred during the previous year. Exactly one year before Anna began her job, Responsible Childbirth faced the beginnings of what would become a six-month battle against a coalition of ultraconservative Christians who wanted to convince the county government to stop funding Responsible Childbirth. It was a vigorous and often acrimonious fight that centered on the issue of abortion. Approximately six months before Anna began her job, Responsible Childbirth won that battle and retained county funding. The impact of the conflict influenced much of what Anna did while working as a writer for Responsible Childbirth.

As a writer, Anna was classified as one of the many volunteers who worked throughout Responsible Childbirth. Officially, however, she was a student intern receiving general elective credit from the University for working ten to fifteen hours a week at the agency. She worked for the public relations operation, which included education services, fund raising, and other public relations activities, such as the publication of a newsletter. (The other major segments of the organization that play a role in this research are the clinical staff—the staff in charge of the medical operations of the agency—and the board of directors.)

Anna's supervisors were Fiona Leeds and Nel Rothwell. Fiona, in her mid-thirties, was a full-time employee serving as the director of fund raising. Fiona was quick-witted and intelligent, assertive but friendly. Anna admired her assertiveness. According to Anna, Fiona was "an aggressive feminist. . . . She is a dominating personality. I wish I were more like her." Nel, in her mid-forties, worked part-time and headed the production of the Responsible Childbirth newsletter. She was very patient with Anna, and Anna believed that she was an excellent on-the-job teacher.

As a writer, Anna was given two major tasks over the six months of her job. The first was to write articles for the newsletter. Each issue of the newsletter, distributed to about 4,000 people, promoted Responsible Childbirth's community services and often featured articles that described community events that Responsible Childbirth supported or sponsored. Anna worked to produce one newsletter, writing or rewriting all of the articles and helping Nel design the layout. Nel gave article assignments to Anna and edited her drafts. Originally, Anna was very unsure of her ability to write for the newsletter, but Nel gave Anna much guidance. Anna began to learn about this new discourse community by working for Nel.

After writing articles for one newsletter, Anna spent most of her time researching and writing a report that documented the county funding fight. Fiona gave Anna the job of documenting the crisis, so that members of this regional office as well as the members of other Responsible Childbirth offices throughout the nation would understand how the crisis arose and how this office handled it successfully. Anna wrote a draft of the report and it was reviewed by Fiona and Nel. Fiona gave final approval to all of the changes to Anna's draft. The final draft of the report consisted of approximately twenty pages of text with nine lengthy appendices of supporting documentation.

## RESEARCH QUESTIONS: THE JOB

Over the course of her time at Responsible Childbirth, Anna evolved from an outsider to a responsible member of the public relations operation. That is, she learned how to play the appropriate institutional role. And yet Anna continually felt uneasy about playing that role in the organization. This uneasiness directly related to the writing that she did as an employee. While she learned how to work as an effective member of the organization, her inclusion into the organization was problematic. She felt a conflict between the ethos of the organization and her own ethos. Thus, this analysis attempts to answer two questions:

1. What did she have to learn in order to become a member of the discourse community? What was her institutional role and how did she learn how to play it?
2. To what extent did Anna allow herself to become a member of the Responsible Childbirth discourse community? What was the source of her ambivalence? What was the nature of the conflict between her ethos and her perception of the ethos of the organization?

## ANALYSIS

The answer to the first question shows that the process of becoming a useful member of this new discourse community was largely a process of learning the politics of Responsible Childbirth. I use the term "politics" in a generic sense to describe factionalism both within Responsible Childbirth and between Responsible Childbirth and other organizations.

The answer to the second question reveals an ethical dilemma that she faced in light of the political nature of her writing. This dilemma centered upon the conflict between her conception of what constitutes ethical discourse and her perception of the organizational demand to produce discourse that furthered the organization's image. Ethical discourse was what Anna called "balanced." It should attempt to give voice to both sides of an issue. Anna realized, however, that unbalanced discourse that promoted a monolithic ethos would further the aims of the organization. Ultimately, Anna produced discourse that furthered the organization and she became an accepted and valuable employee in doing so. That is, Anna played the institutional role that she was hired to play. Yet she never allowed herself to become a completely committed employee. In the process of adhering to the demands of the organization, she, as writer, subordinated her ethical persona to a monolithic one. Thus, in order to function effectively in this particular nonacademic setting, she became, in her terms, inauthentic. In contrast to Rennie, Anna was able to switch masks and play a role through her discourse even though she saw that role as conflicting with the ethos that she wanted to project.

These conflicting roles had little to do with Responsible Childbirth's stated philosophy or actions concerning sexuality, birth control, or abortion. Anna would not have been taken on as a potential volunteer unless she generally knew and accepted what Responsible Childbirth does. Those at Responsible Childbirth who coordinated volunteers made it clear that any volunteer—including the interns from the university—must have at least a neutral or at best a positive attitude toward Responsible Childbirth's activities. Anna believed in Responsible Childbirth's mission. It was Anna's perception of the mission of the public relations operation that conflicted with Anna's ethos, and it was this mission that Anna had to undertake to become a productive employee—that is, a good writer—for Responsible Childbirth. Carrying out this mission as a writer required that Anna learn about the two political dimensions of the public relations discourse community: (1) the relationship of Responsible Childbirth to the community—the external politics of the organization—and (2) the relationships among different factions within Responsible Childbirth—the internal politics of the organization. Anna's perceptions of these political elements influenced her writing.

## What Anna Learned to Become a Member of the Discourse Community

*The External Politics.* Right from the start, Anna learned that Responsible Childbirth's relationship with the community limited the public language of the organization as well as the information that the organization deemed important.

The moment she began to work on the newsletter, Anna began to learn the political limits on the organization's public language. For example, when she first helped Nel design the layout of the newsletter, Anna suggested including a few public service advertisements, one of which contained the word "abortion." Because this word was used, Nel said that the ad could not be included in the newsletter. And, Anna noted, "she was emphatic about this." Nel told her that the local board of directors of Responsible Childbirth would not approve of this ad because of that word. Anna was stunned: "With that, my jaw dropped down to my knees. I couldn't believe what I was hearing!"

Anna then turned to another advertisement as a potential newletter item. This one had the words "safe" and "Roe v Wade" and the date of that Supreme

Court decision. Again, as Anna described, Nel balked at including this ad in the newsletter. "Nel said, 'I'd love to use that but we've never done anything like that.' I said, 'Why?' and she said, 'Because we're not allowed to use the word *abortion* in the newsletter and this made silent reference to the word.' "

Abortion was one of the services offered by Responsible Childbirth. This service had been a central issue raised by the ultraconservative coalition that opposed county funding of Responsible Childbirth. Anna's experience with the use of the word "abortion" was her introduction to the influences that external politics had on the use of language. This politically motivated limitation is further accented by comparing it to the tremendous freedom of language—discussed below—that Anna experienced when learning to communicate with outsiders in a nonpolitical environment.

As a volunteer, Anna was required to take part in an orientation program. During the first orientation meeting, the session leader asked the volunteers to say aloud the most offensive words and expressions that they could think of that dealt with sexual activities, bodily functions, and body parts. They discussed what Anna described as "some bizarre, shocking, and sometimes funny language." The point of this activity was to get the volunteers used to this type of language so that they would not be shocked if and when they worked with clients who explained their sexual activities in such ways. After her experience with the language of the newsletter, Anna said, "I thought that this was interesting in light of the fact that the board of directors will not allow us to use the word 'abortion' in the newsletter." The limits on language varied greatly in political and nonpolitical facets of the organization.

Learning the special limits of the discourse community's language did not end with questions of appropriate vocabulary. These limits also showed Anna that what was meaningful to her was not meaningful in light of the external politics. For example, Anna's first major assignment was to attend Responsible Childbirth's fifteenth annual community luncheon, take notes on the proceedings, and write an article for the newsletter. The featured speaker at the luncheon was the national president of Responsible Childbirth, who spoke about abortion, teenage pregnancy, and the victory of the local Responsible Childbirth over the local conservative coalition. In addition, brief speeches were delivered by several community leaders, such as the mayor of the city and the head of one of the local television stations.

The first draft of Anna's article had to be altered extensively, not because it was poorly written or incorrect—not even because it was not interesting or positive about Responsible Childbirth—but because it focused too much on the serious issues that the president described as central to Responsible Childbirth's mission. Instead, after talking with Nel, Anna came to realize that the newsletter should focus primarily on the "fluff," as Anna called it. This meant that it should include information such as which community leaders were at the luncheon and how the community leaders continue to support the organization. One of the key strategies, according to Nel, was to include as many names of attendees as possible.

Thus, Anna began to learn that external politics determined what was meaningful and what was not. That first assignment had made her witness to Responsible Childbirth's political standing in the community. While she listened to people who were notable on local, regional, and/or national levels speak in support of the organization, she began to get a sense of the political opponents that had attacked the organization during the previous year.

Anna learned the most about the anti-Responsible Childbirth factions when she began working on the report that documented the county funding fight. Anna learned much from Fiona about the tactics of "the opposition," the term Fiona used for the conservative coalition. These tactics influenced Anna's writing; her responses in a discourse-based interview indicate that she attributed some of her rhetorical choices to external politics. For example, one passage of the report described an incident in which a member of the opposition gained entrance to the Responsible Childbirth library and secretly seized and later publicized a booklet entitled *So You Don't Want to Be a Sex Object?* Although Anna had described the contents of other controversial publications in her report, she chose not to describe the contents of this particular one. In the interview Anna explained that an elaboration would indeed clarify the controversial contents of the booklet to members of other Responsible Childbirth agencies who might read the report; however, she added that she believed that Fiona would have deleted the elaboration in editing the document. "If this report got into the hands of the wrong people, it could be used against Responsible Childbirth. . . . Based on past opposition tactics, they could get hold of this report and use anything in it to distort." By identifying the contents of a controversial Responsible Childbirth document, Anna believed that she could be unintentionally providing ammunition for future opposition attacks.

At another point in her report Anna chose to elaborate the description of an antiabortion rally with a quote from one of the opposition leaders. She wrote that this person "used this opportunity to single out Responsible Childbirth as '. . . all that is sick and confused and even diabolical about modern policy making' " (p. 3). When asked if this elaboration could have been deleted from the text, Anna replied that it was very important for future political reasons:

> There were some people in Responsible Childbirth who read this in the newspaper that decided that [the opposition leader] was going to be a problem but there were others who said, "Ah, he's just a nut." This passage is an indication that you should not write off these kinds of people when you hear them saying these kinds of things. . . . This [report] is going to be used as a learning tool for other Responsible Childbirths and there is a tendency to not take the opposition seriously. This passage would help people to tune into the opposition.

When Anna, as a writer, began to take actions that would help sustain that community in future crises, she began to become a productive member of the discourse community.

Yet even though she learned to make rhetorical choices based on her perceptions of external political factors, she did not interpret her rhetorical choices to be as politically sensitive as did her principal editor, Fiona. In separate discourse-based interviews that focused on the same rhetorical choices in Anna's report, Fiona and Anna interpreted some of those choices quite differently. For example, when asked if an elaborative quote from an opposition document could be deleted, Fiona's reply was quite political and Anna's was not. The passage read "Responsible Childbirth is labeled 'the nation's largest chain of abortion clinics. . . .' " Fiona responded by saying that this passage was very important and must be kept in the report because it "shows how inflammatory the opposition's piece on Responsible Childbirth was. It shows how extreme their view was. [By including the passage in the report it] lowers the credibility of the organization making that attack." Anna also stated that the passage was important, but only because she thought it accurately portrayed the opposition's point of view. Anna did not see the passage as an attack on the opposition. Anna had become politically aware, but not to the extent that Fiona had.

While Anna quickly learned about the external political environment, she did not readily recognize the political factions operating within the organization.

*The Internal Politics.* Originally, Anna perceived no clear factions or any political conflicts among segments of the organization:

> Even though this is my first day and nothing really has been accomplished except getting through the formalities, I feel comfortable at Responsible Childbirth. This may have something to do with the fact that I am a woman working in what might be termed a woman's workplace. . . . I sense a strong sense of commitment. There doesn't seem to be any jockeying for position or competition between workers.

Factions started to become clearer when, midway through the internship, she began interviewing agency employees in order to reconstruct what had happened during the county funding crisis. It was during this interview process that she began to see the factionalism, and she felt somewhat intimidated: "This is a touchy subject and people in the organization have diverse and passionate feelings and I am very worried about writing it [the report]."

She first learned that there were differing perspectives on the crisis within the staff. Those who were involved in different aspects of public relations would "respond differently to the same issue: one person looks at it from a political [i.e., county commissioners' activities] point of view; another looks at it in terms of public relations; the director of education services focused on how the issue influenced the education program." While these differences influenced what she learned while gathering information for the report, there were more significant differences between the public relations staff and other internal factions that directly influenced some of Anna's rhetorical choices. For example, when Anna discovered a major conflict between members of the public relations staff and members of the clinical staff, she chose to only briefly mention the conflict and not to elaborate. She did not want to explicitly pit these factions against each other, so in her report she glossed over the conflict by writing "Some staff members stayed throughout the evenings stuffing envelopes, while other staff members did not" (p.

13). During an editorial review of Anna's first draft, Fiona reacted strongly to this description of the conflict:

> You were too diplomatic in your writing. We carried the weight and other parts of the organization didn't. You did not make it clear enough for two reasons: (1) it still pisses me off and (2) we had basically four people (the public relations staff) who fought this battle. The medical people did not help.

In the final draft the sentence cited above was followed by:

> There was some conflict over whose problem the county funding was—some departments within the agency received none of the county funding money, yet worked extremely hard to see that it was received in 1985. Other departments simply felt the county funding was not their concern. The clinic staff did not contribute extra time to help in the direct mailing, etc. They did come to the county hearing. All nonsalaried personnel staff [essentially clinical personnel] was paid to attend the county hearing. [p. 13]

In the preceding instance Anna tried (unsuccessfully) to be apolitical by glossing over the conflict in her original draft. In another instance, Anna chose to enter the political arena with her text: Anna discovered that the county funding battle was waged primarily in public forums: newspapers, county commission meetings, public rallies at churches, etc. Thus, since the public relations staff did most of the work to fight the conservative coalition, those staff members believed that they should have taken on the high-profile leadership role in directing the fight. The president of the agency's board of directors, however, decided that she, the president, and other board members should represent the agency in public during this battle. Fiona wanted Anna to attack that board's actions and argue that the public relations staff should have taken the leadership role. But Anna did not do this. When considering how to report this issue, Anna decided to participate in the internal debate by agreeing with one faction and then trying to express it in a way that ameliorated the conflict. Her text read:

> Any request concerning the use of public funds must have the support of the community behind it. . . . It was essential that the county commissioners feel positive about Responsible Childbirth. With this in mind, the Responsible Childbirth board assumed the "leadership position" during the county funding fight. It was the board's belief that if the staff took the leadership position, it might appear to be self-serving. It was therefore necessary for the board, composed of influential [local citizens], to defend and represent the Responsible Childbirth organization. [p. 9]

With this argument Anna again explicitly entered the ongoing conversation of the discourse community and tried to influence that community. As she explained in an interview:

> Initially, when I started this, I had the impression that everybody banded together to save themselves, but that wasn't the case. You had differences between the

clinic and the [public relations] staff; you had differences within the staff; you had differences between the staff and the board. And it is important for Responsible Childbirth [employees] to look at these differences and not take offense at these differences during a trying time.

In this instance Anna successfully "soothed over some differences between the board and the staff." Fiona grudgingly agreed. In commenting on the above passage, she admitted, "Although at the time I was very resistant to the idea, I think that it is true that the board needs to be the leaders. They are the volunteers and influential [community] leaders."

Thus, Anna served as a productive member of the discourse community by contributing to an internal debate. As such, this instance was an attempt by Anna to produce an ethical message, and it indicates that she was becoming a committed member of the discourse community. Yet, when her commitment is examined carefully, it is clear that her desire to reconstruct the Responsible Childbirth crisis ethically was not consistent with what committed members would see as proper discourse. Therefore, as the following section will show, Anna's participation in the discourse community was quite problematic for her.

## *Conflict Between Individual and Organizational Ethos*

As a writer in the literature course, Anna was an advocate. She constructed an argument that was implicitly related to her personal social life. At Responsible Childbirth she did not want to be an advocate. She wanted to be objective:

> [At Responsible Childbirth] I'm in a totally neutral position, given a bunch of information, supplemented with interviews. I am only reporting, not persuading. . . . In writing for Responsible Childbirth there is no creativity, no interpretation. These are not my opinions, not my perspectives. Responsible Childbirth is documenting the event. With Skip's class, it is more an extension of me personally. It is my point of view supported with the literature of my choosing. It speaks to me as an individual.

Anna wanted to be a conduit through which facts flowed unimpeded. And if she could not include all of the facts, then at least she could provide a balanced set of facts:

> I wanted to interview the opposition. . . . Getting other points of view is not to support that view but to report in a more balanced way. I think that this report would have been different if one of the county commissioners had documented this. . . . I may have still had my own personal opinion of who was right or wrong, but you would have had a more balanced view. . . . the opposition cannot defend themselves [in my report].

Anna included no defense of the opposition in the report; nor did she include any positive statements about the opposition. The closest thing to a positive statement was one passage that avoided saying anything negative about the opposition. She wrote:

> Despite the intensity of the county funding issue, Responsible Childbirth of [the region] was more fortunate than other clinics across the country in some respects. The opposition did not resort to any of the following tactics: picketing of Responsible Childbirth offices, fire-bombing, tire slashing, physical assaults on Responsible Childbirth staff. [p.3]

In a discourse-based interview Anna explained that this passage was important:

> because these [violent] actions were done in other communities. . . . The conflict was essentially a war of words in the newspaper, not a physical battle. It is fairer to the opposition to clarify what they did not do while others in the other communities did those things. Fairness is important to me. I take offense at unfair tactics. For example, the opposition has a very colorful book of aborted fetuses. That is a distortion. . . . I think if you are going to fight you ought to come with facts that are substantiated. I don't want to stoop to distortion like the opposition did.

Ultimately, Anna realized that she could not be an objective conduit and admitted that her selective reporting of "facts" exhibited a Responsible Childbirth bias. For example, at one point in the report she described the circumstances that surrounded the opposition's major report on Responsible Childbirth, entitled "Why Responsible Childbirth Should Not Receive County Funding," which was produced by the Ad Hoc Committee to Oppose the Public Funding of Responsible Childbirth. After identifying the ad hoc document in her report, Anna wrote the following description of its contents and followed that with Responsible Childbirth commentary on the document.

> It contains national and local statistics on abortion, illegitimate birth rates, teenage sexual activity, contraceptive use among teens, as well as Responsible Childbirth's budget and how it reflects their abortion connection (the opposition's assertion that county funds are used to support the abortion clinic). Quotations are liberally used throughout to give credibility to the report. . . .
> According to (a Responsible Childbirth board member), "the depth of the inaccuracies found in the Ad Hoc Report demanded a detailed response from Responsible Childbirth." [p. 15]

In a discourse-based interview, when asked whether the discussions of the content of the opposition report could be deleted, Anna replied that the passage above was useful. It enabled readers to understand the type of information the ad hoc report contained, so that readers would not need to read the ad hoc report if they did not want to.

When asked why she elaborated to some extent on the contents of the controversial opposition document and not on the controversial Responsible Childbirth document (entitled, *So You Don't Want to Be a Sex Object* and discussed earlier), Anna replied that it would have been a "fairer" presentation if she had included specifics from the controversial Responsible Childbirth booklet. She admitted that her report was not, in her terms, fair. She cited two reasons for this: (1) the opposition was not fair in their selective presentation of information about

Responsible Childbirth and (2) Fiona and Nel, as heads of public relations, would not approve of a more balanced presentation: "The image of Responsible Childbirth, they [Fiona and Nel] are almost paranoid about it, and they would construe that (including a description of the controversial Responsible Childbirth booklet) as damaging to Responsible Childbirth."

Anna was uneasy about her selective use of facts to reconstruct a totally positive image of Responsible Childbirth. "I guess this report is slanted toward Responsible Childbirth. Some facts I report and some I don't report and I'm not sure this is appropriate."

She did take one stand that, ironically, undermined her ethical intent. She resisted structuring the report the way that Fiona and Nel first wanted her to. They wanted her to write a narrative—a dramatic story that would be interesting to read and would tell of their triumph over the opposition. Anna did not produce such a story. Instead, she dispensed with any chronological reconstruction and classified events by type. For example, her report was structured upon major headings such as "The Issue," "Tactics," "The Ad Hoc Report," and "The Role of the Newspaper."

Although Fiona and Nel were surprised and initially disappointed when they saw the structure of Anna's first draft, they soon decided that Anna's structure was indeed the best way to organize the report. They both recognized that this structure would serve better as a teaching tool. As Nel told Anna, "A narrative would be used to tell people how wonderful we are, but I see this as a functional piece." Thus, Anna's structure would be more effective in showing others (1) how this particular agency handled the crisis and (2) how other agencies could handle similar crises. Even though Anna avoided implementing the polemical narrative, the structure she developed served to further undermine her own ethos by making the biased report a more effective teaching tool.

Overall, Anna felt a conflict between reporting fairly and yet still promoting Responsible Childbirth. She was writing within a discourse community of members committed to the organization and wary of external threats to that organization. She recognized that because she was writing for a community of advocates, she could not be as neutral as if she had been writing for a less committed community of readers. Thus, she had a conflict between adopting the point of view of her primary readers and keeping true to her own self as reader. As she said, she felt as if she wore a mask at work and was not her authentic self.

After the final draft was completed, Anna, because she was ultimately dissatisfied with the report, refused to put her name on it as author.

## DISCUSSION

The key difference between Anna's experience in both discourse communities lies not in the texts that she produced; nor does it lie in the communities themselves. The key difference lies in the relationship of writing to each community. The two different relationships of writing to community that are exemplified in Anna's experience illustrate the two primary social/institutional roles that writers must play: they can produce discourse that maintains their discourse community or they can produce discourse that changes it. Bruffee (1984) describes these two types of discourse as normal and abnormal discourse (distinctions Bruffee has derived from Rorty [1979] who, in turn, had developed them from Kuhn's [1972] concepts of "normal" and "revolutionary" science).

As Bruffee describes it, normal discourse maintains the community: "Its purpose is to justify belief to the satisfaction of other people within the author's community of knowledgeable peers" (p. 643). Anna's function at Responsible Childbirth was primarily geared to help maintain an organization whose members believed it was threatened. Especially when reconstructing the county funding fight, Anna's role was to promote and conserve the organization. The county funding fight report (and to a lesser extent, the newsletter) communicated a message that said: "Even though others want to destroy us, we will continue to thrive." Because her supervisors collaborated with her and approved of her work, Anna succeeded at this task. Her writing conformed to the conventions and values of the discourse community. But because she did not see herself as a member of that community, she was uneasy about producing normal discourse.

She was not uneasy about attempting to produce abnormal discourse in the literature course. Abnormal discourse does not adhere to the conventional thinking of a community. It is discourse that may be judged to be ridiculous, outrageous, or revolutionary: "the product of abnormal discourse can be anything from nonsense to intellectual revolution" (Rorty, p. 320). If, for example, in her report on the county funding fight, Anna had written "The opposition offered many valid criticisms of Responsible Childbirth—criticisms that the agency should consider and act upon," she most likely would have been seen to be either temporarily insane or the enemy. If she had convinced the others in the organization to believe that her statement was true, then that statement would have been revolutionary.

Whether or not Anna's idea that Rennie committed suicide by choosing to have an abortion was ridiculous or insightful, mundane or revolutionary, is not important. What is important is that the discourse community (as embodied by Skip) privileged speculative—possibly "abnormal"—thinking.

While both discourse communities privileged a different type of discourse, clearly both types of discourse are important to the continued development of any discourse community. As other studies have shown, writing plays a reciprocal role: it both maintains and shapes organizations (e.g., Bazerman, 1983; Paradis, Dobrin, & Miller, 1985; Myers, 1985; Doheny-Farina, 1986; Harrison, 1987; Doheny-Farina, 1988). While we all can agree that institutions foster normal discourse, these studies indicate that institutions which continue to evolve will also foster, to some degree, abnormal discourse.

If we, as teachers of writing, enable our students to become aware of and undertake these types of discourse, we prepare our students to take part in the ongoing development of the institutions that they choose to enter. As Bruffee (1984) argues:

> We must teach practical rhetoric and critical analysis in such a way that, when necessary, students can turn to abnormal discourse in order to undermine their own and other people's reliance on the canonical conventions and vocabulary of normal discourse. We must teach the use of these tools in such a way that students can set them aside, if only momentarily, for the purpose of generating new knowledge, for the purpose, that is, of reconstructing knowledge communities in more satisfactory ways. [p. 648]

Since discourse communities can continually be reconstructed, we need to give our students the tools and awareness to do so. Such advice implies a generally positive picture of what power all of us—not only teachers and students—have in terms of the institutions within which we operate. While I certainly prefer to believe that we do have this power, I must offer a caveat, however, which briefly recasts my findings in a darker light.

It makes for a nice rhetorical structure for me to find that each community in this study fosters a different type of discourse—especially when the type that we see fostered by the academic community seems to privilege critical—even radical—thinking. Such a conclusion is consistent with our belief in the university as a bastion of "academic freedom." But, to use Perlman's term, such an ideal is really an "institutional rule" (p. 475). The freedom to be radical is limited within the institutional boundaries of the academy and its individual disciplines. I do argue that the academic discourse in this case appears to be abnormal in nature. Yet, by privileging discourse that integrates seemingly radical ideas into established thinking, academic communities (and the professors who represent those communities to students) institutionalize that radical thinking, thus stripping it of any revolutionary impact and, in effect, normalizing those ideas. Thus, one could interpret my findings as showing that the academic community privileges normal discourse which is laced with the trappings of abnormal discourse. Indeed, one could use my findings to illustrate the belief that institutions resist revolutionary discourse by fostering such "false" abnormal discourse. These are issues that, obviously, cannot even begin to be resolved through studies of such a narrow scope as mine.

Finally, while the scope of this research may be extremely narrow, it does represent a very small step in what will be a long journey. Bizzell (1986) calls for studies of college writers that provide "in-depth, comparative, ethnological stud[ies] of discursive practices in and out of school, such as we find in the work of Shirley Brice Heath, David Olson, and other researchers into the development of literacy in young children" (p. 7). Clearly, this case study is not an answer to that call. It is merely an indication that such studies can and should be undertaken.

## Notes

1. All proper names cited in this report are pseudonyms.
2. When I use terms such as "new," "original," "radical," or "speculative" to describe concepts, I do not mean that I believe these adjectives describe the concepts. I mean only that the participants viewed the concepts in these ways.

## Works Cited

Barth, John. *The End of the Road.* New York: Bantam Books, 1987.

Bazerman, Charles. "Scientific Writing as a Social Act: A Review of the Literature of the Sociology of Science." *New Essays in Technical and Scientific Communication: Research, Theory, Practice.* Eds. P. Anderson, R. Brockman, and C. Miller. Farmingdale, N.Y.: Baywood, 1983, pp. 156–184.

Bizzell, Patricia. "Academic Discourse: Taxonomy of Conventions or Collaborative Practice?" Paper presented to the College Composition and Communication Conference, New Orleans, March 1986.

Bruffee, Kenneth A. "Collaborative Learning and the Conversation of Mankind." *College English* 46(November 1984):635–652.

———. "Social Construction, Language, and the Authority of Knowledge: A Bibliographic Essay." *College English* 48(December 1986):773–790.

Chabot, C. Barry. "Understanding Interpretive Situations." *Researching Response to Literature and the Teaching of Literature: Points of Departure.* Ed. Charles R. Cooper. Norwood, N.J.: Ablex, 1985, pp. 22–32.

Comley, Nancy R., and Robert Scholes. "Literature, Composition, and the Structure of English." *Composition and Literature: Bridging the Gap.* Ed. Winifred Bryan Horner. Chicago: University of Chicago Press, 1983, pp. 96–109.

Doheny-Farina, Stephen. "Writing in an Emerging Organization: An Ethnographic Study." *Written Communication* 3(April 1986):158–185.

———. "Creating a Text/Creating a Company: The Role of a Text in the Rise and Decline of an Organization." *Text and the Professions.* Eds. Charles Bazerman and James Paradis. Madison: University of Wisconsin Press, 1988.

———, and Lee Odell. "Ethnographic Research on Writing: Assumptions and Methods." *Writing in Nonacademic Settings.* Eds. Lee Odell and Dixie Goswami. New York: Guilford Press, 1985, pp. 503–535.

Freed, Richard C. and Glenn J. Broadhead. "Discourse Communities, Sacred Texts, and Institutional Norms." *College Composition and Communication* 38(May 1987):154–165.

Harrison, Teresa. "Frameworks for the Study of Writing in Organizational Contexts." *Written Communication* 9(January 1987):3–23.

Herrington, Anne J. "Writing in Academic Settings: A Study of the Contexts for Writing in Two College Chemical Engineering Courses." *Research in the Teaching of English* 19(December 1985):331–359.

Kuhn, Thomas S. *The Structure of Scientific Revolutions.* 2nd ed. Chicago: University of Chicago Press, 1970.

Moran, Charles. "Writing from the Inside Out: Reading with Authority." Paper presented to the Modern Languages Association Convention, New York, December, 1986.

Myers, Greg. "The Social Construction of Two Biologists' Proposals." *Written Communication* 2(July 1985):219–245.

Odell, Lee, and Dixie Goswami. "Writing in a Non-Academic Setting." *Research in the Teaching of English* 16(October 1982)201–223.

———, ———, and Doris Quick. "Writing Outside the English Composition Class." *Writing in Non-Academic Settings.* Final Report NIE-G-0224. Troy, N.Y.: Rensselaer Polytechnic Institute, Dept. of Language, Literature, and Communication, 1981, pp. 81–116.

———, ———, Anne Herrington, and Doris Quick. "Studying Writing in Non-Academic Settings." *New Essays in Technical and Scientific Communication: Research, Theory,*

*Practice.* Eds. P. Anderson, R. Brockman, and C. Miller. Farmingdale, N.Y.: Baywood, 1983, pp. 17–40.

Paradis, James, David Dobrin, and Richard Miller. "Writing at Exxon ITD: Notes on the Writing Environment of an R&D Organization." *Writing in Nonacademic Settings.* Eds. Lee Odell and Dixie Goswami. New York: Guilford Press, 1985, pp. 281–307.

Perelman, Les. "The Context of Classroom Writing." *College English* 48(September 1986):471–479.

Raymond, James C. "Fictions and Freedom in Writing about Literature." Paper presented to the Modern Languages Association Convention, New York, December, 1986.

Rorty, Richard. *Philosophy and the Mirror of Nature.* Princeton, N.J.: Princeton University Press, 1979.

Selzer, Jack. "The Composing Process of an Engineer." *College Composition and Communication* 34(May 1983):178–187.

# PROCESS AND GENRE

Mary Ann Eiler
American Medical Association

*Mary Ann Eiler received her Ph.D. in Linguistics from the Illinois Institute of Technology in 1979 after studying with M.A.K. Halliday both in the U.S. and Australia. Since 1982, she has developed and written statistical publications for the American Medical Association. She has given document design presentations for the American Medical Writers Association and the Association for Business Communications and has published and continues to research in the field of document design and graphics theory.*

*Eiler has also served as a lecturer in Technical and Business Writing for the College of DuPage and as an instructor in Italian, as a member of the editorial board of* Training Today *magazine, and as editor for The Society of Midland Authors Newsletter. She is currently a member of the NCTE Committee to Evaluate Curriculum Guides.*

## INTRODUCTION

This paper argues that to discover the dynamics of the writing act, features of both the writing process and written product should be formally studied. That is to say, the act of writing should not be divorced from its goal—the type of discourse the writer is attempting to create. Although this approach insists on the notion of genre or canonical form as a strong determinant of the writing event, it also requires (1) an appreciation of the entire context or conditions in which the event occurs, with demands posed by audience, content or subject matter, as well as physical and non-physical environment, and (2) a clear distinction between procedures used to foster developmental writing in school and processes that characterize the writing acts of professional writers. To ignore these dimensions is to trivialize the totality and uniqueness of each writing act and to arbitrarily "canonize" the popular linear model of prewriting, writing, editing, revision, and the like. It is also to blur what is required to teach writing across the curriculum effectively and to widen the gap between the writing experience in school and writing on the job or in the professions.

To support this argument, three separate case studies involving writing in school, writing on the job, and writing in a science are discussed. More specifically, these case studies include rhetorical and linguistic analyses of (1) the development of expository essays written by ninth graders in response to literature, (2) a statistical monograph written on the job by a sociologist and a professional writer, and (3) a lecture-chapter on physics delivered by a scientist and edited for inclusion in a college textbook.

In the first study, student writers share with their teacher in taped conversations their rhetorical and linguistic decisions as they try to write an expository essay on literature. In the second, in a collaborative writing project, a sociologist and a professional writer share their linguistic, rhetorical, and typographic choices as they prepare a statistical document which, unlike literary analysis, had no traditionally defined or "accepted" canonical form. In the third study, the oral and written features of a textbook chapter on quantum behavior, edited from an oral lecture, are examined. All three studies demonstrate that if we are to speak *at all* of a composing process, we must do so not only in linear and recursive terms but also as being genre- and environment-specific and as highly dependent on variables like prior knowledge of content areas and procedures.

## WRITING ABOUT LITERATURE IN SCHOOL

### Narrative Fiction and Written Exposition

The expository essay on literature is a common assignment in U.S. high schools. It is, however, one that makes extensive linguistic demands on the writer.[1] The writer must first "know how to" read a novel or short story and be consciously aware of its structure. The writer must also know how to undertake a variety of simultaneous roles: reader of the novel, writer for a well-defined or ill-defined audience, and critic of literature. The writer must know how to manage expository prose as it is taught and institutionalized in school, with its deductive, hierarchical mapping of information into an introduction, body, and conclusion. The writer must understand and know how to manipulate the concepts and language of literary analysis like plot, theme, character, setting, symbol, tone, among others. Finally, writers must bridge the gap between an oral discussion of literature—as conducted in class, where they can supply background information to further explain or justify a comment or interpretation *on demand*—and the production of a written essay that must stand on its own without the opportunity of supplying the reader with further or clarifying information.[2]

M. A. K. Halliday in "Text as Semantic Choice in Social Contexts" discusses the demands of genre and situation in linguistic expression. Halliday explains how what we are calling "content area and environment" will determine the choice of language to tell what we have experienced.[3] For example, we cannot write that "Fortunato in Poe's 'The Cask of Amontillado' suffers an ironic fate" unless we first are able to read the story, conceptualize it as being ironic, know how to use the term "irony," and do so in expository syntax. For a student learning how to write about literature—or, for that matter, learning how to write—this is a tall order, for from every direction the task is dependent on sophisticated language skills. In contrast, if the student were writing an expository essay about a dance or football game, the complexity of the task would be greatly reduced, for the dance and the game, unlike literature, are not dependent on verbal language for their existence. One does not need language to watch a game or a dance. When Kinneavy observes that "no text is autonomous . . . it exists within a biographical and historical stream,"[4] he is, I believe, talking about situational context, as is Halliday. If we think about the game, dance, and Poe's story, we can make a similar point. Although in the large sense, the process of writing may be thought of as universal, in its concrete manifestation it cannot be divorced from its goal. Just as I cannot viably engage in the process of dressmaking without conceptualizing the pattern *first*, I cannot write about a Poe short story without understanding the structure of the genre. Unlike the case with the dance or game, however, I have access to that structure only through language.

## *Research Design*

As part of my Ph.D. thesis ("Writing about Literature: A Study of Cohesion in the Expository Texts of Ninth Graders")[5], I tape-recorded my students in composition conferences in which they talked about their language choices and language difficulties in writing about novels they had read for their expository essays. The students had just completed an intensive unit on the expository essay that focused on the hierarchical structure of introduction, body, and conclusion, as well as levels of generality and specificity and other rhetorical principles typically institutionalized in high school textbooks. Also presented were instructions like attention openers, coherence strategies between and among segments of text, background information from literature to understand comments made, conclusions of summation or high points, among others.

To test my hypothesis regarding the difficulty of such writing tasks with their language and genre dependencies, I selected for my case study academically talented ninth graders who were selected for honors English placement by the high school placement office on the basis of (1) scores on the Otis Lennon IQ Test, (2) paragraph and language meaning scores and grade equivalents on the Stanford Achievement Test, and (3) recommendations for placement made by junior high school reading and English teachers—recommendations based on the students' classroom performance. The average IQ score of the research group was 135, a score indicating placement in the top tenth of the class, a top-tenth IQ score consisting of 130 or higher. In the Stanford Achievement Test, in the subtest "Paragraph Meaning," grade scores or grade equivalents for the entire ninth grade class ranged from 2.7 to 12.9. The average grade equivalent of the research population was 11.7; a top-tenth grade score equivalent began at 11.6. In the subtest "Language," the range of grade score equivalents for the entire ninth grade class was 2.1 to 12.9. The average grade equivalent of the research population was 11.5, a top-tenth grade equivalent beginning at 11.2.

Approximately 100 ninth graders out of a total ninth-grade population of 1,200 students were placed in the highest ability group for English—prehonors English. Of the 100 students placed in prehonors English, 32 students—or two classes—formed the initial population selection for the study. All 32 students were assigned three writing tasks at critical junctures in the school year. Writing task 1 was administered in early October, before any instruction in grammar or composition but after an intensive study of the short story. Topic and composition form were left to the students. Students were told that they could choose whatever form they felt most appropriate to discuss the collection of short stories by one author they had chosen to read. For example, they could choose a written strategy they had used before for similar assignments in junior high school or think up a new one.

Writing task 2 was administered in early February, after three months of intensive study in written composition and grammar. Students selected their own novels and topics but were expected to adhere to the hierarchical structure of the expository essay as taught in class. Immediately preceding the submission of this task, each student was taped in a twenty- to thirty-minute composition conference with me, where the students discussed the assignment, the composing problems, and their interpretations or understandings of the instructions in composition as given in class. Writing task 3 was administered in June, after a semester devoted to extensive and intensive study of literature and composition on an individual needs basis. In task 3 students were presented with five similarly structured topics such as the following:

> The leading character in a piece of fiction, a persona in a poem, or a real person in a biography is often confronted with the necessity of making a decision which will influence his fate or the fate of someone connected with or opposed to him. The choice often reveals what the character, persona, or person understands of himself, others, and the world around him.
>
> Considering four or five or more selections of the literature you have read this year, write an essay in which you discuss *decision making* by the characters, the persona(e) or person(s): the choice or choices made, what the choice or choices reveal, the consequences.

Writing task 3 was to represent an optimal literary response to a sophisticated body of literature representative of several genre types—epic poetry, biography, imaginative literature—in a cumulative demonstration of expertise in written exposition.

Of the 32 students making up the initial research population, 10 were eliminated through a control of the student variable. All students were observed for extralinguistic factors of performance (e.g., illness, fatigue, emotional strains, absence on days tasks were assigned, unwillingness to be part of the study, and the like). The essays of the remaining 22 students were critiqued in turn by four teachers in the honors English program from grades 9 through 12 according to a formally devised Composition Scoring Scale which addressed (1) plan of organization and development, (2) sentence structure, (3) vocabulary, (4) style, (5) grammatical mechanics, and (6) literary interpretation and response. As a result of these measures, the student population was further decreased to 15 students for a symmetrical placement of five in the low-scoring group, five in the middle group, and five in the high-scoring group. A representative sampling of observations on the composing process from the taped composition conferences at writing task 2 for these groups follow.

## Taped Conversations on Composition

Each one of the five students in the low group had difficulty conforming introductory paragraphs to the rhetorical conventions of introduction presented in class, with its features of background information, attention-getting devices, anticipation of thesis statement, and formulation of the thesis statement itself. One student writing about *The Ugly American* rejected his first linguistic inclination as too "bookish" and counterintuitive but knew of no other options—"I was trying to use attention-getter words . . . I was thinking of colorful words like 'plateaus,' 'explores.' " The second student expressed difficulty in designing the hierarchical-subordinate relations in the opening paragraph. She had written: "George Orwell uses allegory to show what can happen to Communism if the leaders get too power-hungry. He uses animals in place of people but still achieves the effect of people misusing power." But then she expressed these misgivings: "I was going to say something like the pigs claim that they're the smartest and then take all of the benefits for themselves, but then that's going down to the pigs and for the first paragraph don't we want to keep it sort of general?"

The third, fourth, and fifth students in the group all spoke of difficulty in abstracting background information for their introductions and preventing drifts into narration. That is, when they began to make an expository comment about some aspect of the short story, they invariably began (and ended) by retelling a good portion of the story, so that their essay became more narrative than expository.

Students in the low group also discussed problems and solutions regarding relationships between the introductory and developmental paragraphs that followed. The student of the essay on *The Ugly American*, who had taken "range of characters" as his topic, stated "I don't have trouble with this because the whole book was filled with characterizations." What this student was saying, in effect, was that since the short story was structured by characterizations, he had no problem structuring his essay in the same way, thus using the form of one genre to write another. The second student had difficulty stating a global position regarding the collection. When I asked "Can you give me a larger view of the book?" the student responded "If I put it down I think it'll be narrative." She also had misgivings about injecting herself in the essay through the use of the first person— "It sounds dumb to say 'I'm going to show you. . . .'" Summing up was the major challenge for the third student but the structure of his essay itself was no problem for him, for he had managed, for the organizational structure of his essay, to cull from *The Andromeda Strain* a listing of precautions that the United States should have taken. The fourth student, in effect, reported that *All Quiet on the Western Front* posed problems because its organization was more oblique than what he saw as the temporal and locative structure of *The Longest Day*, a novel he had successfully written about in an earlier assignment: "But like in *The Longest Day* I had the obstacles on the water and then the land . . . on the beach . . . and on the land . . . and then I could go like "Once they got out of the water and onto the beach, they. . . ."  The fifth student had difficulties making generalizations about *A Separate Peace* in essay-length exposition. Having discussed with me the adolescent experiences of Gene and Phineas, she eventually wrote "Gene has a need for recognition and a feeling of importance so he relies on his friend Phineas's opinions." This shows the relation of thought to writing process or thought as an aspect of the writing process. The discussion of Gene and Phineas's experiences was a necessary *inductive* prelude for the *deductive* expository observation regarding Gene's need to recognize his importance.

A review of the low group's reactions to the assignment reveals the wedding of process to specific genre: (1) the attempt to use language of the book review or literary style and then its rejection as stereotypic as seen in the student's reaction to words like "explores" and "plateaus," (2) the making of recursive judgments regarding appropriate levels of generality in a given segment of the essay and the explicit statement of purpose using the first person in light of the "canon" given in class, (3) the dependence on the structure of one genre to form another, and finally (4) the reversal of an inductive thought process in the deductive ordering of the written discourse.

The students in the middle group, like those in the low group, came to the conferences with drafts of the introductory paragraph. Like some members of the low group, they primarily questioned whether their paragraphs were "long enough," thus reacting to a visual aspect of the canon, namely the chunking of information in visually well-developed paragraphs. Unlike members in the low group, they did not have difficulty integrating background information in the introduction. This seemed to indicate a control over the genre interferences which by contrast manifested themselves in the low group as tendencies to rewrite the narrative. Also, while the low group had experienced difficulties with the model or canonical form introduced in the classroom, the middle group, for the most part, felt that such models were helpful. The first student admitted, however, that she did have trouble trying to write around the topic sentence and wrote extraneous verbiage to "fill in" as she was "trying to think of something to say." This type of hedging is not atypical and has counterparts in oral discourse, where expressions like "that is to say" or "well . . ." allow the speaker to formulate his or her statement.

The second student's only concern, as to whether I could differentiate his thesis statement from his background information, indicated his need for reassurance that he had successfully followed canonical form. The third student had drafted a perceptive introductory paragraph about *Brave New World*. When asked how he felt about his work, he replied, "I like it. If I go into too much more, I'm going to be taking away from my other points." This student had clearly conceptualized the superordinate and subordinate structuring of the expository text. Narrative detail was clearly separate from and subordinate to statements of topic and position. He had, in short, mastered the abilities to generalize deductively about the literary text. This student had also mastered the differentiation of genre (unlike the student in the low group who used the structure of the short story to guide the development of the expository essay by using a series of characterizations). The second student, moreover, had learned how to integrate aspects of the literary text into expository text according to the canonical form given in class. What problem he did have was a philosophical one. Having stated that the characters in the novel chose "universal happiness" at the cost of their own individuality, he was hard put to determine what was a human right and what was a human freedom.

The fourth student's only misgiving was length—was his introductory paragraph long enough? Like the first student alluded to earlier, he was concerned about length as a visual aspect of canonical form. The fifth student came to the conference with difficulties reading *Pride and Prejudice,* thus confirming the intense language dependency posed by writing about literature in contrast to writing about nonverbal experiences.

The middle group expressed an assortment of problems with development. One student tried to model her essay as a superparagraph but was uncertain how she could order major points and minor points. She was also confused about the conclusion. A second student also spoke of the longer essay in terms of the single-paragraph composition. Speaking of a development paragraph, he asked, "You'd have then, for the paragraph, a topic sentence followed by supports?" In the course of the conference, he managed to devise a temporal sequence as the organizational principle of his essay. A temporal expository sequence, though canonical, approximates the time relations of narrative. Although not retelling the story, this student was seemingly transferring the organizational principle of a familiar genre (the novel) to an unfamiliar one, his essay. After recognizing the chronological order that was emerging, the student commented "I don't really know how to do the last paragraph." The last paragraph could not be sequenced temporally, thus returning him to the challenge of a hierarchical rather than temporal structure.

A third student had already written three supporting statements for his thesis statement. In the conference he spoke of narrative events he would relate to each observation. His major problem was also the final paragraph. The student ruled out summary as an option because he did not know how to select from the profusion of narrative details. A fourth student, like the others, was mystified by the instructional demands for a conclusion—"kind of how to write it . . . how to sum everything up."

A fifth student in the middle group (the reader of *Brave New World*) continued to have difficulty with a philosophical interpretation of events in the novel and potential definitions and subcategorizations for rights and freedoms. This student, unlike some of his peers, was removed from a locative or temporal ordering schema and ready for rhetorical expression through definition. When asked if he anticipated any difficulty with his concluding paragraph, he replied "I don't think so. I think in my final paragraph I'll probably restate the ideas of rights and freedoms."

When asked how they would have written the book paper a year earlier or before the instruction in expository writing given prior to the assignment, the middle group, like the low group, gave essentially the same type of response—if given the assignment a year earlier, they would have either retold the story or summarized it.

The middle group, however, unlike the low group, demonstrated key advancements in the development of exposition about narrative fiction. For the most part, they did not rewrite narrative. They were responsive to the hierarchical dependencies and levels of generality in the expository essay and sensitive to the visual aspects of the genre, as a poet would be sensitive who visualizes the form of verse on a page. What did trouble them was the conclusion, which required not only higher degrees of cognitive synthesis but also more complex language to express that synthesis. Although taught in class, conclusion models were sparse. It was more difficult also to mimic the anatomy of the conclusion. The students knew that one option was to reflect the position of the thesis or topic statement, but the quandary was how to accomplish this without blind restatement.

Like the students in the low and middle groups, students in the high group came to the conferences with substantial parts of their preliminary drafts written. One student, writing of the characters in a Victoria Holt novel, questioned: "Am I conveying the idea that they're sort of stereotyped in that introductory paragraph or am I just not getting that across to the reader?" She was also concerned that the following was "bad English": "Holt provides the enchanted forest as a background for the story, giving the story an air of fantasy." What she was reacting to so negatively was "air of fantasy." She was selecting options that sounded like the erudite language of the models because she did not have the language resources readily available to say what she meant. Writing process here was directly related to the student's perceptions of the language of literary criticism, but she was astute enough to also recognize its sometimes formulaic and stereotypic tone. She also recognized that such expressions were not her own and were therefore unnatural.

A second student also rejected the language she had originally used in her introduction, which read as follows:

> In *The Return of the Native,* Hardy has frozen forever the life on Egdon Heath. The characters, setting, and plot of this novel intertwine together in order to transport the reader back into Hardy's own time and place. Alone, none of the elements are significant, but when put together, they are in perfect harmony and form a powerful piece of literature.

The student commented that "a powerful piece of literature" was "pretty bad. It just sounds too overused." As did other students, she attempted to model her statement on a lexicon she thought characterized the genre, but she recognized such choices as stereotypic and counterintuitive.

A third student came to the conference with a fully drafted introduction but asked "Is that introductory paragraph the way it should be?" She was, in effect, seeking confirmation that she had adhered to the canonical form of the expository essay as presented in class. The fourth student complained that he was having problems thinking of a concluding paragraph, while the conference of the fifth student in the high group was almost exclusively devoted to talking about *The Return of the Native.* Unlike the other students, she had written journallike notes to herself about what she planned to include in her introduction, notes that included observations like "... different types of characters ... can't exactly decide what to say about them, possibly include the scenery, the heath, the beauty and the mystery, danger and happiness...." Her problem was directly related to literary response. As she commented on the abstractions in her notes, she realized, "They're all those things in one, you know." She expressed difficulties in putting into language the relationships she knew existed between and among elements of narrative typology. As she explained: "... well, like, the heath ... Mrs. Yeobright ... she likes it and so the heath ... most of the time like when it refers to her with scenery it seems like it brings her happiness."

This student's rather sophisticated notion of organic form was complicating the writing process because she seemingly lacked the immediate language resources to express or match her perceptions. She, also, unlike the others in the high group, raised questions about background information and audience—"Are we supposed to write this like no one's ever heard of the book?"—which in turn raised questions of the audience's prior knowledge as a variable that needs anticipation in the writing process. Later, she delineated the order of her introduction: "It seems to me that like it would start off something like "In *The Return of the Native* ..." and it would describe briefly the heath first and then how ... the characters look at it in a different way and that forms their opinion."

She was in effect using setting as an organizational principle and focal point for her essay, thus demonstrating how the genre of the literary text was influencing the developmental process of writing the expository text. However, her approach was more sophisticated than that of the member of the low group, who defaulted to a series of characterizations. For the reader of *The Return of the Native*, setting was a constant around which she made her interpretations.

A consistent problem for the high group was selecting language to express generalizations made or implicit in their introductions so as to relate with precision their intended meaning. One student, having written that "To Hemingway war is not a historic textbook event but a catalyst for all the corrupt, destructive and wasteful elements in the human soul," had both syntactic and semantic difficulty relating Frederick Henry's plight to this observation. She tested alternate options like these:

As a result of war, Henry's own irresponsibility ...
Henry becomes irresponsible ...
Henry's own irresponsibility creates problems ...
no, not problems ... creates suffering?

A second student wanted to discuss symbolism in *This Perfect Day* but did not know how to correlate his perceptions with the elements of the narrative typology. He had spoken earlier about types of Utopian societies and the futility they represented in the novel. When the conference turned to questions of development, he asked "Can you tell me if there is any way I can include symbolism?" This student's dilemma involved an integration of his literary perceptions as a prerequisite to putting pen to paper. In his case, prewriting was governed by his perceptions of the literary genre he had read.

The third student's fear that her development was turning into a summary was justified. When I suggested she might focus on one of the elements, like setting or character, she did not know how to structure a taxonomy within the element. Finally, she decided to focus on characters and the effects the social atmosphere had on them. The fourth student also decided to work with characters, specifically a correlation of character and setting. However, the student had questions about what strategies she should adopt. Referring to her introduction, she asked "How, considering what I said, would I have to prove that the forests here are a good background for my characters?" Throughout the conference her questions centered on taxonomy: "Could you say the enchanted forest includes castles and stuff?"

The fifth student had posited "The beauty and the mystery, danger and happiness of Egdon Heath" but then found difficulty relating specific characters to such abstractions. She wondered whether she could write "Each character's opinion of the Heath, be it good or bad, reflects . . ." She also had difficulty determining a taxonomy: "I've gotta decide which way I'm going to do the paragraphs, then whether I'm going to focus more into the characters or more the opinions." Later, she mused: "You could do a whole thing on happiness, a whole thing on beauty, or you could do beauty and happiness together. There's so many ways in which you can combine it." Her deliberations on process, like those of some earlier students, were directly correlated with her level and sophistication in literary response.

Of these five high-group students, two ended their conferences discussing the strategies they would employ or were already employing to finish their essays, thus leaving no time for questions regarding their earlier writing experiences with literature. The third student, however, when asked if the instruction in general and specific ordering of text was helpful, commented that this approach was new: "I had always thought I needed to explain what was happening and see I really don't have to do that because that's what brings in narration." The fourth student explained "We didn't do much expository writing." When asked what kinds of writing she did do, she replied: "We did a little bit of descriptive . . . once in a while we did narrative." Only the fifth student had had pre-high school instruction in deductive ordering of an expository text with a focus on an introduction, body, and conclusion.

## *Summary*

The high group demonstrated problems of a more sophisticated correlation of process to genre as seen in the complicating factor of literary response and the recognition of the appropriateness of setting up taxonomic relations in text. The high group was able to articulate more successfully than the other groups the relationships that *should* govern the integration of the primary literary text in the secondary expository text, but they too were often hard pressed to realize those relationships in language. In review, the low, middle, and high groups, though all representative of academically talented students, represent a *gradation* in skills in the approach to an unfamiliar genre. The genre of expository writing was new to almost all the students. It clearly required instruction and its realization was for all groups influenced by the content area that informed it, namely the typology and structure of the literary text itself.

The tapes also demonstrate that at every juncture writing about literature is a "language-intensive" process governed by knowledge of *product* and that the delineation of the process is predicated on the writing goal. The tapes also demonstrate that product realization is *developmental*, suggesting not only the role of prior knowledge of content area in a delineation of process but also an understanding of how that content area will configure the "written goal." These are variables, it appears, that teachers must understand and allow for both in curriculum development and in the critical evaluation of student writing.

The on-the-job case study that follows begins with statistical data as content area and demonstrates how text was developed for publication to present that data in the absence of a rhetorically defined canonical form. This case study also includes the visual language of graphic display and its role in the writing process and product development.

## WRITING STATISTICAL DATA PUBLICATIONS ON THE JOB

The second case study focused on the conceptualization and writing of a book on demographics for the American Medical Association that included statistical data on physician location, specialty, and professional activity.[6] The project was designed and authored through the collaboration of a professional writer (myself) and a sociologist. Apart from the fact that the book would contain both data analysis and tabulations, there existed *no prescribed canon* or rhetorical tradition for the genre. The context or environment of writing was, however, defined by extralinguistic variables like budget and time considerations as well as technological facilities. All tabulations were generated off the AMA Physician Masterfile in camera-ready laser-print output. All text was ultimately prepared on a word processor and coded for an outside typographer and printer.

In the project-planning or prewriting stage, the two authors (hereafter John and Mary Ann) reviewed a variety of similar publications in an attempt to determine what appeared to be *obligatory* and *optional* features of the genre or what seemed to approach an "industry standard." The questions they asked were in some ways related to Hasan's study of the structure of the nursery tale, where she differentiates between a bedtime story and a nursery tale and explicitly asks "What are the properties a text must display in order to be an instance of the genre 'nursery tale'?"[7]

For Mary Ann and John there were a variety of questions related to the concept of genre: What should a book on demographic statistics contain within the major components of data analysis and tabulations? What proportions should exist between and among the treatment of specific data variables? What kinds of charts, graphs, and summary tables should be included, if any? How would the structure of the data—numbers and percentages in tables—dictate or influence the analysis? John looked at the data for their "stories." What and how many stories are implicit in these data? What tables should we design to tell these stories? One story, for example, centered on foreign medical graduates and their geographical location patterns by specialty choice in the fifty states. Another concerned U.S. medical graduates and their schools of graduation and choice of activity, be it office- or hospital-based practice. Mary Ann asked how obligatory features of text, namely verbal language, should be integrated with optional but preferred features like charts, tables, and graphics, and how all of this information could be "mapped" in a cohesive proportional way in the publication.[8] Prewriting was characterized, therefore, in large part by considerations of what and how *visual* and *verbal* as well as *numerical* aspects of the book would dictate its design.[9]

The design of tables involved still further considerations like the principles of reducing the universe of data so that patterns could be seen and meaningful summaries made explicit.[10] The authors decided on two types of tables: (1) large, full-page data spreads of cross-tabulations that present aggregated counts of physicians by various professional activities (e.g., office-based practice, hospital-based practice, research, administration, etc., and over 100 schools of graduation as one case in point) and (2) small "chunked" tables integrated in text flow that constitute highlights or reductions of the larger spreads. These, in turn, would reflect data-reduction techniques like ranking of variables from high to low, salient trend data, and so forth. Tabular data would also, where warranted by the data, be given focus in graphics. The decision to draw a graphic was not arbitrary. If the data suggested a more dramatic review in visual form than in verbal language, the graphic was made. The selection of type of graphic was also motivated by the type of data. A line graph is more suited to present trend or time series, while a dissected pie can dramatize the components or relationships in a full complement. All visuals were designed, as was the text, for a mixed audience—some oriented to statistics and others not—of professionals such as physicians, researchers, management consultants, legislators, curriculum planners in medical schools, and others. These audiences would use the book for policy making and analysis, retention studies, forecasting, and membership recruitment and as a basis for more sophisticated statistical studies.

Like writing about literature, the process of writing the statistical text was influenced by the goal, namely an anticipation of the finished product. Also, both the literary discussions written by the students and the statistical text written by professionals were based on *prior knowledge* that served in many ways to "customize" the composing process. In the case of literary analysis, the students needed to understand the structure of the novel. The narrative typology of plot, theme, character, symbol, etc., were determining variables in the approach to the expository essay. In the case of the students, these variables were further integrated in an institutionalized rhetorical tradition.

The statistical text also depended on prior structures of data, graphics, and statistical "storytelling." Unlike literary analysis, however, the statistical document and its components did not always have a clearly defined or mapped visual and verbal rhetoric, thus motivating questions on the part of the authors like: (1) What space and size proportions should exist between tables, graphics, and lines of text on a page? (2) How does eye movement suggest where graphics and insert tables should be placed on a page?

Fowler seems to address the particularization of the composing process toward intended product in his almost philosophical description of what he calls "textual competence": ". . . 'textual competence' is knowledge of the conventions for forming discourse, on the foundation centrally of the grammatical system and additionally on the basis of various other systems of knowledge."[11]

What Fowler seems to be saying is that not only does one need a knowledge of the grammatical system of a language or a linguistic competence to generate a text but a knowledge of other systems or conventions as well. Textual competence includes not only an understanding of canon—if available—and of audience but also of content or subject. We might add here that since the canon for the technical-statistical data text is evolving in concert with technology itself, with the development or approach toward a systematic graphic theory, and with sophistication in statistical theory and method, the *search* for canon is more pronounced. It is this very search and the textual competencies implicit in it that play such a formidable role in the writing process for the types of texts that Mary Ann and John were attempting to produce.

Audience as well as other considerations in the entire contextual environment of the writing event were major determinants toward the final product.[12] Just as prior knowledge of content in all its manifestations were major determinants of the statistical document as written, the audience's level of prior knowledge influenced both the design and writing of the book. John and Mary Ann asked themselves questions like:

- What prior knowledge of the physician population discussed and presented in the book did the audience have?
- What "stories" about this population had already been published in the professional literature?
- How would the audience make use of the book?

For marketing and budgetary purposes, the authors also needed to visualize the completed document before the fact: (1) How many pages were anticipated? (2) What was the anticipated ratio of pages of text to solid pages of large table spreads? (3) How many graphics would there be and how elaborate would they be, given budget constraints for artwork?

The authors decided that the book would focus on those physicians in U.S. medicine who had received their degrees from foreign schools. Through informal field testing, analysis of literature reviews, and manpower assessments, John and Mary Ann determined that the book would attempt to answer questions like the following:

- What years saw the greatest influx of foreign medical physicians? The least influx?
- What foreign schools graduated them?
- Where did foreign medical graduates locate in the United States?
- How did the location patterns of foreign physicians differ from those of U.S.-born physicians who received their medical degrees in the United States?

The data tables and graphics would be "user-friendly," providing optimal access for the mixed audience described earlier with the "range of meaningful design options" correlated to the type of information presented.[13] Types of graphics would be wedded to the data—pie charts when appropriate, etc. In the absence of a "universal optimal table design," as Wright argues, the author or designer must be aware that there is "No appropriate alternative to analyzing the user's requirements in detail."[14]

Users, as indicated, constituted a mixed audience with a variety of needs. Further, it was unlikely that any one readership would "read" the book from cover to cover, but instead would use it as a reference or resource tool, giving more or less attention to segments. Thus three modules of information—trends, characteristics, and location—of physician data were planned. Earlier and later information would require cohesive bonding. Assumptions would need to be made regarding old information or "what the readers were already likely to know" about the topic and decisions made on how new information would build on that prior knowledge and extend it. Thus, document design in its verbal and visual aspects would be dictated by type of discourse with its linguistic options and constraints[15] and type of audience or user requirements.

Specifically, the interplay of text and graphics would directly influence the composing process. Decisions would be made regarding what best could be presented verbally, numerically, or graphically. The presence of graphics and tables on the page would influence how and where text would be placed, its length and proportion, and how best to display all varieties of information for optimal reader access. The composition itself of a statistical data text in a purely descriptive, nonargumentative mode would dictate choice not only of individual semantic items but syntactic patterns as well. For example, the discussion of foreign doctors would not be controversial or "sensational," as is often the case in the popular press, but rather strictly objective, as dictated by the data. Sentence structure would often be controlled by the verb. Elsewhere (see "Semiotics of Document Design"[16]) I have discussed how the "sublanguage" of a specific type of discourse can limit the scope of stylistic variation. For instance, in discussions of counts and percentage distributions of physicians, verbs like "increased," "demonstrated," "accounted for," and "revealed" will predictably prevail and control syntactic strings. These types of linguistic properties of text, as well as others, require continued study and formalization not only as descriptors of genres but for their power to influence and even control the writing process.

## *Summary*

The experience of designing and writing the document on physician data argues strongly for viewing the writing event from the perspective of both process *and* product. Waxler, in his observations in "On Process," clarifies the creative tension that should prevail between process and product in the act of composition. Although he decries the emphasis that most business writing textbooks place on the "product" rather than the "process" of writing, as "emphasizing death rather than life," his contextualization of the tension focuses on the relationship that should exist between the two concepts. Waxler:

> "Process" suggests movement, change, action. It is the life principle itself, a sign of growth, being alive. "Product" may be considered the termination of "process," the end of change, stasis.
>
> In this context, "process" may lead to "product," just as life leads to death. *In fact, in order to understand the meaning of a "process" we must understand the "product,"* just as we must understand death if we are to understand the meaning of our lives. To say that we teach "process" in our writing courses is usually, then, simply a way of describing what we emphasize: the activity of writing, for example, rather than the end result of writing.[17] [italics added]

John and Mary Ann needed to understand as many of the contingencies of the entire document design of their book as possible before writing it. Their experience in many ways was unique in the product/process controversy. There existed no coherent preconceived model or theory of genre as in the case of literature and literary analysis, no product to write toward or artificially "drive" the writing act as some opponents of product-oriented writing might charge. At the same time, they could not engage in "blind" process without investigating the parameters of what they realistically could accomplish in a situation of an evolving rather than "canonized" genre. In their case, the act of writing was both process- and product-governed, much in the way that Waxler philosophically speaks of the tension or relationship between life and death.

## WRITING A TEXTBOOK CHAPTER ON SCIENCE

For the third case study, I began with the features of a *product* and searched for implications of *process* underlying that product by analyzing the sentence openings of a chapter on quantum behavior published in a college textbook. The chapter, from *The Feynman Lectures on Physics: Mainly Mechanics, Radiation, and Heat,* was a written translation of a lecture and thus could be expected to have features of both oral and written discourse in addition to its primary exposition, namely the writing about physics for a student audience. As I indicated in the complete study published elsewhere,[18] I was primarily interested in studying a finished product for its manifestation of linguistic choices as an instance of genre and correlating these choices with their use and function in the discourse. I recognized from the start that for a definitive description of a genre, the isolation of one segment like sentence openings (or for that matter even several linguistic segments) could not pretend in any way to be conclusive. My purpose in analyzing the quantum behavior chapter, however, was to posit (if not establish) a testing procedure for discovering linguistic and rhetorical genre structures, that is to say "the way particular types of information are conveyed and interpreted."[19] Once this information is available, I argue, one can begin to approach a "reconstruction" of the process of writing—however implicit that process is in the text—in a context-sensitive way that reveals the interplay of writer's intention and subject matter or content and the relationship of these variables to form. Once the reconstruction is available, we can perhaps assess more knowingly the complexities of writing tasks and work toward not only teaching methods to present them to students but also develop a scope and sequence of curriculum based on levels of linguistic development and sophistication implicitly required for their creation.

This focus on discovering genre structures revealed a strikingly similar tension between process and product both in the physics chapter and in the physician demographic publication. In these two discourses, the form can be said to reflect a content that "controls" its development. A similar type of "content control" toward development of form is seen in certain types of modern poetry where an "open" form evolves to accommodate the subject or the material of the poem. Conversely, the case of the institutionalized writing about literature in school, discussed previously, has closer analogues to the writing of that variety of poetry that begins with a preexisting form (like that of the sonnet, sestina, or others), where poets order their subject or material in patterns or chronologies that are largely given or established—the octave expressing the speaker's reluctance to surrender to a lover and the sestet showing her overcome by his charms.

As reader and linguist attempting to "reconstruct" aspects of the process of linguistic choice implicit in the quantum behavior chapter, I asked myself the following questions:

1. What linguistic and/or rhetorical properties make the chapter a scientific text on physics for a student audience and how can we identify these properties in a formal way?
2. What specific types of information are conveyed and how are they interpreted[20] through these text-forming strategies?
3. What patterns of linguistic choice in the text also demonstrate written and oral features of language use and how can they be correlated to the chapter's content and intention?

To answer these questions, at least in part, I analyzed sentence openings for linguistic features like nominal and pronominal subjects, nominalizations, coordinators, conjuncts, disjuncts, adjuncts, and other categories occurring in fronted position in the English sentence.[21]

The use of first and second personal pronouns in the chapter reflects the chapter's oral genesis, namely the lecture. The presence of the first person plural "we," however, also functions to unite reader and writer (e.g., student and teacher) in the joint learning venture typified in the classroom genre where, for example, in a different setting, an English teacher might say "As we can see in Poe's story . . ." or "let's turn to the setting described on page 10." Similarly, the frequent use of the coordinator "and" illustrates a variety of functions in addition to its predictable cohesive function of continuance in spoken language. These additional functions in the case of the chapter include (1) *contrast* in telling the story of scientific discovery and (2) teacher *comment* on the information presented. For example, in "Historically, the electron . . . was thought to behave like a particle, *and* then it was found that in many respects it behaved like a wave . . ." we have a report of earlier understandings of quantum behavior with the contrast marker "and" introducing later information of scientific discovery, as a textbook on physics would be expected to do. The use of "and" as comment in the following segment, however, shows a strikingly different function, but one also prototypical of its use in instruction genres: "Even the experts do not understand it, i.e., atomic behavior in the way they would like to, *and* it is perfectly reasonable that they should not. . . ." Here, the coordinator "and" initiates an interjection of teacher comment that contextualizes and interprets information for the reader; in so doing, it reinforces the role relationships of teacher and student evident elsewhere in the text.

This type of analysis does not mean to suggest that we tell our students to use coordinators in writing about quantum behavior. Far from it! Instead, what it can do is sensitize them to how linguistic and rhetorical choice can govern the interpretation of text in different contexts. Another case in point is the research currently conducted by the National Opinion Research Center (NORC) on survey design and respondents' understandings of survey questions. According to the *NORC 1985–1986 Report*, "the research team is investigating how the context in which a survey question is asked—particularly the order of a given item in relation to other items—causes respondents to retrieve beliefs supporting one side of the issue or the other in answering attitude questions."[22] Just as these analyses of how items are worded and ordered in contexts illustrates the genre of the survey questionnaire, so, too, the analysis of markers in the quantum behavior chapter demonstrates the *social interaction* that occurs between writer and audience and the interplay between content and intention in the *process* of creating text.

The use of the coordinator "but" in the physics chapter further illustrates this interaction in its functional correlation with both the form of lecture and content of quantum behavior. In (a) below, the use of "but" advances the lecture:

> (a) We could, of course, continuously skirt away from the atomic effects, *but* we shall instead interpose here a short excursion. . . .

In (b) below, "but" has a different function, namely that of illustrating the method of scientific discrimination.

> (b) We know how large objects will act, *but* things on a small scale just do not act that way.

The use of "when" clauses also demonstrates a functional correlation to the content of physics. In the segment that follows, taken from a section on experiments, the "when" clause expresses the conditional and circumstantial (as well as temporal) meaning associated with scientific testing:

> When hole 2 is covered, bullets can only pass through hole 1. . . .

One could substitute "if" for "when" in this example to further illustrate the contingency of scientific testing procedures that the use of "when" conveys.

Other adjuncts of time also illustrated the functional meaning of the chapter text. "Now" demonstrated the sense of collaborative learning, as in its ruminative use in segment (a):

> (a) *Now*, let us measure the wave intensity for various values of $x$. . . .

In segment (b), "now" conveys a sense of inference typically associated with scientific modes of thinking. Having explicated the wave theory of light, the lecturer comments:

> (b) So *now* . . . we see a *big* [italics in original] fuzzy flash. . . .

In (b) one could substitute "since that is so" for "now" to further underscore the functional meaning of inference.

Like time adjuncts, conditional clauses were functionally expressive of the content of the genre. The vast majority of these clauses in sentence openings were found in descriptions of experiments that involved water waves and electrons and in conclusions or arguments involving experimental procedures. This focus on experimental procedures is seen in the use of the conditional in the following segment:

> *If* one looks at the holes or, more accurately, *if* one has a piece of apparatus which is capable of determining whether the electrons go through hole 1 or hole 2, then one *can* [italics in original] say that it goes either through hole 1 or hole 2.

To summarize, the analysis of the lecture chapter was not intended to result in an exhaustive definition of genre but rather to be indicative of how linguistic choice is *functionally* related to aspects of genre. As *product*, the chapter illustrates the culmination of a *process* of meaningful choice: that is to say, the *realization* of linguistic and rhetorical decisions that characterize writing about quantum behavior for students. If Waxler has told us that to understand the process we must understand the product, we must also focus on what is required of linguistic resources in the process to achieve the goal of a specific product.

## CONCLUSION

In the three case studies discussed in this paper, we have looked "up close" at the tension between process and product and have illustrated that *both* are realities that cannot be ignored. For students writing about literature, where product involved a preestablished form (e.g., expository essay about literature), we saw that knowledge of the literary text itself was a significant variable in the "configuring" of the essay. We also saw that the achievement of the more successful essays involved a synthesis and conscious rendering of information, one that depended on the students' linguistic repertoire to manage and express their understanding of the literature in prescribed ways. Similarly, if the literary subject was understood but the "receiving" form of exposition was not, the narrative typology of the literary text itself became the structuring modus operandi or principle of the essay—e.g., a paragraph each for several characters in the story, or other similar arrangements based on literary elements.

In the case of the statistical data text on physician demographics, we saw still another tension between process and product, where search for canonical form to accommodate not only verbal but also numerical and graphic language was required, as was the interplay of text, tables, and graphics in the composing process. The linguistic properties of "restricted" texts, like statistical writing, was also examined for the extent to which it influenced the process of the writing act. Finally, a "reconstruction" of the process of language choice, however partial or cursory, as in the analysis of the chapter on quantum behavior, demonstrated how process was wedded to the defining features of subject material or content as well as dependent on the writer's intention and purpose, namely instruction in physics for a student audience.

In "Writing Instruction and Assessment: The Need for Interplay between Process and Product," Wolcott observes that "the constraints of a typical testing situation often work at cross-purposes with current writing-instruction theories, curtailing—especially for weaker writers—any potential applications of the process paradigm."[23] In the same discussion she argues that the "product-accountability" that assessment samples impose "may more closely resemble real-world writing tasks than do some other composition assignments."[24] The "dilemma" that Wolcott argues must be resolved is more accidental, it seems, than essential, and can find its solution, as this paper has argued, in formulating a theoretical and instructional paradigm that *allows for* the dynamics of both process and product in *concert.* Just as we would not ordinarily ask a student to "discover" the sonnet form through a writing process, so, too, where an established or preexisting form or genre is a given, it must be presented in instruction and the process toward its achievement must be creatively and formally nurtured. Similarly, in those types of writing tasks where subject or material can "search for its form," the writing process must also be nurtured as well as examined for what it involves and reveals regarding discovery of meaning and linguistic choice.

Wolcott's citations of Marie Jean Lederman's observations in "Why Test?" merit recording here for they target my central argument. While Lederman admits that "The best teachers do help students learn something about their own writing processes," she also argues that

> ... it is a lie to tell students that "product" does not matter.... The brilliant insight that may have flourished briefly before fading in the course of the writing process is of no use to anyone except, perhaps, the writer. What is altered does not matter to the reader, nor does the ease with which the writer composes. In the real world, product is all we can share with each other.[25]

If product is indeed all we share with each other in the real world, it is a terrible and sad anomaly (perhaps even a contradiction) that we do not share as much with our own students. In short, writing cannot be divorced from its goal, be that goal open or fixed in its form, any more than the dancer can be separated from the dance. Only in a context that allows and studies the tension between process and product as an instance of genre can the notion of discovery take on any real and enduring meaning and depth for both teachers and their students.

## Notes

1. Eiler, Mary Ann. Meaning and Choice in Writing about Literature: A Study of Cohesion in the Expository Texts of Ninth Graders. Ph.D. dissertation. Chicago: Illinois Institute of Technology, 1979. pp. 47–49. (#80-03647) University Microfilms, Ann Arbor, Mich., 1979.
2. ———. "Meaning and Choice in Writing about Literature." *Developmental Issues in Discourse.* Edited by Jonathan Fine and Roy O. Freedle. vol. 10 in the Series Advances in Discourse Processes. Norwood, N.J.: Ablex, 1983. pp. 170–171.
3. Halliday, M. A. K. "Text as Semantic Choice in Social Contexts." *Grammars and Descriptions.* Edited by T. A. Van Dijk and J. S. Petofi. Research in Text Theory 1. Berlin: Gruyter, 1977. p. 201.
4. Kinneavy, J. L. "The Aims of Discourse." *A Theory of Discourse.* Englewood Cliffs, N.J.: Prentice-Hall, 1971. pp. 22–24.
5. Eiler, Mary Ann. Meaning and Choice in Writing about Literature. (chap. 15)
6. Eiler, Mary Ann, and John D. Loft, *Foreign Medical Graduates in the U.S.* Chicago: American Medical Association, 1986.
7. Hasan, Ruqaiya. "The Structure of the Nursery Tale: An Essay in Text Typology." *Linguistica Testuale.* Atti Del XV Congresso Internazionale Di Studi. Edited by Lorenzo Coveri. Roma: Bulzoni, 1984. pp. 95–96.
8. Horn, Robert E. *The Information Mapping Course for Writing Procedures, Policies, and Documentation.* Waltham, Mass.: Information Mapping, 1984. *Note:* The concept of mapping information by knowledge type is derived from Horn's research. The specific methods developed in the course, however, were not applied to the statistical data text.

9. Eiler, Mary Ann. "Semiotics of Document Design." *Language Topics*. Edited by Ross Steele and Terry Threadgold. vol. 2. Amsterdam: John Benjamins, 1987.
10. Ehrenberg, A. S. C. *Data Reduction: Analyzing and Interpreting Statistical Data.* 1975. Chichester, England: Wiley, 1978.
11. Fowler, Roger. "Cohesive, Progressive, and Localizing Aspects of Text Structure." *Grammars and Descriptions*. Edited by T. A. Van Dijk and J. S. Petofi. Research in Text Theory 1. Berlin: Gruyter, 1977. p. 70.
12. Eiler, Mary Ann. "Semiotics of Document Design."
13. Wright, Patricia. "A User-Oriented Approach to the Design of Tables and Flowcharts." *A Technology of Text: Principles for Structuring, Designing, and Displaying Text.* Edited by David J. Jonassen. Englewood Cliffs, N.J.: Educational Technology Publications, 1982. p. 329.
14. Wright, Patricia. "A User-Oriented Approach to the Design of Tables and Flowcharts." p. 319.
15. Lehrberger, John, and Kittredge, Richard. (Eds.). *Sublanguage: Studies of Language in Restricted Semantic Domains.* Berlin: Gruyter, 1982.
16. Eiler, Mary Ann. "Semiotics of Document Design."
17. Waxler, Robert P. "On Process." *The Journal of Business Communication.* vol. 24, no. 1, winter 1987. p. 41.
18. Eiler, Mary Ann. "Thematic Distribution as a Heuristic for Written Discourse Function." *Functional Approaches to Writing.* Edited by Barbara Couture. London: Pinter, 1986.
19. ———. "Thematic Distribution as a Heuristic for Written Discourse Function." p. 49.
20. ———. "Thematic Distribution as a Heuristic for Written Discourse Function." p. 67.
21. ———. "Thematic Distribution as a Heuristic for Written Discourse Function." p. 55.
22. NORC Report 1985–1986. Chicago: University of Chicago Press, 1987. p. 55.
23. Wolcott, Willa. "Writing Instruction and Assessment: The Need for Interplay between Process and Product." *College Composition and Communication.* vol. 38, no. 1, February 1987. p. 40.
24. ———. "Writing Instruction and Assessment: The Need for Interplay between Process and Product." p. 43.
25. Lederman, Marie Jean. "Why Test?" *Writing Assessment: Issues and Strategies.* Edited by Karen L. Greenberg, Harvey S. Wiener, and Richard A. Donovan. New York: Longmans, 1986, (41), *as quoted in* Wolcott, "Writing Instruction and Assessment: The Need for Interplay between Process and Product." p. 44.

# FROM THE GARRET TO THE FISHBOWL: THOUGHTS ON THE TRANSITION FROM LITERARY TO TECHNICAL WRITING

*William E. Rivers*
University of South Carolina

*William E. Rivers is associate professor of English and currently director of the freshman composition program at the University of South Carolina. His articles on business and technical writing have appeared in such publications as the* ADE Bulletin, *the* Iowa State Journal of Business and Technical Communication, The Journal of Business Communication, *and the* ABC Bulletin. *His* Business Reports: Samples from the "Real World" *was published in 1981 by Prentice-Hall.*

*In addition to his academic publications, Rivers has written several technical manuals for computer software programs and has served as a writing and communications consultant with several companies and organizations. Currently, he is Principal Investigator for the NCR-USC Document Validation Laboratory, a joint research endeavor by NCR and the University of South Carolina designed to improve the accuracy and effectiveness of NCR computer manuals. The laboratory is supported by a grant from NCR-Columbia.*

One of the most interesting and dynamic of the many fronts along which academic and nonacademic writing confront one another occurs in technical writing. Taught for decades in English departments by people with traditional graduate degrees in British and American literature, technical writing has always pushed English academics to think and write in nonacademic ways. Recently, however, an interesting and challenging change has taken place.

For years the students taking technical writing courses were majors in scientific and technical disciplines. They forced English Ph.D.'s to deal with the writing done in these disciplines but also offered the advantage of distance: instructors could talk about writing in another discourse community and then safely retreat into their own without worrying much about the differences between the two, the difficulties one might encounter in trying to move from one to the other, and how we might improve the writing done in our community (literary) by looking carefully at that done in the other (technical).

In the last five to ten years, however, the increasing market for technical writers with strong backgrounds in language and writing has attracted growing numbers of English majors—both undergraduates and graduates—to technical writing classes. This circumstance poses an interesting challenge, because many of these English majors have serious problems with the transition from literary writing to technical writing. Their problems should push us, I believe, to carefully reexamine the writing done in both discourse communities, especially our own.

The purpose of this study is to examine some of the characteristics of academic literary writing and nonacademic technical writing, to define as specifically as we can the reasons for the transition problems our English majors encounter when moving from one of these discourse communities to another, and, finally, to suggest some things we can do to ease that transition. I have tried to achieve these purposes by soliciting and presenting the perceptions of five individuals now working and writing in highly technical industrial settings who have successfully made the transition from literary to technical writing. Their testimony gives us, I believe, a fresh and revealing look at the strengths and weaknesses of the writing in both discourse communities; their responses also redocument for us the difficulties in the transition from one discourse community to another. In this paper I present and evaluate their insights. Before dealing with their comments, however, we should briefly examine the problems English majors typically have when confronted with technical writing situations.

## LITERARY VERSUS TECHNICAL WRITING SEEN FROM THE ACADEMIC SIDE

When English majors first appeared in my technical writing courses, I expected them to have some initial difficulty with the technical information in the examples of technical writing I use in class and the detailed cases I use for writing assignments; I did not expect them to have fundamental problems adapting to principles of technical writing. I found, though, that many of them have much more difficulty learning to produce good technical writing than do the technical majors in these same classes.

The slowness with which many of the English majors catch on to technical writing principles puzzled me because most are interested in writing and are often pursuing either undergraduate or graduate programs in composition. They are usually good, highly motivated students who bring to their technical writing tasks the strengths we traditionally associate with liberal arts majors:

- Facility with language
- Analytical skills
- Organizational skills

But they have frustrating initial difficulties with technical writing, I believe, because the writing habits they learn and have reinforced in their literature courses simply do not work well in a technical or industrial context. I find three major problems often evident in their academic writing patterns:

1. Excessive verbal complexity
2. Indirect organizational patterns
3. Little if any reliance on visual cues

Although these problems seem easy to solve (do this; do not do this), they are often persistent impediments. I find myself doing as much unteaching as teaching. Once through an initial transition period, most of these English majors go on to produce good technical documents; however, that transition is often slow and frustrating.

## LITERARY VERSUS TECHNICAL WRITING SEEN FROM THE INDUSTRY SIDE

My perceptions of the differences between literary and technical writing and my growing sense of the difficulty of moving from literary to technical writing are largely based on my observations from the academic side. Although I am confident that my conclusions are correct, in the last few years I have increasingly felt the need to check my perceptions against those of people who know academic writing but who are now in industry. They, I thought, might be able to offer some special insights that would help those of us still on the academic side better shepherd our English major technical writing students through this transition.

I therefore wrote five individuals who have moved from being English students and instructors to being writers in highly technical industries and asked them to respond to four key questions about literary and technical writing and their transitions from one to another. All five of these people responded to my request with thoughtful answers which help us, I believe, see more clearly the strengths and weaknesses in both kinds of writing; their comments also verify the difficulty of moving from academic to nonacademic writing and suggest some ways we might ease that transition for our liberal arts students. In addition, they focus on an aspect of the transition that those of us still on the academic side may not have foreseen: almost all of my respondents directly or indirectly call attention to *emotional* stresses in the transition caused by the following:

- The new value system they encountered in the business world and its impact on how they must justify actions

- The new ways of thinking and presenting information to which they had to adjust
- The new "fishbowl" writing environment that differs radically from the private, garretlike writing environment they found and were subtly but persuasively taught to cultivate in an English department

All of these respondents have made the intellectual and emotional transition. They have all become very successful in the different and difficult world of business and technology. But in their responses to my questionnaire and in conversations with them I have seen that the academic world has a clear, nostalgic pull on them. Their success in the business world coupled with this attraction they still feel for literature and academia tends to validate and make more emphatic their observations about the writing done in both worlds.

The five individuals I contacted are, in alphabetical order:

Bruce Castner (NCR—Columbia, S.C.)
Lynn Denton (IBM—Austin, TX)
John Hansen (Xerox—Rochester, N.Y.)
Don Snook (Xerox—Rochester, N.Y.)
Robert Waite (IBM—Rochester, Minn.)

A brief biographical sketch of each person is provided at the end of this essay; however, let me briefly point out some basic similarities and a few differences in their academic and nonacademic experiences which lend authority, I believe, to the parallels in their observations:

- All have graduate degrees in English or American literature (three have doctoral degrees; one has a master's and is ABD; one has a master's).
- None studied composition or rhetoric in a formal academic context.
- All taught literature and writing for several years in a university setting.
- All produced literary criticism as a part of their degree requirements and/or for publication in literary journals.
- All left academia and entered the business world for financial reasons.
- Only Denton and Waite had extensive (more than five years) experience as teachers of business and technical writing. Hansen and Snook taught business writing for a few years.
- All moved into nonacademic employment that required them to write as a major part of their jobs.
- Three (Castner, Denton, and Waite) began as technical writers and editors producing user manuals for computer equipment and have subsequently moved into other areas, including management.
- Two (Hansen and Snook) began as operations analysts responsible for writing and editing extensive internal reports.

In my letter I asked them four basic questions:

- What differences have you noticed between academic and nonacademic writing?
- What characteristics have you noticed in academic writing that make it a *poor* preparation for nonacademic writing?
- What characteristics have you noticed in academic writing that make it a *good* preparation for nonacademic writing?
- What were the most difficult aspects of your own transition from academic to nonacademic writing? What techniques or resources helped ease that transition for you?

In my questions I used the word "academic." However, in their answers it became clear that in most cases "academic writing" carried for them the narrower, more specialized meaning of writing about literature. Since that more specialized meaning helps us define and therefore better understand a specific discourse community, I have used the term "literary writing" throughout my discussion except in those few cases where another kind of writing is clearly involved. I have retained the respondents' phrasing in quotations but have occasionally added in brackets "literary" when the context clearly justifies that clarification.

## Differences Between Literary and Technical Writing

The respondents dealt with this question by calling attention to obvious differences. Within their responses, however, were interesting emphases and patterns. Hansen and Snook, whose writing is done mainly for internal audiences, stressed basic stylistic differences, whereas Denton, Waite, and Castner, whose writing has mainly been done for external audiences (e.g., users of computer products), emphasized special characteristics of their technical writing dictated by specific audiences and purposes.

Hansen stresses that in the writing he now sees and does "stylistics always serve a very utilitarian objective. [His readers] don't have time, inclination, or tolerance for anything (style or content) that isn't required by the business needs or circumstances." In contrast, "academic writing encourages/indulges a fair amount of style, personality, and even content for its own sake or interest. It reflects an element of self-consciousness, an expectation that how something is phrased/organized is of as much interest as what fundamentally needs to be considered."

Snook's response to this question focuses on the stylistic implications of the visual cues found in technical and business writing and how they reinforce organization and logic. He goes on to expand his comments to purer considerations of style and, in doing so, implicitly expresses a preference for the literary style while admitting the functional value of technical style. Technical or business writing "does not value elegance, neat verbal turns, or wit. It is not fun. It is hard work.

But it gets the job done. Academic [literary] writing at its best entertains and instructs, and reveals the writer as a fellow citizen of the world of letters, a humane and civilized person."

Waite provided the most detailed response to this question. He offered a list of ten basic differences that reflect his experience with user documentation. I have reproduced his list and in parentheses have quoted and paraphrased selectively from his comments.

- Purpose. ("The official purpose of academic [literary] writing is scholarship; the unofficial purpose is to avoid 'perishing.' The official purpose of nonacademic [technical] writing is to document products; the unofficial purpose is to increase sales of those products.")
- Content. ("Derives from purpose.")
- Organization. ("Indirect," "inductive" patterns in literary writing versus "direct, deductive organizational patterns" in technical writing.)
- Graphics. (The "photographs, line drawings, figures, tables, graphs, flowcharts, bulleted lists, and numbered lists" that "are seldom used in academic writing" are "essential in nonacademic writing." He goes on to raise an interesting question: "Considering how visually oriented human beings are—TV, movies, *USA Today*—and how effectively graphics communicate information, isn't it odd that freshman composition courses don't teach students to use graphics?")
- Style. (Literary writing is written with the assumption that "because life is complex, writing must also be complex to be true, respectable and interesting. The result, however, is sometimes obscurity and pomposity...." Technical writing aims for a simple, plain, utilitarian style....")
- Individual versus team effort.
- Schedules. (In technical writing, schedules are set and of "paramount importance.")
- Printing, packaging, and distribution. (Technical writers must often be aware of the physical aspects of their published work.)
- Translation.
- Maintenance. (Technical writing must be planned to allow for subsequent changes due to changes in products.)

Denton's comments focus on the "functional," task-oriented nature of technical writing, which produces shorter, more direct documents. Castner also stresses the importance of purpose in technical writing but goes on to mention the varied reading levels found in his audiences and the consequent need to use a simple, direct, active prose style.

Despite their varied ways of saying it, all five of these writers agree that one of the key ways to distinguish academic, literary writing from nonacademic, technical writing is style: in technical writing, style is always regulated by the function of the document and encompasses considerations (e.g., visual cues) that do not figure in literary definitions of style at all. These writers all see that style in literary writing often becomes a self-conscious indulgence that can either delight or frustrate. One interesting divergence of opinion (or attitude) does appear here: the three respondents who produce or have produced computer documentation (Castner, Denton, and Waite) seem to have a more positive attitude toward the technical style. Hansen and Snook clearly still find the style in good literary writing very appealing and perhaps preferable to the flatter, more utilitarian technical style.

## Why Literary Writing Is a *Poor* Preparation for Technical Writing

When asked what characteristics of academic writing make it a poor preparation for writing in a nonacademic setting, my five respondents mentioned a variety of qualities that focused on style, appearance, and purpose.

Hansen furnished a brief but incisive list:

Indirectness
Excessive description
Excessive exactness ("preciousness")
Self-consciousness (overemphasis on the personality of the writer and/or audience versus the message)

Although he did not use the term "self-consciousness," Snook also focuses on the tendency in literary writing to emphasize at times the "niceties [of language] over substance." He also returned to his emphasis on the visual aspects of technical or business writing.

> Academic [literary] writing does not prepare one to present information quantitatively. An academic writer could struggle (and this one did) for hours to present such information in traditional paragraph prose, while a skilled business writer would see the need for a simple bar graph or matrix as the immediate solution. "English teacher" types also tend to overemphasize niceties over substance, e.g., anathematizing the use of "however" as a conjunction without a semicolon, or shuddering in horror at words like "dollarize" and "effectivity." Nonacademic writers are also seldom allowed to have fun with their writing; puns and other plays on words are distinctly unwelcome.

After his long, detailed list and discussion of differences between literary and technical writing, Waite simply listed three key characteristics that impair the effectiveness of literary writing as a preparation for writing in the business world: verbal complexity, indirect organization, and lack of visual cues.

Castner focused on essentially the same characteristics; however, his experience as a writer and editor of technical manuals led him to emphasize special elements. He stressed that the purposes of literary writing exercises make their character very different from the technical writing he must produce:

> *Argumentative/Persuasive.* Most academic [literary] writing tends to be one of these two types. This is not the type of writing that nonacademics [technical writers] do the majority of the time. True, there are times when we are trying to convince someone to take a particular action. Even then, the type of arguments tend to be business/money/time oriented rather than idea oriented.

*Wordy.* Literary criticism tends to be too wordy. The basic sentence idea is too qualified by phrases and clauses. Good nonacademic writing tends to be very "lean"—the basic information in the sentence is evident to the reader immediately.

*Ideas.* Academic writing deals with ideas and interpretations. Often there is more than one way of believing. Nonacademic writing tends to be more focused. We provide information on doing one thing at a time.

Because he taught business and technical writing in an academic setting for many years, Denton is the only respondent who touches on the difficulty of creating writing assignments in an academic environment that truly mirror the situations students will later find on the job. For this reason his definition of "academic writing" was usually broader than that of "literary writing." Like Castner, he also focuses on how the different purposes inherent in academic and nonacademic writing create impediments:

Little academic writing focuses on some of the common types of nonacademic writing, including task analysis—analyzing the actions necessary to perform a certain set of tasks and then writing instructions for performing those tasks.

Also, in nonacademic writing, more attention generally is given to *justifying* actions that have been taken or that are being recommended.

Much of nonacademic writing is, again, more *realistic* than is academic writing. That difference is not unexpected, I'm sure. But it remains difficult to make academic writing assignments as realistic.

All five respondents point to major differences in purpose as a key reason that academic writing is a poor preparation for nonacademic writing. Even in the more realistic, task-oriented assignments designed for a technical writing class, the purpose finally is always to *prove* (from the student's point of view) or *improve* (from the instructor's point of view) the writer's ability to write effectively. Therefore, the writing is often evaluated separately—an act which draws special attention to the language in a way that is unusual in the world of work. Analytical writing done in most literature courses is assigned to allow the student to demonstrate his or her ability to analyze a work of literature. It is usually evaluated largely on the basis of the writer's insight and how persuasively, even how cleverly, those insights are presented. Success often depends on verbal ingenuity. Clearly, there is a place for this ingenuity: insights, especially in literary studies, are often inextricably tied to language. However, it is easy to see how this purpose often leads to an overemphasis on language—to a situation in which language is valued for its own sake. We therefore do often get (as Hansen says) "niceties over substance" and "self-conscious" writing or (as Snook says) an "overemphasis on the personality of the writer and/or audience versus the message." We also see (as Castner, Denton, and Waite suggest) writers from this discourse community preferring indirect, deductive organizational patterns instead of direct, inductive ones. When English majors get into business and technical writing courses, these habits are hard to break, because the writers are still trying to perform with language instead of using language to solve problems.

## Why Literary Writing Is a *Good* Preparation for Technical Writing

The replies of my five respondents to the question of what makes literary academic writing a good preparation for nonacademic technical writing all suggest that literary writing can offer a good foundation for later writing on the job if the basic tenets usually taught in the classroom are applied in a sensible way. For example, Bob Waite accepted my list for this category:

- Facility with language
- Analytical skills
- Organizational skills

But clearly he had in mind these skills wisely applied, especially facility with language, for earlier he pointed out the tendency of that facility to degenerate into "obscurity and pomposity" in literary writing. Similarly, we can in literary writing be overly analytical or become too subtle and/or complex with our organizational patterns. But the potential strengths are clearly there and, according to these nonacademic writers, frequently drawn upon.

This potential is evident in the way Hansen set up his list of *transferable* values well stressed by academic (literary) writing:

- Coherence/logic
- Organization (at minimum, good topic sentences)
- Accurate word choice
- Correct grammar
- Ability to amplify and/or illustrate

Castner listed and explained three ways in which writing about literature helps develop skills useful in technical writing:

*Analysis.* The analysis that should be a part of forming an academic [literary] argumentative writing piece is definitely needed in nonacademic writing. Understanding the pieces and how they fit is a requirement before I can start trying to explain them to a reader who has never seen them before.

*Examples.* The reliance on examples from the text to prove a point carries over into nonacademic writing, since examples and diagrams are the clearest way of getting points across to a reader. Often a reader/user will use the examples in the book to get started on his own computer system.

*Deadlines.* I know this may sound contradictory, but I want to mention deadlines again. As a graduate student trying to write papers for three courses at the same time, I experienced the type of pressure in the nonacademic environment that results from trying to get 5 to 10 manuals written and published within a specified time. The knowledge that I can write under pressure, under the gun, helped me cope with the pressure once in the nonacademic environment.

In his response, Snook mentioned several of these same basic points, but then moved into a telling comparison:

> Academic [literary] writing, done well, emphasizes substance, critical analysis, and structure. It respects both complexity and simplicity. Academic writing, at its worst, makes the simple appear complex through excessive verbal complexity. Nonacademic writing, at its worst, oversimplifies the complex, and sacrifices substance for a misleading clarity.

Finally, although Lynn Denton focuses at first on the value of a good sense of grammar and style and the importance of learning quick yet effective rewriting skills, he does go on to break the pattern we have seen in the other four respondents. He calls attention to the skills taught in all writing courses but then stresses the positive impact on the writing and writing habits of those in his workplace from courses in business and technical writing courses:

> The attention generally paid to correct grammar, good style, etc., is certainly worth the effort, because in nonacademic writing one sees probably more mistakes than in the usual college classroom. Emphasis on revising in the classroom pays off on the job, where there is little time for several rewrites but, at the same time, correctness and good style are valued commodities.
>
> I also see that those who have taken technical and business writing in college are better able to write descriptions or analyses than those who did not have those courses in college. Many of those who took courses years ago still depend heavily on what they learned there, and may even keep their old textbook on their desk for easy reference.

So despite the differences, literary writing and the academic context do build many basic patterns and skills that are useful, even essential in a nonacademic context. These writers have seen patterns and skills transfer to their own writing and to the writing of those around them.

## *The Transition: Specific Difficulties and Successful Techniques*

This question, for my purposes the key one among those I raised, produced the most interesting and reflective answers. The most appropriate response to begin this discussion is Bob Waite's, because he explicitly divided the issue into intellectual and emotional aspects. Although the other respondents did not organize their responses in this way or address directly the intellectual-emotional nature of their adjustment, their answers do all deal with both intellectual and emotional problems generated by learning to write and work in a different environment—we might even say a different culture with different ways of doing things and even different values. Many of their comments intentionally or unintentionally call attention to attitudes that are especially strong in or even unique to students of literature.

Waite's response suggests that the intellectual transition may have been, initially at least, easier than the emotional transition:

- Intellectually, the most difficult was understanding the technical subjects I had to write about. Most helpful in easing that difficulty was talking with programmers

whose code I was writing about. Talking with other writers, reading existing manuals, and taking courses were also helpful.
- Emotionally or psychologically, the most difficult was learning to identify my own interests with those of the organization. Academic life had conditioned me to be cynical about capitalism and big business. Most helpful in easing that transition was repeated evidence that the company's objective is not merely to make money but to create products that meet customers' needs so well that customers are eager to buy the products.

John Hansen's subtle but repeated use of military metaphors in his response strongly suggests the emotional adjustments he had to make. Even though the issues he discusses all involve mechanical and stylistic questions that he had to resolve rationally, he was also clearly involved in an emotional battle of sorts:

> After one month I surrendered any intolerance of split infinitives. That and other selected stylistic "rules" seemed too arbitrary. I learned to focus on the nonnegotiable requirements of organization (direct) and word choice (including jargon as long as it unambiguously communicated to the audience at hand). I learned not to wince at verbs like "to status" or "to incent" (motivate) and decided only to fall on my sword for the important issues like reasonable parallelism or mapping phrases that are key for revealing logical organization. You need to pick your battles/standards or lose credibility with the folks whose writing you are trying to improve. You need to have a supportable practical reason for editorial choices, not just stylistic preferences or elegance.

In his response, Don Snook outlines a major shift he made in the way he organized information that required a basic change in thinking—from indirect and inductive to direct and deductive. Although the change was in many ways intellectual, it also involved a reassessment of values and therefore some difficult emotional adjustments. His comments constitute an unusually clear analysis of the differences between literary writing and business writing:

> The conventions of business writing generally demand a deductive structure, e.g., this is so, here is why it is so, here is what to do about it. My practice had been to write inductively, and somewhat discursively, to lead the reader imperceptibly to my conclusion. I valued indirection, nuance, rhetorical cleverness. Business writing demanded (unless one is deliberately trying to be evasive) a straightforward, clearly structured form that uses the audience's time effectively. The prose thus generated may be ugly, but at its best it communicates quickly and accurately. It took me a long time to really believe that the new was better than the old; being made regularly to rewrite what I submitted was a sobering experience, but I responded quickly. My help came from colleagues and examples of presentations and reports, as well as from my use, for the first time, of word processing.

Bruce Castner provided a list of five things that were either problems he had to overcome in his transition or that helped him in his transition. Two of the five considerations on his list, good writing skills and knowledge of typesetting/photography, are fairly straightforward intellectual matters that I shall not quote. The other three items in his list clearly deal with aspects of technical writing that require both intellectual and emotional adjustments by a writer initially trained to write about literature. They also reveal the major adjustments Castner had to make in his composing process:

> *Ability to Take Criticism.* In the nonacademic environment, there is not room to be defensive or possessive about one's writing. My manuals are reviewed by 5 to 10 people each. Their comments are incorporated into the final draft. Sometimes I ignore their comments, but often they spot something that I have overlooked and that makes the manual better. My approach has been to almost totally divorce myself (my ego) from what I write. The writing is intended to make my company's product better, so I need to keep my own feelings about it in check.
>
> *Ability to Make One's Writing Fit In.* It is important to be able to adapt one's writing style—to make it fit in. Often several people work on the same project and we write different manuals or pieces of the same manual. Our styles have to mesh and look as if one person wrote the manual(s) for a particular product.
>
> *Working with Others.* In academic [literary] writing, one usually works on a project alone, researching it, planning it, and writing it. In a nonacademic environment, I work with at least five people on every manual I write. I work with computer programmers, quality assurance and test personnel, distribution personnel, and production assistants. My project is public knowledge from the beginning. I have to report on its progress at weekly schedules meetings. Getting used to this "fishbowl" type of writing was difficult for me.

Moving from the privacy and quiet of the garret to the noisy public scrutiny of the fishbowl is difficult indeed.

Of all the respondents, Lynn Denton expressed the least difficulty making the transition from teaching writing and literature to working as a technical writer. Perhaps the relative ease of his transition derived from his years of experience teaching business and technical writing and the better knowledge he therefore had of basic practices in business and technical contexts. But even he reports a certain degree of culture shock:

> I had several difficulties—especially learning the need for task orientation (for technical manuals), the need to justify almost everything in terms of financial savings, and (as an editor) to realize that absolute correctness often is less important than technical accuracy.
>
> It was fairly easy to make the transition, and I relied heavily on looking at manuals and reports, etc., that had been produced within the company. Also, I took two or three week-long courses offered for writers and editors by IBM. Once immersed in the way IBM does things, it was easy to make the transition.
>
> I now see myself as a professional writer and editor.
>
> I think that the whole spectrum of writing experience through college courses has been invaluable to me—knowing typical ways to structure a product description or an analysis or an executive summary, etc. Also, the foundation of good grammatical and rhetorical stylistic practices has helped me tremendously. Those particular strengths that one picks up, perhaps not from any one course, are the most meaningful.

Denton moves from this statement to make a call for writing internships as a way of easing the transition and improving business and technical writing courses.

Internships would make the necessity of making a transition from literary writing to nonacademic writing very real and emphatic, but would also keep that transition in a semiacademic context where the culture shock could be softened and the emotional and intellectual problems often confronted by English majors worked out in a more leisurely and, we would hope, effective way. Such internships, though admittedly difficult to set up for even a few students and impossible to arrange for everyone, would help address what Denton sees as the "greatest weakness of academic writing . . . [:] the lack of realistic situations to work within."

## Some Suggestions to Help Ease the Transition

The comments of our respondents offer no easy answers about how we can help ease the transition between literary and technical writing for our students. They do, however, offer valuable information—differences, weaknesses and strengths in both kinds of writing, experiences with the transition—that can help us better understand the nature of the transition. That understanding we can pass on to our students. From what these writers have told us, I think that we should emphasize several key things when we teach students who are trying nonacademic writing for the first time:

- Most students with a strong background in literary writing do have the skills they will need to become effective writers in business and industry. They will have to accommodate their writing to the different styles, organizational patterns, visual techniques, and purposes employed in nonacademic writing, but the basic considerations that make for good writing in an academic setting make for good writing in a nonacademic setting. We should be emphatic about this fact.
- Moving from literary to technical writing does require a transition that for most English majors involves both intellectual and emotional adjustments; however, many have made that transition—successfully. The testimonies of these respondents can help us make this point more emphatically and effectively.
- The world in which the technical industry operates is a culture with a value system that differs in significant ways from the value system students (and faculty) have encountered in the academic world. Although the goals and therefore the reasons for doing things are different, we need to keep in mind and to remind our students that this other value system is, in most companies, as humane as the value systems practiced in academic contexts.
- We should require students to complete as many realistic writing assignments of a nonacademic type as they (and we) can get in during a course in business or technical writing. They should be given the opportunity to make their mistakes and adjustments to nonacademic writing in an academic context where more time is allowed for analysis, reflection, and growth—where both theoretical understanding and practical adaptation are encouraged.

- We should provide assignments and exercises that push students out in the open with their writing. We must give all our students, but especially our English majors, a taste of the "fishbowl" environment they will face in industry.
- Finally, we should keep in mind that not all of our English majors—graduates and undergraduates—are temperamentally and/or intellectually cut out for a career in technical writing. For these students we should diplomatically suggest other alternatives.

As more and more English majors appear in our technical writing classes, I believe we should rethink our courses with their special needs in mind. Many of the changes we make upon considering their needs would probably even help our technical majors. The comments of these English majors turned technical and business writers should help us not only to review how we teach writing but also what we value in writing. Their comments should force us to look carefully at the writing we do in our discourse community and consider how we might change and improve it based on what we learn from the writing done in technical and business contexts. Leaving the privacy of the garret and looking carefully at what happens on public ground should help us do our work better—whether we stay on the ground or again seek the garret.

## BIOGRAPHICAL SKETCHES

**Bruce Castner**

**POSITION AND COMPANY:**

Product/Manager/Competitive Information Analyst
Systems Engineering—Columbia, S.C.
Office Systems Division
NCR Corporation
West Columbia, S.C.

**ACADEMIC TRAINING:**

Ph.D. English, University of South Carolina, Columbia (nineteenth-century British literature)
M.A., English, Fairleigh Dickinson University, Rutherford, N.J.
B.A., English, Fairleigh Dickinson University, Rutherford, N.J.

**TEACHING EXPERIENCE:**

Adjunct Instructor, University of South Carolina, Columbia
Adjunct Instructor, Francis Marion College, Florence, S.C.

Graduate Teaching Assistant, University of South Carolina, Columbia
Graduate Teaching Assistant, Fairleigh Dickinson University, Rutherford, N.J.

**Lynn W. Denton**

**POSITION AND COMPANY:**

Staff Communications Specialist
IBM Corporation
Austin, Texas

**ACADEMIC TRAINING:**

M.A., English, Eastern New Mexico University, Portales (American literature)
B.A., English, Abilene Christian University, Abilene, Texas

**TEACHING EXPERIENCE:**

Associate Professor and Director, Applied Writing Program, Auburn University, Auburn, Ala.
Instructor, Texas Technical University, Lubbock
Instructor, Colorado School of Mines, Golden

**John T. Hansen**

**POSITION AND COMPANY:**

Project Audit Manager
Corporate Audit and Operational Analysis
Xerox Corporation, Rochester, N.Y.

**ACADEMIC TRAINING:**

Doctoral candidate—English, University of North Carolina, Chapel Hill (eighteenth-century British literature)
M.A., English, University of North Carolina, Chapel Hill
B.A., English, Fordham University, Bronx, N.Y.

**TEACHING EXPERIENCE:**

Instructor, University of North Carolina, Greensboro
Graduate Teaching Assistant, University of North Carolina, Chapel Hill

**Donald G. Snook**

POSITION AND COMPANY:

Manager, Project Audit and Operational Analysis
Xerox Corporation
Rochester, N.Y.

ACADEMIC TRAINING:

Ph.D., English, University of North Carolina,
Chapel Hill (American literature)
M.A., English, Auburn University, Auburn, Ala.
B.A., English and philosophy, Augustana College,
Rock Island, N.Y.

TEACHING EXPERIENCE:

Division Chair, Communication and Languages
Gadsden State Community College, Gadsden, Ala.
Assistant Professor, University of Alabama,
Tuscaloosa
Instructor, University of North Carolina
Chapel Hill
Instructor, Wright State University, Dayton, Ohio

**Robert Waite**

POSITION AND COMPANY:

Information Developer
IBM Corporation
Rochester, Minn.

ACADEMIC TRAINING:

Ph.D., English, University of Kentucky, Lexington
(American literature)
M.A., English, University of Kentucky, Lexington
B.A., English, Lehigh University, Bethlehem, Pa.

TEACHING EXPERIENCE:

Assistant Professor, University of Maine, Orono

# PART TWO

## INTEGRATING WORLDS: ACADEMIC INSTRUCTION FOR NONACADEMIC WORK

# ADAPTATION: BUSINESS WRITING AS CATALYST IN A LIBERAL ARTS CURRICULUM

*Janette S. Lewis*
*University of California, Los Angeles*

*Janette S. Lewis has taught business writing at the University of Hawaii, at Pepperdine University, and at UCLA, where she is a lecturer in UCLA Writing Programs and T. A. Coordinator. She holds the M.A. in American Literature and the Ph.D. in Renaissance Literature. She has delivered papers on writing at the Association for Business Communication, the Conference on College Composition and Communication, and the UC Council of Writing Programs. She has also written on Shakespeare, Benjamin Franklin, and American women writers. Lewis is a member of UCLA Writing Programs' Business and Technical Communication Group, whose members serve as liaisons between the university and the business community.*

> *Only 60 miles to the south, there's a vast city, and here you find civilized man. Civilized man refused to adapt himself to his environment; instead, he adapted his environment to suit him.*
> 
> *So he built cities, roads, vehicles, machinery, and he put up power lines to run his labor-saving devices. But somehow he didn't know when to stop. The more he improved his surroundings to make his life easier, the more complicated he made it.*
> 
> *So now his children are sentenced to 10 to 15 years of school just to learn how to survive in this complex and hazardous habitat they were born into.*
> 
> *And civilized man, who refused to adapt himself to his natural surroundings, now finds that he has to adapt and readapt himself every day and every hour of the day to his self-created environment.*

In the film *The Gods Must Be Crazy,* this voice-over narration provides the background for a prelapsarian bushman's hilarious and telling excursion into civilized society. Perhaps the film exaggerates the civilized person's need to be constantly adapting and changing to suit the urban environment he has created for himself—but not by much. Certainly, academicians trying to prepare students for the complicated world waiting for them outside the collegiate Kalahari Plain will detect in the film's wry humor more than a little truth. Unlike the bushman, who attained his end, shook the dust of civilization from his naked foot, and returned to his simpler, saner life, graduates *cannot* return—not for long anyway, not most of them. They must *adapt* to the bewildering thicket of rules, regulations, modes, and norms created by the discourse communities they enter. And to an extent, their ability to function as communicators will determine their success or failure, even their survival, within these communities.

But how is this adaptation to be accomplished? In all the writing about business communication courses, too little attention seems to have been paid to one essential question: What do students *really* need from those of us who teach the undergraduate business writing course? What adaptive mechanisms can we reasonably be expected to provide for them—as opposed to what they must obtain when they enter their particular discourse communities? How far can we go toward approximating a business situation without neglecting the more basic and important knowledge they can acquire only at the university—their version of the distinctive survival tools the bushman possessed that allowed him to triumph in a strange environment. For even if we try to approximate that outside world, how successful can we be, functioning as we are in an academic, not a real-life situation?

Probably no single answer could supply a satisfactory solution to any, certainly not to all, of these problems. About business writing courses, particularly, thinking falls into two sometimes warring camps. On one side are those who view discourse-specific curricula (and especially business classes) as an erosion of the humanistic, liberal arts tradition of the university. Far from being considered a humanizing tool, business writing courses are seen by this group as the trout in the milk—blatant evidence of the watering down of the humanistic education (see Bloom's indictment of the M.B.A., for example; 369ff). On the other side stand those (notably students and employers) who clamor for *more* practical training; their perception is that educators are failing to prepare students to function in the workplace (Hirsch, 5). These two sides can perhaps be brought together, however, if we approach business writing from a different perspective. Rather than settling for one approach or the other, we could reach a significant compromise if we encouraged students to view business writing on a continuum with their other courses, as a part of the rhetorical tradition, and to adapt the knowledge they have acquired in these courses to a business context (Sidley). If we can resist the (very seductive) temptation to allow students to believe that this is a course somehow more real and therefore more valuable than others they have taken at the university, we can begin to show them that business writing need not be dehumanized to be effective. As a result, the students, the curriculum, business, communication, and—one hopes—the larger community will be enriched.

The assertion that business writing need not be narrowly defined in order to equip graduates to write in the workplace is borne out by a recent survey of major employers who have hired numbers of UCLA alumni (UCLA Writing Programs, 1987). In response to the question, "What qualities do you look for in a new employee who will be doing a significant amount of writing for you?" employers most often specified that work should be "clear," "concise," and "correct." One employer added that "basic writing skills, plus the ability to adjust to the audience, are more important than specific types of reports." This latter statement, especially, reinforces Teresa M. Harrison's observation that "teachers of writing should equip their students with analytic capabilities that will guide them in [a] particular writing context" (4). And while these analytic capabilities may be taught in discourse-specific contexts, they are a far cry from the word-processor-based, quasi-secretarial course students sometimes expect business writing to be and many academics disparagingly perceive it to be.

In fact, the survey suggested that cumbersome adherence to, or exhaustive coverage of, the various *specific* types of discourse possible in a business setting is less useful than simply employing those types of discourse to reinforce basic *general* principles of good writing. For example, one employer's remarks included these observations:

> Our biggest complaint is lack of attention to detail. In school, students aren't penalized for "typos" or spelling mistakes. These items are *crucial* in our business. Also, students should be taught to be very critical of their own work, and should be forced to *rewrite* papers (since junior people here do it all the time!).

Although this respondent did not use pedagogical terms, the case for editing, revising, and proofreading is clear. Another complained of "a high 'Fog Index' " and suggested, "Students need to be trained to start with a clear outline of what they intend to write." While good spelling and proofreading skills, even when linked to clarity and organization, may not seem the loftiest of goals, employers' awareness of their importance—and of employees' deficiencies in these areas—suggest a respect for language and form that is seldom appreciated by academics.

On the other hand, only 3 of the 49 respondents alluded to specific business forms in any way, and these comments were in themselves general. One cited an understanding of "proper business form" as desirable, while the other two mentioned "ability to draft memos, letters, reports . . . cogently and concisely" and "knowledge of how to compose a business letter or a concise memo." Far from urging that coursework be tailored to specific vocational needs, these comments suggested, over and over, that—to these businesspeople at any rate—a *good* writing foundation counted for more than a *business* writing foundation.

While this conclusion does not invalidate the business writing course, it does free instructors to think of the course's content in broader terms and liberates them from a cumbersome, overly specific, and ultimately isolating approach. If teachers have the time and inclination, together with a class roster of homogenous and single-minded business majors, they might want to instruct them in the differences between "Writing Direct Requests," "Writing Routine and Good-News Messages," "Writing Bad-News Messages," "Writing Persuasive Messages," and "Writing Goodwill Messages"—all chapter headings from a respected, typical, and widely used current text (Bovee and Thill). Such distinctions might even be useful in giving students an idea about the variety of writing demands they may face on the job. However, if these distinctions fit into neither the timeframe nor the pedagogical philosophy of a particular instructional milieu, then teaching students how to write a clear, correct, effective, even graceful letter suited to both audience and method should serve them just as well. (Teaching a short essay would probably do similarly well except for the perception of context that the business class supplies.)

In fact, overindulging the tendency to compartmentalize business writing, to treat it as somehow separate from other writing the students have done, only fuels "the contemptuous dismissal of business writing as unworthy of inclusion in a university curriculum" (Mitchell, 545). Being overly specific can also mislead students by giving them a false sense that they have learned exactly how to respond in a particular context when, in fact, such understanding is achieved only through experience in and familiarity with that community:

> The rhetorical choices made by the writer must be based upon knowledge about the nature and characteristics of the organization itself that does not already exist ... and must ... be acquired. In an organization, the purposes of the text may be apparent only with an appreciation of organizational activities, motives, and goals. Audience members' attitudes and beliefs are likely to be well understood only as one comes to appreciate what it means to be a member of that particular organization. [Harrison, 17]

Nowhere has this fact been more dramatically illustrated than in the work by Fennell, Miller, and Herndl on the failures in communication prior to the Three-Mile Island and Challenger disasters (1987). In each of these situations, territorial and hierarchical considerations literally canceled rhetorical competence; that is, the social and organizational contexts rendered impotent the communicators in each situation who had insight into—and expressed concern about—existing dangers.

What is more, even *within* the business community, novices may find that the organization they enter "has an in-house language and certain local discourse conventions" (Faigley, 238). The rhetoric of the banker, for example, is not that of the stockbroker; large corporations impose different writing demands than do small companies; the manufacturer, the wholesaler, the distributor, and the retailer in the same discourse community may find themselves facing different types of composing tasks. So while a general introduction to business discourse will doubtless prove useful, for students should "learn those forms socially necessary for effective communication within the society in which they live" (Coe, 21), no class can prepare all students for the specialized demands their various professions will make on them. In fact, trying to do so can even be counterproductive, instilling in students the false notions that business is an arcane world speaking in its own mysterious tongues and that this course has somehow provided them with secret knowledge and entree into that closed society. Further, we reinforce the notion that other writing courses—and, in fact, most other courses they have taken in their undergraduate careers are irrelevant, not applicable, useless in the corporate fraternity they are about to enter.

These notions are not only false; they also suggest the misconception that perpetuates and fosters some of the worst crimes committed by business writers: that phrases, words, clichés which would be eschewed in normal discourse are somehow acceptable, desirable, or even necessary in this community. The dichotomy, or even schizophrenia, that results from this approach is immediately apparent in the letter form. Letters have long been accepted as a respectable, even literary genre. Business letters, on the contrary, seem to be perceived as something separate and distinct. The result has been a plethora of business letters that range from boringly forgettable and mechanically formulaic to embarrassingly inept and, sometimes, even incomprehensible. In spite of business texts' and teachers' persistent attempts to rid letters of phrases like "per your previously received communication please find attached" and in spite of employers' complaints about bad writing, atrocities still abound. Here is a recent example, the opening sentence of an actual letter written by a mortgage broker to his clients:

> We are corresponding with you so as to make you aware of specifically what is currently precluding us from placing closure as to that of finalizing our processing in conjunction with that of providing you with new First Trust Deed financing as to your purchase of the property as referenced above.

There is no need to suffer through further examples of this type, though many could be produced. All of us have been the victims of such odious prose hiding in the guise of "professional jargon" at one time or another. Since this mortgage broker is informing his clients that their loan is on hold, perhaps he believes he must diffuse his "bad news" in a cloud of verbiage. But if, while telling students this kind of writing is unacceptable, we also treat business writing as somehow special or separate or exempt from traditional rhetoric, we sabotage our own efforts in this area. We should not, therefore, be surprised when we continue to produce these word-processor Frankensteins.

Perhaps a second example, dramatically different from the first, will suggest an answer and at the same time lend support to the argument that business discourse and the liberal arts are not necessarily incompatible bedfellows. The following is another opening sentence, representing one of the most onerous tasks of business discourse, the solicitation letter:

> It doesn't exactly secure my ego to recognize that the most important letter I write each year is in a genre appropriately labelled junk mail and, worse, falls in the category of the infamous solicitation letter that urges you to remember that without your check or money order today some cause you allegedly believe in deeply will perish from the earth. [Cubeta]

It might be argued that pitting the director of a notable language school against a small-time mortgage broker does not constitute a fair fight. Nevertheless, both passages *are* from business letters, and the greater success of the latter underscores the desirability of bringing humanistic skills and values to a business context. While both opening sentences are long—fifty-one words each—the latter's use of tone, control of language, and richly allusive prose captures and holds the reader's attention. The sense of a human voice, of a person speaking to his audience rather than writing from a formula, makes the message palatable. Alumni may actually reach for their checkbooks, not toward the trashcan; the recipient of the mortgage broker's missive can only reach for the aspirin—even if the news, as here, is not really all that bad.

While most writing for business may not sink to the depths of the first passage, little of it rises above the mediocre. Why can't we help our students to carry the riches of their education into the marketplace, to buy goodwill and good feelings, rather than shedding their knowledge to don pinstripe flannel prose and proffer clichés and formulas as currency? This possibility finds an unlikely ally in E. D. Hirsch, who, in bemoaning the poverty of a common cultural background among young men and women today, makes the following point:

> My father used to write business letters that alluded to Shakespeare. These allusions were effective for conveying complex messages to his associates because, in his day, business people could make such allusions with every expectation of being understood. For instance, in my father's commodity business, the timing of sales and purchases was all-important, and he would sometimes write or say to his colleagues, "There is a tide," without further elaboration. These four words carried not only a lot of complex information, but also the persuasive force of a proverb. In addition to the basic practical meaning, "Act now!" what came across was a lot of implicit reasons why immediate action was important. [9]

While integrating business writing more closely with the liberal arts will not immediately provide the cultural coherence Hirsch longs for, such an approach would at least enable students to recognize and to use some of the background information they do possess. To insist on business writing as a form of discourse that exists outside the traditional rhetorical context, one that makes strange and alien demands of its own, denies this possibility. Such an approach does everyone a disservice: the student, the universities, professional communities. Disenfranchising the business writing student results in the kind of discourse represented by the mortgage broker's pathetic attempt at communication—what Richard Lanham refers to as the bureaucratic style (here disintegrating further into "octopus prose" [1987]). While we cannot expect to produce budding Mesdames de Sévigné or Earls of Rochester, we can at least turn out students with heightened sensitivity to language and its possibilities—even in business discourse.

Teaching business writing at the university is justified to the extent that such a course prepares students to think and write in their future professional communities, but this preparation need not take the narrow and pedestrian form many of the endless and interchangeable texts that pour from publishers would suggest. Even a document as utilitarian and rigid as the resumé can provide a synthesizing and humanizing experience for students. For one thing, resumé conventions dictate that writers take hard, cold inventories and evaluate themselves in light of their own histories. This kind of self-examination may not quite measure up to the renaissance dictum of *nosce teipsum* but still affords a valuable and new exercise in self-awareness for these eighteen to twenty-year-olds. Next, creating a resumé forces students to use language (and in some cases to violate traditional rules of grammar) in ways they have not before: arguably, this necessity can provide the instructor with a means of bringing the students to greater rhetorical awareness—not simply self-awareness. Finally, since the resumé form and format is, for most discourse communities, inviolable, considerable creative effort is required of the writer who wants to rise above the herd. Good resumés, though they may use fragments, eschew articles, and seem excessively parallel, require canny selection of detail, careful attention to connotation, and a keen eye for organization.

So the business writing class can provide a forum for bringing together—rather than dividing—the academic and professional worlds. If this is to happen, however, the emphasis must be on the broader concerns that both communities share, not on the mechanical aspects of writing a particular type of document that students will have to relearn on the job anyway. While students entering the business community will find it helpful to know how to compose a memo, for example, this instruction can be dispensed in a manner that builds on what students already know about writing. For instance, it seems appropriate to point out to students that the subject line of a memo resembles the thesis of an essay in purpose and use: focusing the writer's and the reader's attention on the message. On the other hand, it seems inappropriate to devote much time to purely mechanical considerations such as where the date goes in relation to the "to" and "from" lines (though students often prefer to dwell on these less-than-challenging aspects). Format is usually dictated by the particular organization the new worker finds him/herself in. In this case, students would profit from learning how to adjust style to audience, as Fielden has shown, since more specific techniques "cannot be divorced from the circumstances under which something is written" (129).

This point can be applied to other business forms as well. The business report, like the academic essay, can take a number of approaches: persuasive, descriptive, argumentative; like the research paper, it can require that information be gathered and synthesized from a variety of sources. There is no reason that a business writing project—whether in a class or on the job—should be less challenging and stimulating than assignments in a typical college writing class. What the business emphasis can do is enable the instructor to reach students who have been skeptical about the value of their other writing courses. What we have to offer them is what these courses have been offering all along; it is just that in these classes we supply an apparent context beyond the instructors themselves as sole context. Through this, we command the student's attention.

If we view these courses as reinforcement, as helping students to use what they have learned, business writing should be neither at odds with the liberal arts nor an anomaly in the college curriculum—a victim of the "orphan syndrome" (Hagge). Knowing how to adapt what they have learned is the final step students must take to complete their education, and too often it does not get taken. Good preprofessional courses can help them to take this step by providing a heuristic of "roles, specific assignments, and class activities designed and sequenced to facilitate students' movement from college majors to professional communities" (Anderson). Still, it is wrong to pretend that we can duplicate the students' future experiences in their jobs—that we can somehow cover all the bases for them. Courses that try too narrowly to follow this path are in serious danger of being the collegiate analogy to children putting on their parents' clothing, dressing up, and playing "junior executive" or "business person." Some textbooks especially fall prey to this fallacy and are tireless in their attempts to be an exhaustive resource; instead, they become merely exhausting. Similarly, the case approach to teaching business writing—though it can be useful—requires specialized knowledge on the part of both teacher and students to be really effective. What is more important than simulated reality is giving students the tools to adapt to whatever rhetorical situation they find themselves in. Too much specificity reinforces the fallacy mentioned above: that bureaucracies outside academe are somehow different from the one they have encountered from time to time inside the university, that there is a special, secret language that exists and that they will be initiated into, and that this will be "real" writing—as opposed to whatever it is that they have been doing.

Instead of reinforcing this false and detrimental notion, we should be telling students that good writing is good writing in any discourse community. While they may have to abide by certain conventions of their particular field (many of which they will have to learn when they are actually on the job), they will be one step ahead of the game if they are comfortable with themselves as writers going into their jobs, if they know how to convey a message clearly and correctly, if they understand the importance of audience. Textbook writers for these communities should convey this message, rather than pandering to students' desires for simple solutions and presenting themselves as the keepers of the keys to these separate, mysterious realms. The dearth of usable textbooks pointed out by Blyler (in her 1987 article, "Process-Based Pedagogy in Professional Writing") continues, for the most part, though some improvement has been made.

Perhaps, if we are very good, or very lucky, it is also possible to nudge our students toward thinking about how to make their professional communities better, about the meaning of work; perhaps we can use the writing course to start them thinking about business ethics. Although this is a lofty goal, the course certainly should not exist merely to help them to master the technical aspects of formatting or a particular kind of document design any more than a poetry course should be merely about metrics and poetic techniques. The class should at least suggest to graduates that they can adapt the knowhow they have acquired in their four or more years of college to these new discourse communities. And, at its very best, it can help them to carry other humanizing elements from their education into those communities. This approach should allow them to link the skills and knowledge they have acquired to the requirements of the discourse community they enter. In this way, the business writing course becomes the connecting road between the university and the professional world outside.

Adapting skills, then, need not be empty exercises in getting-by:

> For example, if the day is called Monday and the number seven-three-zero comes up, you have to disadapt yourself from your domestic surroundings and readapt yourself to an entirely different environment.
>
> Eight-double-zero means everybody has to look busy. . . . Ten-three-zero says you can stop looking busy for fifteen minutes, and then you have to look busy again. . . .
>
> And so your day is chopped up into little pieces, and in each segment of time you have to adapt to a new set of circumstances. No wonder some people go off the rails a bit. [Prologue, *The Gods Must Be Crazy*]

In the film, the bushman's story had a happy ending. Leaving the Kalahari Plain, he took with him special talents that not only kept him on the rails but enriched the lives of the urban dwellers he touched. We can similarly equip our students to survive. While they will never completely master forms until they reside entirely in the community that dictates and assesses those forms, students will start to achieve mastery and impose coherence if they have begun to learn some of these forms in the familiar academic setting. After all, the academic context is the first and most memorable discourse community a writer experiences. In leaving it to join a new discourse community in a specific business context, students must adapt their communication skills from the old to the new—just as they must adapt decision-making skills, behavior, even clothing.

More importantly, adapting communication skills to new contexts remains an ongoing activity, involving continual adapting and readapting because of the topical, transient, and ever-changing nature of business. At the university, students have successfully adjusted, going from one instructor's requirements to another's or from the seemingly arbitrary forms of one discipline to another—encountering what Bloom labels "the imperial and imperious demands of the specialized disciplines unfiltered by unifying thought" (337). Since much of their experience in the professional communities they enter may be similarly disjointed, fulfilling these academic demands may have given them coping strategies they don't even know they have—strategies that can stand them in good stead in adapting to the forms imposed by their professional discourse communities.

In the prologue to *College*, Boyer asks, "Is the academic major simply a means to prepare specialists with narrow technical skills? Above all, can the liberal and useful arts be blended during college, as they must inevitably be blended during life?" (4) At its best, the business writing course can provide the kind of synthesis Boyer hopes for by offering students a validating and empowering experience. It can reaffirm the worth of what they have already learned in the academic community by showing them how this knowledge can be adapted to a nonacademic setting while at the same time preparing them to succeed in the workplace and perhaps even to improve writing there.

While it would be pleasant to pretend that, 600 miles to the south, the natives are not slugging it out, tooth and nail, for jobs and advancement, we cannot. As writing teachers, we see the marketplace infringe more and more on our territory; employers complain about graduates who are unable to write or think and are thus unprepared for the world they will have to function in for the remainder of their lives. These voices demand to be heard, and we cannot choose to ignore them or hope they will go away. They are our students' futures. We have an obligation to instill in our graduates the best values of our own Kalahari Plain: the basic knowledge that can keep them on the rails in the world to which they must and can adapt.

## Works Cited

Anderson, Chuck. "The Major Meets 'The Real World': Professional Discourse in Upper Division Tech Writing." Conference on College Composition and Communication. Atlanta, March 20, 1987.

Bloom, Alan. *The Closing of the American Mind: How Higher Education Has Failed Democracy and Impoverished the Souls of Today's Students.* New York: Simon & Schuster, 1987.

Blyler, Nancy Roundy. "Process-Based Pedagogy in Professional Writing." *The Journal of Business Communication* 24:1 (1987): 51–60.

Bovee, Courtland L., and John V. Thill. *Business Communication Today.* New York: Random House, 1986.

Boyer, Ernest L. *College: The Undergraduate Experience in America.* New York: Harper & Row, 1987.

Cubeta, Paul. Letter to Bread Loaf Alumni. November 1981.

Faigley, Lester. "Nonacademic Writing: The Social Perspective." Odell and Goswami, 231–248.

Fennell, B. A., Carolyn R. Miller, and Carl G. Herndl. "Mapping 'Discourse Communities': Linguistic, Rhetorical, and Ethnographic Analysis." Session at Conference on College Composition and Communication. Atlanta, March 19, 1987.

Fielden, John S. "What Do You Mean You Don't Like My Style?" *Harvard Business Review* (1982): 128–138.

*The Gods Must Be Crazy.* A film by Jamie Uys. Twentieth–Century Fox, 1984.

Harrison, Teresa M. "Frameworks for the Study of Writing in Organizational Contexts," *Written Communication* 4 (1987): 3–23.

Hirsch, E. D., Jr. *Cultural Literacy: What Every American Needs to Know.* Boston: Houghton Mifflin, 1987.

Lanham, Richard A. *Revising Business Prose.* New York: Macmillan, 1987.

Mitchell, Ruth. "Shared Responsibility: Teaching Technical Writing in the University." *College English* 43 (1981): 543–555.

Odell, Lee, and Dixie Goswami. *Writing in Nonacademic Settings.* New York: Guilford Press, 1985.

Sidley, Gay. " 'Hellenizing' the Interoffice Memo." *Record of the Proceedings of the 1984 Canadian Regional Business and Technical Communication Conference.* New Westminster, B.C., 1984.

UCLA Writing Programs Employer Survey. Los Angeles, 1987.

# RHETORIC AND THE DISCOURSE OF TECHNOLOGY

*Theresa Enos*
University of Arizona

*Theresa Enos is the founder and editor of* Rhetoric Review. *She has taught freshman composition, basic writing, and scientific and technical writing for fifteen years and has published various articles on rhetoric and composition. Editor of* A Sourcebook for Basic Writing Teachers *(Random House, 1987), she currently teaches rhetoric at the University of Arizona.*

> *In grave Quintilian's copious work, we find*
> *The justest rules and clearest method joined.*
> —Alexander Pope
> *Essay on Criticism*

## CHANGING TIMES AND SHIFTING VALUES

An airplane flies to Iran, its belly full of weapons; a hostage is released shortly thereafter; concurrently, our president is assuring us that he will not deal with or sell arms to terrorists. The insider-trading scandals spread as Boesky and Levine demonstrate fraud as the key to riches. Revelations abound about falsified scientific research; scientists at Harvard and Emory produce misleading papers. U.S. employees alter their educational and career credentials. Duplicity emerges within NASA before and after the *Challenger* tragedy. Defense contractors admit to false charges, overcharges, or kickbacks in dealing with the government. Scandals multiply in university and professional athletics. Liberace's lawyer and doctor both lie about the cause of his death. The embassy sex-and-spy scandal tarnishes Marine Corps honor. The climate of mistrust between individual and institution is the norm. As times change, values shift, and ethics erode, the distrust swells. And in the American workplace, a value system based on loyalty has changed to a climate of moral grayness.

## SCIENCE, TECHNOLOGY, AND SOCIETY

Alarmed by questionable ethics and outright dishonesty, institutions are reacting. Some companies are hiring outside specialists to formulate and write ethics policies and codes and then try to enforce them. Because the biggest problems in the workplace are human ones that arise in decision making and leadership, professional schools are trying to broaden and humanize their specialized courses. For example, recognizing that the "science" of business is but a myth, the Harvard Business School is requiring students to read from literary classics. Other M.B.A. schools in their own business and professional curricula are following Harvard's inclusion of the classics. The logic behind this movement is that Shakespeare's plays, for instance, can call attention to and shed more light on many management problems than the most critical, and traditional, case studies. By this management approach, King Lear ends up as one of literature's more tragic figures because of his decision making: Lear is offered to M.B.A. students as an example of a poor delegator.

Some of the approaches in this educational renaissance, however, are intelligent and not so solidly based on practical concerns (as the reductionist approach to Lear suggests). In 1985 A. Bartlett Giamatti, then Yale president and literature professor, lectured business managers on Machiavelli's *The Prince,* emphasizing the text as an invaluable aesthetic approach to managing rather than a moral one. By this approach *The Prince* becomes more than a handbook for monsters.

Other schools are drawing on literature to help individual professionals confront career dilemmas and moral issues they face in their daily work. Brandeis, as part of its continuing education program, offers a technology and literature course to doctors, legislators, corporate executives, and various other professional groups. (Offering this course does require the training of faculty, because they come from different departments and colleges.) Still other institutions are combining technology and liberal arts in a single course. Interdisciplinary programs like the program at Brandeis require professors to teach outside their departments, often causing problems in crossed or blurred departmental boundaries.

This increasing recognition of technology as a human activity may cause "science, technology, and society" to become a discipline in itself. The recent movement questions modern technology's insistence on the tenets of specialization and objectivity that has led to a certain collective consciousness. Carolyn Miller already has written of this particular technological ethos that reflects narrow-mindedness and nonresponsibility (234). Yet at the same time that professional schools are trying to bridge the humanities-science split, many technical communication courses housed in English departments do not go beyond a skills approach. Such an approach is hardly a positive response to recent movements that are deemphasizing the narrow focus on practical skills.

Indeed, if professional schools and interdisciplinary university programs are connecting literature to technology for professionals well established in their careers or specialized studies, then teachers of English, by their very backgrounds, are especially qualified to teach humanities-based courses in technical communication. And technical communication is the fastest growing area in English departments, if not the fastest growing area in the entire university curriculum.[1] More and more literature teachers will join writing teachers as instructors of these courses housed in English departments. Instead of graduate or continuing education courses that attempt to remedy problems in ethics, then bringing such issues to students in an undergraduate liberal arts course may be the logical and ultimately more successful approach.[2]

## THE HUMANITIES-TECHNOLOGY SPLIT, QUINTILIAN, AND RHETORIC

Even though C. P. Snow called the humanities-technology split to our attention again in this century, we can trace the split back much further, even back to Quintilian's division of the kinds of knowledge as he tried to deal with an arts-science split already evident in ancient times. Instead of a two-category division that invites an either-or kind of thinking, he classified the arts of learning into a harmonious and inclusive triad. Into the first category Quintilian placed those arts that aim toward knowledge for its own sake, a group in which today many would lump all of the humanities. Into the second category went the kinds of learning that lead to the making of a tangible product, a group in which we can place technology. Into the third category Quintilian placed the kinds of learning whose end results in some kind of action. Quintilian realized the problem of placing rhetoric within such a taxonomy of the theoretical, productive, and practical because rhetoric, being both a substantive art and a methodology, involves both theoretical and productive aspects. Because of rhetoric's centrality in forming and reflecting the ethos of any person or organized group, Quintilian finally placed rhetoric in the third category, the practical arts. Quintilian valorized the inclusiveness of rhetoric, its usefulness in creating connections and interrelationships among the theoretical, the productive, and the practical. To Quintilian rhetoric represented the highest of human achievements. Through rhetoric, he believed, we can locate the basis for ethics and culture in any society. Like this master of pedagogy, we too can recognize rhetoric's usefulness in drawing technology and the humanities closer together by placing the voice of the individual and the good of society in a dynamic balance, the informing principle in humanist rhetoric (Leff, 7). A liberal arts approach to professional writing, then, would be philosophically based on the most inclusive discipline in the humanities: rhetoric.

In our recent history, many English departments have not perceived rhetoric as spanning across disciplines; furthermore, many traditional English departments do not consider rhetoric as truly belonging to the humanities, even though it has formed the core of their writing programs. The result is that such departments are actually two sharply divided nations, another manifestation of the arts-science split, even though we may call it the aesthetics-skills split. Ironically, English teachers have compounded the problems, too often reducing Quintilian's three-part structure into two, thus failing to recognize rhetoric's centrality. A further irony is that some departments of English only grudgingly offer courses in technical communication—or any writing courses beyond the freshman sequence—and resist outside demands for increasing the number of sections of professional writing. (At the university where I previously taught, department curricular changes in 1984 eliminated "Advanced Expository Prose," "Business Writing," and "Scientific and Technical Writing," replacing these three courses with two additional creative writing courses and an additional literature course entitled "Gay and Lesbian Literature." The argument was that these three new courses would emphasize writing; thus, leaving only the freshman writing sequence intact was justified to some. Later, one section in technical writing was reinstated because of pressure from the university's business school; the other upper-division writing courses were erased from the department's curriculum.)

So here is yet another level of the arts-science split: the perception here being that scientific and technical discourse, characterized by the tenet of objectivity, is even more skills-oriented than "regular" writing courses. If teachers of literature and writing characteristically live uneasily next to each other in separate camps, teachers of scientific and technical communication are viewed as camp followers, somehow hardly part of rhetoric and composition studies. Literature teachers often view technical writing courses as "alien intruders unrelated both to the established goals of an English department and to the attempt to encourage and preserve the study of humanities and aesthetics [and as] intellectually arid, controlled only by format and mechanical approaches to clarity" (Tebeaux and Kroiter, 28). And some of us have heard these charges made by our own colleagues in composition studies. These attitudes toward different kinds of writing and the implication that some are outside the liberal arts tradition suggest that different *levels* of the humanities-science split have invaded English departments. The implications can be dangerous for an educational system already fragmented by increasing specialization.

## QUINTILIAN, RHETORIC, AND THE CITIZENRY

In *Institutio Oratoria*, Quintilian formulates his philosophy that rhetoric should be the center of a society's educational system. Here he justifies and sets forth a system that educates and forms a citizen into a full member of society. Rhetoric creates a balance between the theoretical and the productive categories of knowledge; an educational system with rhetoric at its center thus can build moral awareness between the individual and the institution. A citizen who is expected to be productive in any field is also expected to develop and project a strong consciousness of character. And how good character is developed cannot be separated from a rhetorical consciousness, which is developed through the art of writing and speaking.

This ideal citizen must be knowledgeable about all that has formed a society: civil law, customs, religion—all that is just and honorable. The citizen then, regardless of vocational goals, must address the morals and ethics that make up the collective consciousness of any group or institution or of society itself.[3]

Teachers of professional writing in liberal arts colleges can draw from Quintilian's system, which places rhetoric at the center of the course of instruction. Making rhetoric the center of an educational system means placing before students every kind of discourse subject matter. Quintilian's ideal citizen is one who best represents his or her society. The ideal citizen must be not only an excellent communicator but also one who communicates human values along with any subject matter. Thus, teachers of professional writing are in a unique position to help students see the complementariness rather than the separateness of the humanities and the sciences.

Some English teachers new to technical writing at first believe the course content to be unchallenging. Perhaps part of this problem comes from the conviction that they are bound, in part because of their inexperience, to teach the assigned textbook. But most technical writing books are written out of current-traditional rhetoric and composition of the nineteenth century, emphasizing a rigid forms approach organized around reports and letters. New teachers also may depend too much on the forms/skills approach, because students come into the classroom with the attitude, "Just show me the form, the technique, and I'll be able to use these skills to communicate professionally." Indeed, teaching skills is part of what we do, and such work is not incompatible with critical or ethical ambitions. But we should resist teaching skills without intellectual content. We can do both, and our backgrounds make us particularly prepared to help these future professionals see that imagination, expression, and rationality are part of all of us as human beings. For many of these students, their technical writing course may be the only upper-level English course and their only writing course besides freshman composition. We can urge these students to think seriously about the world around them, inspiring them to look for solutions to its problems. Such goals are the ultimate goals of all humanities courses, and they should be the ultimate goals of technical communication courses that are offered as part of the liberal arts curriculum.

## VALORIZING VOICE AND METAPHOR IN TECHNICAL WRITING

A liberal arts approach to technical communication must go beyond the techniques outlined in some of the more recent technical writing textbooks that suggest how we might deal with the criticism of too much emphasis on objectivity (i.e., put *people* in, use personal pronouns, work with tone, use more narrative). Few, if any, have solid sections on style, voice, persuasion, or ethical concerns. A liberal arts approach to technical writing, then, places more emphasis on the writer's voice than the traditional technical writing textbooks do.

Our technical writing textbooks are even slower to change than freshman writing books. Most of the technical communication books come straight out of nineteenth-century writing instruction in specialized engineering schools, instruction that focused on the forms approach. The two-culture split had been established in colleges by 1900, and the forms approach evolved from the familiar science-arts split in these specialized schools. For a while many courses in these schools were humanities-based, but the recognizable battles broke out and advocates of the humanities-based curriculum lost. Robert J. Connors in "The Rise of Technical Writing Instruction in America" traces the field's evolution from its beginnings in land-grant colleges of the nineteenth century to current praxis in technical writing textbooks. Knowing how technical writing instruction and textbooks evolved from the two-culture split helps us understand why the tenet of objectivity underlies current technical writing courses in liberal arts colleges.

The tenet of objectivity creates dangerous ethical issues: personality devaluation, the suppression of the author, no discernible voice. The result is a nonresponsible attitude, intended or not, an abdication of human responsibility for what humans have created. It is only by the act of separating oneself from personal values, emotions, and biases that an "objective" voice can be maintained. While studying a problem so as to come up with a solution, and then while producing technical discourse (letters, reports, proposals) about this problem and its solution, the writer is supposed to stay neutral so that what is said looks the same to everyone. This adherence to objectivity is the primary reason that writing in technological fields reflects a voice impersonal, nonresponsible, narrow-minded. Furthermore, the implication that it is desirable to ignore the writer's identity, voice, or stance devalues the individual as both reader and writer, at the same time establishing some kind of anonymous corporate voice. No one and no real human being is responsible. Philip M. Rubens argues in "Reinventing the Wheel?: Ethics for Technical Communicators" that character devaluation, conscious or unconscious, stemming from too much emphasis on objectivity in language is unethical. It isolates the writer—and too often the reader—from the text, thus reinforcing this "corporate anonymity." The attempt to make everything read the same to every reader also raises interesting questions in reader-response theory. Other than simple step-by-step instructions or graphic warnings, the idea that a report's or proposal's message is simply transmitted to a programmed reader is shaky.

After all, objectivity is not really possible. Even if we think we are reporting—presenting—what is out there in the world, we still cannot present a real objective history of anything. All kinds of writing, even in science and technology, call for a variety of creative techniques—of representation. We can readily see the difference a strong, responsible voice makes when someone in technology speaks in a real voice that reflects both the person and the corporate ethos. Lee Iacocca, for instance, more than once has clearly avoided the usual voice of "corporate anonymity," most recently when he published the Chrysler letter taking responsibility for the "dumb" mistake of turning back odometers on tester cars later sold as new.

Georges Dusdorf in his philosophy of language sets up a language spectrum. On one end are "objective" kinds of technical writing; on the other, pure expressive writing. On the "objective" side is the kind of language that actually says the least, according to Dusdorf, because it is based on the objectivity of things, not on the personality of human beings. It is an "inhuman language." If we take away all of ourselves, our own ways of expression, the form we adhere to "degenerates into formula." Our selves, our styles, become empty imitation, a whole "jumble of conditioned responses in which [we become] victim rather than . . . master" (75).

Besides allowing language to degenerate into conditioned responses, objectivity cannot respond to the ever-growing range of technical communication today. Much technical writing involves the adaptation of messages for audiences unfamiliar, or relatively unfamiliar, with the subject being presented. We may communicate to educate others, create public awareness, persuade a supervisor, address a group of employees. A real voice helps arouse interest, and interest sharpens awareness and understanding.

Using figurative language in technical communication projects voices that arouse interest *and* understanding. Metaphor adds individuality to discourse; it creates a distinctive voice, making the writer more visible. Metaphor also can support several logical interpretations.[4] For any or all of these reasons, many technical writers avoid metaphor in their insistence on objectivity. But, as Richard Weaver reminds us in *The Ethics of Rhetoric*, abstract conceptions require model building. Analogy and metaphor cannot be eliminated from technical communication, because models must be explained and understood. Visualization through use of metaphor helps the reader to see relationships. Technical writing, even more than other kinds of discourse, *requires* pictures and concreteness that only metaphor can supply. Einstein presents a universe by showing the picture of an orange. Or a writer helps us understand the concept of entropy by showing us Arabs riding their camels here and there across desert sands. Valorizing voice in technical writing, then, allows us consciously to use figurative language, particularly metaphor, when our purpose and audience appropriately call for it.

More importantly, Weaver argues that metaphor is itself a means of discovery. Because metaphor can lead us from the unknown to the known, it is an important, perhaps the most important, heuristic. Analogy, for instance, can both formulate and direct inquiry (203–204). If we can regard metaphor as a means of dramatistic presentation, Weaver further suggests, then scientific writing might *really* bring together writer, reader, and subject. Dramatistic presentation is the only kind of writing that truly gets people involved because the argument comes out of narrative or metaphor. Dramatism, because it requires a dichotomy of opposites, solves the problem of reading difficulty in abstract writing. Yet it is not so concrete that it fails to accommodate hard-to-grasp ideas. We recognize dramatistic writing, for instance, in essays by Lewis Thomas and Loren Eiseley.[5]

Because current textbooks do not valorize voice—because they do not address the issues, theory, and praxis that are essential to a liberal arts approach to technical writing—they should be used as references rather than models. Using "models" would not, in any case, work well in the course I envision. But students and teacher can build their own portfolios of "examples" from written communication, which they collect from scientific and technological fields. The textbook forms they then can use as reference matter, as they see how the books' rigid forms transform under purpose and audience considerations and corporate ethos in the "real" world.

By deemphasizing the "textbook" of technical communication, the technical writing class can become a discourse community where students see technological language in a broader context. Specifically, the liberal arts approach to technical communication I envision combines reading a body of literature on science and the humanities, keeping personal notebooks, maintaining portfolios of writing in nonacademic settings, and doing collaborative work on campus and community projects. Such an approach enables students to place the scientific tenet of objectivity in another perspective as they work on a variety of correspondence, reports, and proposals during the semester. Instead of the usual forms approach, this combination of reading and writing would inform a rhetorically based, ethical technical-communication course.

## USING LITERATURE TO EXPLORE ETHICAL ISSUES IN THE SCIENCES

A liberal arts technical writing course must include a variety of reading assignments along with writing assignments that require students to produce a variety of letters, reports, and proposals. More important than establishing a canon of readings in technology and the humanities is allowing flexibility in the readings, because, typically, technical writing courses housed in English departments attract diverse majors. Students come from engineering, computer science, the hard sciences, and business as well as from economics, communication, psychology, and political science, and, many times, from history and English. Reading and responding to a core of readings on both technology and the humanities is appropriate for a classroom with this kind of diversity.

Before I suggest one possible classification of subject matter and some reading examples, let me stress that this approach does not emphasize the readings over the technical writing assignments; rather, the students' writing would be informed and influenced by the absorption of ideas. These connections are little different from those governing any writing-intensive course.

This part of the course approach requires a reading core, journal-type writing, and peer collaboration. As students work independently through the core, they write responses to the readings. Using the dialectical notebook, they respond to the readings dialogically, summarizing on the left page and responding on the right page. Writing analytical summaries is an effective rhetorical strategy, because while students are exploring the author's major ideas—historical, ethical, stylistic—they are learning not only how to read critically but also how to become conscious of the repercussions of ideas in their own writing. The notebooks contain good material on which to base a final exam. Students connect the analyses and dialogical inquiry to their own writing processes of completed course assignments.

Following the usual technical-communication practice in oral presentation, students also can give brief "reports" during the semester on these readings, reporting individually or by team. Team presentation has the further advantage of drawing on collaborative learning, and it frees more time for class discussion.

Just as in any writing class, there are a variety of ways to incorporate a body of readings into the curriculum. The difference is that the writing assignments do not come out of the readings; the students' writing comes out of a learned sense of historic, stylistic, and ethical considerations. Thus, the core readings and the technical writing assignments strongly connect. Here are several suggestions for a reading core, grouped by subject matter. I intend this classification to be suggestive, not exhaustive, of the kinds of issues meaningful within a liberal arts technical writing course.

## History of the Idea of Metatechnology

Readings in the history of ideas prepare students for later readings in science and the humanities and give them a historical sense of opposing philosophical ideas on the making of knowledge: reason alone versus experience. Because Wordsworth grew up and wrote in a scientific age, selections from his work are useful, along with selections in rationalism. These readings enable students to see how Wordsworth sets the active mind that sees and orders observations against the Lockean mind that passively records observations onto a piece of blank white paper. Students are ready to read Carlyle on rescuing society from materialism and irresponsibility (e.g., "Latter-Day Pamphlets"). Selections should include Emerson on man as the center of the universe—a view that is in opposition to rationalism. Such selections speak to how we gain knowledge and develop world views. They serve as a philosophical basis for further readings.

## Imaginative Technological Improbabilities

Selections from H. G. Wells, de Tocqueville, and Jules Verne are of particular value, apart from their obvious subject interest. Such readings generate discussion on the issue that science should be directed toward human ends. These kinds of readings introduce students to further reading and exploration into contemporary controversies on whether or not technological "advances" are always synonymous with human "progress." Peer groups, for instance, can formulate lists of twentieth-century technological advances in their fields and then discuss actual and possible repercussions.

## The Split between Science and the Humanities

This topic is rich with possibilities. Numerous essays on the subject are anthologized in popular readers used in freshman writing courses. Because of this rich variety, I prefer not to assign the same readings each semester, and I like to include some topical issues as well. Whatever the list, it should include both old and new essays. Bacon's essays (e.g., "The New Atlantis") are a good beginning, for these students' immediate concern, especially when they first enter a "technical" writing class, is efficiency, not morality. Other writers that students who are going into public life respond to are C. P. Snow, Marshall McLuhan, and Richard Selzer. Another way to structure this assignment is to require a smaller list of common readings, then require additional, independent reading so that students can read on this subject out of their own particular interests or disciplines and from their own independent research.

## Views of the World as an Ordered Machine

Pope's *Essay on Man* fits this subject because it is an effort to reconcile the rational and the subjective, a view of the possible totality in each of us. And I. A. Richards, in *Science and Poetry*, argues that humankind is not just an intelligence but a whole system of interests. In opposition is Thomas Huxley's "On a Piece of Chalk," which emphasizes the value of science at the expense of the humanities curriculum. Other possibilities include Mary Shelley's *Frankenstein* and selections from Matthew Arnold, George Orwell, and J. Bronowski. The rationale behind these readings is that students begin some synthesis of science and the humanities.

## Mechanistic Thinking Reduced to Absurdity

Any of Jonathan Swift's works developing this idea would be both enjoyable and informative to students, who would, within the structure of this particular course, see Swift's ideas from a different perspective.

## The Morality of Science

This subject has long been debated, but perhaps at no time in humankind's history has it become more important. Our planet's very survival is increasingly threatened by technological advances. Numerous historical and topical writings address such threats. Hawthorne's "The Birthmark" will give students an historical context of how humankind attempts to control nature through science. And "Rappacini's Daughter" illustrates that the extreme arrogance of caring more for science than people can result in isolation. John Cheever's "The Enormous Radio" describes a technology that destroys through its invasion of others' intimate lives. Students then are prepared to explore issues that carry morality beyond the individual and communities to whole societies and the world. The cataloguing of representative moral grayness with which I began this article points to appropriate reading matter. Such contemporary issues recorded in newspapers and current periodicals address how our rapidly changing culture is causing values to shift even more dangerously than in past times.

## Defining What a Scientist Should Be

Readings on and by scientists persuade students of the reality and importance of creativity and individuality in science as well as the humanities. Satirical writings such as Mark Twain's "The Artist of the Beautiful" help them realize the importance of creativity rather than technical proficiency. And "Some Learned Fables for Good Old Boys and Girls" satirizes illustrious scientists building a body of demonstrated fact from a very little bit of supposition. Then, reading Einstein on creativity and intuition in the scientist, students see an intelligent and sensitive synthesis of proficiency and creativity.

Though demanding, Douglas Hofstadter's *Gödel, Escher, Bach* brilliantly shows the syncretic relationship between science and the arts. As Hofstadter traces the strange loops in these men's work, ultimately representing endless process, we see how the human mind is a maze of interwoven threads, an "eternal golden braid." Different disciplines in science and art play out copies of the same theme.

## Emerging Voice of the Scientist

James Watson and Francis Crick's article in *Nature* on DNA (1953) together with S. Michael Halloran's articles on the rhetoric of science help students realize how ethical argument can lead to the making of a field—in this case, molecular biology.[6] Studying Halloran's rhetorical analysis of Watson and Crick's seminal article helps students learn to analyze other scientific and technical discourse as well as their own and classmates' letters, reports, and proposals written during the semester.

## USING THE WRITER'S NOTEBOOK

Along with the readings, students use their notebooks in various ways during the semester. First, they create a dialectical section in which they critically summarize and subjectively respond to the reading core. With the notebook pages spread open (looseleaf notebooks work best), students write précis, critical analyses, or some form of disciplined implementation on the left side. Then on the right side, they respond to the précis or analysis in a subjective way, drawing on imagination and dialogic inquiry. The facing pages of the notebook support within them a dialogue, enabling students to continually think about thinking. Their notebooks themselves become forums wherein students speculate, investigate, test, respond, define, compare—all kinds of thinking that Ann Berthoff calls "dialogic action" (122).

Second, during their research for semester reports and proposals, students use the notebooks as learning logs. For instance, when they are investigating a problem or potential problem that will be the subject of an informative report or a persuasive proposal, they write descriptive narratives of their research that become the basis of later investigative, progress, informative, or feasibility reports. Learning logs are good starting places for students to begin "functional prose" because they can put problems, policies, or whatever, in narrative or even dramatic form, at the same time experimenting with figurative language. These strategies help students to recognize the value of concrete details and to make conscious use of them to anchor observations and support assertions in their reports and proposals. Working with narrative helps them see that it does not have to be subordinate to argument; they see how arguments can grow out of narrative.

Third, students use their notebooks as journals wherein they write self-evaluations of particular composing processes and note what part ethical considerations play in the processes.

The juxtaposition of these imaginative and disciplined approaches injects enough subjectivity so that technical writing students can avoid voices of false authority. These ways of using notebooks also enable them to see themselves *not as observers who are independent of the process but as observers who are participants in the process.* They learn for themselves that technical communication is not just what is left when everything but objectivity is taken out. The tenet of objectivity gives way, we hope, to a heightened consciousness that technology does not have to create a nonresponsible and detached ethos.[7]

Here is a verbatim extract from an engineer's lab notebook that describes the first snow-making outside the GE Research Lab:

> Curt flew into the cloud, and I started the dispenser in operation. I dropped about three pounds [of dry ice] and then swung around and headed south. About this time I looked toward the rear and was thrilled to see long streamers of snow falling from the base of the cloud through which we had just passed. I shouted to Curt to swing around, and as we did so we passed through a mass of glistening snow crystals! We made another run through a dense portion of the unseeded cloud, during which time I dispensed about three more pounds of crushed dry ice. . . . This was done by opening the window and letting the suction of the passing air remove it. We then swung west of the cloud and observed draperies of snow which seemed to hang for 2–3000 feet below us and noted the cloud drying up rapidly, very similar to what we observe in the cold box in the laboratory. . . . While still in the cloud as we saw the glinting crystals all over, I turned to Curt, and we shook hands as I said, "We *did* it!" ["Why Study English?" 3–4]

Here the writer is projecting to others individual progress and potential worth. Historically, the notebook report is significant because it was *used* for much of the subsequent theory and research in weather control. Students can emulate this extract, drawing on their own research process, or they can find other research narratives to emulate or record in their notebooks.

Certainly our backgrounds—whether in rhetoric or literary studies—can help counteract some of our students' belief that technology demands objectivity over all else. We can help them see both ways of learning in each of us: the artist with sudden flashes of insight not yet based on facts and the scientist/researcher with experiments based on observation. The two are interlinked.

We particularly embrace complementariness in our own discovery and composing processes. But then so do many technologists. An often-told story has Einstein asking a poet how he works. The poet describes to Einstein how the idea of a poem came to him and grew, with an important part being played by the intuition and the subconscious. Einstein, delighted with this answer, says that the process is the same for the scientist. The mechanics of discovery are neither logical nor intellectual. Often, there is a sudden illumination. Later, intelligence and analysis confirm the intuition. But initially there is a great forward leap of the imagination. We can appreciate and recognize what Einstein and the poet were talking about. The point is that we help our students see artists as people who penetrate into secrets of nature whether they write poetry, novels, or papers on unified field theory.

The principle of complementariness permits us to accept both as valid, maybe not simultaneously, but at least alternately. Our students, who will be going into a diversity of fields, can learn to balance the two kinds of knowledge and to recognize that the knowledge of most worth is never wholly external to the knower. And is this not the mission of the humanities?

## USING COLLABORATIVE LEADERSHIP

Career planners stress that leadership and working with others are qualities that employers are looking for today, even more than individual achievement. If those outside academe are stressing the social context in business and technology, then we can no longer focus on formalistic approaches in technical writing courses. If we truly respond to who we are and who our students are—and what we both envision and strive to become in our increasingly complex worlds—then we can instill in them the value of mutual cooperation and social harmony when they enter the world of technology.

Academe has begun emphasizing the social context in business courses. In 1985 several U.S. universities offered courses that stress group cooperation and leadership development through social exploration, although none of these were technical-communication courses.[8] The new courses are coordinated with community activities in order to develop and encourage the students' participation in all levels of society. Moving the instruction of technical communication into surrounding communities enables students to recognize language as social construction. Moving some course work out into the public arena also makes us participants in the rhetorical tradition.

Emphasizing collaborative learning in technical-communication courses helps to instill these values of both leading and working with others. In addition to group discussion on the readings and in addition to group oral presentations (this last activity giving them valuable practice in speaking before groups), students should also collaborate as they work toward solving real problems. Both the campus and its surrounding community are fertile ground to find real problems to solve. Such shared work that does not rely on simulated case studies sharpens a concern with the value of mutual cooperation and social harmony and emphasizes not only language *in* its social context but also language *as* social construction. Working on some real problem along with discussing their core readings helps students, both individually and in groups, see that technology always should be directed toward human ends. Collaborative leadership, furthermore, helps them learn that any one human problem might be solved through the combined efforts of technology and the humanities.

If we agree that technical communication has to arise from a rhetorical context, we can structure our classrooms along corporate lines so that students can work in groups on real projects, projects they have chosen after close observation and investigative reporting on buildings, land, facilities, systems, policies, and procedures on campus or in the local community, worlds in which they already participate. But these real projects must address an issue's or problem's history, politics, and sociology as well as its technology. Thus students enter into a real context that requires cooperation, sharing, and participation in real situations that are further strengthened by sequential assignments.

Student peer groups can work together to come up with real projects to report on in sequential reports throughout the semester. Even their working together to choose a real problem to tackle helps them to become more conscious of the importance of close observation, narrative investigation, analysis, and, of course, social cooperation. Active participation in real problems/projects enables students to see their school work as "real" when they can be instrumental in bringing about some needed change in the campus community. And out of real-world collaborative projects in which students participate because they have a real interest—or real stake—come real voices.

In my technical writing classes, students have eagerly worked on real projects instead of the usual simulated case studies outlined in textbooks.[9] For instance, a team in one class worked all semester with faculty from other departments and the administration to set up and get approved a policy whereby plus and minus grades would be incorporated into student grade point averages. The sequential assignments came out of actual situations requiring correspondence, a proposal, a progress report, and a feasibility report. The sequence was an organic one, each piece of written discourse arising from a real rhetorical context as the team worked through their project. Another team worked on getting approval for the restoration of a long-broken stone fountain outside the Divinity School chapel and the planning and construction of the fountain's surrounding area into a "philosopher's garden." Working closely with the Divinity School and the Physical Plant Department, the team worked for and got formal approval for repair and construction to begin. Again, their oral and written technical communication on their semester project came out of a real situation and purpose.

Yet another team through its effective semester sequential reports, which culminated in a feasibility report, succeeded in getting a sidewalk outside the business and engineering schools widened. The sidewalk had long been of inadequate width for the increased numbers using it, resulting in soil erosion, groundcover destruction, and constant complaints every time it rained. Students had to slog along the muddy areas on either side of a sidewalk if they lost their "right of way." And in the community outside campus, other student teams worked with city transportation on synthesizing opinion surveys on a mass-transit-system referendum. Still another team enthusiastically worked with (and sometimes against) various city bureaucracies to turn a city-owned vacant lot into a small but well used inner-city park. These are just a few examples from my own teaching experience that show what peer groups can and will accomplish enthusiastically when they become interested in solving problems connected to real instead of simulated projects. A technical writing course that requires students to participate within a real social context prepares and encourages them to shape the world that will be theirs.

## CONCLUSION

Several new emphases in business and technology are suggested by the educational approach of many professional schools as they try to deal with alienation, dishonesty, mistrust between the individual and institution. We seem to be at the beginning of several related strong movements toward

- Partnerships between public and private sectors rather than any one governing body
- Consensus building rather than hierarchical command
- Inclusionary rather than exclusionary strategies
- Collaborative rather than dictatorial leadership

All of these movements are reflective of cooperation and collective action. Thus, disciplinary lines in accounting, engineering, marketing, manufacturing, and so on—fields that can be just as ivory-tower insulated as academic lines—are beginning to blur along with those same disciplinary lines within some academic communities. If M.B.A. and other professional schools are trying to develop in graduate or postgraduate students the moral fiber that holds us together as a society, then can we, in English studies, do less for students who may be just beginning their undergraduate specializations? For some of these undergraduates, a course in technical communication may be the only English course they have taken since freshman writing. By our very backgrounds, who more than we are qualified to teach writing and reading grounded in both the humanities and science?

Far too often our students come to us perceiving the split between science and the humanities to be irreconcilable. And perhaps too often we ourselves concentrate overmuch on these discipline differences, living in one camp or the other formed out of departmental splits that have exacerbated the views of writing as nothing more than technique, thus divergent from the aesthetics of literature. But the application of creative intelligence at full stretch—whether in the making of works of art, in scientific discovery, or simply in the search for understanding and wisdom—is essential for any civilization worthy of its name. We can help our students make such connections, so that they can see the poem, the essay, the chemical formula *all* as achievements and thus, in the proper sense of the term, creations. We are, as teachers of English, uniquely qualified to help our students not only see the complementariness of our diversities but also make connections between voice and subject, individual and community, technology and art. And because rhetoric rests on the presumption that discourse is a generative force central to human thought and social conduct, we can strive to instill this rhetorical consciousness in our technical-communication students.

## Notes

1. In a recent survey, those English departments that offer undergraduate technical communication programs reported an 80 percent growth. See Slevin, 192.
2. The approach I describe here could also realize course goals in schools with large and well-developed writing-across-the-discipline programs.
3. See Merrill D. Whitburn's "The Ideal Orator and Literary Critic as Technical Communicators: An Emerging Revolution in English Departments," for a brilliant and thorough conceptualization of technical discourse as rhetoric.

4. For a challenge to these objections to metaphor, see Halloran and Bradford's "Figures of Speech in the Rhetoric of Science and Technology."
5. See Winterowd's "Dramatism in Themes and Poems" and Chris Anderson's "Dramatism and Deliberation." Also see "Figures of Speech in the Rhetoric of Science and Technology" for Halloran and Bradford's argument for using figurative language in technical writing. Students in scientific and technical writing courses should first work with the rhetorical principles upon which the writing norms of a field rest, then go on to work with schemes and tropes in solving certain problems in a given scientific or technological field (183–85). Douglas M. Catron also has argued for using metaphor as an heuristic in technical communication. His "Creation of Metaphor: A Case for Figurative Language in Technical Writing Classes" outlines specific heuristic assignments requiring students to write a technical description, a definition of a technical principle, a description of a mechanism or procedure, and instructions—all based on metaphor as a heuristic.
6. See Halloran's "The Birth of Molecular Biology: An Essay in the Rhetorical Criticism of Scientific Discourse" for a discussion of ethical argument in the Watson and Crick article.
7. See Powell's "A Chemist's View of Writing, Reading, and Thinking Across the Curriculum," especially 416.
8. Harvard, Princeton, Columbia, Rochester, Northwestern, Wisconsin, Minnesota, Stanford, Colorado College, Texas, Pace, and Maryland.
9. For an extended discussion of this collaborative approach, see Enos's "Aristotle, Inc.: Corporate Structure in the Technical Communication Course."

## Works Cited

Anderson, Chris. "Dramatism and Deliberation. *Rhetoric Review* 4(Sept. 1985):34–43.

Berthoff, Ann E. " 'Reading the World . . . Reading the Word': Paulo Freire's Pedagogy of Knowing." *Only Connect: Uniting Reading and Writing.* Ed. Thomas Newkirk. Upper Montclair, N.J.: Boynton/Cook, 1986, pp. 119–30.

Bump, Jerome. "Metaphor, Creativity, and Technical Writing." *College Composition and Communication* 36(Dec. 1985):444–453.

Catron, Douglas M. "The Creation of Metaphor: A Case for Figurative Language in Technical Writing Classes." *Journal of Advanced Composition* 3(1982):69–78.

Connors, Robert J. *"Actio:* A Rhetoric of Manuscripts." *Rhetoric Review* 2(1983):64–73.

———. "The Rise of Technical Writing Instruction in America." *Journal of Technical Writing and Communication* 12:4(1982):329–352.

Dusdorf, Georges. *Speaking.* Trans. Paul T. Brockelman. Evanston, Ill.: Northwestern University Press, 1965.

Enos, Theresa. "Aristotle, Inc.: Corporate Structure in the Technical Communication Course." *The Technical Writing Teacher* 13(1986):71–77.

Halloran, S. Michael. "The Birth of Molecular Biology: An Essay in the Rhetorical Criticism of Scientific Discourse." *Rhetoric Review* 3(1984):70–83.

———, and Annette Norris Bradford. "Figures of Speech in the Rhetoric of Science and Technology." *Essays on Classical Rhetoric and Modern Discourse.* Eds. Robert J. Connors, Lisa S. Ede, and Andrea A. Lunsford. Carbondale, Ill.: Southern Illinois University Press, 1984, pp. 179–192.

Hofstadter, Douglas R. *Godel, Escher, Bach: An Eternal Golden Braid.* New York: Basic Books, 1979.
Leff, Michael. "Acting and Understanding: A Note on the Relationship Between Classical and Contemporary Rhetoric." *Federation Review: The Journal of the State Humanities Councils* 8(1985):6–10.
Miller, Carolyn. "Teaching as a Form of Consciousness: A Study of Contemporary Ethos." *The Central States Speech Journal* 29(1978):228–236.
Murphy, James J. (Ed.). *The Rhetorical Tradition and Modern Writing.* New York: Modern Language Association, 1982.
———. *A Synoptic History of Classical Rhetoric.* New York: Random House, 1972. Rpt: Davis, CA: Hermagoras P, 1983.
Peterson, Linda. "Repetition and Metaphor in the Early Stages of Composing." *College Composition and Communication* 36(1985):429–443.
Powell, Alfred. "A Chemist's View of Writing, Reading, and Thinking Across the Curriculum." *College Composition and Communication* 36(1985):414–418.
Quintilian. *Institutio Oratoria.* Trans. H. E. Butler. In *Readings in Classical Rhetoric.* Ed. Thomas W. Benson and Michael H. Prosser. Bloomington, Ind.: Indiana University Press, 1972.
Robertson, Linda R., and James F. Slevin. "The Status of Composition Faculty: Resolving Reforms." *Rhetoric Review* 5(1987):190–193.
Rubens, Philip M. "Reinventing the Wheel? Ethics for Technical Communicators." *Journal of Technical Writing and Communication* 11(1981):329–339.
Rutter, Russell. "Poetry, Imagination, and Technical Writing. *College English* 47(1985):698–711.
Stoddard, Eve Walsh. "The Role of Ethos in the Theory of Technical Writing." *The Technical Writing Teacher* 11(1984):229–241.
Tebeaux, Elizabeth, and Harry Kroiter. "Bringing Literature Teachers and Writing Teachers Closer Together." *ADE Bulletin* (Summer 1984):28–32.
Weaver, Richard M. *The Ethics of Rhetoric.* Chicago: Regnery/Gateway, 1953. Rpt. Hermagoras Press. Davis, CA: 1985.
Whitburn, Merrill D. "The Ideal Orator and Literary Critic as Technical Communicators: An Emerging Revolution in English Departments." *Essays on Classical Rhetoric and Modern Discourse.* Eds. Robert J. Connors, Lisa S. Ede, and Andrea A. Lunsford. Carbondale, Ill.: Southern Illinois University Press, 1984, pp. 226–247.
"Why Study English?" General Electric Bulletin. In *Ideas and Patterns for Writing.* Ed. Carle B. Spotts. 2nd ed. New York: Holt, Rinehart and Winston, 1967, pp. 1–8.
Winterowd, W. Ross. "Dramatism in Themes and Poems." *College English* 45(1983):581–588.

# PART THREE

# UNDERSTANDING CULTURES: WRITERS AS AGENTS OF CONSERVATION AND CHANGE

# WRITERS IN ORGANIZATIONS AND HOW THEY LEARN THE IMAGE: THEORY, RESEARCH, AND IMPLICATIONS

*Jean Ann Lutz*
Miami University

*Jean A. Lutz is an associate professor of English at Miami University in Oxford, Ohio, where she teaches in the graduate and undergraduate programs in technical and scientific writing. Her two undergraduate courses focus on the preparation of resumés, letters of application, solicited and unsolicited memoranda of recommendation, instructional materials, proposals, and reports. Her graduate seminar requires students to work with clients to prepare documentation for a process or instrument, proposals (often to state funding agencies or national organizations), articles on scientists or technicians for local distribution, and a series of short assignments that include writing for media other than print. Lutz's research interests focus on the effects of the writing process in various environments. She has published widely on the effects of computers on writing and on the influence of organizational socialization on writers' processes. She regularly serves as a consultant to business, industry, and government.*

*Lutz is an associate in a California-based communication consulting agency, Hamlin-Harkins Ltd. in San Jose. She has done consulting work for General Electric and the United States Department of Labor.*

Theorists in organizational communication generally agree that members of organizations share similar values, that these values are identifiable, and that they are the genesis for a theoretical construct known as *corporate culture*. Although Desmond Graves (following Evan, 1968, and Guion, 1973) argues that the construct is "at best a 'commonsense' and at worst a 'fuzzy' concept" (1986, 150), even he asserts that "culture is not a concept invented by academics to increase . . . publications. Whether it is called 'atmosphere,' 'company spirit' or 'ethos,' it is part of the tissue of organizational life and would deserve to be studied if only as a phenomenon of leadership" (126). When attempting to sharpen the concept of corporate culture, researchers typically define it in terms of values, the patterns of thought, beliefs, feelings, attitudes, behaviors, products, and publications that result from the experiences and common goals shared by people working in the same organization.

In addition to identifying these generic features, researchers often study them in individual cultures, since they agree that each organization is recognizably different because the manifestations of the generic features are also distinct (Deal and Kennedy, 1982). Further, these differences are revealed in two ways: an internal manifestation of values which I will call the climate (I borrow the term from Graves, though he defines climate as the patterns common to individual work groups within the same organization) and the external manifestation of these same or different values, usually termed corporate or public image.

The features that make up a culture—its climate and image—*may be* consciously (and *will be* unconsciously) imparted to all who join a company. That is, successful new employees will learn about an organization's climate and image—they will be socialized. Organizational socialization is thus "the process by which an individual comes to appreciate the values, abilities, expected behaviors, and social knowledge essential for assuming an organizational role and for participating as an organizational member" (Louis, 1980, 229–230). The duration of this interactional process, its stages, and any conflicts that arise from it will—because of its essential nature—affect the organization's and employee's stability and the ability of the employee to act in the organization. Employees who are socialized will usually become supporters of and contributors to the organizational environment they have joined.

Thus, the definition and effects of these concepts and considerations are important to organizational theorists—but not just to them. The concepts are also important for writing theorists and for technical and scientific communicators: communication is the primary tool through which members participate in an organization, through which nonmembers learn about an organization, and through which a corporation's climate and image are codified. In this article, I, therefore, discuss the means, effects, and conflicts related to writers' socialization processes. My observations are drawn from literature in technical and scientific communication and from my experience advising professional writing majors with their internships and jobs. They are supported by evidence from responses to questionnaires by ten graduate students who were then completing their course work in Miami University's Master of Technical and Scientific Communication Program. From these various sources, I tentatively conclude that the processes through which writers are socialized into an organization are crucial because of the writer's unique background and organizational function. I also conclude that the writer, once socialized, has the potential to support or change the organization according to his or her degree of responsibility and personality. Finally, I note that identifying these processes raises important implications for organizations, writers, and academic institutions responsible for educating professional communicators.

## DEFINING AND UNDERSTANDING CORPORATE CULTURE AND ITS SOURCES

We can begin with the premise that "every business—in fact every organization—has a culture" (Deal and Kennedy, 1982, 4), a widely shared system of values, beliefs, attitudes, and philosophies that constitute the essence of the company. Employees must understand it either to join it *or* to change it, for, as I will explain later, advance attention to the prevailing culture will "have a vital impact on the degree of success of any efforts to alter or improve the organization" (Porter, Lawler, and Hackman, 1975, 489). At any given time, however, the values held in common by employees are synonymous with what their organizations stand for: "Shared values define the fundamental character of their organization, the attitude that distinguishes it from all others." "[Thus] management pays a great deal of attention to shaping and fine-tuning these values to conform to the economic and business environment of the company and to communicating them to the organization" (Deal and Kennedy, 1982, 23, 22).

Presumably, Deal and Kennedy are referring to the way business is conducted—to what is valued by managers and other employees in any particular firm or any specific organization. However, what is valued inside an organization may be consistent wholly or only partially (or less typically, not at all) with another aspect of its culture, the image the company projects to its clients, customers, or consumers.

These groups learn (or are taught) to recognize companies by the slogans consciously promoted as the company image. At GE, "We bring good things to life," or "Progress is our most important product." DuPont produces "Better things for better living through chemistry." And Monsanto, in a statement more overt than its corporate slogan ("We challenge tomorrow, every day"), encourages us through a 1986 copy headline to believe in its concern for the environment: "At the present rate of erosion, much of our farmland could become wasteland. We're helping make sure it won't." Through such identifiers, an organization teaches us to connect specific values with the company name. Corporations (and/or their advertising agencies) make conscious decisions about the way they want to present themselves to their public—and also possibly, but not necessarily, to their employees.

Typically a company's publicly espoused values are consistent with its internal values and climate—because such consistency both motivates employees and contributes to their commitment (Buchanan, 1974; Deal and Kennedy, 1982). However, an organization's climate may conflict with its public image: employees may be encouraged or required to maintain a public image that is not supported by the organization's capabilities or services. Such a company may lose or frustrate employees who cannot work well in the ambiguity inherent in the dissonance between the two expressions of culture. Consistent or not, an organization's values are most often initiated and promulgated both internally and externally by its chief executives, whose values act sometimes as "a large lens held up by high priests through which the worshippers may examine their gods, the stars: 'you shall see things thus' " (Graves, 1986, 157). Values also allow reciprocity, "a means by which participants [may] communicate and coordinate their efforts" (11). Culture, recognized as both internal values and external image, is usually perceived as a downward-and-outward-moving phenomenon that permeates, drives, and constrains the awareness of all, from top-level managers to clerical staff or production workers and even to staff in outlying divisions or satellite companies.

Most importantly, managers rely on workers being aware of these values, for only through becoming socialized (that is, learning about, identifying with, and accepting these values) can employees help perpetuate a company's climate and image. If culture is, as Schein (1985) defines it,

> ... a pattern of basic assumptions—invented, discovered, or developed by a given group as it learns to cope with its problems of external adaption and internal integration—that has worked well enough to be considered valid and, therefore, to be taught to new members as the *correct* way to perceive, think and feel in relation to those problems. [emphasis mine] [9]

then, socialization is one of the principal mechanisms by which culture and corporate control are maintained.

## THE STAGES, MEANS, AND EFFECTS OF SOCIALIZATION

Although organizational and employee effectiveness are dependent on socialization, it does not, actually *cannot*, occur all at once. Accordingly, most organizational theorists identify stages in the process (Buchanan, 1974; Feldman, 1976; Jablin, 1982, 1984; Porter, Lawler, and Hackman, 1975; Van Maanen, 1976; and Wanous, 1980). Initiation most probably begins when workers are being hired, a "prearrival" stage (Porter et al., 1975) when the employee and company make preliminary judgments about compatibility. If the two find each other suitable, this stage is followed by a "breaking-in" period (Jablin, 1982), when the employee receives the most conscious and intensive orientation to the firm's policies and practices. A third and final stage follows, an acceptance or metamorphosis phase in which the employee becomes an insider, a supporter and promoter of the organization's philosophy and image. So substantial is what the employee learns during this process that Graves suggests that culture cannot be objectively observed by those outside of the organization—outsiders simply do not have the same sense of culture as insiders. Yet, some values must be evident, for persons do choose organizations that they believe suit them, where they believe their own personalities, self-concepts, values, and needs will be realized, thus engaging in a process of self-fulfillment or even self-selection (Graves, 1986, 48). Organizations, for their part, want people who will fit in. Hence, they typically devote considerable time and money to finding appropriate employees—people whose goals, and hence commitment, will be consistent with the organization's expectations (Schneider and Reichers, 1983, 27).

To attract appropriate employees and increase their ability to become a part of the organization's values, companies carry out the socialization process through various informal and formal means. In the initiation stage, the means are most likely to be informal and oral—interviews, conversations, question-and-answer periods. (The degree of formality of this stage, of course, can give important information about both internal climate and organizational goals that affect public image.) Typical informal means may be accompanied by the more formal ones that usually come in the next stage of the socialization process. Once hired into an organization, workers are often officially introduced to its preferences by such means as worker orientation programs and meetings or sessions with other employees. Newly hired managers may be requested to participate in management training sessions or to watch training films depicting essentials of the company's philosophy, products, and management style. The new employee may also be asked to read annual report(s), training manuals that explain relevant procedures or give instructions for specific tasks, or any of a multitude of day-to-day documents—internal and external memoranda, letters, and reports—that have been written to carry on the company's business but from which the employee may infer the company's philosophy and public image. The employee will also begin to hear about the "heroes" and "heroines" of the organization and about the "rites and rituals" and "myths" that have evolved into the present organizational milieu (Graves, 1986, 48; Deal and Kennedy, 1982, 13–84). Deal and Kennedy note, in this regard, the importance of the cultural network, "the primary 'carrier' of the corporate values and heroic mythology" (15).

Schein offers a useful summary of the means of socialization:

- Formal statements of organizational philosophy
- Design of physical spaces, facades, buildings
- Deliberate role modelling, teaching, and coaching by leaders
- Explicit reward, status system, and promotion criteria
- Stories, legends, myths, and parables about key people and events
- What leaders pay attention to, measure, and control
- Leader reactions to critical incidents and organizational crises
- How the organization is designed and structured
- Organizational systems and procedures
- Criteria used for selection, promotion, and retirement of people

Clearly, as Harrison (1972) suggests, socialization plays a large role in *organizational* effectiveness. "It determines how decisions are made, human resources are used and the external environment is approached . . ." (23). Van Maanen and Schein (1979) add, "New members must be taught to see the organizational world as do their more experienced colleagues, if the traditions of the organization are to survive" (211). But Schein's summary also suggests that socialization works by having a profound effect on organizational members: it helps them know what matters to managers, how to be managers, what the organization's public expects and, consequently, how high and how fast they can be promoted. It is a means by which an employee can move from being an outsider to being an insider, a participating member of the organization (Van Maanen, 1976, 67). Socialization influences, at least indirectly, commitment, motivation, and job performance—all critical factors for any employee but particularly for the employee whose job it will be to represent the company in print.

## THE INFLUENCE OF CORPORATE CULTURE AND SOCIALIZATION ON WRITERS

Because the kinds of knowledge writers bring to organizations is unique and because writers do or should play a key role in assessing and recording a corporation's culture, the issues raised by theory in organizational communication are particularly crucial to the situation faced by technical and scientific communicators.

Most employees must integrate two kinds of knowledge when they join an organization: knowledge of their discipline (or career field) and knowledge about their profession. Writers who join an organization must also integrate a third kind of specialized knowledge, an awareness of that organization's culture and image.

In discussing disciplinary knowledge, let me begin with an assumption: Many members of certain *kinds* of organizations—or certain groups of people in *various* kinds of organizations—have in common knowledge affiliated with a discipline. Members of chemical companies, Dow and Monsanto for example, or computer firms such as IBM and Apple, share interests common to the scientific or technological orientation of the firm. In addition, members in different firms (research chemists in epoxy resins at General Electric and Kodak, for instance) share what Toulmin, Rieke, and Janik (1984) would call field-dependent knowledge, a set of commonly held issues and questions based upon disciplinary affiliation or formal education. Most professional communicators share such field-dependent scientific or technical knowledge. They are encouraged or required to have technical or scientific knowledge in their field of choice, and they bring such knowledge as an asset to the firm they join.

This specialized kind of field-dependent knowledge gains them entrance to specific "discourse communities," groups whose members can be characterized by their familiarity with discipline-related knowledge and language and by the specialized kinds of discourse competence that enable them to participate in their groups. "Members [of these groups] know what is worth communicating, how it can be communicated, what other members of the community are likely to know and believe to be true about certain subjects, how other members can be persuaded and so on" (Faigley, 1985, 238). For example, the publications referred to in *Chemical Abstracts* and the trade journals of the chemical industry demonstrate that chemists speak a language in some ways demonstrably theirs alone. A professional writer's technological or scientific disciplinary affiliation, and hence membership in that discourse community, will enable him or her to speak its special language and communicate with and for its participants authoritatively.

But many professional writers will also belong to a second discourse community that will influence their approach to a writing task. As professionals, they typically will acquire the theoretical perspective, the practical knowledge, and the metalanguage particular to those concerned primarily with the communication of technology or science. This knowledge will be different from disciplinary knowledge related to a scientific or technical field. In the ideal, technical and scientific writing has a broader-based disciplinary knowledge, a rhetorical foundation which demands a contextual approach to language use that always accounts for the particularities of audience and purpose. As a result, technical and scientific communicators' second discourse community, language about issues and questions in communication, has field-*invariance* that other disciplines do not have. Connors, Ede, and Lunsford explain the field invariance of rhetoric in the following passage: "Rhetoric [and technical and scientific communication] is perhaps less suited than any other subject to specialization. Its major function . . . [is] as a synthetic art which [brings] together knowledge in various fields with audiences of various kinds; its goal [is] the discovery and sharing of knowledge" (1984, 3).

Thus, a good deal of a professional writer's educational preparation focuses on what constitutes "good" writing. Ideally, as I suggest, good is often dependent on context and situation, but writers do learn rules and guidelines that are appropriate for discovering the best available means of communicating in almost all situations. Writers must know these guidelines as well as the conventions of a particular scientific or technological discipline if they are to make effective choices apart or in conjunction with organizational influences.

Finally, it is evident that as organizational members, writers draw on a third kind of knowledge, a "variety of social resources, including personal interaction and the culture of the organization in which they read and write" (Odell and Goswami, 1985, ix; Odell, 1985, 250). Thus they potentially belong to a third discourse community, the organization they join—and to a fourth community, the division, department, or group in which or for whom they perform their work. Referring to the organizational specificity of the writer's task, Dobrin asserts "the way they handle technical writing at Kodak is very different from the way they do at Corning, and each way is tied up with the corporation's organization, its self-image, its decisions about what is acceptable behavior, its valuations of judgment and knowledge, and so on" (248). Clearly, that each organization has a culture, that this culture may be different inside and outside the organization, and that divisions and departments may also have "cultural" differences must, of necessity, affect the strategy inherent in writers' documents—their content, structure and appearance. These aspects of organizational culture may also affect the value placed on writing (and hence on the writer's organizational function and potential influence) and even on the specific documents that are planned and produced. They may even influence a writer's style by requiring the writer to prefer the house style over—or in combination with—his or her own.

The complex interrelationship among the kinds of knowledge a writer brings *to* an organization and the kinds of knowledge a writer gains *in* an organization complicates the writer's task—a task which requires the writer to integrate this knowledge and still be a reliable "spokesperson" (Debs 1984) for the organization, resolving at times its internal climate and external image as well as its subdivisions. Since the writer's role can entail writing documents that record or perpetuate aspects of the organizational culture (how things are or should be done) and more frequently representing the organization to its public (how the organization wants people to think it does or has done things), the writer is essential to the stasis, change, and ultimate success of the organization as it works to achieve its goals. Thus it is that socialization has some of its most profound effects on the job performance of writers hired to prepare documents for organizational and public use.

If we take as a given that culture (climate and image) are important to organizations, then we can also assume that preserving and codifying that culture is essential—that organizations will want to consciously preserve, and in some cases create or recreate, the best of their cultural heritage. More and more this task is falling to professional writers, individuals hired for the express purpose of conveying information and image to those inside and outside the organization. Information, of course, can be conveyed in a wide range of documents: manuals, scientific manuscripts, standard operating procedures, proposals, publicity pieces, and informational pamphlets. In developing a strategy for these documents, writers become maintainers of an organizational status quo, or culture makers, who must, because of this role, be very rapidly socialized to the organizational culture they have joined.

For writers as culture shapers or agents of change, I contend that their art is synthetic (in the sense defined above). Writers stand at the juncture among disciplines and among various interests and perspectives outside and inside their organization. They may enter the organization, come to understand its values, and with or without encouragement from those in charge, come to differ with either the organization's values or how communication about these values should occur, perhaps in response to audience or employer needs. Insofar as writers are effective in convincing those within the organization to change, they become effective agents of that change and advocates for the organization's audiences.

Finally, if culture *is* the organization and if communication represents, makes, and shapes the organizational culture, communication is one of an organization's most important products. Internally, effective communication contributes to the solidity of organizational goals and to employee commitment and satisfaction. Externally, it sells the organization to its public.

A primary difference, then, in the socialization processes of writers (and those of other organizational members) is that they must be rapidly and effectively socialized if they are to become primary spokespersons for the organization's climate and image: they are usually intimately and immediately involved in being culture makers at the same time they are assimilating the culture which they have joined. In addition, writers are partially socialized, as are other employees, through documents produced by the organization; but they may also be the employees who provide—in the breaking-in or the acceptance phases—the communications that are used in the socialization process. If the writer's essential role and potential contribution to the organization are perceived by managers, then managers will consciously attend to the socialization of newly hired communicators. They will want to constrain and direct the orientation of these new members, but they would also do well to consider suggestions by them. However, if managers do not perceive the writer's role as vital and do not facilitate their socialization, writers will, in order to enhance their performance, have to learn about the organization from other sources, and perhaps on their own initiative.

## HOW WRITERS LEARN THE IMAGE

To encourage a dialogue between the organization and new writers—to facilitate writers coming to know, carry out, and responsibly influence the communication policies and practices of a firm—I describe below the specific means, effects, and potential conflicts that may occur during the socialization process. The theoretical framework laid out above is particularized to these three issues by referring to literature in technical and scientific communication and by extrapolating from my experience in advising students in internships, on jobs, and on preparing progress reports and theses on their internship experiences. Each issue—means, effects, and conflicts—is supported by data collected from ten graduate students in Miami University's Master of Technical and Scientific Communication Program, who had, when the data were collected, just finished fourteen-week writing internships with various organizations. Five of these students left their organizations after the fourteen weeks; five performed their internships as the first fourteen weeks of full-time employment. In addition, one of the ten has provided data (using the same questionnaire) about two full-time positions she has held since her internship, each in different kinds of organizations.

## DESCRIPTION OF WRITERS' ROLES

Before I discuss the issues of writers' socialization processes, I give a context for the excerpts from the responses to the questionnaire (which is reprinted at the end of this paper) by providing below an overview of the writers' working environments, addressing in each case their setting and/or subject-matter focus, the documents they typically wrote, and their role within the company. Students who were responsible to a client as well as to the organization that employed them are marked with an asterisk. Those who were interning as full-time employees are marked with a dagger.

Three of the interns wrote documents in computer-related environments.

> As an intern, *LB*\* worked as a writer on a project team (with a director, editors, and other writers) for her firm, a large and well-established

writing consultancy, that produced documentation for an also large, multinational hardware and software development firm.

As the first fourteen weeks of a full-time job, *WB*† wrote documentation (to be used internally) for a company that offers electronic database services to government agencies, corporations, and individuals.

As the first fourteen weeks of a full-time job, *CK*† wrote scripts for videotapes to be used internally to publicize the services of the computer support division of her large consumer goods company.

Three of the interns wrote documentation or standard operating procedures in technical or laboratory settings.

As a fourteen-week intern, *VF* was the sole communicator responsible for documenting standard operating procedures for employees in a scientific research lab affiliated with a government agency.

As a full-time writer, *BS*† wrote publicity materials and documentation for the manufacturer of high-technology products such as jet engines.

*WM*\*† was hired full time to document standard operating procedures to be used by members of his firm (and potentially by its clients) who required information on techniques used by his firm to determine the composition of soils and waters.

Of the remaining *technical* writers, *KL*\*† was hired full-time as an account executive and technical copywriter for one of the Midwest's largest full-service advertising agencies. Her job was to meet the technical literature needs (product specification sheets, industrial advertising brochures, catalog inserts, and so on) of a large industrial client.

The three remaining interns, all *scientific* writers, prepared documents for the health or medical field.

For his internship, *KS* edited articles prepared by scientists and wrote grant proposals to secure funding for a cancer research laboratory affiliated with a medical school.

Also for her internship, *NW* wrote TV and radio public service announcements, articles for publications directed at specialists and nonspecialists, and a brochure (publicizing the medical and support services of a department) for the Division of Public Affairs of a nonprofit teaching, research, and treatment medical foundation.

*KK*\*† interned as one of a team of writers who wrote documents for the Information and Publications Division of a scientific firm. The division was under contract to a health-related federal agency whose communication needs included letters to patients and their families, research reports, and general information pamphlets on specific types of a certain disease.

In her first full-time job, VF, † as a senior technical writer/editor, wrote proposals for a contract organization that provides technical and scientific support to a federal agency concerned with environmental quality.

VF, † in her present full-time position, is one of many technical communicators in a firm that specializes in providing customized computer systems and quality documentation.

## THE MEANS BY WHICH SOCIALIZATION OCCURS

Consistent with the framework provided earlier in the article, new writers, like other employees, typically have print and oral, formal and informal means to help them learn what and how to write in a way that is acceptable to the organization. Frequently, organizations provide these means—the orientation and training materials mentioned earlier. But some materials are designed especially for writers: style guides, for example, may give information about special abbreviations; specific, sometimes idiosyncratic, rules about diction, usage, grammar, and style; and the often organizationally based advice about format and design. In addition to influencing the so-called form of a document, style guides and other organizational documents may influence the content and its relationship to a prescribed form. Miller and Selzer might call these "company-specific sources of persuasion." In discussing the *topoi* (special topics) associated with a particular report genre, they note, "Quite often, . . . an organization will specify that particular things be included in its proposals and reports, things that go beyond superficial matters of format and appearance. 'Every company has something unique it wishes to emphasize' says one manager. That something might be codified in company guidelines or manuals" (Miller and Selzer, 1985, 327). In addition to or in lieu of guides or manuals, writers may be given and encouraged to follow rhetorical models. Writers may have freedom in adapting these to particular rhetorical situations, or they may simply be encouraged to imitate an organizational canon with codified approaches to arrangement, style, audience, purpose, format, and design.

The ten interns who completed my questionnaires were all exposed to some of the formal and informal mechanisms for socialization to the organization and to writing practices that I mention above.

As is predictable, most interns were socialized through oral discourse or printed documents that explained organizational policies and practices during their interviews and the first few weeks of their jobs. Orally, interns were told "what was expected" by "the boss" or by "management," "by employees during conversations," "by colleagues," or "by support staff during discussions." Print means included "an employee handbook signed by the president," "documents prepared for the new employee by the company," "marketing brochures," "formal memos from management," "annual reports," "a brochure describing the medical function," "a proposal describing the nature of [the] company's contract with the federal agency," and "an employee handbook put together by many people at the agency."

Two methods of this type of orientation stand out as good examples of a top-down management style of socialization: one intern was sent monthly memoranda on the company's incentive program and was exposed to ideas from management at monthly company cookouts; another received "circulated policy statements" which had to be signed by each employee. This same employee was required to watch videotapes on the company prepared by senior and midlevel managers and to read the weekly (company) newspaper; and another, also oriented in part by videotapes on the company, learned "who [had] won what writing award," and that "writers are essential to the company's success."

Of the ten interns, all said that they learned by "observing"—both positive and negative interactions; "by paying attention to office politics"; "through the general comportment of personnel"; and "by reading publications [not for new hires] put out by their organizations." Of course, those who worked for both an organization and a client were told, during orientation, that they "were expected to know the client's wishes"; the intern who worked at the advertising agency, for example, and the one who worked for the organization performing work for the health-related federal agency were both told that they should be able to meet client demands at the same time they enhanced the contract organization's image. Two other interns, as will be discussed later, were also told how to project their organization to the client; but this projection contradicted their perception of the values of the organizations for which they worked.

It is noteworthy that two of the interns learned *only* by observing, noting that there were no formal means for orientation to the organization made available to them. And of the eight noted above who read materials on the organization, only three were asked to read the materials they found helpful. Suggesting that organizational commitment can affect socialization practices, the five who were not specifically asked to read materials were those who ended their internships after fourteen weeks, internships that were not part of full-time positions.

Socialization to writing practices was, in this group, apparently not accomplished by using style guides, though one intern did mention that she spent two days in an orientation seminar to learn the "X Company way of writing." As one of the interns who experienced dissonance between internal climate and external image, she also felt as though everything she wrote "had to be put through the company style filter before it could go to the client."

A second means of socializing writers to writing practices was most often accomplished through imitating rhetorical models and through planning meetings that initiated work on a new or modified document.

Three interns were hired to develop either a process for producing the document they were to write, to develop a prototype for that document, or both; therefore, these interns had no models to follow. Four others did have models and used them in the conventional way—to see how those before them had analyzed similar situations with similar audiences, purposes, and constraints for writing. Quite naturally wanting to excel, to help the organization reach its goals, they noted that they consciously tried to follow the models, perhaps discerning, as did managers in a study by Brown and Herndl, that what was "good" was what met the complex needs of the language culture (1986).

Three other employees encountered particularly prescriptive situations in the way in which their company used rhetorical models. In a circumstance where the aim of the organization was to produce winning proposals, VF found that she was asked to imitate proposals that she felt "left in false information, that presented a false image of highly trained, expert scientists" and that showed "no concern for good writing." KK, writing for the federal health agency, was asked to use models of letters that were a collage of paragraphs preapproved by the agency; since the contract organization did not want to have to have other material approved, she was not allowed to change any words or take any initiative with style even though she felt changes would have improved the letters' effectiveness with the client's audience. Finally, LB felt that her "creativity" in planning and arranging the materials for her documents was "constrained" by having to follow a "method of presentation" that was typical of her organization but which she thought did not cater to "audience needs." It might be argued, since all three of these writers worked in organizations whose incomes depend on outside clients, that there is something inherent in the type of situation which requires managers to control external communications more aggressively. Perhaps, in fact, the newly hired writers did not understand the complexities of their situations. Nevertheless, the writers' points of view are well taken; put in a position to evaluate the ethics or effectiveness of the documents in relation to the constraints of the rhetorical situation, all felt that they had knowledge about the organization, communication practices, or client needs that made their position uncomfortable, perhaps eventually untenable.

In contrast to these writers who encountered a prescriptive method of socialization in connection with models, writers who were initiating new documents or document types in their organizations had to consciously seek information about audience needs, purpose, and constraints for writing. As master's students in professional communication, they had been taught a problem-solving approach (Anderson, 1984) which demanded their aggressively seeking information before writing. Therefore, they had been trained to methodically consult such sources as managers, supervisors, members of their prospective audience, and "gatekeepers" of the information they needed for their documents, including clients and technical or scientific personnel. This group's experience with the problem-solving approach provides some insight into the effectiveness of using a systematic approach to gathering information (for writing) that, in the process, facilitates socialization. However, it is important to note that the success of a systematic approach to information gathering can be affected by at least three factors: (1) by the degree of cooperation the writer might or might not receive in gathering essential information—of our interns, some received minimal support, particularly in being able to talk to members of the intended audience whereas others received strong support; (2) by the degree to which the writer can become an advocate for the audience; and (3) by the conscientious use of a systematic method of gathering information by writers. In spite of these factors, all of these writers did use the problem-solving approach to writing and found it to be an effective *method* of socialization to writing practices. For example, at planning sessions (designed to provide information about writing tasks) writers were able to learn much about the role of writing and writers in the organization, the public image the organization wished to project to customers or clients, the image that clients wished to project through documents written by their organization, and the values that drove writing policies. Of course, a problem-solving approach is also useful even when models exist.

A third means of socializing writers to writing practices included editing sessions, peer reviews, and advice from mentors or supervisors.

We know that writers gain much of their socialization through collaborative efforts. A writer may be asked to work with a group or a partner to prepare a document. Such collaboration helps the writer form a consensual view of what the organization expects in a given situation—it is another means of socialization. Or, if the writer composes alone, he or she may still learn a great deal from mentor and peer review. Usually, these processes are a kind of informal and preliminary evaluation of the document that precedes the document's validation with its potential internal and external audience(s). These reviews, too, reveal much about organizationally approved rhetorical and stylistic strategies and the political climate of the organization. As Miller and Selzer point out, "the something unique" that companies wish to emphasize "might be explicitly directed in meetings between managers and top executives. . . . it might be imposed by a manager whose responsibility it is to oversee all report-writing functions . . . or [it] might be the product of a supervisor's wishes" (1985, 327).

These issues were played out for all ten interns. All were assigned to a mentor who reviewed their documents, particularly during the early stages of their tenure with organization. In addition, all writers asked, and some were instructed to ask, for peer reviews. (No writers wrote in a group, though some were part of a team effort.) Most frequently, writers' styles were altered to "be more readable," to "reflect the party line," to "clean up quotes" (to be more grammatical or precise), and to "refine technical accuracy." The division director of the medical foundation had a more specific purpose in mind during reviews: he wanted to make sure that "above all, [documents] were accurate and reflected the high-quality research and care provided by the institution." Similarly, the technical writer who produced videotapes for internal explanations of the services offered by her computer support division found that reviewers "were interested in representing her division fairly, in showing the company as having a competitive edge, and in not stepping on any other division's toes." Less frequently, for example in KS's case, his word choice was changed to reflect vocabulary more on "the cutting edge" of cancer research and to be more "stilted or scientific"; and KL's advertising copy was altered (by agency personnel) to convey "high-technology sophistication." In the latter's case, she often found herself, as did others, negotiating "nuances of language" with her reviewers. To build her confidence in these negotiations, she "had several meetings per week" with the client to check "style, diction, tone, and strategy." Only then did she have her writing reviewed by someone at the agency.

As might be expected, reactions to reviews were mixed. In an effort to please, most writers tried to achieve what reviewers recommended; some felt more confident and others more constrained in the process. At least one writer was "disappointed at not having really critical reviews" and one who wrote only internal documents was not reviewed but "did the best possible." Only the full-time employee who felt she was preparing proposals (VF) with false information believed that her attempt to "include accurate information" put her in an "uncomfortable position"; in fact, she believes she was demoted as a result of these review sessions. All other writers felt that these socialization processes, over time, increased their confidence.

## THE MAJOR EFFECT ON WRITERS OF SOCIALIZATION PROCESSES

Culture, and I would add socialization, "satisfies the basic needs for affiliation and security in attempting to describe as unified a grouping that may seem to be random" (Graves, 1986, 157); and Brown and Herndl add about writers "both common sense and theory recognize the tight bond of language, culture, and self" (1986). Noting that writers must "balance clarity with political grace" and that "writing style" makes "groups," these authors support the interns' impressions that the major effect of writers' socialization processes was that they gained confidence through learning and adhering to organizational and writing practices and preferences.

As spokespersons (since this is the way I couched the question), three writers "felt more confident" and others "felt more respect for company and colleagues," "understood more about what [her] role was about how much authority [she] had," "felt more able to represent the lab," "found that recommendations [about her writing] decreased and [her] confidence increased as [she] learned to follow company policy," and "found that confidence increased as familiarity with clients' preferences increased, credibility grew, and people gained confidence in [her] and [her] instincts." Another described the effects of socialization this way: "I grew more confident as I became more familiar with our audience and purpose. Over time I became more confident because of feedback that said I was delivering a product that met the expectations of my supervisors."

These responses attest to the power of feedback from the "high priests of the culture" and the employee's general desire to fulfill what the company expects. Say Brown and Herndl, "In our view of things, ostensible core conventions of 'good' writing go the way of standard dialects in sociolinguistics: The conventions shift and change, to be replaced by other conventions, all dictated by contextual criteria" (1986). The interns' experiences and these authors' views speak to the power of political and psychological forces to motivate language behavior. As persons whose role is to speak effectively for the organization, writers no doubt have a desire to do this job well, to fulfill the expectations of the company; for meeting expectations generally elicits positive feedback, a loop which is completed by the employee's increased sense of confidence and desire to please.

## POTENTIAL CONFLICT AND CHANGE DURING WRITERS' SOCIALIZATION

Though the above review of the effects of socialization on these ten writers might suggest that the process is one-way, that the writer is a kind of *tabula rasa* onto which is written the organizational lore and preestablished preferences about writing, I address below the potential for writers to change the policies of the organizations they join, both in terms of writers' roles and writing practices. In essence, this section of the paper asks and responds to the questions "Are there some undesirable aspects of socialization?" and "Are there some potential advantages to an organization if the employee, after socialization, resists company policies and as a result seeks to change the organization?"

As I argued earlier, writers come to organizations with beliefs developed during academic training in their technical or scientific areas, their profession, and their former work experience. Thus, writers have their own views about what constitutes good writing in general, about how a specific document should be prepared—and after some time with an organization—about what is an appropriate rhetorical or organizational strategy. The process may be one-way, I would assert, but is almost always interactional—a process wherein the writer has the potential to affect the organization, just as the organization has the potential to affect the writer. Says Graves, "People . . . are continually joining [an] organization and impregnating it with their own cultural background. All this is not abandoned upon joining the firm, but helps to create a new culture for that cohort of entrants" (1986, 156).

The extent to which writers can help to create a new culture depends in some part on the function they inherit when they join the organization and to some degree on the function they create for themselves according to their personalities and prior experiences.

Generally, a writer's function (or ability to function) is contingent upon a writers' prestige in his or her company. These functions fall into three overlapping categories: first, the writer is regarded as neutral—the writer has been hired to do a job and is expected, like other employees, to do it the best way possible. Second, the writer's function may be privileged. As described by one intern:

> Writers are treated well; they are paid well; the company feels like good writers are essential to its success. They are committed to writing computer documentation that works, that enables users to make the most of the company's products. Technical writing and writers are important, documentation is an essential part of the product, and we are provided with and encouraged to read the latest in the technical communication field.

In the third position for writers, they may be, as one employee puts it, "expendable" in a "profit-oriented company." Of the ten interns, two felt that they were held in high esteem; a third felt this way in her full-time job but not in her internship. The four others, I infer, felt that writers were reasonably important in their organization. However, four interns, including VF (in both her internship and one full-time position), felt that writers were held in low esteem; in one case, "the boss acted as if writing were important, but the staff acted as if it were unnecessary." Unfortunately, until the gatekeepers of organizational information—in addition to managers—come to realize the marketing and morale value of communication, this latter case may be most typical. Of course, the degree to which writers are accepted and more or less highly regarded has direct bearing on the writers' need to conform to socialization practices and to attempt to effect change.

Personality, another major factor in the compatibility of company and communicator, is inseparable from the experience of the employee and the flexibility of organizational policies. All of these affect the writer's assimilation into and accommodation of writing practices. The aggressive, highly motivated employee will have potentially very different effects on organizational policy than will the one who "wishes not to make waves." In fact, as Graves puts it, " 'decisive' people destroy organizational cultures because they do not allow 'custom and practice' to weigh in a decision. Thus culture is a constraining activity in heavily traditional organizations" (1986, 10). Employees, he suggests, will need to be particularly alert to the effectiveness of cultural and communication values in traditional organizations. If effective, the values will have to be learned so that they may act as a heuristic for the writer's work; if ineffective, the values will still have to be learned so that the writer will know where, when, and how to argue for change.

The decisiveness of a writer may be determined not only by personality but also by the individual's prior experience. These factors may have a direct influence on the perceived and actual need for change in the organization and the organization's perceived and actual flexibility and receptivity to change.

As has been suggested above, most of the interns did not perceive a need for change or come into conflict with members of their organization. Of those who did perceive a need to change policy or writing strategy, several attempted to negotiate change but finally agreed that the organizational policy ("the squeaky clean conservatism," "the subtle-advocacy rhetoric," "the discarded editing suggestions because of set standards by the client") should prevail inasmuch as the organization seemed to have a good idea of what would be effective under the circumstances. The employees perceived change to be necessary; upon coming to know the organization's views more accurately, the employees agreed that the organization was better attuned to the best practices in its setting and how the employees could best further its organizational goals and the writing practices developed in light of these goals. Thus, the employer and the employee agreed that no change was needed.

In other circumstances, the employees perceived change to be necessary and were able to effect the change because organizational members concurred with them. The technical account executive/copywriter had several years' prior work experience and was hired into the agency, in part *because* of this experience. Therefore, as soon as she felt comfortable with her organizational role, she also felt quite comfortable in arguing for new types of documents that she felt would be beneficial to her client. She had no trouble convincing the agency that her changes would positively affect their goal, profit and client satisfaction. By carefully fitting her recommendations to the goals of her organization, this writer was able to argue effectively and change writing policy.

Even an experienced employee, however, might argue unsuccessfully in an organization that requires change, but is unwilling to consider it. Two examples stand out in the data: one employee felt conflict because the public image she was to project to the client ("we write well and fast; anything can be written about simply") did not mesh with the internal climate of the organization ("we were disorganized and documents were poorly thought out; we had to work hard in a chaotic environment, but we were to make it look easy"). Attempts on her part to change the process, to ask the client for help, to be upfront, were met with an admonition to "help maintain the public image at all times." In another organizational context, VF, in one full-time job, found that writing proposals in which she felt encouraged to "include false information" not only raised conflict between internal climate and external image, it also raised ethical questions and challenged her feelings about belonging to the organization. When she chose not to include what she believed to be false information, she "was considered naive and moralistic." Ultimately, the conflict became too great and she left her job. In both cases, these writers' tasks were probably made more difficult because they were arguing for changes that would affect clients' perceptions and in the end the profits of their companies. Thus, over time, both employees were better socialized—they understood the organization and therefore were more *able* to do what the organization required. However, understanding organizational values and implications and their own ethics and sense of responsibility made them less willing to accept the organization's values and thus write as they required.

That socialization does occur for newly hired writers, that its means may have to be actively pursued by them, that it may result in both long-term and/or short-term comfort and/or dissatisfaction—are some of the tentative implications of the theoretical perspective and supporting evidence presented above. These observations are valuable because they offer insight into what might, does, or should happen in an organizational context. They help to explain the day-to-day events that are so influential and are keys to success (or control) on the job. However, these implications have a potentially different impact on different groups: organizational members, writers, and academicians who help prepare communicators for their professional roles.

## IMPLICATIONS FOR ORGANIZATIONS, WRITERS AND TEACHERS

This final section addresses implications of the theory and generalizations presented in the first two parts of the article and supported by the evidence presented in the third part. It suggests that managers in organizations, professional writers, and teachers in academic institutions who prepare professional communicators might all benefit from paying conscious attention to the organizational interactions explored above.

First, culture is an important aspect of every organization, and writers are central to preserving one of the most visible internal and external manifestations of culture. Since all writers experience and seem to depend on socialization processes to help them know the organizations they represent in their documents, organizations might wish to make conscious efforts to assist writers as they learn to identify company values, and to do so early and thoroughly. Managers will want to make sure that written materials about organizational policies are made available to writers; that writers are acquainted with any formal processes or policies about writing documents; and further, that writers have an appropriate and formal mentor to work with.

But organizations also will want to be open to change. Remembering that writing is a product of the company, that the company benefits or suffers according to employees' and the public's perception of it (gathered through its documents), managers will want to pay attention to the advice of the experts they have hired. They will want to resist the typical reaction to suggested changes predicted by Graves: "When some stimulus . . . causes [organizations] to change direction, the atmosphere becomes thick with confusion and morale falls" (Graves, 1986, 127). If organizational members remain aware that writing is just as much a product of their organization as whatever technical or scientific product bears their name, they may be more willing to examine critically the values and processes that govern writing and even the writing itself. A new organizational member with a fresh perspective may be an appropriate agent for this examination and potential change.

One particularly appropriate way in which organizations could evaluate the effectiveness of their present communications or suggestions for changes in future ones would be through validating documents by testing them with members or representatives of the target audience. Internal documents such as memos to employees, statements or guidelines about new policies, reports to upper management, and so forth could benefit from an informal testing phase in which other writers or organizational members acted as members of the potential audience and read the documents for strategy and clarity. More formal documents, internal and external proposals, feasibility studies, documentation, and so forth could go through this same type of preliminary testing. But they could also be tested, again for strategy, clarity, and usability with simulated or real members of the potential audience. Such testing has the potential, at best, to increase the documents' effectiveness, and at least, to initiate a dialogue about them. Routine testing could enable managers to have some assurance about the effectiveness of their communications. It might also be a guarantee against a war of wills between writers and managers.

Since writers obviously benefit from the information they gain during the socialization phases they encounter upon joining an organization, and since they need this information quickly, they will want to consciously and aggressively pursue information about the organization's values and the values it wishes to express in its writing. The writer's contribution to the success of the organization depends on his or her ability to assimilate and assess the culture, to document it, to present it to the public, and to aid in implementing change. Additionally, part of the writer's job may be to convince managers of the importance of corporate culture and of his or her role in creating it and, as a consequence, increasing organizational effectiveness. Writers also need to seek out rhetorical models, yet they need to look at them critically, to make sure that they solve the present rhetorical problem in the best possible way. They also need to make sure that the organization uses a process for writing that includes systematic information gathering, focusing on audience analysis, testing, and evaluation. If the organization does not, writers may wish to point out the value of these processes in enhancing one of the organization's most important products, its documents.

Importantly, too, writers should seek reviews from their mentors and peers. Such reviews will help them learn about an organization's preferences, will build rapport with company personnel, and will give them the opportunity to negotiate important differences. They will want to remember to analyze changes for strategy, not to be defensive about them, and to negotiate what they perceive as the most important changes with their colleagues.

Educational institutions—teachers of undergraduate and graduate students in professional writing—can make writers aware of the difference between the generic kinds of information that can be learned in writing classes and the contextual kinds of writing that can only be learned in an organization and usually only in a specific organizational setting. On the other hand, as Miller has pointed out, the academic institution has its own special function, and its role is not to attempt to imitate or be simply responsive to the marketplace. Academic institutions must maintain an integrity and contribution of their own (Miller, in press). However, teachers can more adequately prepare writers for their professional roles by sensitizing them, as prospective corporate employees, to the theoretical notion of corporate culture and to the issues surrounding socialization. Such sensitization would provide a theoretical framework for students to analyze and work within the constraints of particular cultures and ultimately to contribute fully to documenting, enhancing, or, if need be, changing the organization's writing policies and practices.

In addition, teachers can provide opportunities for writers to work with case studies that simulate organizational settings and with clients, who will often demand that the student weigh client preferences against theoretical instruction, cost, or the advice of peers or professors. Both kinds of writing experience are not meant to substitute for the complexity of an organizational setting, but they *are* meant to prepare the student for the kinds of heuristics and constraints that such settings typically provide. Teachers can enhance the value of assignments by pointing out how contextualized writing is a kind of steppingstone to the kind of experience the communicator will face on the job. Such assignments also require orientation to more than one person's preferences, and often require reconciling these with personal, peer, client, and instructor feedback—all good experience for the professional's interactions in an organizational environment.

Directors of undergraduate and graduate programs might also consider the worth of internships as another vehicle for preparing students for future organizational roles (Lutz, in press). By guiding students' progress during internships, instructors can teach them how to "read" an organization (Debs, 1984), how to learn the issues so that they will benefit from any socialization process, and how to seek information that will enhance their ability to represent the organization, the organization's client, or themselves in a document. Learning such values will enable them to balance the degree of certainty and stability that comes with knowing what is expected with the flexibility that comes with being able to challenge—then accept or change—the way things have always been done in the past.

## Works Cited

Anderson, P. (1984). What technical and scientific communicators do: A comprehensive model for developing academic programs. *Institute of Electrical and Electronics Engineers Transactions on Professional Communication,* PC-27, 161–167.

Brown, R. & Herndl, C. (1986). An ethnographic study of corporate writing: Job status as reflected in written text. In B. Couture (Ed.), *Functional Approaches to Writing: Research Perspectives* (pp. 11–28). London: Frances Pinter.

Buchanan, B. (1974). Building organizational commitment: The socialization of managers in work organizations. *Administrative Science Quarterly, 19,* 533–546.

Connors, R., Ede, L., & Lunsford, A. (1984). Revival of rhetoric in America. In R. Connors, L. Ede, and A. Lunsford (Eds.), *Essays on Classical Rhetoric and Modern Discourse* (pp. 1–15). Carbondale: Southern Illinois University Press.

Deal, T. & Kennedy, A. (1982). *Corporate Cultures: The Rites and Rituals of Corporate Life.* Reading, MA: Addison-Wesley.

Debs, M. (1984). The social rhetoric of technical writing. Unpublished manuscript. Presented at Modern Language Association Conference.

Dobrin, D. (1983). What's technical about technical writing? In P. Anderson, R. Brockman, and C. Miller (Eds.), *New Essays in Technical and Scientific Communication: Research, Theory, Practice* (pp. 227–250). Farmingdale, NY: Baywood.

Faigley, L. (1985). Nonacademic writing: The social perspective. In L. Odell and D. Goswami (Eds.), *Writing in Nonacademic Settings* (pp. 231–248). New York: Guilford Press.

Feldman, D. (1976). A contingency theory of socialization. *Administrative Science Quarterly, 21,* 433–452.

Graves, D. (1986). *Corporate Culture—Diagnosis and Change: Auditing and Changing the Culture of Organizations.* New York: St. Martin's.

Harrison, R. (1972). Understanding your organization's character. *Harvard Business Review, 50,* 119–128.

Jablin, F. (1982). Organizational communication: An assimilation approach. In M. Roloff & C. Berger (Eds.), *Social Cognition and Communication* (pp. 255–286). Beverly Hills, CA: Sage.

———. (1984). Assimilating new members into organizations. In R. Bostrom (Ed.), *Communication Yearbook 8* (pp. 594–626). Beverly Hills, CA: Sage.

Louis, M. (1980). Surprise and sense making: What newcomers experience in entering unfamiliar organizational settings. *Administrative Science Quarterly, 25,* 226–251.

Lutz, J. (in press). Understanding organizational socialization: The role of internships in helping students acquire strategies for writing effectively in organizations. In W. Coggin (Ed.), *Establishing and Supervising Internships.* Lubbock, TX: Association of Teachers of Technical Writing.

Miller, C. (in press). What's practical about technical writing? In B. Fearing & K. Sparrow

(Eds.), *Advanced Essays on Technical Communication.* New York: Modern Language Association.

Miller, C. & Selzer, J. (1985). Special topics of argument in engineering reports. In L. Odell and D. Goswami (Eds.), *Writing in Nonacademic Settings* (pp. 309–338). New York: Guilford Press.

Odell, L. (1985). Beyond the text: Relations between writing and social context. In L. Odell & D. Goswami (Eds.), *Writing in Nonacademic Settings* (pp. 249–281). New York: Guilford Press.

Odell, L. & Goswami, E. (1985). Preface: Writing in nonacademic settings. In L. Odell & D. Goswami (Eds.), *Writing in Nonacademic Settings* (pp. vii–ix). New York: Guilford Press.

Porter, L., Lawler, E. & Hackman, J. (1975). *Behavior in Organizations.* New York: McGraw-Hill.

Schein, E. (1983). The role of the founder in creating organizational culture. *Organizational Dynamics, 12,* 13–28.

———. (1985). *Organizational Culture and Leadership.* San Francisco: Jossey-Bass.

Schneider, B. & Reichers, A. (1983). On the etiology of climate. *Personnel Psychology, 36,* 19–39.

Toulmin, S., Rieke, R. & Janik, A. (1984). *An Introduction to Reasoning.* New York: Macmillan.

Van Maanen, J. (1976). Breaking in: Socialization to work. In R. Durbin (Ed.), *Handbook of Work, Organization, and Society* (pp. 67–131). Chicago: Rand McNally.

Van Maanen, J. & Schein, E. (1979). Toward a theory of organizational socialization. In B. Staw (Ed.), *Research in Organizational Behavior, Vol. 1* (pp. 209–264). Greenwich, CT: JAI Press.

Wanous, J. (1980). *Organizational Entry: Recruitment, Selection, and Socialization of Newcomers.* Reading, MA: Addison-Wesley.

## QUESTIONNAIRE

Thank you for taking time to help with this project. Please answer the following questions with as many examples as come to mind. Answer on separate paper and return your answers and the questionnaire to me at the English department, Miami University.

1. a. With what kind of company did you perform your internship?
   b. For how many weeks?
2. How would you describe your company and your role as a writer?
3. a. Did you have the same impression of your company when you ended your internship as you did when you began it?
   b. If not, how did your impression change?
4. Would you please list some of the values conveyed by this company to its employees?
5. How were you made aware of these values?
   a. Were you told them? Informally? Formally? By whom?
   b. Did you read about them? In what document(s)?
   c. Were you asked to read about them? By whom? In what documents?

6. a. How would you describe the image your company attempts to convey to the public?
   b. Does this image represent the company fairly?
7. How were you made aware of this image? (Refer to #5.)
8. Do you feel your access to privileged information and/or your responsibility to those outside your immediate work group increased or decreased as you became more aware of your organization's values and image?
9. Were you ever conscious of having to change features of your documents to accommodate the company values you describe in #4 or the organizational image you describe in #6?
   a. What feature of your writing?
   b. What documents?
   c. What organizational values/aspects of image?
   d. On whose recommendation?
   e. How frequently?
10. Did such recommendations increase/decrease during the internship? Why?
11. Were features of your documents ever changed by someone else to accommodate or project the company values you describe in #4 or the image you describe in #6?
    a. What features of your writing?
    b. What documents?
    c. What organizational values/aspects of image?
    d. On whose recommendation?
    e. How frequently?
12. Do you feel conveying company values in documents you wrote was less important, equally important, or more important than consideration of audience or purpose or content? Answer the same question for image. Explain, please.
13. Were you more confident as a spokesperson for your company as your internship continued? Please explain your reply.
14. What, or who, was the source of this confidence?
15. Did you encounter any instances (in documents that you wrote) in which your personal values or the image you thought the company should project conflicted with what you have come to understand as company policy, values, or image? Please explain.
16. Can you estimate what percentage of your writing time was spent on documents used within the organization? Outside the organization?

**Thank you for taking the time to answer these questions.**

# THE TEXT AND THE TRADE ASSOCIATION: A STORY OF DOCUMENTS AT WORK

*Elisabeth M. Alford*
University of South Carolina

*Elisabeth M. Alford is pursuing a Ph.D. in English (composition and rhetoric) at the University of South Carolina, where she teaches freshman composition. She has also taught technical writing and a practicum in communications skills for staff of state and local government.*
*For eighteen years, she was an executive with the South Carolina Hospital Association. She currently consults with health-care organizations and governmental agencies.*

In composition circles, trade associations evoke images of lobbying and special-interest public relations campaigns. This narrow view is probably unavoidable, since few writing teachers have seen the inner workings of an association. But trade associations and professional associations, their close cousins, have broad roles in shaping American society. The American Medical Association, the American Dairy Association, the American Bar Association, the American Chemical Manufacturers Association, and countless others provide both services to their memberships and information for public decision making. Obviously, they are partly political. However, they also develop technical standards, conduct research, provide statistical information, and promote and encourage professional and ethical behavior within their memberships. Most important for scholars and teachers of rhetoric and composition, they generate a variety of texts that they use to negotiate and achieve consensus, to interpret the impact of technological change on broad segments of society, and to influence public policy.

A study of the writing done within a professional or trade association does more than explain why one congressman may receive scores of identical letters on an issue.[1] From such studies, we can see how specialists write collaboratively to produce a unified association response on issues that cut across disciplines. We can also learn about the emotional reactions of professionals to the demands of writing for a group and with a group. Association staff members must adopt an association persona and translate highly complex information for nonspecialists. Often, as part of the group process, staff members' texts are edited by officers, supervisors, colleagues, and even adversaries. Since most association staff were educated to work as individual practitioners of a profession rather than as association personnel, many are acutely aware of the influence of the association environment, or the group's culture, on their writing. This heightened awareness, sharpened by the consensus-building processes characteristic of associations, leads them to consider "association culture" throughout the stages of the writing process.

An association's culture differs from corporate culture because it includes both a staff located within central offices and a geographically dispersed membership, which interacts with staff periodically through meetings, correspondence, and other forms of communication. The members resemble stockholders of a corporation in that they are owners of the association and elect officers to govern the association and direct the staff. But unlike corporate stockholders, members participate in the association's work. And association members receive no monetary profits; the benefits are the perceived results of the collective actions taken by the association. Such benefits are more difficult to measure than bottom lines on a financial statement; thus, the value of association activity must be lauded frequently. As a result, staff must not only perform the work which supports the consensus-building process but also praise the value of the process. At the same time, staff members must minimize their own roles in the activity. Consensus is a product of the members' work, regardless of who writes the texts through which it is achieved and by which it is expressed publicly.

Staff members do not own the texts they produce. To write those texts, the staff must enter into dialogues with members and other groups and then write with the collective voice and mind of the membership. The individuality of the staff member must be submerged. Because the staff's experiences so clearly illustrate the role of environmental influences on the production of texts, an analysis of their adaptive responses can add much to modern composition pedagogy and discourse theory. And because a trade association is an interpretive community employing a diverse group of specialists, it provides an ideal laboratory for studying the interface between cognitive and social theories of writing.

A trade association is an ideal laboratory for almost any kind of research on nonacademic writing and modern rhetoric, both spoken and written. Writing in an association includes both business and technical writing. Staff members write in a variety of forms, some of which will seldom be found in a textbook on business or technical writing. They use forms flexibly, adapting conventional forms for special purposes and creating new ones when necessary. They use all rhetorical genres flexibly too, but most especially epideictic rhetoric. Since association texts must often either praise or blame complex technology and economic factors, association discourse combines epideictic rhetoric with technical writing in a way that may be uniquely characteristic of this type of organization. Finally, since association personnel constantly translate oral rhetoric into written forms and written material back into speech, the association environment provides a twentieth-century setting in which to examine the orality-literacy connection.

The rhetorical and writing activities of the South Carolina Hospital Association (SCHA) illustrate how heavily associations rely on texts to carry out their work and how much of the organization's resources are devoted to producing these texts. Staff members perform a variety of writing tasks, as do professional staff members of any organization, but in the association context, their drafts often supersede speech in accomplishing daily activities and long-range objectives. Drafts provide a means for members and staff of the association to interact with each other, with other organizations, and with the larger society. Drafts become final only when agreement is reached or compromise achieved. Final drafts distributed to members often become industry standards. They become part of the canon of American health care. When they are adopted by regulatory agencies, as they often are, the final documents of associations become part of administrative or statutory law.

These same processes occur in other trade and professional associations; the voluntary standards of associations are often adopted by regulatory agencies. Thus, any discussion of intertextuality and dialogics in the working world must include an examination of association texts, for these represent collective voices of major influence groups within society. And these voices speak to each other. The texts of a trade association are clearly dialogic, written in response to other texts, developed through a sequence of dialogues, and precipitating broader dialogues after they are distributed or spoken to larger audiences. The SCHA offers a rich model of these processes.

The SCHA is both a trade association and a professional organization. Its voting membership includes ninety-two community hospitals, specialty hospitals, and nursing homes. In conducting business and formulating policy, members of the institutions are represented by their chief executive officers or other administrative and professional personnel. The association employs seven professional staff members: a president, two specialists in hospital finance, one lobbyist, and one specialist each in hospital planning, professional services, and public relations. The other thirteen staff members include administrative assistants, data and graphics technicians, and a printer. All of the professional staff are deeply involved in the production and use of texts. The president and the lobbyist generate fewer texts than other staff, but the president assigns, critiques, and edits subordinates' writing, and the lobbyist uses SCHA policy statements and briefing papers in his discussions with lawmakers and representatives of regulatory bodies.

I worked at SCHA from 1961 until 1979. In 1985, I went back, along with my partners, to teach a writing seminar there and to consult on the development on the association's annual report. Later, to collect data for this article, I interviewed staff, observed several committee meetings, attended the association's 1987 annual meeting, and read stacks of minutes, reports, letters, and similar material. The association's technical vocabulary has changed dramatically since I left in 1979, but in spite of efforts to reduce paperwork through technology, the volume of texts produced has not diminished. The association continues to rely heavily on texts in accomplishing its work, and the staff continues to write extensively. Textual influences pervade the atmosphere; all executive offices have wall-to-wall bookshelves, and most are overflowing. The office has a centralized word processing system, so that administrative assistants can edit and format drafts generated by executives. However, since drafts are the tools used by the association in developing consensus among members, reaching compromises with other agencies, and debating with opponents, the organization cannot reduce the number of drafts needed to produce a final document. Staff members must accept this process.

Staff members writing in this environment have enormous adjustments to make. They must work with a constantly changing vocabulary, a blend of governmental jargon and high-tech terminology. And since the small staff includes a variety of specialists, each member must have at least a smattering of knowledge about a wide number of subjects in order to communicate with his or her colleagues. Staff members write for a number of audiences: hospitals' chief executive officers, professional staff, physicians, government agency personnel, elected officials and legislators, and the general public. They write an extensive variety of forms: memos, reports, letters, policy statements, minutes, technical briefs and analyses, newsletters, manuals, technical schedules, instructions, speeches, and white papers. Though the association values good writing, the quality of an individual text is judged by its performance rather than by its style. Consequently, staff members must write to satisfy committees and often must rewrite prose that is well written but somehow not quite what a committee member had in mind.

To find out how one learns to write in such an environment, I interviewed two new professional employees and tracked two projects they were working on at the time of my investigation. I interviewed other staff members and read other materials to gain additional background, but I believed that studying the work and responses of new employees would show me most clearly how the environment influences writers and their writing.

The first professional staff member I interviewed, the vice president for research and planning, had joined the SCHA staff eighteen months before I began my research. She previously worked for another state hospital association, so she was familiar with the types of activities conducted by such organizations. However, I chose to watch her work on an assignment that was peripheral to her field: the development of a position statement on educational preparation for nursing practice.

## TEXTS AND CONSENSUS

The issue of nursing education is a national one. Some groups of nursing educators and leaders believe that the educational system should prepare two types of professional nurses, a basic or technical (associate degree) and an advanced (baccalaureate degree) level. The associate degree would prepare basic practitioners who would be licensed as "technical nurses"; the baccalaureate degree would be the minimum requirement for entry into professional practice. Only baccalaureate degree holders would be licensed as R.N.'s. The scope of practice permitted to each of the two categories would differ. Technical nurses would be employed to carry out less-complex functions. Under the proposed two-level scheme, nurses holding diplomas rather than college degrees would no longer be eligible for licensure as professional nurses. The nursing profession views these proposals as a means of upgrading the professional status of nurses and responding to the increasing complexity of nursing practice.

The hospital industry supports all the existing forms of nursing education which currently prepare candidates for professional practice and licensure as R.N.'s. In its view, the baccalaureate degree is "a voluntary attainable goal" but should not be mandatory for entry into professional nursing. Hospital administrators say further that limiting practice to two levels of licensure would cause problems in staffing hospitals. They also fear that eliminating diploma schools of nursing would make the nursing shortage worse.

Negotiation of the nursing education issue is complicated because hospital associations, both nationally and at the state level, include societies of nurse executives under their organizational umbrella.

This national issue must be debated at state levels because nurses are licensed by states. Early in 1986, the South Carolina Statewide Master Planning Committee on Nursing Education, an interdisciplinary group in which the majority of members are nurses, published a plan recommending two levels of licensure in the state. Later that year, the South Carolina Organization of Nurse Executives (SCONE) adopted a position supporting the "plan to upgrade the educational preparation of nurses for entry into practice" contained in the Statewide Master Plan. The SCONE position did not specifically mention two levels of licensure, and it stressed cooperative action with SCHA and other groups in assuring "an adequate supply of appropriately prepared nurses." Nonetheless, SCONE's statement implied support for the two levels. And this position was potentially divisive to SCHA. SCONE is an affiliate of SCHA, and the SCHA board of trustees supports all existing educational paths leading to licensure as an R.N.—a diploma, an associate degree, or a baccalaureate degree. Obviously, group solidarity was threatened when the affiliate unit adopted a position contrary to the stated policy of the larger group. Thus, internal negotiation was necessary. SCHA created the Ad Hoc Committee on Educational Preparation for Nursing Practice to conduct the discussions, and the vice president for research and planning was assigned to staff the committee.

To assist the committee, the vice president prepared a discussion draft which she labeled "Policy Briefing." In order to write the one-page draft, she reviewed the following texts: minutes of the SCHA board meeting at which the original SCONE position was discussed; the original SCONE position; the *Policy Strategy Bulletin on Nurse Education, Titling, and Licensure* prepared by the American Hospital Association (AHA); two issues of the *The Nurse Executive,* a newsletter published by the American Organization of Nurse Executives (AONE, an AHA affiliate); an AHA memo regarding diploma nursing education; a resolution prepared by the Michigan Council of Associate Degree Nursing Directors; a statement from the American Association of Community and Junior Colleges and the Council of Associate Degree Programs of the National League for Nursing; a letter from the School of Nursing of Weber State College, Ogden, Utah; a position statement from the Oregon Association of Hospitals; a summary of a survey conducted by the Idaho Board of Nursing; an AHA analysis of issues related to advanced degrees for registered nurses; a newsletter from the Wisconsin Hospital Association; and *The South Carolina Plan for Nursing Education: 1985–1990.* The vice president's draft was not an abstract or summary of any of these documents. Instead, it was a response to them, a dialogue between the members of SCHA and all the organizations that had previously prepared texts on the central issue and related concerns.

As the vice president's work shows, association writing is heavily intertextual. And the texts of other organizations continue to influence staff members writing throughout the negotiation and editing process. When the discussion draft was reviewed at the meeting of the ad hoc committee, representatives of SCONE brought new texts with them. One of their spokespersons had recently attended a meeting of AONE, at which the AHA *Policy Strategy Bulletin* had been discussed. The national discussion made it obvious that no definitions of the proposed two levels of nursing had been developed. In addition, no guidelines existed for determining the scope of practice for the two levels. In short, there was no text describing exactly how the proposed two-level scheme would work. Because definitions and guidelines had not been written, according to the SCONE representative, SCONE realized that neither work nor discussion on the issue could proceed. SCONE therefore decided to rescind its previous position. The SCONE spokesperson then told members of the ad hoc committee that SCONE had "no philosophical difference with the intent of the SCHA position" that the vice president had drafted. The clearly philosophical draft apparently helped the participants achieve consensus on the nursing education issue.

The ad hoc committee then proceeded to edit the draft, word by word. Both the original draft and the changes show how association texts use epideictic rhetoric to reaffirm values dominant in the association's culture and to interpret the significance of technological and economic change within the context of those values.

## VICE PRESIDENT'S DRAFT

### *DRAFT*

### *Policy Briefing*
### *Nurse Education, Titling and Licensure*

Nursing practice today is facing an increasingly complex environment in the delivery of quality patient care. With the evolution of prospective pricing and corresponding changing incentives, nurses are faced with a "sicker" patient population that is subsequently discharged sooner than under the traditional cost-based reimbursement scheme. At the same time, changes and sophistication in technology cloud and complicate the nurse practice arena.

The nurse is the mainstay of any hospital human resource supply and is the primary resource in service delivery and patient care. It is therefore essential that there is an adequate supply of nursing personnel available to hospitals in order to fulfill the mission of all hospitals in the State.

Accordingly, the American Hospital Association has adopted a Policy Strategy on Nurse Education, Titling and Licensure which supports all forms of nursing education, with the baccalaureate degree as an attainable goal, regardless of the source of entry into practice, to ensure an adequate flow of nurses into the hospital environment.

Consistent with AHA Policy Strategy, The South Carolina Hospital Association supports all forms of nursing education with the baccalaureate degree as a voluntary attainable goal and emphasizes the need for flexibility in the achievement of this goal to ensure educational mobility in nursing and thus, an adequate supply of nurses in the State.

In South Carolina the vehicle for the provision of educational mobility is through arrangements with the colleges, universities and hospital schools of nursing for all levels of nursing. In South Carolina there is only one Diploma program and therefore the baccalaureate degree as an attainable goal should not create a problem.

It is the belief of the South Carolina Hospital Association that the development of educational standards remains the responsibility of the profession of nursing and of educational institutions. It is the hospital's primary responsibility to handle issues of employment and utilization of nurses prepared at different levels and to develop standards that assure quality of practice within the institution.

Because the supply of nurses is affected by changes in environmental conditions with respect to the nursing profession having to compete with other professional opportunities for the potential nurse, it is essential that all interested parties work cooperatively with educators, the appropriate licensure Boards and state agencies and organizations to make the nursing profession an attractive, price competitive option for all those interested in pursuing a nursing degree.

## AD HOC COMMITTEE'S EDITED VERSION

### THE SOUTH CAROLINA HOSPITAL ASSOCIATION
### POLICY BRIEFING
### NURSE EDUCATION, TITLING AND LICENSURE

Nursing practice today is facing an increasingly complex environment in the delivery of quality patient care. With the evolution of prospective pricing and corresponding changing incentives, nurses are faced with a "sicker" patient population that is subsequently discharged sooner than under the traditional cost-based reimbursement scheme. At the same time, changes and sophistication in technology and the creation of community alternative delivery settings cloud and complicate the nurse practice arena.

The nurse is a primary resource in service delivery and patient care. It is essential that there is an adequate supply of nursing personnel with appropriate knowledge and skills to meet the needs of individual hospitals.

Accordingly, the American Hospital Association has adopted a Policy

Strategy on Nurse Education, Titling and Licensure which supports all forms of nursing education, with the baccalaureate degree as an attainable goal, regardless of the source of entry into practice, to ensure an adequate flow of nurses into the hospital environment.

Consistent with this AHA Policy Strategy, The South Carolina Hospital Association supports all forms of nursing education with the baccalaureate degree as a voluntary attainable goal, and SCHA emphasizes the need for flexibility in the achievement of this goal to ensure educational mobility in nursing and thus, an adequate supply of nurses in the State.

It is the belief of the South Carolina Hospital Association that the development of educational standards remains the responsibility of the profession of nursing and of educational institutions. It is the hospital's prerogative to develop staffing patterns consistent with its individual needs and state laws and regulations.

It is essential that all interested parties work cooperatively with educators, the appropriate licensure boards and state agencies, employers and other organizations to make the nursing profession an attractive option for all those interested in pursuing a nursing career.

## EPIDEICTIC RHETORIC AND CONTEXT

Both versions are largely epideictic and highly abstract, yet in the association world this genre serves to resolve a concrete issue: must a nurse hold a college degree to be licensed? A close look at the first paragraph uncovers clues to the draft's effectiveness.

In both versions, the first paragraph provides the context in which the policy is to be interpreted. It describes the environment as hospital leadership perceives it and incorporates a set of value statements that reveal the association's beliefs about the environment. Perhaps not by accident, the value statements are ordered according to the hierarchy of values characterizing SCHA's culture. The first value, "quality patient care," appears in the first sentence. If SCHA officials were asked to rank the organization's values, they would undoubtedly name "quality" first without hesitation. Quality, however, in the view of hospital leadership, is inextricably linked with money to finance hospital operations. The second sentence reflects this view: The prospective pricing system and incentives to discharge patients sooner, according to the statement, result in a "sicker" patient population. Though it is not stated in the briefing, nurses and health-care officials know that a "sicker" patient population requires more intensive and specialized nursing care.

By contrasting new prospective pricing systems adopted by federal programs, state agencies, and other third-party payers to the "traditional" cost-based reimbursement scheme, the association can place the blame for current nursing problems without blaming its colleagues, the nurses. Third-party payers, government especially, are the main culprits. The vice president had added technology as a second complicating factor; the committee added community alternative delivery settings (i.e., HMOs, surgicenters, primary-care clinics, etc.) as a third environmental factor that complicates nursing practice. In this classic example of epideictic rhetoric, the first paragraph begins to reunite the hospital family, which finds itself within a changing, uncertain environment.

The vice president, with her experience in hospital association activities, had selected the appropriate environmental factors related to the issue and connected the issue at hand to the association's value system. Consequently, the committee made only one change. That change, however, was significant. By adding a reference to alternative delivery systems, the committee calls attention to major restructuring within the health-care environment. "Restructuring" is an increasingly prominent term today in hospital jargon. The industry is experiencing revolutionary changes. Federal payment programs and declining admissions are forcing hospitals to compete, both with one another and with "alternative delivery systems," such as HMOs. In the committee's discussion, one member commented that "prospective pricing creates the alternative delivery system," clarifying the culpable factor in the complex, cloudy, complicated environment.

Most of the remaining editorial changes were prompted by audience considerations and concerns about readability and conciseness. The committee felt that some words in the second paragraph were "editorial comment," and "could be inflammatory." They decided that the fifth paragraph was superfluous and that the sixth and seventh were hard to read. As the edited version demonstrates, the committee does not edit a text as a composition teacher would. For example, it did not comment on the sentences that begin "It is essential," "It is the hospital's responsibility," etc. Composition teachers correctly point out the wordiness of sentences that begin with expletives, but writers of epideictic rhetoric, policy, and legal decisions use them frequently. Although Perelman does not mention this structure when he discusses the expression of universal values in epideictic rhetoric to appeal to the universal audience (31–35), I believe Perelman's concepts explain the form's prevalence in the epideictic genre. Such structures suggest that the statement is self-evident or expresses a belief or value that any right-minded audience should accept as indisputable. The expletive construction, of course, is often the structure of choice for legal and authoritative speech acts, such as "It is the intent of Congress" and "It is the judgment of this court." The structure, no matter how wordy, frequently appears in rhetoric whenever the writer wishes to emphasize a purpose, a belief, or a decision. Understandably, the committee saw no need to delete these phrases in a document emphasizing beliefs and values, even though they made several changes to achieve conciseness.

## THE TEXT IN DIALOGUE

The editorial changes, as illustrated above, reflect the members' understanding of the audience as well as their concern about textual effectiveness. But the editorial session also revealed the role of texts in achieving consensus. The discussion in the meeting was a dialogue between members and the text more than between members. The text of the draft was the main speaker. Members questioned its meaning in one paragraph, its logic in another, and its words in a few sentences. Not once did they ask the vice president what she had meant when she drafted it. The vice president herself commented on the draft in a detached manner, not as the owner of the words.

Apparently, when she created the text, the vice president viewed it as a speaker in a dialogue. The title "Policy Briefing" is not a standard name for a particular type of document at SCHA. The organization has no standard nomenclature for the background materials they write for use in continuing discussions of policy issues with other groups. The choice of title seems pertinent: "briefing" implies a continuing dialogue rather than a final statement. When I asked the vice president about her choice of terms, she had no ready answer. She thought awhile and then told me that the draft was "an educational piece . . . advisory. The issue is so touchy." She later elaborated on the "educational" aspects of the draft: "It explains the issue at hand while at the same time provides SCHA's position on the issue." She apparently recognized that the voice of the text in a sensitive dialogue must be explanatory or advisory rather than dogmatic. The text, which concludes by emphasizing a cooperative approach to resolving the issue, is structured to keep the dialogue going rather than to end it.

Thus far, the Policy Briefing has had a successful life. After the editing session, the SCONE representative expressed her approval and the ad hoc committee voted to recommend to the association's board of trustees that the statement be adopted as official policy. The conflict over means to achieve the goal of upgrading nursing education was resolved in the context of the higher values shared by SCHA and SCONE. The unanimous vote at the committee meeting demonstrated that consensus had been achieved. In addition, the committee took two other significant actions. They recommended that SCHA appoint a hospital association member to the Statewide Master Planning Committee on Nursing Education and establish a "mechanism . . . for ongoing dialogue between SCONE and the SCHA board of trustees." The board approved the Policy Briefing and accepted the two recommendations. The entire issue concerned dialogue, and the Policy Briefing was a persuasive force in keeping lines of communication open so that new ones could be developed. The nursing education issue at SCHA is now dormant, at least temporarily. SCONE members are devoting their energies to correcting the nursing shortage, a problem that concerns hospital and nurse executives alike and one that requires cooperative action.

## EPIDEICTIC RHETORIC AND SURVIVAL OF THE GROUP

Cooperative action and continuing dialogue rank high in any association's hierarchy of values. Consensus-building groups that must influence other groups in order to achieve their purposes depend on cooperation and communication for survival. And the benefits of cooperation and communication motivate the formation of associations in the first place. Understandably, the association's epideictic rhetoric will stress these two values whenever appropriate.

In the composition field, we do not fully appreciate the critical function of epideictic rhetoric, and we neglect to teach it. Indeed, we often disparage it, calling it slanted prose, propaganda, and similar epithets. The association's dependence on epideictic rhetoric illustrates a major point in Perelman's theory of argumentation. All societies rely on epideictic rhetoric to reinforce adherence to values that are critical to the existence of the group. Without this constant reinforcement, values might "not prevail against other values that might come into conflict with them." Perelman's explanation of epideictic rhetoric explains SCHA's text perfectly:

> The very concept of this kind of oratory . . . results in its being practiced by those who, in a society, defend the traditional and accepted values, those which are the object of education, not the new and revolutionary values which stir up controversy and polemics. . . . In epideictic oratory, the speaker turns educator. [51]

As the vice president said, the Policy Briefing was "educational." "Educational epidictic speeches," according to Perelman, "create a mere disposition toward action," not action itself (54). But the epideictic genre plays a critical role in society. As Perelman asks, "Without such common values, upon what foundation could deliberative and legal speeches rest?" (52–53).

Perelman describes epideictic rhetoric as the foundation for the subsequent acts and decisions of the group. The genre could also be classified as the *context* that influences writers within the group, or it could be given another apt label: corporate culture. Perelman did not, of course, equate epideictic rhetoric and corporate culture, since the latter term is new jargon for an age-old reality. But epideictic rhetoric is one of the main vehicles through which such culture is expressed and maintained. Keynote speeches and award ceremonies at annual meetings of associations and corporations serve much the same function as the Greek *eulogiai* (good-speakings, praises, blessings) and *agōnes* (assemblies, games, contests for prizes). The keynote speaker, who is always someone exemplifying the virtues prized by the society, praises values and illustrates them with stories of heroic achievement. The award presentations echo the praise of values in recounting the accomplishments of present-day heroes and heroines. Outsiders, much like newscasters at political conventions, dismiss all this talk as "rhetoric" in the pejorative sense. But what appears as "mere rhetoric" to an outsider is life-renewing ritual to members of the group. Without this annual renewal through epideictic rhetoric and the constant reinforcement of epideictic writing in the intervals between, associations would be unable to prevail against competing values.

## TEXTS AND CONFLICT

Association texts are vital agents in achieving cooperation between organizations with divergent goals. However, association texts sometimes become the focus of conflict. The texts themselves may be attacked. Texts written by the second new staff member I interviewed were singled out for sharp criticism by a representative of another agency.

The second new staff member, the vice president for professional relations, had joined the SCHA staff less than a month before my first discussion with her. Two months later, her texts and her methods for distributing them were criticized by the spokesman for a relatively new regulatory agency. When the agency first started its activities, SCHA created an advisory committee to meet periodically with agency representatives to discuss the agency's programs and hospitals' concerns. The vice president's predecessor, who staffed the committee, had routinely submitted drafts of committee minutes to the agency director for comment before distributing them. This practice was consistent with the association's early posture toward the regulatory organization, an attempt at open dialogue and cooperation. The predecessor also used a format for the minutes that differed from SCHA's customary form. The advisory committee minutes contained large segments of quoted statements and resembled transcripts. SCHA minutes normally summarize discussions and record actions. The names of individuals making motions or seconding them are omitted and discussion is generally reported in indirect statements rather than by quotation.

I do not know why the predecessor chose a transcript format for the minutes. He certainly had that option, since SCHA does not mandate formats for any of its documents. Perhaps he suspected that communication with the regulatory agency was inherently sensitive. In fact, a few months after the agency began operations, SCHA grew dissatisfied with communication from the agency, questioning its clarity and timeliness. Its posture toward the agency changed at about the same time the new vice president for professional relations joined the staff. The head of the regulatory body attributed the change in SCHA posture to the change in vice presidents and cited specific problems in relations between the two organizations. All of the problems pertained to communication; one of them was "unreliable documentation of committee proceedings as reflected in the minutes. . . ."

The new vice president had indeed changed the format of the advisory committee minutes, using the summary style used in most other SCHA minutes. She also discontinued sending a draft of the minutes to the agency head for approval. When I first met her, before she had attended her first meeting of the advisory committee, she was orienting herself to her new job by reading minutes— SCHA board minutes written under the SCHA president's direction and minutes of advisory committee meetings written by her predecessor. Ironically, she complained to me that reading the latter was a chore. "They're like transcripts. It takes forever to find out what happened." She also told me that she did not think drafts of the minutes needed the agency director's approval before they were distributed, since the advisory committee was created by and reports to SCHA.

These changes in the text of the minutes, both the form and the control of the content, brought latent conflict into the open. But the text itself was attacked. Since the agency director mentioned no specific words, sections, or actions in the minutes but criticized "unreliable documentation," he apparently was reacting to the form. The vice president had been unable to interpret the meaning of previous meetings from the transcripts. The agency director raised objections when dialogue was summarized. Obviously, the new vice president and the director belong to two different interpretive communities. Communication between the two communities will inevitably be a problem because language used in both may not have the same meaning to the two groups. Verbatim transcripts of one group's words do not communicate clearly to the other group; a summary of a dialogue may seem accurate to one group yet misconstrued to the other. When two different interpretive communities come together in dialogue and they have not yet learned to translate so that they understand each other, the minutes of the meeting will hardly satisfy both sets of participants.

Minutes are greatly misunderstood texts. Many organizations consider them a necessary nuisance, reminders of previous actions and records for the archives. In an organization with little conflict, minutes are history. They usually reflect actions and agreements but seldom passion and conflict. In minutes, the living speech of the meeting becomes a voiceless record. No matter how well written the minutes may be, they cannot show the emotion and drama of debate. Not even a transcript can do that. Thus, the minutes of interorganizational meetings characterized by opposing views and interests are quite likely to become targets of criticism. They may even instigate further conflict, rather than promote cooperation and mutual understanding. Giving participants a chance to preview drafts before distributing the minutes allows them to edit their oral texts as well as the written record. Of course, an oral text cannot be edited unless it is first written, and then it is no longer an oral text. One begins to wonder where the dialogue takes place. Does it occur in meetings where people talk to one another? Or does it happen in the written text where one edited written speech responds to another?

The dilemma of minutes creates mammoth problems for organizations such as SCHA. The life and dialogues of the organization are distilled into these records. The minutes are cited in other texts, become speakers in other dialogues, and occasionally, as in the case explained above, provoke criticism. The writer of the minutes is not only expected to provide a synopsis useful to all future readers who will interact with the text but also to summarize a drama to the satisfaction of all the characters. The expectations become impossible when all the characters are not playing to the same audience. Neither the new vice president for professional relations nor a more experienced staff member could satisfy such requirements. But since she was new and had not allowed participants to edit the minutes before distribution, she and the minutes were obvious targets for criticism.

The new vice president was fully supported by SCHA, which immediately began formulating a letter responding to the criticism. The vice president herself created the first draft, a draft she admitted was "angry." She asked a colleague with longer tenure (the vice president of finance) to critique her draft and recommend changes. His draft of the vice president's letter was then sent to the committee chairman, who made further changes. The vice president next incorporated the main points of all three drafts into a fourth version and returned it to the chairman. The chairman made minor changes and sent the letter. Collaborative writing in associations often follows this pattern: collaborators revise one another's texts in order to arrive at a single document that best reflects the organization's thinking. Collaborative writing is to be expected in an organization that values cooperation so highly, but the nature of the collaboration is perhaps unusual. The collaboration is based primarily on texts rather than talk.

In recent years, collaborative writing has sparked interest in the composition field. And the orality-literacy connection has too. Both of these theoretical interests come to life in the saga of the advisory committee minutes. And the SCHA experience shows that we have not yet fully appreciated how these theories work. Many of our textbooks and case studies, for example, describe groups of student and co-workers talking to each other throughout the development of texts. Or, as an alternate pattern, they may describe the production of a report by a group of writers who parcel out the pieces and put them together after the individuals have drafted certain sections. At SCHA, one text leads to another text, or one text merges with another. Of course, the writers talk to each other, but most often their texts do the talking.

The relationship between talk and text at SCHA catapults the theory of the orality-literacy shift into the twentieth century. The written text at SCHA is primary, and many of the organization's texts are "written speech." Havelock, in his analysis of the literate revolution, shows the consequences of writing speech. Our written texts have lost the music of the human voice and the drama of human action. Instead, they have become conceptual and difficult to understand (290–292). Havelock's description is accurate, but are these consequences necessary? Must organizational prose mute all the collective voices that create the texts? And must individual writers stifle their own voices as well?

## LEARNING TO WRITE AT SCHA

Experienced writers at SCHA often write impersonal, conceptual prose. Much of the writing they must do falls in that category, and staff members frequently regard this kind of writing as a chore. Still, they take pride in their writing and are eager to improve it. They like to talk about writing. They occasionally joke about it. They often ask one another's advice on style, punctuation, and mechanics. And occasionally they derive personal satisfaction from their writing.

I asked several experienced writers to tell me how they learned to write at SCHA. They could not tell me how they absorbed an association persona. So I asked them to tell me about specific occasions when they felt good about their writing at SCHA. The vice president for public relations, who was educated in journalism, told this story:

> We'd invited a very important speaker to speak at our annual meeting. He sent an advance copy of his speech, so I wrote a summary for the promotion. And during his speech, he complimented me. He said it was the first time anybody had ever written an accurate summary of his ideas.

The vice president for finance told his story:

> [The SCHA president] let me write the letter to [a top state official]. This was after a trip to HCFA. It was a nice, nasty letter. We copied the world [sent photocopies to many individuals] and laid everything on the table. It felt good to say exactly what you meant.

The vice president for finance then described another situation in which he had written collaboratively with a committee, saying "we didn't have the opportunity to be creative."

The staff members' stories show that they care about accuracy, voice, and style. And obviously they occasionally feel stifled by the requirements of association writing. Both stories also show that the writers value their individual voices and being able to use them, though staff members told me that they did not mind when committees, other staff members, and even outside consultants changed their drafts. They accept the constraints as part of the job. But when asked to tell their success stories, one remembered praise from an important guest speaker and the other remembered writing to an important official. Even though association officers value good writing, the organization rewards staff members for accomplishing objectives, not for the perfection of the texts they write in order to achieve those goals. Possibly, association members do not consciously think about the individual authorship of the group's texts, since they regard the text as both an object and as a participant in the consensus-building process. Staff writers eventually absorb that perspective. They do not write for self-expression; they write for results. And they are rewarded for those results. But when the occasion permits, they still feel pride of authorship and pleasure in speaking with their own voices.

## IMPLICATIONS FOR TEACHING

The experiences of writers at SCHA and the organization's use of texts suggests some changes in the composition and rhetoric curriculum. Obviously, we cannot and should not try to prepare students to function as association staff writers any more than we try to prepare legal writers, but we should be aware that associations are dominant factors in our society. The majority of our students may never work for an association, just as the majority will not enter law school or serve in a legislature. But many of our students will join associations and participate in their deliberations. Our teaching will have given them only a partial view of the rhetoric they will encounter and use in these societies. At present in teaching argumentation, we stress forensic and deliberative models and disparage epideictic rhetoric. This neglect of epideictic rhetoric shortchanges students. It distorts their view of what responsible persuasion should be and how necessary it is in a society.

Students' views of writing and rhetoric at work are distorted in other ways by some of our practices and biases. Romantic approaches to teaching composition often lead students to think that writing can only be good if it springs from the individual's unique perspective. Students also come to believe that the only effective voice in writing is a single voice, their own voice. And students know the dire consequences of taking another person's draft and incorporating large chunks of it into the papers they submit. How well would these students perform at SCHA?

Would students who had completed an advanced course in pragmatic writing do any better? Not unless they were taught to adapt standard business forms for a variety of purposes and to create new forms when the rhetorical situation demanded it. Unfortunately, one short course in business or technical writing can only teach the basic forms. But the emphasis on the basics often gives students the false impression that memos, letters, and reports constitute the entire spectrum of nonacademic writing. Who would ever think to teach students how to write minutes? (Perhaps we still think that only secretaries—or the female members of the committee—write minutes, so the form must be unimportant. People in corporate circles once thought that. But then they heard the story about the woman, the only female on the committee, who reluctantly agreed to write the minutes when her male colleagues automatically assumed she was the logical choice. Her minutes were never longer than one page. And she became president of the company in less than two years.)

We do not need to abandon all our traditions and values in order to prepare students to write at work. We do need to emphasize some new approaches that are gradually working their way into the curriculum and to use some old theories in new ways. Reader-response theory, the concept of dialogics, and the notion of collaborative writing should inform all composition courses, so that students will learn how to respond to corporate texts, write in response to them, and write with and for corporate groups.

Burke's pentad will also serve us well in teaching students how to put life into dying corporate prose. I recently heard a law professor use a version of the pentad in showing lawyers how to put action into their statements of facts. The pentad helped the attorneys see how their passive sentences and wordiness buried the facts and slowed the pace of the action. This heuristic, which focuses on facts and action, belongs in any classroom where the contexts of writing are emphasized. It not only calls attention to the scene and to the drama of human action but also requires the writer to examine the act within the scene and all the complex relationships between the pentad's five elements.

Another neglected heuristic, the tagmemic matrix developed by Young, Becker, and Pike, can help advanced students in pragmatic writing courses clarify the immense complexity inherent in much organizational prose. The vice president of finance at SCHA particularly likes this heuristic. People who deal with systems find it helpful in pinpointing system dynamics and relationships. This heuristic also belongs in any classroom where contexts of writing are stressed. It makes writers examine the meaning of events from several perspectives, to see the action not only in isolation but as part of a system interrelated to other systems. Corporate writers cannot survive without this type of thinking.

Corporate writers also cannot survive unless they write in a corporate voice. The corporate voice, however, need not sound like an inhuman signal filtered through channels of bureaucracy, but negotiated texts often sound that way. In the composition classroom and in advanced courses in pragmatic writing, we need to give students practice not only in writing *with* a group but also in writing *for* the group. They need to experience at first hand what happens to their texts when group members disagree, when they do not want to appear too critical, or when they want to praise an action but not the actor. To satisfy these typical responses of a group, writers frequently use more and more abstractions to gain group approval. They resort to passive structures and to euphemisms. To satisfy the group, achieve the group's goals, and still produce a lively text is a masterful accomplishment. Sometimes style must be sacrificed for a larger goal, but the astute writing teacher can help writers develop strategies for resolving many of the problems provided she or he never loses sight of the context of the writing.

To develop realistic group writing assignments, evaluate them, and reward them when done well will require the composition teacher to think and act both like a writing teacher and like a corporate manager, a role that few of us have been educated to fill. This dilemma, I believe, is the crux of the problem in teaching nonacademic writing. Correcting the problem is not as simple as reading articles that prove how greatly employers emphasize good writing skills. We know they do, but we do not fully understand how they characterize good writing. Frequently the managers themselves cannot articulate their criteria in language we understand. Managers and writing teachers, after all, dwell in distinctly different interpretive communities. And this fact we must recognize first. Before we can teach students to write well in the corporate community, we must learn what writing means in that interpretive community, how it works, and how it is valued. The collected articles in *Worlds of Writing* will help us begin that investigation and encourage us to engage in dialogues with leaders of the communities in which writers work.

## Notes

1. Legislators say they pay little attention to the identical letters they receive from members of associations. Apparently, legislators value the unique voice of the individual writer and view identical letters as instances of "group think." Progressive associations discourage such "group" letter writing campaigns, although they do encourage members to communicate with representatives on an individual basis.

## Workes Cited

Havelock, Eric A. *The Literate Revolution in Greece and Its Cultural Consequences.* Princeton, N.J.: Princeton University Press, 1982.
Perelman, C., and L. Olbrechts-Tyteca. *The New Rhetoric.* Trans. John Wilkinson and Purcell Weaver. Notre Dame, Ind.: University of Notre Dame Press, 1969.

# THE FILE CABINET HAS A SEX LIFE: INSIGHTS OF A PROFESSIONAL WRITING CONSULTANT

## Lee Clark Johns

*Since 1978, Lee Clark Johns has headed Professional Writing Consultants in Tulsa, Oklahoma, teaching writing seminars in the oil industry, banks, government, computer industry, and other businesses. With a B.A. from Duke University and an M.A. from the University of Kansas, she has also taught composition and advanced grammar at the high school, community college, university, and graduate school levels.*

*Committed to establishing writing consultancy as a profession, Johns was founding president of the Association of Professional Writing Consultants. She has also presented workshops on consulting and teaching business English to other writing consultants throughout the United States. In addition, she is an active member of the American Society of Training and Development and, in 1987, received an ASTD Chapter Award for Excellence for her seminar "Managing Other People's Writing."*

Ask anyone "When you were given your first writing assignment on the job, how did you know what to do?"

"I looked in the file cabinet." "I asked how they had done it before."

The exact answers differ slightly, but the sense is the same. When facing new writing tasks—in new jobs, new companies, or new professions—most employees "go to the file." They are looking for writing models that have succeeded in the past, models that they can efficiently copy, models that their supervisor will approve. Because of this practice, however, the organizational patterns and style of documents in the file cabinet resist change. Old formats and stylistic preferences continue to thrive long after they have outlived their usefulness. The evidence is overwhelming:

The file cabinet has a sex life; it reproduces itself.

This article examines the nature of that reproductive cycle. What are the models that are being reproduced? What is their parentage? Are these useful models or have they outlived their usefulness? How are the models evolving and what are the sources of change? Who is responsible for "cleaning up the bloodline"? I do not claim to have all the answers to these questions. In fact, the greatest danger in an article of this sort is to overgeneralize. But I do want to identify patterns and cite typical examples that illustrate the nature of the writing done in the workplace.

How do I know about these issues? Since 1978, I have been teaching writing seminars to employees in a wide variety of organizations—in both the private and the public sectors. I have worked with oil companies and banks, with engineering firms and accounting firms, with the police department and university administrators, with the water and sewer department, a federal agency, a computer company and a hotel/motel management company. The individuals within these organizations make up almost a what's what of professions: executives, secretaries, attorneys, accountants, computer specialists, manufacturing supervisors and managers, marketing specialists, pipeliners, engineers, technical writers, police officers, juvenile justice social workers, city government employees, bankers, architects, and so forth. The article draws on this broad experience to share my understanding—and very informal research—of how people write in the workplace. In my opinion, they all face the *same* writing problems. And they seem to solve their writing problems in amazingly similar ways.

Instead of looking specifically at the nature of writing in a particular discourse community, I am interested in the writing patterns and behaviors that cut across discourse community boundaries. I see far more similarities than differences in the writing that different professionals produce. Of course, people do write within the narrow constraints of their professional fields and produce documents that satisfy those communities. But more frequently, they write for people outside the discourse community. Or more accurately, they operate within several "discourse communities" at the same time. For example, oil company accountants write to other accountants, work with computer programmers to plan and understand on-line accounting systems, address legal and taxation issues—all within the oil industry. And they write to gain management approval, to inform royalty owners, and to negotiate with other oil companies. Just which is their "discourse community"?

That's where the file cabinet comes in. Instead of operating within the narrowly defined boundaries of one discourse community, employees operate within several. So the writing they do relies on a variety of models. Some models literally come out of the departmental file cabinet: company formats, organizational patterns imposed by the particular department or by a manager, stylistic preferences dictated by a reviewing supervisor. Other models are drawn from the writer's own experience: from formats learned in school or from thinking patterns developed in professional studies. Whatever the source, these writers turn to what's been done before to produce an adequate document efficiently, get it approved, and move on to the next task.

Unfortunately, many of these old models have outlived their usefulness. They simply do not meet the needs of the readers who must use them or the organization that must move information productively and efficiently. They are dinosaurs. To stretch the analogy, many business documents—from short memos and letters to very long research reports—have very tiny heads, huge bodies, and weak tails. But they are prolific. Instead of becoming extinct, they multiply. No change in climate or reduction in food supply threatens to destroy them. In fact, these dinosaur models are nurtured in their academic infancy, groomed in professional adolescence, and rewarded in working adulthood. And they will continue to reproduce unless significant changes take place in that nurturing environment. These are fairly strong claims. But the thousands of documents that I read each year testify that when people go to the file cabinet for models, they find these outmoded, sometimes ineffective dinosaurs. Let us examine the old models themselves, their sources, and the problems they cause in modern business and industry.

## PARENT: THE ACADEMY

The proto-parent is the academic essay and its longer version, the research paper. Most people learn to write in school. Thus, the models taught there become extremely powerful in shaping their perception of "what writing ought to be." In English classes, these models are primarily personal essays, arguments on public issues, literary analyses, and term papers. Most secondary school teachers are getting their students "ready for college," and college teachers are preparing students for other college writing. Thus, writing academic papers becomes an end in itself.

Leslie Moore and Linda Peterson, in describing their writing-across-the-curriculum program at Yale, reveal this goal: that students should be prepared to write within their academic disciplines. As is typical, students in both freshman and advanced writing classes "are expected to observe a series of conventions agreed upon by members of a scholarly community" (Moore and Peterson, 474). While the move toward writing across the curriculum broadens the previously narrow concerns of English department classes, it is only a first step because it is still inner-directed.

However, very few students remain in academic life. When they graduate, most take jobs in organizations that are non-academic in nature. Unfortunately, many feel they have not been prepared for the writing they do on the job. Recent surveys and leaders in our field increasingly question the adequacy of college writing courses in preparing students for on-the-job writing tasks (Harwood et al.). My consulting experience supports this criticism. In every seminar, I hear, "Why wasn't I taught this in school?" "This" includes alternatives of organization and style that differ from traditional academic models.

Part of the answer is that the writing requirements in an academic environment usually do not match the requirements of the workplace. J. C. Mathes and Dwight Stevenson, in their 1976 article in *Engineering Education*, outline these differences and suggest an alternative approach for engineering professors. (Mathes and Stevenson, 154–156). But progressive teachers in all departments need to recognize the differences. In school, students learn to write to one audience (the teacher), to work alone, to reveal what they know about a subject, and to achieve a high grade as the only result. In the workplace, the same students must write to many different audiences, often work in groups or must receive a supervisor's approval for the document, should focus on what the readers *need* to know about the subject, and hope to achieve very specific results from the document. Thus, the total context—audience, method, content, and purpose—differs significantly between academic and workplace writing. And even though many business and technical writing classes recognize and address these differences, the fact is that most students do not take upper-division writing classes.

## *The Models*

Of course, traditional academic writing is an important first step in learning a model. It teaches students to shape incomplete and unruly thoughts. Some students also learn to value clarity and conciseness. Finally, the academic organizational model—introduction, body, conclusion—is perfectly adequate for short memos and letters. Writers who have stored that model produce clear, short documents that satisfy their readers.

The problem arises when the same model is imposed on a long report. The term paper approach simply does not meet the needs of workplace readers. A typical banking document illustrates the problem. In the banking industry, loan decisions are based on documents called credit analyses. In these normally lengthy documents, the analyst presents this information about the company requesting the loan: background, operating results (earnings, profits, losses), financial position (debts, assets, liquidity), and industry comparisons. Many of these analyses run over eight pages. Generally they are written by inexperienced employees, credit analysts who are essentially management trainees in their first banking position. The credit decisions are made by the senior loan committee, often the most experienced executives.

The combination of writers who are insecure about their technical understanding (but confident in their college-learned writing ability) and readers who must make important decisions in a short period of time produces the problem. The writers, having learned their lessons well in undergraduate school and often in their M.B.A. studies, produce "data dumps." Unsure about what information is significant, they include everything. With no alternative format to follow, they rely on the academic model: short introduction, background, a story about the company's operations and financial position, etc., until they reach the conclusion about credit risks involved in the loan. Such documents do not carry specific recommendations; they are essentially resource documents that help the loan committee make a decision.

But senior executives do not have time to sort through all this data. One executive of a major regional bank holding company explained what happens:

> The Senior Loan Committee meets every Friday morning. I usually receive the analyses we will discuss about 4:00 P.M. on Thursday and take them home for review that night. We may be looking at six to ten potential loans, and there is no way I can

read these long, rambling reports. So I do the best I can. I review the ones that I already know something about and hope for the best on the others.

Every Thursday evening he is frustrated, and every Friday morning decisions of major importance to the organization are being made on the basis of poorly organized reports. Other banks have developed a credit analysis format that has an executive summary at the beginning (a model that appears later in this article). But my point here is that the writers—using the only model they know—are doing the best they can.

## *The Thinking Processes*

In the absence of an academic model, writers fall back on their thinking processes, often the same process that the old file models reveal. For example, minutes and trip reports are almost invariably narratives: "What did we do?" Within an organization, these reports can be very important because problem solving and interdepartmental negotiations often occur in meetings or on trips to the regions. But the narrative approach buries the significant decisions and becomes an exercise in frustration for the writer and an ineffective reference for future readers. A classic three-page meeting report shows the problem; in outline form, it reads:

> On March 3, 1982, a meeting was held at the Research Center . . . The purpose of the meeting was . . .
>
> Personnel in attendance were: . . .
>
> DISCUSSION
>
> *Morning Session*
> John Smith reviews his presentation of March 2 . . .
> At this point, Jones says . . .
> Thompson and White leave to attend interviewee seminar. Johnson addresses questions four and eight . . .
>
> *page 2*
> The physical properties questions of four and eight were taken up . . .
> Thompson and White return. Philosophical discussion of _____ the problem resumes . . .
> Frank takes up question six . . .
>
> *Afternoon Session*
> Frank continues . . .
>
> *page 3*
> The following outline in the form of major tasks along with dates is presented . . .
> Charge to Research . . .
> The discussion turns to how to proceed with . . . There is no plan put forth . . .

This report, written by a senior research scientist, is all too typical. I rarely see either meeting minutes or trip reports that use substantive headings or any sort of executive summary. Most are narratives. In the absence of alternative models, writers fall back on "the way it's been done before" or on their most primitive communication skill—telling a story.

The *academic discourse community* rewards students for documents that reveal their thinking processes. But in the workplace, the decision makers are not interested in "how the watch was made." They want to know "what to do with it."[1]

Both senior employees and novices often *think* they are writing to others within the discourse community, and they follow the models of that community. For example, several years ago I began to notice the many inductive paragraphs within long research reports from one oil industry laboratory. Most followed this pattern in the discussion section: "Figure 1 presents the findings of the x test. (several lines of factual data) Therefore, it is concluded that. . . ."

The pattern was too prolific to ignore because it consistently violated the topic-sentence-first model for writing effective business paragraphs. I finally realized that these scientists were modeling the scientific method on paper—paragraph after paragraph. When I pointed that out to them, most answered, "But that is what our readers [other scientists] expect."[2]

However, the assumption that documents are read only by those within the narrow discourse community is simply wrong.[3] Other scientists are the primary audience for the discussion section of a report. But so are operational engineers and other nonscientists. *All* could read a deductive paragraph more efficiently.

## The Results

Employees who are blindly committed to the academic discourse model face frustration and sometimes career disappointment. Recently, one scientist told me wistfully:

> Before I came to Company X, everyone always praised my writing. My professors said I did an excellent job on my papers. Then I went to work for Company Y and they loved the way I write. One boss even said, "Finally they give me someone who knows how to write." But then I came to X and have been criticized ever since. I didn't know what they wanted until I took your writing seminar. At Y, Ph.D's become top management. They understand the scientific paper. But Ph.D.'s don't become the Director at X.

His assessment of promotion opportunities may be wrong, but he has identified the source of his writing frustrations. His current management wants results-oriented research reports, not the methods-oriented scientific paper. Obviously, the "discourse community" in each of the companies—both in the same industry—is different.

Gregory Colomb and Joseph Williams sum up these differences in addressing the needs of different readers:

> Readers who are pressed for time or who for other reasons are unwilling to give their time to the writer tend to prefer Point-first structures, since these structures make the reading process as quick and efficient as possible. . . . On the other hand, readers who are willing or who must give their time to the writer and who expect in return the kinds of pleasures we associate with fine, belletristic writing generally feel more rewarded by Point-last structures, since only in such structures are they accorded the pleasures of the chase. . . . Very few readers in professional settings are willing to allow writers the kind of claim on their time and energy that is inherent in Point-last structures. [Colomb and Williams, 111]

Thus, when scientists *assume* their expert readers will enjoy "discovering" the conclusion with them, they miss the needs of management and even of other experts who could read more effectively with point-first structures. The result of relying on these academically based thinking and writing models is frustration—for both reader and writer.

## PARENT: THE PROFESSION

The first-generation offspring of the academic proto-parent are the models students learn for their professions. These, too, are academically based. Some, such as legal formats, are learned in the professional school itself (where students also learn a method of reasoning that may later appear in documents). Others, such as accounting models, are learned in preparation for certifying examinations such as the CPA exam. Finally, some are set by the professional system itself. Court report formats in the juvenile justice system are established by statewide guidelines and reinforced by judges, essentially the chief executive officers of the system. Whether required or simply traditional, these models powerfully shape the specific types of written discourse within the field. Many that I have seen look amazingly like the proto-parent academic report. These three examples from different professional discourse communities illustrate the resemblance.

### *The Patent Application*

Figure 1 shows a patent application that is traditionally arranged. The most important part of the application is the claims section. The applicant is not required to tell *how* the invention works, just that it does. In a sense, the claims are the "bottom line" of the document.

### *The Internal Audit Report*

The format for internal audit reports is also set by tradition. Irvin N. Gleim's *CIA Examination Review* (for Certified Internal Auditors) acknowledges that "internal

| | |
|---|---|
| Abstract | Brief statement of the invention. |
| Background | Sometimes called Prior Art; what previous related inventions exist. |
| Summary | The uses of the invention. |
| Description | Detailed explanation of the invention's components. |
| Figures | Drawings (may precede the description). |
| Claims | Summary of major advantages of the invention; each claim must be a single sentence; the sentences are *extremely* long (several paragraphs). |

*Figure 1*

audit reports do not have a prescribed format" (Gleims, 318–319). However, it presents samples from Sawyer's 1981 textbook entitled *The Practice of Modern Internal Auditing,* as the model to follow in preparing for the certification examination. Young auditors, without experience in the companies whose internal operations they will audit, learn the textbook model of Figure 2 as they prepare for their first professional hurdle. This model is closer to an executive summary, but it still places information of primary interest to the *accountant* before information of primary interest to *management.* The accountant is concerned with the status, goals, and scope of the audit. Management wants the results. In practice, this audit format *is* useful to management, but not as useful as it could be. (A more useful format for internal audit reports appears later in the article.)

| | |
|---|---|
| Summary | Brief overview of findings. |
| Introduction (Foreword) | Status of the audit. (Has it been completed?) |
| Statement of Purpose | Goals of the audit. |
| Statement of Scope | What was examined. |
| Statement of Opinion | Major conclusions. |
| Audit Findings | The body of the audit report discusses each opinion in detail. |
| | These are presented in this order:<br>    Summary<br>    Criteria<br>    Facts<br>    Cause<br>    Effect<br>    Recommendation<br>    Corrective action taken |

*Figure 2*

## The Certification Report

The final example of a prescribed professional format comes from the Oklahoma juvenile justice system. A certification report, written by a probation officer, is used by the judge in deciding whether or not a juvenile offender should stand trial (be certified) as an adult. The format is established in the state guidelines for court-related social workers and reinforced by most judges in the system. In Figure 3 the prescribed format is on the left and the heading outline of a typical report appears on the right. Both follow a modified chronological pattern, with recommendations coming at the end of the document: The 4½-page report reads like a story—just as the prescribed format intends.[4] Oklahoma social workers testify that the judges want to accumulate detail and form their own opinions as they read.

These three examples of professionally prescribed formats confirm several points. First, they exist and they are extremely powerful. Most people who write such documents insist that they *must* follow the format—even if it is not as useful for readers as it could be. Indeed, the expert readers in each discourse community expect information in the prescribed order and read accordingly. Second, most of these professional models are direct descendants of the academic term paper—background first, conclusions last. Only the internal audit report comes close to a

**Prescribed Format**

A. Any involvement in the juvenile justice system:
  1. Adjudications
  2. Deferred prosecutions
  3. Informal probation
B. Psychological evaluation
C. Assessment of family and community environment:
  1. Family relations
  2. Peer associations
  3. Academic experience
  4. Employment history
  5. Outside interests
D. Physical or mental impairments
E. Diagnostic impression the worker may have of the child
F. Worker's opinion of the reasonable prospects of rehabilitation and the protection of the public

**Actual Report**

*Nature of Offense*
"Prosecutive merit found indicating that _____ did commit an act, which if committed by an adult, would constitute the offense or murder . . ."

*Previous Record*

*Psychological Evaluation*

*Family Background*
(Parents and siblings)

*Academic History*
*Work History*

*Psycho/Social Summary*
(two full pages)

*Summary Analysis and Diagnostic Impressions*

*Treatment Potential*
(almost a full page)

cc: Judge
    D.A.
    Attorney (for youth)
    Family
    File—agency office

*Figure 3*

point-first structure, and even it presents the auditor's information (scope and objectives) first. Finally, these models spawn offspring in the other documents the same professionals write. Because these writers define their discourse community narrowly, they assume that clients, management, or other departments will understand and tolerate their professional model.

## The Result

The frustration this narrow definition of audience produces is illustrated by a fascinating, heated exchange that occurred one day in a seminar. The spark was the use of jargon, but I hear that the format of computer documentation is a comparable problem. The two employees served on a task force that brought together accountants and computer specialists to design computer programs for the accounting department of their oil company. When we began to discuss some computer jargon, the accountant exploded, "You throw all those terms at us in the meetings and don't explain what they mean. Or we become invisible. It doesn't seem to make any difference that we're there." The systems analyst shot back, "You don't need to understand the technicalities. Besides, explaining everything would take too much time. Just tell us what you want and we'll do it." The moral: Discourse-community boundaries blur in organizations. Nonexperts *want* to understand the information that affects them, and they want the information to be easily accessible.

## PARENT: THE ORGANIZATION

Because of the blurring of these professional boundaries, the immediate progenitor of the models in the file cabinet is the organization itself. In some cases, the models are set by company fiat. The famous Proctor and Gamble one-page memo is an example. Corporate style sheets are another. However, I find that sort of top-down control to be rare. Most of the models are set at the department level or by supervisors who impose their personal preferences on the writing of their subordinates.

Companies do have unique—often unrecognized—conceptions about what "writing" should be. Richard Freed and Glenn Broadhead argue that different companies have different norms: "Each organization is a different culture and each has different rules. And though each will use the English language and write the English language, the writing (and the attitudes about and behaviors during the writing) may very well be different" (Freed and Broadhead, 157). The earlier story about the scientist who moved from Company Y to Company X illustrates the difficulties these differences produce. In her 1987 CCCC presentation, Carol Lipsom told a similar story. In her "Company X," the rule was, "Do you want to get fired? Don't use 'I.'" The source of the rule was a 1955 memo. When a new young manager took over a lab unit, he tried to impose a deductive organizational format and an informal, lively style. The staff refused to change and began to seek transfers. They were concerned that outside readers would object. Furthermore, they had made the company a success, and the young upstart was going too far when he attacked their writing. They knew how to write *proper* scientific reports (Lipsom, 1987).

I hear the same story, although generally it is from subordinates who would like to use a deductive, informal approach that their older *supervisors* will not permit. But I have *never* seen a *companywide* prescribed format or style. In fact, the diversity of formats within a company can be the source of communication problems and employee frustration.

## *The Research Report*

A sequence of memos establishing the research-report format for technical laboratory divisions illustrates the historical resistance to standardization and the autonomy of group managers in establishing their personal preferences. In 1960, the head of the Production Research Division issued a memo establishing "a revised format" for their research reports (documents that may run up to 100 pages). His goal was to make the reports more useful to their primary audience: "Many

| *Headings* | *Paraphrase* |
|---|---|
| Purpose and Introduction | This will orient the reader as to why the study . . . was conducted. Brief, pertinent background material can be included. (6 to 8 lines) |
| Summary (or) Summary and Conclusions | This would briefly recapitulate the highlights of the Discussion part of the report. (A few lines to perhaps a page) |
| Conclusions | Certain specific conclusions should be set forth and enumerated. General conclusions can be incorporated under "Summary and Conclusions" in a short report. |
| Recommendations | If recommendations are made, they should be specifically set forth under this heading. |
| Pertinent Assumptions | The basic or controlling assumptions which limit the applicability of the conclusions should be listed. |
| Discussion | This is intended to elaborate on the "Summary and Conclusions" presented with the idea of emphasizing applications and limitations. |
| Appendix | The Appendix will include theory or mathematical development, procedure, and results. |

*Figure 4*

operating engineers only need and use certain portions of our reports as now prepared. This new format is intended to assist the operating engineer in using our research developments." Figure 4 summarizes his prescribed format.

In 1982, a different manager of the same research division issued a memo, again prescribing a format for the section's reports and memorandums. He attached a copy of the older memo and other reprints of articles about writing research reports. Figure 5 shows his format.

The first laboratory employees who attended my seminars *insisted* that this was the prescribed company format: introduction, summary, discussion. They were convinced that they could not use more descriptive headings or vary this format in the slightest. Later someone gave me a copy of the format from a different division (see Figure 6). Written in 1983, it defines the continuing problems with research reports and closely models the 1960 memo. Because of its concern for

| Headings | Paraphrase |
|---|---|
| Introduction | The "Introduction" should contain (1) the problem definitions in terms of the "big picture" to the company, (2) background information necessary to support the content of the report, and (3) a clear, concise purpose of the report. References to work or written documents closely related to the subject should be included. |
| Summary | The "Summary" section includes summary and concluding statements. It conveys to the reader in nontechnical terms . . . the highlights or most significant results of the work being reported. It shows how these results are of benefit to the company and therefore *sells* the report to the reader. |
| Discussion | One purpose of the "Discussion" is to provide less relevant and/or more detailed background information required by the reader but not included in the "Introduction" . . . The most important purpose of the "Discussion" is to provide sufficient information through verbiage, references, tables, figures, and appendices to technically support the statement within the "Summary" section. |
| Signature | The author signs the report . . . |
| References | Typed in the proper format used by SPE for technical publications. |
| Figures | |

*Figure 5*

## The File Cabinet Has a Sex Life · 165

Subject: Organization of Research Reports

During the last meeting we had some forthright feedback on our recent research reports. Perhaps the comments can best be paraphrased as "Some reports read like a mystery novel: one is left guessing until the very end."

I believe that this is a legitimate complaint and we should realize that many of our reports, while being given a wide distribution to promote accessibility, are often designed for a fairly limited audience. It is therefore not unreasonable to expect that a reader can, by scanning the abstract and early sections of a report, obtain a capsulated understanding of the entire volume. I request that reports be organized along the following lines:

| | |
|---|---|
| Abstract | Two or three main points of significance that result from the work being reported. . . . Abstracts which merely outline the nature of the work without providing conclusions are inappropriate. |
| Brief Introduction | This should cover, in summary form, the reason why the work was undertaken and a clear statement of who, we think, will be interested in the results. |
| Summary | This should be as brief as possible but include the key conclusions, recommendations and results. It should also include one to several sentences on procedures unless these would be obvious or of little or no significance. |
| Conclusions | This should be an itemized list of conclusions and should not contain any lengthy discussion material. It should be written in language that anyone, including managers, can understand. |
| Recommendations | This should be an itemized list of recommendations for action by Operations and also for continued or new research. Again, it should be brief, to the point, and in plain English. |
| Discussion | This is the body of the report and may be subdivided as appropriate. . . . This is the place you can write for other research scientists, specialized users, etc., as appropriate. Clarity is still a virtue. By all means keep in mind the objective of shortening the "Discussion" by using appendices when appropriate. |

*Figure 6*

both organization and style, it is the format I suggest in my seminars for this company.

One would think that this model was widely known and used in the organization. Unfortunately, that is not the case. Many scientists discover it for the first time in my seminar (and a few still insist that the model would not be accepted in their groups). Just as the 1960 format did not permanently standardize the company or even the division format, so too this model is prescribed only for the particular manager's group. Thus, despite the long existence of a superior model, the "format of choice" often remains the point-last structure of the academic model.

## PARENT: THE SUPERVISORY REVIEW

The most powerful control of organizational writing comes from the widespread practice of supervisory review. In many companies, the immediate supervisor must approve a document before it is sent. Thus, the personal preferences of supervisors (and/or their superiors) determine both the organization and the style of many employees' documents. The most local file cabinet literally rules.

There are several good reasons for having supervisors review subordinates' documents. Often the supervisor's name is at the bottom because protocol demands that people of equal rank correspond with each other. Thus, employees who ghostwrite for their supervisors try to emulate the writing practices of the "author." Also, supervisors want to ensure at least minimal uniformity in the documents that issue from their groups. Finally, they bring important company experience to the review; they understand corporate issues or politics that subordinates—especially new employees—may not know. One manager, in a memo on "Effective Writing," reveals the department's need for "better planning of reports, reviewing the content, and critiqueing the document before it is issued":

> Our written product is our sales tool to explain results, persuade others, defend our work, and to ask for money. Your success, and mine, is based firmly on the quality of your effort and the clarity with which that effort is communicated to management. Unreported or poorly documented work is lost forever; hence, my insistence that we report our work completely. To paraphrase General Electric's corporate motto: "In Research, paper is our most important product."

Many employees report that they have learned their successful writing techniques from strong supervisors who literally taught them how to write in the workplace.

However, the critiques on supervisory review are usually less glowing. Far too many employees are told, "This is the way we've always done it. You will, too." So outdated formats and style proliferate, protected by the supervisory review process itself. Several problems result. Because each supervisor has a different idea of what constitutes good writing, employees must change to meet the expectations of each new supervisor. One young man told me that in the eighteen months he had been with the company, he had had six different supervisors—each with a different style. "I don't know who I am," he said. Some supervisors insist on rewriting everything. Thus, the employee loses ownership of the document, doesn't learn revision techniques, and often develops an "I-don't-care" attitude. The time wasted in recycling perfectly adequate documents because of personal preferences of supervisors is a major cost to the organization. Ultimately, employees learn simply to accept the changes, get the needed approval, and send the document. The frustrations for both writer and reviewer are obvious.

This detailed explanation of the problems of supervisory review reveals why the file cabinet reproduces unrestrained. First, the *system* of writing in the workplace usually prevents change. It is safer and more efficient for writers to follow the old models rather than to suggest new ones. Therefore good models survive, but so do poor ones. Second, although employees draw on their own academic and professional experience in defining the nature of good writing, they are also *instructed* by their superiors. Thus, the real training in workplace writing is being conducted by "teachers" untrained in either rhetoric or pedagogy. It is a journeyman system in which the "master" controls powerful incentives for the "apprentice."

## THE EVOLUTION OF NEW MODELS

Since the system of writing in the workplace both creates and protects the models in the file cabinet, changing those models requires employee initiative and the rare willingness to take risks. Permanent change of writing throughout the organization also requires power. Thus, the solutions to writing problems evolve from some of the same sources as the old models: from individual choice, from strong managers, occasionally from a central corporate group. Change also can come from outside writing consultants. However, change rarely comes from academic or professional sources. Nor do I see it imposed from the top down in large companies. Therefore, most new formats remain localized. They are used within a small group which accepts them either because all agree that the new way is better or because a manager or supervisor has decreed that change will occur.

Most changes are solutions to audience problems; they are reader-based. Usually they are born because an individual is dissatisfied with "the way it's been done before." Sometimes the birth occurs because outside readers are complaining that they cannot understand documents. The recent, hesitant changes in computer documentation attest that eventually someone does listen to readers.

The creative models that follow reveal this reader orientation. All are examples of creative problem solving by individuals or managers. Except for one example from a central policies and procedures group, they are not widely used formats within the company (even though they may be widely read). Thus, their life spans within the file cabinet family may be limited by the longevity of their creators. These models do, however, illustrate the potential for improvement that exists in the workplace. They also reveal what we can learn from the problem-solving abilities of these writers.

### *The Paragraph*

One academic model employees carry reflects what a paragraph should look like. They "see" information presented in blocks of black type. Yet when asked how

**PRODUCTS, Inc.**

Date:
To:
From:
SUBJECT: Kit Alternatives

The original Log Plan for the _____ controller used 6 Regional offices for the _____ Kit distribution centers due to the high cost of the Third Program stated below. The 6 Regional Kits would cost $_____ dollars. But, one exposure in regards to that plan is establishing only 6 sites for _____ Kits [which] would be insufficient saturation of spare parts in the field.

Attached are three alternative Kit distribution cost analyses. The first program would consist of 12 centers, located at key Air Freight Hub Distribution sites at a cost of $_____. Second program consists of 14 centers, located at our own 6 Regional sites plus 8 addition Zones. Cost to establish this program would be $_____. The third program is the most costly at $_____. They would be distributed to all 129 Service Centers forecasted in the _____ Maintenance Plan.

---

**PRODUCTS, Inc.**

Date:
To:
From:
SUBJECT: Kit Alternatives

The original Log Plan for the _____ controller used 6 Regional offices for the Kit distribution centers due to the high cost of the Third Program stated below in "Alternatives." But, one exposure in regards to that plan is establishing only 6 sites for Kits [which] would be insufficient saturation of spare parts in the field.

Original Plan:
  6 Regional Kits = $_____

Alternatives:
  *First Program* = $_____
    Consists of 12 centers, located at Key Air Freight Hub Distribution sites.
  *Second Program* = $_____
    Consists of 14 centers, located at 6 Regional offices plus 8 addition Zones.
  *Third Program* = $_____
    Consists of all 129 Service Centers forecasted in the Maintenance Plan.

You will find attached cost analyses of the three Alternative programs for Kit distribution.

*Figure 7*

they prefer to receive information, everyone says, "with white space." Figure 7 shows what happened when a manufacturing supervisor was not satisfied with a simple memo he was writing. He went to his manager for help, who suggested listing the alternatives. Within thirty minutes, the employee produced the revised version, which is not only easier to read but also more complete. (Obviously it *does* still need some sentence-level revision.) The employee not only had not thought of using white space but also needed "permission" to change what a paragraph looked like.

## The Problem Report

The next examples show improved computer problem-report formats. Both formats were created by individuals dissatisfied with the old models. Figure 8 shows one approach. Written for an expert audience, its jargon is dense, but the format is extremely useful to the readers who need to know in a glance what has happened.

### Current Status of Reported DFHSM Problems

Below is a short description of the current DFHSM-reported problems, along with their status. I have also provided an impact statement which indicates the severity of the problem. If you require more information, please contact me.

| | |
|---|---|
| PROBLEM: | Abend S878 during automatic backup of VSAM volumes. |
| STATUS: | This problem has been reported to IBM and they have accepted an APAR (OYO5894). The documentation has been forwarded to IBM. The problem has been recorded as #00169 in the TDC problem database. |
| IMPACT: | Approximately every 72 hours, DFHSM will terminate with an Abend S878, typically during automatic backup of our VSAM volumes. At that time Operations will restart DFHSM, with little impact to the Operating System or client applications. |

| | |
|---|---|
| PROBLEM: | Message ARC1139I and ARC1239I (GDG Rollover problem and HMIGRATE failure respectively) |
| STATUS: | This problem has been reported to SSS/SKK. Providing the required documentation has proven to be difficult due to the amount of data required. Escalation of this problem has just begun, with the actual problem assignment to SSS. For more detailed information, refer to problem #01165 in the TDC problem database. |
| IMPACT: | These two error messages began after installation of the new release of ACF2 and have been nothing more than a nuisance. The user with the ARC1139I (GDG Rollover) would not terminate but just receive the message, and the ARC1239I message (HMIGRATE) was found during testing, and widespread user command awareness has yet to be accomplished. |

*Figure 8*

FILE: TLS      DOC0409   A      VM/SP CONVERSATIONAL MONITOR SYSTEM

UPDATE DESCRIPTION: ---------------------------------------------------------------
   DATE:         04/01/87 - CHECKED OUT
   DATE:         04/09/87 - TO PRODUCTION TEST
   DATE:         04/09/87 - THIS DOCUMENTATION FILE.
   FIX-ID #:     ----------
   CSS PROB #:   08347
   CSS PROJ #:   _____
   TYPE:         SOURCE FIX (FOR TLS).
   CHANGES BY:
   CHANGES TO:
      TLS.TSK ------------------------------------------------------------------- (UPDATED).
OTHER MODULES AFFECTED: (NONE).
PROBLEM:
   TLS sometimes gets into 'LOGGING' mode because of bad data in its copy of tape request information.
   This requires manual intervention to patch the TLS 'LOG' file in order to proceed out of LOGGING mode.
SOLUTION:
   TLS.TSK has been modified to validate the tape MCB information that it receives. (This data is checked only to verify that it is in the valid ASCII character range.)
   If invalid data is detected, the request is handled as follows:
      (1) If the request is for a 'CLOSE', a good return code is given back to TMS, but the information is NOT transmitted to the VM system.
      (2) For any other request, a bad return code is given back to TMS indicating that the request is INVALID.
   In either case (1) or (2) error messages are sent to the operator's console indicating that this situation has occurred.
   The following console messages are produced:
      .TLS: !!! -INVALID MCB DETECTED xxxxxxxxxxxxx    - !!!
      .TLS: !!! -FD=ffffffffff TSK=ttttttt             - !!!
      .TLS: !!! -REPORT THIS TO SSS MINI/MICRO,TULSA - !!!
   where . . .
      xxxxxxxxxxxxx = BEFORE VM MSG
                   or AFTER VMREPLY
                   or AFTER FILEDEF
      ffffffffff   = the file descriptor of the request
      ttttttt      = the task id initiating the request

IMPACT: USERS - (none)

IMPACT: PGMRS - (NONE)

IMPACT: OPERATIONS -
   If the above messages appear, operators are to record the information displayed in the first 2 messages.
   A copy of the console log should be retained.
   This information is to be reported to Software Support Services, Mini/Micro Systems, Tulsa.
   (No operator intervention is required.)

SPECIAL INSTRUCTIONS FOR INSTALLATION:
   (A) It is merely necessary to replace the old TLS.TSK by this new version.

*Figure 9a Original Version*

*The File Cabinet Has a Sex Life · 171*

FILE: TLS     DOCO824   A     VM/SP CONVERSATIONAL MONITOR SYSTEM

UPDATE DESCRIPTION: ------------------------------------------------------------------- 08/20/87
    CHANGES TO: TLS.TSK - (UPDATED).
    CHANGES BY:
    OTHER MODULES AFFECTED: (NONE).

    DATES:
        04/01/87 - Checked out for changes.
        08/19/87 - Sent to production test.

    PROBLEM:
        TLS sometimes gets into 'LOGGING' mode because of bad data in its copy of tape request information.
        This requires manual intervention to patch the TLS 'LOG' file in order to proceed out of LOGGING mode.

    SOLUTION:
        TLS.TSK has been modified to validate the tape MCB information that it receives. (This data is checked only to verify that it is in the valid ASCII character range.)
        If TLS detects invalid data, it handles the request as follows:
            (1) If the request is for a 'CLOSE', a good return code is given back to TMS, but the information is NOT transmitted to the VM system.
            (2) For any other request, a bad return code is given back to TMS indicating that the request is INVALID.
        In either case (1) or (2), TLS writes error messages to the operator console, as follows:
            .TLS: !!! -INVALID MCB DETECTED xxxxxxxxxxxx    - !!!
            .TLS: !!! -FD=ffffffffff TSK=ttttttt           - !!!
            .TLS: !!! -REPORT THIS TO SSS MINI/MICRO,TULSA - !!!
        where . . .
            xxxxxxxxxxxx  =  BEFORE VM MSG
                            or AFTER VMREPLY
                            or AFTER FILEDEF
            ffffffffff        =  the file descriptor of the request
            ttttttt           =  the task id initiating the request

    IMPACT:    OPERATIONS -
        If the above messages appear, operators should record the information displayed in the first 2 messages.
        A copy of the console log should be retained.
        Report this information to Software Support Services, Mini/Micro Systems, Tulsa.
        (TLS processing will proceed normally; no operator intervention is required.)

    IMPACT:    USERS - (none)

    IMPACT:    PGMRS - (NONE)

    SPECIAL INSTRUCTIONS FOR INSTALLATION:
        It is merely necessary to replace the old TLS.TSK by this new version.

---

*Figure 9b Revised Version*

Figure 9 reveals the evolution of a problem/solution format. The author, who is not at all reticent about changing inadequate models, had already modified the file-cabinet model to produce the document on the left. After the discussion of audience, purpose, and format in my writing seminar, he reworked his own improvements. He said, "When I looked at my report, I realized there wasn't any reason to have all those introductory lines. They weren't there for any purpose." He also made some stylistic changes, tightening and clarifying his instructions by replacing passive verbs. The result is a much cleaner and clearer report.

## *The Management-Oriented Report*

The next two samples function in similar company contexts and offer similar reader-based solutions. The sources of poor models for both the credit analysis and the internal audit report are discussed earlier in this article. In both improved models, the managers established the format for reports emanating from their departments. In both cases, the documents are read by higher managers and executives who base important decisions on the information contained in the report. Therefore, both formats begin with an executive summary, just as the successful research report format did.

## *The Credit Analysis*

This credit-analysis format entered the bank's file cabinet when a new manager of the Credit Department arrived. He had used it in the bank he came from.[5] The four-page description of the format closely details the contents of each section. Figure 10 is an abbreviated outline, with my comments in parentheses.
    This format not only permits the senior loan committee to understand the significant credit issues at a glance but also helps the young analysts who write the reports. As participants in a management training program, they are inundated with new information about the banking industry and about credit issues. Deciding what information is important from the mass of data is difficult enough. They would be lost without a report format. In their training, their supervisor and I use a case-study approach to teach them how to analyze the data concurrently with how to write the reports. We work through the *process* of writing a credit analysis. Thus, when they write their first real reports, they have already practiced with a solid model rather than having to grope for their own.

## *The Internal Audit Report*

The process of writing is also important in the following internal audit report format. The format itself improves upon the traditional pattern outlined in the *CIA Examination Review* cited earlier. But the manager of this audit department has also set up a system in which the auditors meet with key "clients" in the department being audited to go over the rough draft of the report. His goal is to eliminate the image of auditors as policemen who raid, looking for crime. Discuss-

**Analysis Format**

I. **PURPOSE** (of the loan)
   A. Name of Borrower
   B. Purpose of Loan
   C. Amount of Loan
   D. Participation Details
   E. Description of the Commitment
   F. Price of Loan
   G. Date of Maturity
   H. Secured or Unsecured
   I. Source of Repayment
   J. Guarantee
   K. Anticipated Level of Usage (If Credit Line)

II. **BASIS OF ANALYSIS**
   A. State financial statements reviewed
   B. Did these statements provide the proper basis of analysis for this request? . . .

III. **SUMMARY AND SIGNIFICANT CREDIT ISSUES** (Executive Summary that covers key points from the discussion)
   A. Operating Performance
   B. Strengths and Weaknesses of Financial Condition assessed in terms of cash flow
   C. Debt Serviceability
   D. Significant Factors which may affect the company's future performance and/or ability to service its debt obligations . . .

IV. **CONCLUSION**

   Determination of risk based on the company's financial strength and repayment ability as reviewed in your analysis and in consideration of the type of credit request.

V. **BACKGROUND**

   (Information about the company's history and products.)

VI. **OPERATIONS**

   Begin with a conclusive topic sentence pertaining to the performance of sales and of income. The first part of operations should give main reasons for changes in the income statement.
   A. Sales/Revenues
   B. Cost of Goods Sold
   C. Changes in General, Selling and Administrative Expenses
   D. Interest Expense
   E. Operating Profit/Net Profit After Tax
   F. Recap of Major Factors Leading the Net Income Changes
   G. Appraisal of Operations

VII. **FINANCIAL POSITION**

   The cash flow should be used to explain the liquidity and leverage sections. Each of these sections should begin with a conclusive topic sentence. If each of the sections is long, then a beginning summary of financial position could be a lead into this part of the analysis.

*Figure 10*

*Figure 10 (Continued)*

      A. Liquidity (several detailed sections)
      B. Leverage (several detailed sections)

VIII. **DEBT SERVICE**
Interpret results of the debt service analysis in view of the credit request . . .

IX. **COLLATERAL QUALITY**

X. **STRENGTH OF GUARANTEE**

XI. **INDUSTRY OUTLOOK**

XII. **APPENDICES**
(financial worksheets and calculations)

ing the report at a draft stage reveals possible misunderstandings and permits revisions. Since the "clients" are one of the primary audiences of the report and have a major stake in what it says, the review step is the ultimate in reader sensitivity. Interestingly, this is the second environment where I have heard the statement, "Paper is our most important product." The other was the Research Center manager.

Figure 11 shows the improved format of these audit reports. With permission from the manager, I am reproducing several pages of an actual report. Notice the one-page, action-oriented summary, the second page introduction and conclusion, the recommendation-first organization of each finding, and the delay of scope and objectives until the last page.

This report format meets the needs of all its readers: the executives who need to know the big picture, the departmental managers who need to improve methods of operation within their responsibility, individuals within the audited department who are responsible for only one of the findings, and the team of auditors who need a consistent report format that their supervisor and manager will approve. Even with the good model, these reports go through a thorough review process—including the preliminary review with the "client" department—before being issued.

## *The Procedure*

The final example of a successful format is the offspring of a central policy and procedures department. It is based on Playscript, a technique that I encounter only occasionally. Most procedures I see follow the old block-paragraph format, with no introduction and the action buried in passive verbs in midsentence. However, this company is imposing a different format because it is in a unique position to do so. The company is growing rapidly. It is no longer an everybody-knows-everybody size. As a result of this growth—both in geographical distance and in corporate size—extensive policies and procedures are being written for the first time. (However, the same standardization does not extend to other company documents.) Although I have serious problems with the clarity of the headings, Figure 12 reveals a very useful format.

These examples show that change can occur in the file cabinet. The docu-

*The File Cabinet Has a Sex Life · 175*

# CONFIDENTIAL
## INTERNAL AUDIT REPORT

| COMPANY | Petroleum, Inc. | AUDIT SUBJECT AND LOCATION | Petroleum, Inc. — Supply and Distribution and Wholesale Marketing City, State |
|---|---|---|---|
| AUDIT NO. |  | | |
| AUDIT DATE | August 26, 1986 | | |

**SUMMARY AUDIT RESULTS:**

Our audit of the Petroleum, Inc., Supply and Distribution (S&D) and Wholesale Marketing Departments indicated excellent compliance by both departments to internal and operational controls in the areas of exchange and spot contract administration and documentation, supply forecast and inventory control information systems and wholesale product pricing.
Our review, however, indicated the need for Management attention to:

Utilization of data base software to operate current department information systems more effectively,

Implementation of a refined products quality control program,

Expansion of retail sales forecast procedures, and

Establishment of freight verification procedures.

Mr. _____ and Mr. _____ agreed to the audit comments and recommendations. Mr. _____ indicated that the implementation of improvements relative to quality control, sales forecasting and freight verification procedures would depend on involvement by the Retail Division and the Accounting Department. Presently, the S&D Department has been assigned neither the specific responsibility nor the manpower to direct such activities.

| Please read and reply as indicated **using the response format set out on the reverse side.** Forward your reply and other comments to:<br>(Please provide copies of the response to each report recipient.) | GENERAL AUDITOR |
|---|---|

| COPIES OR EXCERPTS TO: | LOCATION | PARAGRAPHS | REPLY REQUIRED |
|---|---|---|---|
| Name | City, State | All | No |
| Name | City, State | All | No |
| Name | City, State | All | No |
| Name | City, State | All | Yes |
| Name | City, State | All | No |
| **Deloitte Haskins & Sells** | Tulsa, Oklahoma | All | No |
| —Central Files | Tulsa, Oklahoma | All | No |

| ▶ YOUR COPY | APPROVED BY | Audit Manager | DATE | August 26, 1986 |
|---|---|---|---|---|

*Figure 11*

*Figure 11 (Continued)*

TO: Audit Manager                                                      DATE: August 26, 1986

FROM: Auditors

SUBJECT: Petroleum, Inc.                                    Reference: PE-00-00
          Supply and Distribution
          and Wholesale Marketing of
          Finished Product

---

I. *Audit Summary*

*Introduction*

An internal audit of the Supply and Distribution and Wholesale Marketing Departments of Petroleum, Inc., was performed during the period of June 9 through July 25, 1986. The audit was completed by _____ and _____ and included three weeks of fieldwork at the _____ Refinery.

The audit scope and objectives are summarized in Section II of this report.

*Audit Issues: Control Practices and Procedures*

The results of our audit indicated excellent compliance by the two departments, Supply and Distribution and Wholesale Marketing, in carrying out their functions in accordance with Management's directives.

During the first quarter of 1986, the efforts of both departments were plagued significantly by ESI software problems affecting the truck rack reporting system, unfavorable variances in exchange, wholesale, and retail demand, volatile market prices, and the performance of a refinery turnaround. Continuing attention, however, appears to be directed toward each of these areas as well as toward developing integrated strategies of inventory control and marketing.

Audit issues requiring Management's consideration and action noted during the audit were as follows:

*Figure 11 (Continued)*

| | |
|---|---|
| Subject: Supply, Distribution & Wholesale Marketing of Finished Product Audit | To: Audit Manager<br>Prepared by: Auditors<br>Date: August 26, 1986 |
| Ref: PE-oo-00 | |
| Page 2 | |

A. *The Supply and Distribution Department should evaluate the feasibility of networking department microcomputers or using Data Base software to operate current department information systems more effectively.*

During our audit, we reviewed the Supply and Distribution (S&D) Department's various information systems relating to forecasting, inventory control, and product scheduling. We noted several instances in which the same information is used repeatedly and input to different microcomputers.

Presently, these S&D systems are not integrated and an information data base does not exist. Consequently, all communication of information between staff members must be done manually. The data used at each microcomputer workstation must be input separately into each spreadsheet or report used by that system.

In the absence of an integrated system, the potential exists for the following:

- Input error
- Inconsistent information
- Inefficient time usage
- Inadequate response time needed to analyze changes in production or the marketplace

Consolidation of data across the functional areas of forecasting, inventory control, and scheduling should improve the quality of information in addition to streamlining information gathering procedures.

*Discussions with Management*

Since the audit Mr. _____ has initiated discussions with a consultant currently contracted to establish data base systems for the _____ Transportation Department. Mr. _____ has also emphasized input quality control procedures to improve information generated by the current systems.

## Figure 11 (Continued)

| | | |
|---|---|---|
| Subject: | Supply, Distribution & Wholesale Marketing of Finished Product Audit | To: Audit Manager<br>Prepared by: Auditors<br>Date: August 26, 1986 |
| Ref:<br>Page 4 | PE-00-00 | |

II. Audit Scope and Objectives

Our audit scope encompassed _____ supply, distribution and marketing activities during the twelve months preceding the audit, with particular emphasis on January through May 1986. Also included was a limited review of _____ International spot market transactions.

The primary objectives of the audit were to assess the reasonableness of:
- Supply forecast and inventory control information systems,
- Exchange and spot contract administration and documentation,
- Wholesale product pricing and marketing procedures, and
- Exchange accounting procedures.

III. Audit Conclusion

A draft copy of the report was reviewed by Messrs. _____ and _____. General concurrence to the audit recommendations was expressed. To complete the audit process on a timely basis, a written response is requested from Mr. _____ by September 26, 1986.

We wish to express our appreciation to the staff members in both the Supply and Distribution and the Wholesale Marketing Departments as well as in _____ International for the excellent cooperation and assistance we received during our audit.

_____     _____
Internal Audit Manager              Senior Auditor

_____
Associate Auditor

Prepared by:

Date:

Subject:

Reviewed by:

| | |
|---|---|
| Statement: | This procedure outlines the steps to be followed for a Policy Replacement unit. |
| Applicability: | This procedure applies to all sales office locations, Central Order Processing, Customer Administration, and Traffic. |
| Definition: | A Policy Replacement is the replacement of units, features, or parts at _____'s option at no cost to the customer, when the replacement is not required by warranty or other contractual obligation. |
| Related Documents: | Procedures Manual<br>Form SO33 — Field Equipment Deinstallation and Move Authorization |
| Procedure: | Responsibility        Step/Action |

| Responsibility | Step/Action |
|---|---|
| Customer | 1. Notifies Sales Office to request a change of equipment. |
| Sales Office | 2. Obtains necessary approvals from Central. |
| | 3. Cuts a new Sales Order for requested equipment per OEP Procedures. |
| | 4. Makes a note in the Special Comments section of the sales order, "Policy Replacement" and records the serial numbers of the units being replaced. |
| | 5. Forwards sales order package to Central Order Processing.<br>NOTE: The Sales Office DOES NOT release the sales order to Manufacturing. |
| Central Order Processing | 6. Processes sales order according to OEP Procedures. |

*Figure 12*

ments are more effective because they meet readers' needs to acquire information efficiently. Not one of them looks like an academic paper, nor do they follow the prescribed professional formats. But they are good because they work within the organization.

## The Role of the Writing Consultant

One source of new models deserves comment: Some companies are beginning to turn to writing consultants for improved models. With the increasing recognition of the importance of moving information efficiently in an information society (almost a cliché these days), the demand for writing consultants is increasing. But the demand usually takes the form of seminars for employees, not a communications audit or redesign of departmental formats. Janice Redish, herself a protoparent of document design, echos the resistance to change that I, too, see in companies:

> Our initial projects with new clients are often conducted as exceptions to company standards. This requires a strong project leader on the client's side who will justify the exception in the first place and will then work with us to convince reviewers throughout the project. . . . Although we have written manuals that are exceptions to company or agency standards in several fields, the new reader-oriented style has caught on only in the computer field. Marketplace pressures operate here, but they do not operate in the field of military technical manuals, government policy manuals or employee benefit handbooks. [Redish, 149]

Even when a consultant is hired to improve the communication system, the resistance to change is enormous.

Thus, the influence of consultants is limited, often because we work at the same local level that the problem-solving employees do. We generally work with individuals in seminars rather than with the corporate system. Top management may pay lip service to improvements in company writing, but they rarely take the time either to attend the training itself or to set up management briefings. Even in reviewing sample documents, we see only pieces of the whole communication system. We are hired to improve "skills" rather than to attack productivity issues. Finally, we have little influence within the organization because good writing is not quantifiable; it is not seen as a bottom-line issue. Thus, our influence in solving company writing problems remains personal and localized.

## *The File-Cabinet Style*

So far my primary concern has been the sources of document formats that the file cabinet reproduces. However, the same forces establish the style of workplace documents. In fact, the resistance to change in style is even more powerful than to change in format. From one industry to another, in private and public sectors, I see conformity to the pedantic style: formal vocabulary, excessive nominalization, passive verbs, long sentences. The plain style is the refreshing exception rather than the rule. Thus, I was amazed to read, in *The Journal of Business Communication*, that "There is no doubt that the plain style of short words in short sentences is the 'house character' of the contemporary business community" (Mendelson 15). That simply is not the case.

The resistance to the plain style does *not* come from the top. I know of no corporate executive who says, "Impress me with big words and long sentences." I know of many who complain about the complexity of the documents they must read. Yet employees often think that writing that goes up the authority ladder must be impressive—that is, formal and complex. No company style book (or composition textbook, for that matter) promotes a wordy, difficult style. Quotes from the Air Force Academy's Executive Writing Course are typical:

> Obscure, pretentious, wordy, indirect language obscures thought and fact. Use plain ordinary English. Be economical with words. Use active voice.
> —General William G. Moore, Jr.
> Be selective. Be concise. Don't tell someone what you know; tell them what they need to know, what it means, and why it matters.
> —General David C. Jones
> Informal writing is now the Air Force writing style.
> —AFP 1302, p. 34.

Most company directives echo these statements. They assert, as the research manager did, "Write in language that anyone, even managers, can understand."

But the pedantic style prevails. A few examples will suffice.

From the oil industry:

> Gentlemen:
> The necessary attention has been rendered the division order afforded this office affecting the captioned, and the same is returned herewith for your further handling. The extra copy of the form has been retained for our file completion.

From an attorney:

> Therefore please find enclosed herewith a copy of our authorization to examine those accounts. It is requested that we be allowed to examine, from a period beginning January 1, 1981, through and including July 30, 1981, any and all accounting statements of account, record of transactions, etc., of the above referenced and numbered accounts. Further, it is requested that we be provided with a list of all accounts which have or are maintained at your institution, together with the account numbers thereof, for
> either _____ and _____ Corporation.

From a lobby sign in a New York bank:

> All checks presented for encashment must be endorsed in the teller's presence.

Fortunately none of these examples comes from my clients. Seminar participants have passed them along for my amusement. But they are not much worse than some samples I see every day.

### *Stylistic Parents*

Why, then, do people write this way? They *think* they are supposed to. Lee Odell says that the writer may be influenced by the culture of the organization, by internalized values, attitudes, knowledge, and ways of acting (Odell, 250). Indeed, companies often have a perceived "semantic environment" that maintains the formal, wordy style. For example, one middle manager's defense of his almost unintelligible prose was typical: "I know that the vocabulary muddies the meaning, but that's what my superiors want. I have to write that way." Although I doubt the accuracy of his assessment, his *perception* remains. I hear the same sort of comments from individuals in every field.

What are the sources of that perception?

1. *Individuals want to sound professional.* They fear that they will not be taken seriously if they use short words in short sentences. The younger or more insecure they are, the more likely they are to cling to the safety of the impressive pedantic style.

2. *The academic world rewards complexity.* Students learn early on that big words and long sentences produce longer papers and higher grades. J. Scott Armstrong, a Wharton School professor, tested his theory that written complexity increases academic acceptance. He gave easy or difficult versions of four passages to management professors to rate "the competence of the research that is being reported." The professors were not told the name of the journal or the author. Consistently, the professors rated the easy versions lower than the more difficult ones (Horn, 12).

3. *The professional discourse community requires the style.* For example, the patent application claims cited earlier must be one sentence each, even if each sentence runs several paragraphs long. However, professional guidelines sometimes encourage the plain style, as does the *CIA Examination Review* for internal auditors: "The writing should be kept simple, letting nothing get in the way of the transfer of ideas from writer to reader. . . . Writing should be kept lively, using action words to command attention." (Gleim, 322). But the prevailing use of professional boilerplate convinces most accountants that professional standards require a ponderous style.

4. *The supervisory review process reinforces the older, more formal style.* Even if employees want to use a more direct, concise style, their supervisors change it. Sometimes, supervisors fear clarity; they cannot be held accountable if no one understands the document. More often, they insist on the formal style because it is "professional." After all, they have gotten to their current positions using it. Why change now?

Thus, in spite of widespread recognition that the plain style is more efficient and, therefore, increases productivity, the file cabinet continues to reproduce an inflated, verbose style. However, stylistic change is also possible—but not without management support. According to one technical writer, for at least eight years users had requested computer documentation that was easier to read. The style began to change only after the manager attended my writing seminar and accepted the idea that documentation could be clear *and* professional. Now the programmers who write the manuals use "you," active verbs, etc. The resulting "new" style is much more reader-sensitive:

> This being your first time to log on, you will have no files in your library. Type "list" and hit enter to see if you have any files (this is just for your information.)
> . . .
> Type in your log-on password.

The screen will go blank for a few minutes. Then you will see a screen full of PF key selections . . .

In the past the programmers followed an established "computer style." A manager had to give them permission to change. Changes in style, as well as in format, often require a champion.

## *The Future: Selective Reproduction*

Who is responsible for cleaning out the file cabinet?

Everyone.

Because teachers, the academic world, individuals in the workplace, supervisors and managers, and the corporate culture all contribute the models that thrive in the file cabinet, they must all cooperate to replace archaic models with superior descendants. Consultants, too, must accept the challenge.

## *The Challenge for Teachers*

Teachers of composition should examine their academic heritage, course content, and teaching methods. Most of us chose to be English teachers because we loved literature and valued the liberal arts tradition. However, according to Freed and Broadhead, our own "culture" imposes blinders: "We taught and perhaps even believed [the sacred rhetoric text] because it was given, there before us, and there before our being there, though we rarely recognized its sacredness because it was a code without saying" (Freed and Broadhead, 163). Many of us teach the way we were taught. But we do not have to abandon these values to recognize the broader needs of our students.

Increasingly, voices in our profession are promoting change (Flower, 1981; Holcombe and Stein, 1981; Odell, 1985; Redish, 1985; Halpern, 1985; Hairston, 1986). These writers suggest that the goal of writing instruction should be broader than simply preparing students for academic writing. We should teach strategies for solving both academic *and* professional writing problems. Students should become the creative problem solvers who improve the content of the file cabinet.

How can we achieve that broader goal?

1. *Students should learn a variety of models instead of the limited models of the academic tradition.* They should learn to use executive summaries, white space, visual cues such as headings and figures, the icons that are coming with the electronic revolution, etc.

2. *The classroom should duplicate the context of the workplace.* I do *not* mean that students should be writing letters and memos. But they should write to real audiences, for real purposes. They should learn techniques for collaborative writing. They should practice constructive critiqueing techniques to prepare for the writing review process. They should pay real penalties for poor or sloppy writing. As David Lauerman and his colleagues report, such a change in classroom practices "made us alter some preconceptions: writing became practice, rather than a test;

prose models (i.e., essays?) were replaced by samples; rules gave way to strategies. The classroom became a busier and noisier place" (Lauerman et al., 450).

3. *Writing assignments should test students' problem-solving skills.* Students are pragmatic; they value realistic assignments. Lauerman, Barbara Couture et al., and Anderson report considerable success with writing assignments that duplicate workplace problems. I concur. After I began consulting, the methods I used in teaching freshman composition changed significantly for the better. So did the results.

4. *Teachers need to understand the writing requirements of the workplace.* Experience is the best teacher, but many teachers have only academic experience. Some colleges are instituting writing internships for their writing majors. Perhaps future teachers of English—both secondary and college level—should have practice in the workplace as well as practice in teaching.

These are not new or startling recommendations. Most have been proposed elsewhere. But I must add my voice: We *must* change the traditional methods of teaching writing. They are failing our students.

## The Challenge for the Academy

The academic world should examine its own models. The academic essay, term paper, and thesis enjoy a distinguished history. They have worked well in shaping students' ideas. But the old models assume a narrow result: the scholar graduate. How can we broaden (not replace) that limited goal?

1. *Writing requirements should change throughout the academic community.* Writing-across-the-curriculum programs have been an important beginning, but they have not gone far enough. Armed with new understanding of the writing students will do when they graduate, we should help other departments design writing assignments and contexts that duplicate the workplace environment. For example, M.B.A. theses and scientific lab reports that focus only on method rather than results should be placed on the endangered species list.

2. *The academic community has much to learn from the creative writers in the workplace about more effective ways to communicate ideas.* Perhaps the traditional scholarly paper needs to be examined. Recent changes in the MLA Style Sheet are a first step, but what about different uses of visual clues, the appearance of paragraphs, summary pages, and readable style? Just as parents can learn modern ideas from their mature children, so, too, the proto-parent can learn from its precocious offspring.

## The Challenge for the Workplace

Companies and agencies should understand that clear writing is a bottom-line issue. Many companies worry about correct expression as a reflection of the corporate image. But their corporate culture does not promote effective formats or efficient style. They fail to recognize that productive information transfer is as important as a productive assembly line.

1. *Companies should examine the models in their file cabinets.* These models

should face the same standards of productivity as do the manufactured or service product of the company: standards of efficient production, high quality, and cost-effectiveness. The resulting better models will lower communication barriers instead of creating them. How can we become a modern information society if we are operating with archaic equipment?

2. *Companies should also evaluate the supervisory review process, not to abolish it but to improve it.* If the real "teaching" of writing in the workplace occurs at the supervisory level, that teaching should focus on shared corporate goals and objectives, the standards mentioned above. Also, supervisors who review subordinates' writing should learn techniques for productive reviews. Reducing the length of the rewriting cycle and the frustration of all participants will increase employee efficiency.

## The Challenge for Consultants

Writing consultants should change their self-image from trainers to true consultants. Since many of us come from an English department background, we carry a service-course mentality. We must recognize the value of our knowledge and, thus, "see" ourselves differently. A consultant is a change agent.

1. *Our role will change if we understand that writing is central, not peripheral, to a company's success.* We will still present writing seminars for employees. But we will also dare to approach top management about improving the communication system. This step requires the courage to push for significant change; it is the same courage required of the problem-solving employees who change the models in the file cabinet. Certainly, we better serve our clients if we apply all our expertise, not just our teaching skills.

2. *Consultants should become the pipeline of improved models.* We have the opportunity to draw on the exciting research being conducted in rhetorical theory and practice. We also have the rare advantage of access to the creative but localized models such as those shown in this article. But we need a mechanism for sharing these new models without violating our ethical responsibility of confidentiality to our clients. Last year, at a leadership conference of the Association of Professional Writing Consultants, we discussed publishing an annual digest of "good models" submitted by consultants around the country. Such a digest, when it becomes a reality, will allow access to new models for writing consultants and for their clients.

3. *A word of caution: Consultants should not become too comfortable within one discourse community.* In her CCCC presentation, Carol Lipsom cautioned, "Consultant beware." But her advice was that we need to listen to and attend to the local culture, to gauge the internal corporate politics in which employees refuse to change. Although I share her concern for self-preservation, I reject the notion that my job is simply to fit into the local system. In a sense, I'm in trouble in my consulting role if I am too comfortable with the company jargon, formats, and style. As change agents, we should be *improving* the old models, not simply nurturing the reproductive cycle.

The file cabinet will continue to reproduce. Employees—both novice and experienced—will turn to it for models of what has been done before. Our concern as teachers of writing, as members of the academic community, or as writing consultants in the workplace should be the quality of the models being reproduced. Will the old dinosaurs continue to thrive, or will creative evolution occur?

## Notes

1. Paradis et al. explain the problems created for a new employee who tried to reproduce on paper the *process* of his problem solving; his manager and supervisor criticized his eight-page report because the recommendations were buried in the final section. But the employee wanted his reasoning to be reviewed; "his logic was as important to him as the recommendation itself." Because students learn in college writing assignments that the quality of the writing *effort* counts, they are left with no alternative model oriented to the organization's needs (300–302).
2. Lester Faigley, in defining "discourse communities," seems to agree with the scientists. He strongly implies that documents are used only within restricted professional or company contexts. "Texts are almost always written for persons in restricted groups" (238).
3. Robert Bataille's questionnaire results from Iowa State engineering and industrial administration alumni underlines the importance of audiences outside the writer's field of expertise. These alumni said they wrote 33 percent of their documents to co-workers or superiors somewhat or more outside their field. After adding the documents they wrote to the public or to customers, they estimated that 54 percent of all their writing was directed to a lay audience (278).
4. Russell Rutter reports a similar format for presentence reports in Illinois. He states that some judges do not *want* evaluations and recommendations (291).
5. I have not seen a similar format in my other banking clients' files. In fact, credit analysts at a rival bank resisted adopting it because "that's not the format we use here." As far as I could tell, the rival *had* no established format. In contrast, the regional bank executive I quoted earlier liked the approach because it would solve his Thursday evening reading frustration.

## Works Cited

Anderson, Paul V. "What Survey Research Tells Us About Writing at Work." *Writing in Nonacademic Settings.* Ed. Lee Odell and Dixie Goswami. New York: Guilford, 1985, pp. 3–83.

Bataille, Robert R. "Writing in the World of Work: What Our Graduates Report." *College Composition and Communication* 33(1982):276–280.

Colomb, Gregory G., and Joseph M. Williams. "Perceiving Structure in Professional Prose: A Multiply Determined Experience." *Writing in Nonacademic Settings.* Ed. Lee Odell and Dixie Goswami. New York: Guilford, 1985, pp. 87–128.

Couture, Barbara, Jone Rymer Goldstein, Elizabeth Quiroz. "Building a Professional Writing Program Through a University-Industry Collaborative." *Writing in Nonacademic Settings.* Ed. Lee Odell and Dixie Goswami. New York: Guilford, 1985, pp. 391–426.

Faigley, Lester. "Nonacademic Writing." *Writing in Nonacademic Settings.* Ed. Lee Odell and Dixie Goswami. New York: Guilford, 1985, pp. 231–248.

Flower, Linda. *Problem-Solving Strategies for Writing.* New York: Harcourt, Brace, Jovanovich, 1981.

Freed, Richard C., and Glenn J. Broadhead. "Discourse Communities, Sacred Texts, and Institutional Norms." *College Composition and Communication* 38(1987):154–165.

Gleim, Irvin N. *CIA Examination Review*, 2nd ed. Gainesville, Fla.: Accounting Publications, 1984.

Hairston, Maxine. "Different Products, Different Processes: A Theory About Writing." *College Composition and Communication* 37(1986):442–452.

Halpern, Jeanne W. "An Electronic Odyssey." *Writing in Nonacademic Settings.* Ed. Lee Odell and Dixie Goswami. New York: Guilford, 1985, pp. 157–201.

Harwood, John T. "Freshman English Ten Years After: Writing in the World." *College Composition and Communication* 33(1982):281–283.

Holcombe, Marya W., and Judith K. Stein. *Writing for Decision Makers: Memos and Reports with a Competitive Edge.* Belmont, Calif.: Lifetime Learning, 1981.

Horn, Jack C. "Bafflegab Pays." *Psychology Today* May 1980: 12.

Lauerman, David A., Melvin W. Schroeder, Kenneth Sroka, and E. Roger Stephenson. "Workplace and Classroom: Principles for Designing Writing Courses." *Writing in Nonacademic Settings.* Ed. Lee Odell and Dixie Goswami. New York: Guilford, 1985, pp. 427–450.

Lipsom, Carol. Conference on College Composition and Communication, Atlanta, Ga. March 1987.

Mathes, J. C., and Dwight W. Stevenson. "Completing the Bridge: Report Writing in 'Real Life' Engineering Courses." *Engineering Education* Nov. 1976: 154–158.

Mendelson, Michael. "Business Prose and The Nature of the Plain Style." *The Journal of Business Communication* 24 (1987):3–18.

Moore, Leslie E., and Linda H. Peterson. "Convention as Connection: Linking the Composition Course to the English and College Curriculum." *College Composition and Communication* 37 (1986): 466–477.

Odell, Lee. "Beyond the Text: Relations Between Writing and Social Context." *Writing in Nonacademic Settings.* Ed. Lee Odell and Dixie Goswami. New York: Guilford, 1985, pp. 249–280.

Paradis, James, David Dobrin, and Richard Miller. "Writing at Exxon ITD: Notes on the Writing Environment of a Research and Development Organization." *Writing in Nonacademic Settings.* Ed. Lee Odell and Dixie Goswami. New York: Guilford, 1985, pp. 281–307.

Redish, Janice C., Robbin M. Battison, and Edward S. Gold. "Making Information Accessible to Readers." *Writing in Nonacademic Settings.* Ed. Lee Odell and Dixie Goswami. New York: Guilford, 1985, pp. 129–153.

Rutter, Russell. "Teaching Writing to Probation Officers: Problems, Methods, and Resources. *College Composition and Communication* 33 (1982): 288–295.

U.S. Air Force Academy. *Executive Writing Course.* USAF Academy, Co., 79/0726.

# WRITING IN THE MILITARY: A DIFFERENT MISSION

*Nancy G. Wilds*
Armed Forces Staff College

Nancy G. Wilds is a professor of English at the Armed Forces Staff College in Norfolk, Virginia, where she has directed the writing program for the past ten years. Her students are military officers at the midcareer level who are taking a six-month course in preparation for joint staff assignments at the Pentagon and worldwide. She also serves as consultant to other agencies in the Department of Defense in their development of writing programs for adult professionals.

For a variety of reasons, the armed forces constitute one of the better-hidden discourse communities in American society. Ask any group of college composition instructors how much they know about military writing, generically or specifically, and you are likely to get responses ranging from "very little" to "less than nothing." The isolation of the military from the rest of this society is nothing new, of course. America's founders built that isolation into the documents that codified the new nation's values and aspirations; and except during rare periods of national emergency, the concept of separateness has prevailed. Certainly World War II forced an extraordinary coalition of effort; the Vietnam conflict, on the other hand, led to deep estrangement, especially between the defense and the academic communities. Now, although that breach appears to be healing, the absence of a peacetime draft reduces the opportunity and inclination for interaction between the military and the public at large.

Under these circumstances, it is not hard to see why—despite composition researchers' current interest in examining the influences of social context on organizational writing—little attention has been paid to the types and purposes of writing done in the armed forces. Furthermore, a certain invisibility results from the fact that very little military writing is "public" in the way that business, legal, or other government writing often is. Under ordinary conditions, the armed services do not have to deal with broad client groups as do, for example, the Internal

The views expressed in this chapter are solely those of the author and do not necessarily reflect those of the Department of Defense or the Armed Forces Staff College.

Revenue Service, a large insurance company, or a state educational system. The fact remains, however, that with some 5 million members, the military is this country's largest employer; and its written output—even though removed from the purview of most of us—represents a significant portion of the organizational discourse in our society.

The most interesting aspect of all this writing—for taxpayers as well as for researchers—is the fact that it is currently the subject of internal controversy. A movement is under way to bring about a radical change in both the quantity and the quality of military writing. Top-level military leaders are recognizing the inefficiencies and waste involved in the way military writing has "always" been produced. To eliminate that waste, service writing will have to rid itself of the characteristic defects of bureaucratic discourse—turgidity, woodenness, repetitiousness, and abstraction. Certainly no one could defend an all-too-typical example like this:

> Lack of discipline in and control over utilizing government phones for unofficial purposes is an area extremely vulnerable to abuse. Reimbursement to the government for personal commercial phone calls does not constitute legality. Unauthorized use of government phone circuits is a punishable offense under the Uniform Code of Military Justice.

To become more readable, such writing must be more straightforward, clear, concise, and human ("Don't use government phones to make personal calls"). That kind of change, of course, is the essence of what the "plain English" movement is trying to accomplish in nonacademic discourse communities of all types.[1] In the military, simply because it is a bureaucracy based on tradition and custom, the struggle between the old style and the new one promises to have far-reaching effects; and the outcome is far from certain.

One thing is sure, however. The obstacles that stand in the way of needed reform in military writing will not be overcome except by extraordinary means, effort, and determination. But recognition, now, of the sheer size of the problem can have a powerful effect on what happens in the future.

## HOW MUCH WRITING?

Every large bureaucracy seems to float on a sea of paperwork, at least in the popular imagination, and the military is no exception. Accurate figures are impossible to come by, but a few calculations from the services themselves indicate the truth underlying the folklore. The Air Force, for example, estimates that it turns out 500 million pages of writing per year[2]—and it represents just 23 percent of the total defense population. For the U.S. Navy, a vice admiral recently calculated that, on one of the smaller surface-warfare ships, the day-to-day paperwork and the file cabinets to hold it added 20 tons to the weight of the ship.[3] And high technology has contributed to the proliferation of information manuals employed throughout the services: for instance, more than "one million pages of documentation are required to support the operation and maintenance of the B-1 bomber."[4] The massive total output indicated by these approximations is not surprising; it is no sudden accumulation. But what is being seen clearly now are the unacceptable costs of all this writing in terms of time, storage, and human effort. Budget constraints are forcing the armed services to try to reduce the bulk of what is written and at the same time to improve its readability, essentially through change to a more accessible style and structure.

## WHAT KINDS OF WRITING?

It would be a mistake to think of all this writing as the outpouring of a single-focused monolith. The Army, Navy, Air Force, and Marine Corps (and in many respects the Coast Guard) share the responsibility of maintaining the nation's defense; but they go about their day-to-day missions in very different ways, including those missions that involve writing. While their types of writing resemble each other in broad purpose and format, there is little standardization across service lines. Each service perpetuates and communicates its own ethos, traditions, and concerns in its own way. In many respects, each service, with its separate customs and outlook, is a separate discourse community.

Furthermore, to compound the problem of identifying kinds of writing, each service is made up of a multitude of subcommunities—each with its own work characteristics. Civilians who are little acquainted with the military environment beyond the stereotypes of recruiting posters (which show mainly crews of ships, tanks, and planes) may fail to recognize that the military world is also populated by their own professional counterparts: personnel people, managers, engineers, lawyers, auditors, nurses, chaplains, air traffic controllers, and so on. Each of these subspecialties generates writing with its own occupational peculiarities of expression, format, metaphor, and jargon—all influenced in turn by the branch it belongs to (Army, Navy, etc.) as well as by the overall mission and ethos of military service. And military subcommunities form horizontally as well as vertically: to a degree, all flag and general officers (admirals and generals) share the perspective of their rank; similarly, all Air Force members, from the newest recruit to the Chief of Staff, subscribe to the common Air Force "code."

With these caveats in place, it should be possible to say something useful about the main categories of military writing. Work in the military context is divided into two basic types—operations and administration—with most of the paperwork, as might be expected, coming out of the latter. Operational writing is that done by line officers and their subordinates in carrying out the daily duties of the operating forces—conducting training exercises, flying surveillance missions, performing submarine duty, and so on—all of which require documentation of some kind at some time. Administrative writing is that produced (in very large quantities) by staff personnel in *their* daily activities—drafting, coordinating, and producing policy statements, reports, plans, orders, staff studies, staff estimates, and the like. And of course memorandums and correspondence are as inescapable in the daily business of both operations and administration as they are in the civilian sector.

A more specific listing of types of military writing, but by no means an all-inclusive one, may help to indicate their respective functions:

- standing operating procedures
- information papers
    - memorandums for record
    - fact sheets
    - position papers
- discussion papers
    - subject issue papers
    - background papers, "bullet" backgrounders
    - talking papers
- decision papers
    - summary sheets
    - staff summaries/routing sheets
    - action summaries
- newsletters
- policy statements, letters, and supplements
- citations, recommendations for awards
- mission orders and guidance
- messages
- military letters
- training manuals and bulletins
- directives, letters of instruction, regulations
- training reports, academic reports
- trip reports
- progress reports
- after-action reports
- operations orders and plans
- administrative plans
- personnel reports, fitness reports, efficiency reports

As this list suggests, some of these forms overlap; for instance, the performance evaluation called a fitness report by the Navy and Marine Corps is known as an efficiency (or effectiveness) report by the Army and Air Force. The important thing to recognize is that these writing requirements take many forms, all with well-established formats, and that they do not divide strictly along an operational-administrative boundary. Staff members not only plan, research, and write—they also investigate plane crashes, conduct personnel and material inspections, and try court-martial cases. Similarly, operational units must always perform at least some staff functions: whatever is "done" must be written up. Messages must be sent, correspondence handled, personnel performance evaluated.

Added to staff and operations writing (but often paralleling it) is academic writing, that is, the writing required for military-education courses. With a quarter-million adults being trained and educated in any given year, the U.S. military runs the world's largest educational system (quite apart from its worldwide schools for dependent children). Far more than any other occupation, military service involves a return to schools—or correspondence courses—at specified intervals for career advancement. During these academic tours of duty, writing assignments are designed to anticipate the ones the students will have when they return to the "real world." For example, midlevel officers attending the command and staff colleges learn to write staff-action papers because they are going to need that skill in the next stages of their careers. They also write research papers, military essays, warfare case studies, and "think pieces," the best of which the students are encouraged to submit for publication.

Of course, writing for publication may also originate in operations or staff work. But whatever its origin, this is the writing that receives widest attention, visibility across service lines in some cases, and recognition for its authors. The 600 or so military magazines and journals have readerships that extend through all the many subspecialties and range in circulation from the tiny (1,600 subscribers to the Navy's *Shock and Vibration Digest,* for the turbine people) to the considerable (a half-million readers of *Army Reserve Magazine*). Taking a look at some of these publications at a nearby military installation library would help the prospective mapper of military discourse to get an idea of the range of defense-related topics under current discussion, the vocabulary of that discussion, and the rhetorical strategies commonly used in military problem solving and decision making. But since these periodicals are well edited, for the most part, such an examination would not reveal much about the quality of the great bulk of military writing in the day-to-day workforce.

## HOW GOOD IS ALL THIS WRITING?

Since there is so much military writing, any generalizations about it will necessarily be suspect. As might be predicted, some military writing is very good, much of it is passable, and some is pretty awful. Among the best sources of overall assessment (because they have "the big picture" as well as the greatest propensity for candor) are the top-ranking military people themselves. Some strongly criticize what they have to read. To all his subordinate commands, Army General Carl E. Vuono recently directed the following message: "Army leaders must be able to read, write, and speak effectively. If they cannot, and overwhelming experience tells us too many cannot, they will not function effectively on the battlefield."[5] Of the writing in his own service, an Air Force four-star general has said, "We are really bad. Not in the least professional. . . . And our business demands precise writing, probably more than any other. . . . We are in the wrong business to be oblique, obtuse, confused, indecisive."[6] The fact that not all such criticism is recent shows that today's problem was yesterday's too. For example, not much improvement has been seen in the twenty years since a Navy captain—deploring the then "normal Navy mode of expression," which too frequently "bores, confuses, or annoys"—felt that a reminder of John Paul Jones's eighteenth-century edict was in order ("Nor is any man fit to command a ship of war who is not also capable of communicating his ideas on Paper in Language that becomes his Rank").[7]

To get an added perspective on the issue, we might consult the military historians, who, amid the innumerable lessons of military battles, can point to a sizable number of cases in which the failure to communicate properly led to severe losses of life and property. To cite a mere handful: the Charge of the Light Brigade at Balaclava might have ended much less disastrously if Lord Raglan's order to "attack immediately" had been more specific as to how and where.[8] At the Battle of Fredericksburg, a brilliant victory is said to have slipped through the hands of Union General Franklin, who misunderstood the "vague and inconclusive" orders of his commander, General Burnside, and thus incurred thousands of needless casualties.[9] And in our own time, it has become apparent that the Japanese attack on Pearl Harbor was much more devastating than it should have been because "the commanders and their staffs in Hawaii . . . misinterpreted the information they received" from Washington. "The Army Air Corps commander, for example, thought he was receiving a warning against sabotage and so had his planes all lined up so they could be more easily watched."[10] Failed communication in wartime situations has led—and will lead—to the most adverse outcomes. Whereas in business a misunderstood message may lead to loss of sales, profits, or clients, in the military—and this is true of peacetime exercises as well as on the real battlefield—such misunderstandings can result in the loss of highly sophisticated multimillion-dollar equipment and—especially—human lives.

But what about the general run-of-the-mill daily writing that frustrates the generals and wastes the time of everyone who must attempt to decode that writing and respond or comply? A few examples will demonstrate the nature of the problem. Here's a real (and not untypical) notice in a military installation's Daily Bulletin:

> ATTENTION ALL PERSONNEL. [This installation] has shifted to the interim mode of heating and cooling in [Blank] Hall, Building XX-1. The mode is characterized by temperature fluctuations from 40 degrees at night to 75 degrees in the day time. Accordingly, the heating and cooling plant in [Blank] Hall has been set on automatic which will allow it to shift from heating to air conditioning depending on outside temperature. Also, thermostats throughout the building have been unlocked so they can be adjusted according to prevailing weather conditions. On days when neither heating or cooling is required, all personnel are encouraged to adjust windows to achieve environmental conditions. The [installation] will remain in the interim mode until weather conditions dictate a continuous cooling requirement.

The first question the reader of this message has to ask is this: was it really necessary? Its purpose is unclear, it is loaded with anonymous passives, and its audience orientation is minimal. None of the information contained in the notice seems to require any action or decision by the "All Personnel" being addressed. The objective—achieving "environmental conditions"—seems absurd. Possibly an invitation to open one's windows in order to be comfortable indicates "management" concern and is thus of some benefit, but most decipherers of this long-winded message would consider their net gain to be insignificant.

In cases in which the reader is being asked or ordered to do something, however, accurate message decoding is more critical. Example A below shows a more urgent candidate for revision, in that it requires definite action—once the reader understands what action is wanted, that is. Unlike the first example, this memorandum obviously does have a message that needs to be communicated. But in order to comply with its direction, the reader first has to work hard to learn what the main point is and precisely what action is being directed. The problems here are not so much wordiness, pointlessness, and poor word choice as lack of audience focus (again) and illogical structure. Limiting the information presented to what is essential and putting the specific request at the top rather than at the bottom would save time and effort for everyone concerned, as Example B shows.

HSXN-          **_Hearing Loss Prevalence Study_**
To     Admin Div, USXXXX      FROM MEDDAC     DATE 4 Nov 8X CMT 1
        ATTN:

1. In accordance with AR 40-5 and TB med 501, all military personnel regardless of noise exposure are required to have baseline audiogram (DD Form 2215, Reference Audiogram) entered in their health record and a copy sent to Commander, U.S. Army Environmental Hygiene Agency.

2. The need for greater range and firepower together with design constraints for proposed weapon systems will eventually result in greater noise exposures. Because the potential auditory hazards to our soldiers will be greatly increased as weapons systems now under development are fielded, OTSG has directed development of a mechanism to study the prevalence of hearing loss in soldiers and establish trend comparisons.

3. Request you have the individuals listed below report to Occupational Health Section (OHS), Preventive Medicine Service, Bldg 88, on the date and times indicated below. _This is the second appointment scheduled for these individuals. Please ensure they keep this appointment._ Health records will be pulled prior to appointed times and available at OHS.

4. POC for this action is
DATE: 12 November 198X

_Example A_

Now this memorandum states up front what it is that the recipient is supposed to do. The "why" follows, very briefly, along with a reference to a source of additional information if any is needed. This kind of straightforward, plain-English message gets the job done faster, with less frustration for the reader and with less margin for error.

### Hearing Loss Tests

1. Please tell the persons listed below to report when indicated for a hearing test at Bldg 88, Occupational Health Section (OHS), Preventive Medicine Service.

2. They all missed their first appointments, causing extra effort to get the job done.

3. AR 40-5,          , and TB Med 501,          , require all Army personnel to have a baseline audiogram in their records and on file with the U.S. Army Environmental Agency.

4. If you have any questions, call SFC          at 5555/7777.

Date of test:   12 November 198X.

*Example B*

# WHAT IS BEING DONE TO IMPROVE MILITARY WRITING?

As a result of complaints like those cited earlier from enlightened top-ranking officers, reinforced by scattered subordinates exerting pressure at lower levels, the armed forces have begun to take measures to improve the quality of their written discourse and also to reduce its quantity wherever possible. At the moment, all such measures are intraservice only and do not represent an attempt at standardization (and improvement) throughout the Department of Defense. Each of the services has, however, set in motion initiatives to persuade its members to relinquish the cumbersome and inefficient bureaucratic style and adopt a more readily understandable one.

Leading the effort, not surprisingly, perhaps, have been some of the service academies—the Air Force Academy in particular and the U.S. Military Academy (West Point)—followed by the intermediate service schools (the command and staff colleges) and the senior service schools (the war colleges), with varying degrees of emphasis. Both the Air Force Academy and West Point send out teams of uniformed writing instructors to give lecture-workshops on the "new" style at installations across the country. More extended instruction is furnished through a far-reaching program of testing and teaching now being implemented by the Army Communicative Skills Office in all the Army's professional military-education schools, with results just beginning to come in. And through the normal service distribution channels, instruction booklets and correspondence manuals serve to spread the word to the target audience (which includes almost everybody). All these manuals use examples taken from "real world" writing situations to show the before-and-after of the revision process; in fact, the second example given above (calling for hearing tests) was used for that purpose in an Army staff writing course booklet. The Air Force has its own very popular and widely used book, *Tongue and Quill: Communicating to Manage in Tomorrow's Air Force*. And an excellent commercially published book, *Guide to Effective Military Writing*, by Lt. Col. William McIntosh of the West Point English Department,[11] offers clear and concise suggestions for improving content, style, and organization in all kinds of service writing (and, incidentally, it encourages the would-be writer to ask first whether the communication even needs to be written at all).

In at least one respect, newer forms of usage have already been mandated to supersede the traditional ones: all the services, as well as the Joint Chiefs of Staff, have issued instructions to remove sexist bias from military terminology (thus "crewman" becomes "crew member," and whatever was formerly "manned" is now officially "staffed"). Granted, it is much easier to direct this kind of singly focused change than it is to direct, say, across-the-board improvement in conciseness. But in general, it can safely be said, some widespread attempts are being made to increase awareness at all levels that writing improvement is needed.

## WHAT FACTORS SUPPORT WRITING IMPROVEMENT?

Given the size of the task—the military's need to persuade 5 million people to write more clearly and more efficiently—the outcome will probably not be known for several years. Besides the number of people involved and their vast geographical distribution, a variety of "political" factors come into play which make predicting the end result very risky. Some of these factors clearly favor the desired change. As Janice Redish and her colleagues at the Document Design Center point out, the kind of change we have been talking about here "seems to occur primarily through one or a combination of four motivations: altruism, legal requirements, economics, and pressure of competition."[12] The first and third of these motives are probably applicable to the military—that is, concern for the troops (recognition that people's lives may actually depend on accurate communication) and budget constraints (the necessity to save time, effort, money, and material). Redish and the others also maintain that attitudes and thus actual practice are most likely to change when "top management is convinced that economics favors [such change]."[13] We have already noted evidences of that conviction among some highly placed military leaders over the years, but it is by no means one that is universally held.

Nevertheless, pressures toward writing improvement are beginning to prevail at lower levels as well as at the top. In the military-education schools where plain English is already a part of the curriculum, students are receiving the new gospel and being urged to spread it to the nonbelievers out in the field when they depart. At the Armed Forces Staff College, where majors/lieutenant commanders from all the services attend a half-year course to learn how to become effective joint staff officers, we encounter and have to respond to all kinds of excuses for the prevalence of the "official style," as Richard Lanham and others call it.[14] A major in his (or her) mid-thirties will scarcely remember the content of his last English course (which was probably freshman composition seventeen years ago), even if it did emphasize clear, concise writing—and that cannot be taken for granted. Furthermore, Major Blank will say, "I've learned to write like everyone else in the Army [Air Force, Navy, etc.]. This is the way my boss writes and wants me to write." We have to show these highly motivated overachievers that there are practical reasons for forsaking the protective coloration of the old-style bureaucratic language—reasons that have to do with economy and safety in an increasingly fast-moving and technologically complex world. The fact that high-ranking military guest-speakers at the Staff College often mention their need for plain, to-the-point reports from their subordinates also helps. It is not easy for our students to relinquish in just a few months the fluency in Pentagonese it took them years to acquire, but in many cases they are doing just that. And again, economics enters the picture: these students recognize, as several of our surveys show, that improved writing skills are essential to their professional advancement.

But perhaps the best indicator of the potential for a major change in military writing involves the nature of the institution itself. Since "bad writing results mostly from bad habits rather than from bad motives," as a recent study of the effects of the plain-English movement on Army legal writing recognizes,[15] awareness of the problem should work in favor of its resolution. No one wants to be identified as a proponent of inefficiency and waste. Furthermore, as the same study points out, "in an ordered environment such as the military the chance for meaningful institutionalized change to occur is far greater than in more eclectic surroundings."[16] In other words, in the armed services an order is an order. If the military were to decree a wholesale shift to plain English paradigms in its written discourse, with appropriate emphasis throughout the chain of command, the same kind of successful turnaround could be achieved in military writing as has been achieved, for example, in the services' drug and alcohol programs. Thoroughgoing institutional change is demonstrably possible.

## WHAT SITUATIONAL FACTORS WORK AGAINST IMPROVEMENT?

Unfortunately, the political economy of all large institutions and bureaucracies also exerts a powerful pull toward maintaining the status quo. It should not be necessary to disclaim that we are focusing on the military in a discriminatory way as we discuss this point. *All* bureaucracies share certain distinguishing characteristics, just one of which is the institutionalized perpetuation of what outsiders would consider poor writing habits. The essays in *The State of the Language* collected by Michaels and Ricks (1980) show beyond doubt the unfortunate commonalities of contemporary discourse in many fields. But however much critics may rail, internally or externally, against bureaucratic abuses of language, the (mostly unarticulated) aims of the bureaucracy function to preserve the very forms that appear to be so dysfunctional. Putting the best face on the matter, we can call those aims "consistency, predictability, [and] stability,"[17] but the fact remains that in all large institutions stasis—not social change—is a hallmark. And "We've always done it that way" is likely to be the motto.

In the armed services specifically, other factors tend to militate against an across-the-board movement toward clear and concise writing. First, *time constraints* work against change. A paradox universally acknowledged as true is that it takes longer to write shorter. Ease for the reader usually requires hard work on the part of the writer. For this reason, in the pressure-cooker atmosphere of the Pentagon and some higher-headquarters staffs, harried writers often find it expedient to release a verbose and poorly organized report rather than take the time to clean it up. An even less desirable alternative is just to get an old memorandum out of the files and doctor it to fit the immediate situation. Time and extraordinary determination would be needed to purge those files of convoluted, abstract, and badly organized writing.

*Personnel turbulence* is another fact of life in the military. With tours of duty that normally last three years at most, offices undergo constant turnover in the people assigned to them. Thus it is likely that just as an organizational unit gets everyone "up to speed" on the new style of writing, some of its members will move on to other jobs across the country or across the world. Then training will have to start from scratch again with the newcomers. (On the other hand, those who leave may be able to teach what they have learned about effective writing to their new units.)

*Inertia* and *perceptions of what the boss wants* are also maintainers of the situation as before. If doing it "the way we've always done it" has been acceptable so far, any change that involves hard work and the acquisition of new attitudes and new habits will meet with resistance. Again, it is easier to get an old tried-and-true letter out of the files than it is to construct a fresh one to fit the present context and recipient. As for the boss's requirements, those always take precedence over the ones found in writing manuals. Military staffers frequently have to write for a superior's signature, a difficult task even for confident writers. Unless they can comprehend and assume, temporarily, the role of the higher-ranking signer, their writing will be sent back for revision until it does reflect that role. Unfortunately, military bosses have the reputation—whether this perception is accurate is not important—of *wanting* a depersonalized, strictly formal style in their on-the-job communications. In this kind of situation, it takes great courage to point out the defects of a superior's preferred style and challenge his judgment. It usually makes more sense to reserve the challenges for the most critical issues.

Such issues will almost certainly relate to *the warrior mission*, a factor which works against improvement but is, after all, the reason for the military's existence. It should come as no surprise, then, that the war-fighting mind set prevails and that writing is viewed as a sissy activity. Popular culture certainly encourages and reflects this attitude: in the current spate of very successful war films, how many heroes do we find holding down desk jobs, turning out brilliant memos, and drafting faultless policy? Everything "heroic" takes place in the line, not on the staff. What is needed is a certain long-standing and in-depth perspective of military affairs, such as several military leaders have shown, to recognize that although writing represents a *different* mission from the conventional warfighting one, its importance is still critical. In the words of General Vuono again, "At the very foundation of warfighting is the ability to communicate the commander's intent."[18] Strategy and tactics, plans and policies, messages and orders—all have to be formulated in words and then written in ways that ensure communication. Warriors sometimes find that truth to be unpalatable.

## WHAT IS THE PROGNOSIS?

The military has not needed close examination by civilian academic researchers to become aware of its own characteristics as a distinct discourse community, or federation of discourse communities. It recognizes what must be done if its discourse is to become more effective. The clearly articulated objectives of the plain-English movement, already published in military regulations and directives and incorporated into much of the writing instruction that goes on in military schools, represent the direction that military writing ought to take. However, plain English and its paradigms are clearly "countercultural." If they are to prevail, they will have to overcome the traditional paradigms of the bureaucratic style, which, over the years, have become well entrenched in military writing. The armed services *are* a bureaucratic, hierarchical body; but unlike most bureaucracies, they undergo continuous self-appraisal, with a focus always on improvement (as in the Army's slogan: "Be all you can be"). Innovation and countercultural trends are not seen as inherently bad, at least by those with the power to make change occur. What makes the conflict between these old and new values such an interesting one is that, at this point, the outcome is so dependent on the action taken by military leadership that it cannot be reliably predicted. If strong command emphasis can be mandated—jointly, across the entire Department of Defense—then the rest of this society's bureaucratic communities may have a model program to emulate.

## *Notes*

1. See, for example, Janice C. Redish, "The Plain English Movement," in *The English Language Today,* ed. Sidney Greenbaum (New York: Pergamon, 1985).
2. Department of the Air Force, Air Force Pamphlet 13-5, U.S. Air Force Effective Writing Course, 2 January 1980: v.
3. "Navy Admiral Wages War Against Ocean of Paper," *Washington Times,* 4 May 1987: 4-D.
4. Thomas M. Duffy, "Literacy Instruction in the Military," *Armed Forces and Society* 11 (1985): 439.
5. General Carl E. Vuono, USA, Message 17198Z, Subject: The Army Writing Program, July 1986.
6. General Bryce Poe, II, USAF, "Let's Be Professionals," *Supplement to the Air Force Policy Letter for Commanders,* September 1980: 15.
7. Captain Carvel Blair, USN, "Effective Writing, Navy or Civilian," *U.S. Naval Institute Proceedings,* July 1968: 132, 134.
8. Christopher Hibbert, *The Destruction of Lord Raglan: A Tragedy of the Crimean War 1854-55* (Boston: Little, Brown, 1961) 143.
9. Edward J. Stackpole, *Drama on the Rappahannock: The Fredericksburg Campaign* (Harrisburg, Pa.: Military Service Publishing Co., 1957) 192.

10. Arthur T. Hadley, *The Straw Giant* (New York: Random House, 1986) 43.
11. LTC William A. McIntosh, USA, *Guide to Effective Military Writing* (Harrisburg, Pa.: Stackpole, 1986).
12. Janice C. Redish, Robbin M. Battison, and Edward S. Gold, "Making Information Accessible to Readers," in *Writing in Nonacademic Settings*, ed. Lee Odell and Dixie Goswami (New York: Guilford, 1985) 147.
13. Redish et al. 147.
14. See, for example, Richard A. Lanham, *Revising Prose* (New York: Scribner's, 1979).
15. Thomas W. Taylor, "Plain English for Army Lawyers," Research Report, Industrial College of the Armed Forces (1987) 24. A somewhat modified version of this report appeared under the same title in the *Military Law Review* 118 (Fall 1987): 217–241.
16. Taylor 22.
17. James MacGregor Burns, *Leadership* (New York: Harper & Row, 1978) 296.
18. Vuono.

# PART FOUR

# WRITING IN THE WORLD OF INDUSTRY

# STORYBOARDING AN INDUSTRIAL PROPOSAL: A CASE STUDY OF TEACHING AND PRODUCING WRITING

*Muriel Zimmerman*
University of California, Santa Barbara

*Hugh Marsh*
Santa Barbara Research Center

*Muriel Zimmerman is director of the Interdisciplinary Writing Program at the University of California, Santa Barbara. She has taught writing at Temple University; Drexel Institute of Technology; the College of Engineering at the University of California, Santa Barbara; and the Massachusetts Institute of Technology. She was the editor of* Energy Review *from 1974 to 1981 and consults in varied industrial applications, including software documentation.*

*Hugh Marsh is publications supervisor of Santa Barbara Research Center, and he is a lecturer in technical writing in the College of Engineering at the University of California, Santa Barbara. He has worked as a technical writer and editor for more than twenty-five years, has conducted many seminars on the subject, and is the author of several papers on various aspects of professional communication.*

## PROLOGUE

### Overview

This paper describes a month-long effort in which a group of employees at a California company that specializes in infrared and electro-optical technology wrote a proposal to the U.S. Air Force. The only real names are our own; we call the company General Specifics Research Corporation (GSRC), and we call the proposed technology Automated Telemetry with Laser-Assisted Sighting

(ATLAS). We chose the ATLAS effort for our study because it became the occasion for teaching the engineers and technical managers a new technique for proposal preparation and thus an opportunity to look at how industry both produces and teaches writing.

The ATLAS proposal required the full-time efforts of eight engineers, five technical managers, and two editors and the part-time efforts of six text processors, seven artists, and two photographers. The completed proposal was 225 pages long, and total production costs were $200,000. The ATLAS proposal was not successful. If it had been, the eight engineers would have worked on the project for the next three years and would not write another proposal until nearer the time at which the ATLAS contract expired. Whether the proposal is successful or not, the technical managers, editors, text processors, artists, and photographers soon turn their attention to new proposal initiatives, as it is by means of successful proposals that anyone at GSRC continues to work.

We are interested in describing and assessing both the process by which the proposal got written and that by which the proposal team learned to produce the document. We try to specify how the ATLAS proposal writers learned to write in a new style and a new format through what is an exceptionally powerful pedagogy of the proposal room.

We want to speculate about whether the way that writing skills are taught in the proposal room would be useful in university classes in writing. Many writers at work learn, quickly, to produce a variety of documents that they have never written before at a level that is at least adequate. By contrast, many university students take quarter after quarter of composition classes without much evident increased competence in writing purposeful, rhetorically sensitive papers. Rapid improvement in writing is not always the emphasis in academic writing classes: "No one but a psychiatrist would spend the amount of time that writing teachers often do trying to talk students out of lousy ideas," write Rose Norman and Marynell Young (1985). In contrast, *rapid* improvement in writing is always the goal of the proposal manager.

## *How This Paper Came to Be a Collaboration*

One of us, Muriel Zimmerman (MZ), is presently a university teacher and writing program administrator. Before returning to academic work, MZ had worked for nine years as a technical writer. She felt herself to be reasonably well suited to the task of observing the ATLAS proposal team learn to produce a document in a new way. She was familiar with an industrial environment for writing, she had read widely in recent studies of writing in nonacademic settings, and she had taught both academic and industrial classes in technical writing.

The ATLAS effort was, of course, not a decontextualized, researcher-designed experimental task. What happened early on put more than a little strain on her research plans. The Air Force was asking for a fixed amount of work at a predetermined price of $3 million, and the GSRC proposal team discovered that such an amount of work could not be done for less than $6 million. The team then decided to offer the Air Force *half* the work that had been requested for the $3 million. They abandoned the persuasive strategy that had been developed in early planning stages and rapidly developed a new argument, the goal of which was to make the proposal evaluators believe that less was even better than more.

The social processes involved in reworking the line of argument in the proposal were complex, and MZ no longer had full access to discussions. At that point an insider, Publications Supervisor Hugh Marsh (HM), coordinator of the ATLAS and most other GSRC proposal efforts, agreed to become a collaborator in MZ's study.

## How This Paper Is Constructed

The first part is background: We provide information about GSRC; we describe essential features of the kind of proposal that GSRC produces; we describe the storyboard technique used to write ATLAS; and we describe the Request for Proposal (RFP) to which ATLAS was a response.

The second part is case study: We describe preproposal, proposal, and postproposal activities for the ATLAS project.

The third part is theoretical: We assess what the ATLAS case has confirmed or added to our knowledge about how texts are produced in industry.

The fourth part is pedagogical: We focus on that gap between traditional English instruction and the needs of writers in the world of work, which is the subject of the essays in this volume.

# BACKGROUND

## General Specifics Research Corporation

GSRC is a division of a major aircraft company. It has been located in southern California since 1952, and it specializes in infrared detectors and electro-optical technology. In 1986 it employed 2,450 and had sales of $200 million. The major customer for GSRC concepts and products is the U.S. military.

GSRC gets new business in two ways: (1) it prepares "white papers" describing new concepts and products and sends them to likely customers, hoping to receive from the customer an RFP to provide exactly the items described in the white paper, and (2) responds to proposals advertised in *Commerce Business Daily*, trying for as much advance information as possible because the RFP rarely reaches GSRC more than thirty days in advance of the proposal due date.

Success at presenting proposals is the major factor in staying in business for GSRC, and it is also a major expense of doing business: the ATLAS proposal cost $200,000 to prepare, and it was one of the cheaper initiatives. Some engineers involved in the ATLAS effort—and everyone in publications at GSRC—feel that management is not suitably responsive to the space and time needed for proposal writing.

## Proposals at GSRC

Proposals at GSRC are overt sales documents written with one goal: to beat the competition and thereby to win the opportunity to work. They are always written under pressure; they are always written to an audience that is both knowledgeable and critical; they are always written by more than one person; they are usually written in response to an RFP.

Proposals at GSRC are narratives. The illusion that a proposal must foster in its reviewers is that it represents work that will be done and for which *there is already a plan*. It is always wrong to say "The work described in the RFP will be performed as specified." Novice writers sometimes come to the task of proposal writing convinced that clever business people do not give away secrets until they have won the contract. But a good proposal creates a plan and describes the project in much the same way that a realistic novel describes the world, though the proposal will be more succinct and narrowly focused. The proposal needs to be complete—to convince readers that if they read through to the end, they will know what happens at every stage. The obligation of the proposal preparation team is, in James Tracey's term (1982), to "storybuild."

A group of writers designs and produces a written product that proposes the design of a technical product, one task governing the other. The tasks involved in writing the proposal are often analogous to the tasks involved in doing the work described in the proposal. Both require a systematic method of approach; both require knowledge of what constitutes logical work units; both require careful estimation of completion time; both require allocation of responsibility. The same project management tools are often used to monitor the progress of the writing of the proposal and later to monitor the work defined in the proposal.

## Rhetoric of GSRC Proposals

The proposals that GSRC prepares in order to achieve new business are only distant relatives of the decorous documents that philosophy professors write in pursuit of travel grants from the American Council of Learned Societies.* Their rhetoric might seem rather astonishing to someone unfamiliar with the genre, with cover pages announcing "win themes" like "Miniaturized," "Realizable," "Deliverable," "Affordable," and "Optically Efficient" (see Figure 1). Neither do GSRC proposals resemble very closely the proposals written by Dr. Bloch and Dr. Crews in Greg Myers's (1985) study of the composing and revising processes of two academic biologists. The strategy of the academics is to understate claims, while the strategy of the industrial proposal writers we describe is to make overt, even blatant claims.

Greg Myers chose the preparation of grant proposals for his study because such writing "is the most obviously rhetorical writing scientists do, and the writing that has the most immediate effects on the structure of the discipline" (220).

---

*For a particularly informative account of the kind of industrial proposal we are describing here, see Weiss (1982).

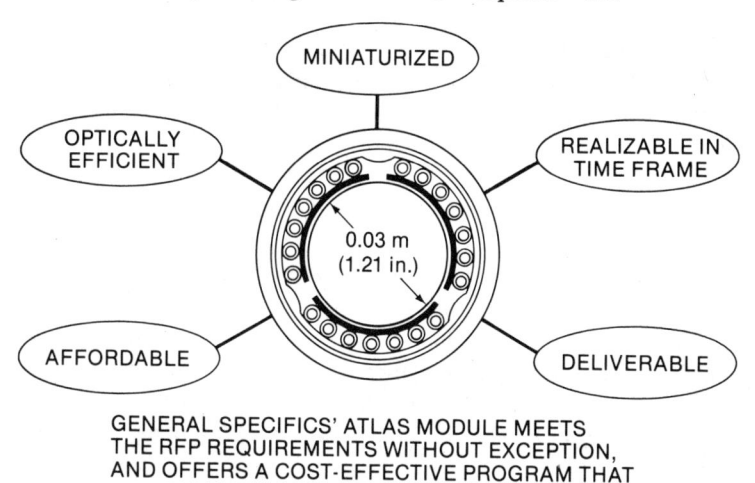

```
        MINIATURIZED
OPTICALLY              REALIZABLE IN
EFFICIENT              TIME FRAME
         0.03 m
        (1.21 in.)
AFFORDABLE             DELIVERABLE
```

GENERAL SPECIFICS' ATLAS MODULE MEETS
THE RFP REQUIREMENTS WITHOUT EXCEPTION,
AND OFFERS A COST-EFFECTIVE PROGRAM THAT
CAN BE COMPLETED ON AN OPTIMUM SCHEDULE.

*Figure 1 Cover page for ATLAS proposal.*

Crews and Bloch "learn the rhetoric of their discipline in their training as graduate students and postdocs, but they relearn it every time they get the referees' reports on an article or the pink sheets on a proposal" (240). Crews and Bloch want to write winning proposals. The most important factors in funding decisions in their field are the applicant's status in the research community as determined by institution, publications, citations, and previous funding. Crews and Bloch cannot change these facts,

> but the tone of almost every sentence of a proposal can be revised to show that one is cautiously but competently scientific. Often, because of the contradictions of self-assertion in scientific prose, the most effective means of self-presentation is understatement, toning down—not one's claims for one's research, but one's language. [227]

Crews and Bloch deliberately constrict their vocabularies; "words like *new, fundamental,* and *important* are all but forbidden, and even *interesting* seems to provoke some readers. Claims of originality are risky, and criticisms of opposing views can seldom be explicit" (237–238).

In contrast—in an environment considerably closer to GSRC than to the academic science laboratory—Broadhead and Freed (1986) study the proposal preparation processes of two management consultants in their book *The Variables of Composition: Process and Product in a Business Setting*. In this discourse community, proposal writers are not expected to sound modest or unassertive. Instead, they decide in advance on unique selling points that will differentiate their offer from the competition's, and they try to express those selling points as themes or key ideas—"short, simple words and phrases that will trigger a reader's affective as well as cognitive response" (53).*

Proposals written at GSRC are meant to sound both like *technical* documents

---

*For another study of proposal rhetoric in a business setting, see Freed (1987).

and like *sales* documents. Managed modesty is out of order, but so is out-and-out hustle. James J. Hill recommends working "win themes" into a proposal in as many places and in as many dimensions as possible, but cautions that in doing so, "we must maintain the ambiance of a technical document, lest it smell too much of a sell" (1985). The proposal writers construct a set of arguments that represent all of the technical, managerial, and cost factors that they want the customer to consider in choosing the winning bidder. The arguments are summarized in key words and theme sentences and repeated in as many parts of the document as possible, as the proposal may be divided for review by several different reviewers. "Make sure you're using the right lure . . . and work it naturally so that your quarry salivates with the knowledge that it's just what he wants. Then have your net and frying pan ready" (Hill, 1986). The reticence of Bloch and Crews is out of place at GSRC; engineers and scientists here need to write openly persuasive sales documents.

All proposal efforts at GSRC are collaborative, involving large numbers of people. By contrast, Greg Myers's scientists write alone. And in the Broadhead and Freed study, after a proposal manager meets with the team members at a strategy meeting, a draft of the entire proposal is usually generated by one writer. Until ATLAS, GSRC proposal managers presented the engineers with an outline and sent them back to their offices to write. Various pieces of the proposal were stuck together at the end, with as much editing as possible (often very little).

## *Storyboarding*

It was for two goals that storyboarding was established as the method for writing ATLAS: getting a better sales story out of the engineers was one goal; managing collaboration was the other.*

The history of storyboarding is somewhat shrouded in myth, but one popular explanation is that Howard Hughes, connected with both film and aeronautics, brought the technique from the movie studio to the aircraft company. In the storyboard process, the writing group receives preprinted proposal storyboard forms, each page representing what will be a two-page spread in the final proposal. Individual authors are assigned specified sections of the outline. They fill in the left side of the storyboard form with a thesis sentence and notes about the point that will be made, and they fill in the right side of the form with rough drawings of illustrations that will be used to support the point as well as captions for the illustrations (see Figure 2). Authors then pin their storyboards to the walls of a large room, quite literally walking and talking their way through the proposal as they move around the room.

Proposals produced by way of storyboards can help both authors and readers. As Tracey explains, "What we do . . . is to break the story into two-page theme units. Each unit consists of a text passage and its illustration on a facing page. A thesis sentence is provided to emphasize the main point of the unit. When you

---

*Proposal preparation methods incorporating storyboarding are sometimes called STOP techniques: *S*equential *T*opical *O*rganization of *P*roposals. The term is used by Tracey (1982, 1983).

# Storyboarding an Industrial Proposal

**STORYBOARD**

NAME: A.N. OTHER
PHONE: 4321

VOL/PART: 1.2
SECTION: 1.2.3
SUBSECTION: 1.2.3.4
TOPIC: ADVANTAGES OF ATLAS ANGLE-OF-ARRIVAL CONCEPT

THESIS SENTENCE (WRITE LAST — SUMMARIZE THEME BODY)

GSRC's concept meets or exceeds all RFP requirements, yet uses the minimum number of detectors and simple processing electronics.

START HERE (STATE POINT OF EACH PARAGRAPH, BEGIN WITH PROBLEM STATEMENT)

1 — Show how GSRC concept meets or exceeds requirements (Fig. 1.2.3-1)

2 — Discuss alternative approaches to system measurement.

3 — GSRC has built and tested this concept
 • Test results (Fig. 1.2.3-2)
4 — Concept selected is smallest, lightest, and comparatively inexpensive.
 • ATLAS photo (Figure 1.2.3-3)
5 — • Schematic (Figure 1.2.3-4)

FIGURE TITLE: GSRC's ATLAS SYSTEM
2ND CAPTION: Our angle-of-arrival concept is simple, but elegant

Fig. 1.2.3-1 Design meets or exceeds requirements

| REQUIREMENTS | RESULTS |
|---|---|
| 1. | |
| 2. | |
| 3. | |
| 4. | |
| 5. | |

Fig. 1.2.3-2 Test performance proves concept.

TEST RESULTS

MAXIMUM CAPACITY OF PRINTED 2-PAGE TOPIC: 110 LINES (4-1/2 SHEETS) OR 'STOP DRAFT'; LESS SPACE NEEDED FOR VISUAL

Figure 2. Storyboard

---

Figure 2 Storyboard

turn the page, you find another thesis, theme body, and visual. And so on through the document" (1983, 68). The reader receives the message three times: in the thesis sentence, in the left-side text, and in the right-side visual and caption.

The proposal story is created and reviewed before it is "cast in the concrete of manuscript." For storyboarding authors, the process provides a mechanism for the proposal team to comprehend, critique, and improve the story at an early stage: "The traditional method of reviewing and revising after the manuscript is written wrong is doomed, because in proposal development there is insufficient time to analyze all the misunderstandings and create better information" (72).

## *How the ATLAS Team Learned Storyboard Technique*

The ATLAS team learned to storyboard by reading a detailed memo from proposal manager Paul Kroger; by attending a seminar on storyboarding led by an experienced editor from the Los Angeles area; and by general prodding from publications manager HM, who had worked in storyboard environments on other jobs. Kroger's memo to the technical team that had been selected to work on ATLAS asked them to employ storyboarding to "help eliminate our usual unstructured and unplanned (well virtually!) approach to generating a proposal." Our "normal" approach, wrote Kroger to his team, "usually culminates in a frenzy of unorganized activity a scant few days before proposal delivery, which results in an unfinished product that is not commensurate with our technical excellence."

In his memo, Kroger included three pages of explanations about storyboarding, a sample storyboard (see Figure 2), and a detailed schedule for storyboard review. He asked the team to pin all drafts to the walls, and he urged each author to "make a habit of walking the walls and reading the other sections."

The seminar on storyboarding was well attended. The presenter, JT, contrasted the new approach with what he called "river-raft discourse"—discourse whose goal is to "flow." With two-page storyboard modules, reviewers can "jump in" and critique at any point. With river-raft, "you have to wait for the whole thing to accrete before you review."

One engineer was skeptical about the benefits of visuals on every two-page spread:

> *Engineer:* I've got my technical content, but you are telling me that the presentation is 50 percent of it?
>
> *JT:* It's not technical input we're looking for, it's a *story about technical input*, written to sell your ideas.

By the end of the seminar, everyone seemed both convinced and excited, though JT had warned that a company's first storyboarding experience could be traumatic.

## *The Request for Proposal*

Advance notice of the ATLAS solicitation was published in the federal *Commerce Business Daily* on March 6, 1986. The RFP reached GSRC on September 24,

1986; it allowed for approximately one month of proposal preparation. The RFP for ATLAS is 128 pages. It includes instructions for the format of the proposal, a detailed statement of work required, evaluation factors for awarding the contract, and a good deal of miscellaneous information such as what color and size identification badges the winning contractor personnel must wear while on Air Force property.

Unlike many proposals, ATLAS was a Best-Proposal-for-Price initiative; offerors are told up front what maximum price the government is willing to pay for the effort. The selection effort is directed at choosing the best technical proposal within that price. The format and content requirements for the ATLAS proposal are these:

1. Table of Contents
2. List of Tables and Drawings
3. Short Introduction and Summary
4. Technical Discussion of Approaches
5. Program Organization
6. Personnel Qualifications
7. Facilities and Equipment Data
8. Program Schedules
9. Supporting Data and Other Information

In his seminar, JT had explained to the ATLAS team that it is not enough in a proposal merely to tell the government to send money. On that point, the RFP reads as follows: "The proposal shall not merely offer to conduct an investigation in accordance with the technical Statement of Work, but shall outline the actual investigation proposed as specifically as possible."

## CASE STUDY

### *The Decision to Storyboard*

The decision to storyboard the ATLAS proposal was made by the Systems Division Manager, Robert (Dr. Bob) Bracken. He had seen the technique used for proposals when he worked at GSRC's parent company. The method had worked well. Dr. Bob was aware that the technical team at GSRC had never done a storyboard proposal, but he felt that they would buy into the process once they saw the advantages it offered. Furthermore, HM, publications manager assigned to the ATLAS proposal, had worked on storyboard proposals at other jobs and was trained by the editor who is credited with developing the storyboard technique in the 1960s.

Paul Kroger, designated manager of the ATLAS proposal effort, is an engineer. If things go well he, like most GSRC engineers, is not involved in proposal preparation and writing more often than every third year or so, when a project is nearing completion. His area of expertise is technical; expertise in proposal preparation at GSRC is in the publications department. Initially, Proposal Manager Kroger was reluctant to deviate from the writing method he had always used: develop an outline, assign sections to the right people, and get them writing. Dr. Bob was persuasive: he convinced Kroger that the storyboard process was worth a try, assuring him that storyboarding would actually save money by making proposal writing more efficient. In any case, the mechanics of the process would be handled by HM. Kroger would be free to address development of the ATLAS technical concept and the admittedly difficult budgetary constraints of the proposed program.

What finally clinched it for Kroger was a visit by the "guru" of storyboarding, the editorial manager of a division of a well-known aerospace firm in southern California and author of several papers on the process. HM arranged for him to conduct a seminar for the ATLAS proposal team.

The seminar occurred during the first week of the proposal effort and was attended by most of the team members; notable absentees were Kroger himself, who was unavoidably called to another meeting, and Merle Blake, physicist and writer, who subsequently played a significant part in the restructuring and preparation of the ATLAS proposal.

The seminar on storyboarding generated considerable enthusiasm among the team members. They were impressed with the ease with which the structure of the proposal could be visualized, and they liked the fact that they would constantly be able to review the contributions of the other writers.

The following morning Kroger introduced a detailed outline for the ATLAS proposal at a meeting called specifically for the purpose. Kroger went over the outline thoroughly with the proposal team. Proposal sections were assigned, and relative importance and emphasis for each section was discussed and agreed to.

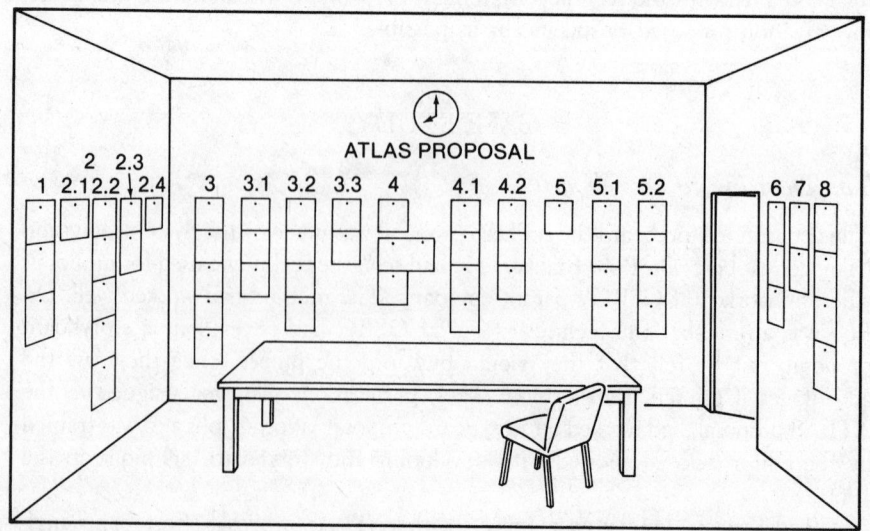

*Figure 3* The "war" room

HM distributed a supply of storyboard worksheets with printed preparation instructions. He explained that drafts of the storyboards would be kept updated and tacked to the bulletin boards that lined the walls of the proposal "war" room (see Figure 3). After some procedural questions were resolved, Kroger asked the team to reconvene two mornings later for the first formal storyboard review.

## The Storyboard Review

Of the planned 27 storyboards, 22 were prepared in time for the review meeting, and HM posted them sequentially around the room with blank pink comments sheets tacked below each storyboard. Most team members were at the meeting, including Merle Blake. Five other new faces were at the meeting: Kroger had decided to include as many members of the Red Team[*] as were available that day, reasoning that the earlier they became familiar with the content and direction of the proposal, the more productive their formal proposal reviews would be.

Kroger announced that instead of a customary storyboard process of reviewing each board in turn and leading a discussion by all team members of ways to improve each board, he would zero in on three or four of the most critical technical areas. He hoped that the experience of the Red Team members would help to shortcircuit some of the more difficult technical questions. What happened was a situation that a more experienced proposal manager would have anticipated and avoided at all costs: the meeting turned into a technical bull session, and the storyboards were not reviewed. One hour beyond scheduled closing time, Kroger called a halt to the argument, apologized for not getting to the storyboard reviews, and announced that he would review each storyboard over the next few days with the individuals who had prepared them.

HM counseled against individual reviews, pointing out that the group would lose the benefit of the collective critique. Kroger compromised to the extent that he agreed to a group review *after* he had talked to each member separately. Kroger did manage to talk to team members individually, and he called a review meeting for Wednesday, now a week and a half into the four-week schedule. Despite the absence of several of the team, including Merle Blake, the review went well. Most technical points of misunderstanding were cleared up, and there was continuing enthusiasm for the storyboard procedure. Most members stayed after the meeting, talking with the others, asking further questions about storyboarding, and taking notes.

At this point, HM had the sense that the proposal and the storyboarding process were going well. For the most part, team members were using storyboards

---

[*]"Red Team" is the name given to the committee of senior technical and management people whose task is to review the proposal critically at least once before the proposal reaches the final preparation stages. In one sense, the Red Team functions as a surrogate customer; in another, it protects the company by making sure that no commitments are made in the proposal that cannot be lived up to by the company. Most importantly, the Red Team uses its collective experience to ensure that the best possible technical proposal is prepared. In the authors' experience, these groups function best if they are not closely involved in the day-to-day work on the proposal.

as they were designed to be used, and two of the key writers of the most complex and critical technical portion of the proposal had even moved into the offices provided just outside the war room. They brought their personal computers with them and settled down to serious writing. By the end of Friday, virtually a complete first draft of the technical proposal, excluding the systems analysis section, was posted on the war-room wall.

## The "X" Factors

Three factors now surfaced that, in retrospect, undermined the success of the storyboarding and of the entire proposal effort. While only one of the factors actually led the customer to reject the proposal, all three factors affected the writing process.

1. It became clear—belatedly, to be sure—that ATLAS could not be completed for the $3 million that the customer had specified as the only possible price. The first pricing exercise had pegged GSRC's ATLAS design at almost $7 million and, even with the sharpest pencils, the cost could not be reduced below $6 million. Clearly the scope of the program had to be scaled back drastically, or GSRC would have to commit its own money in the hope of recouping the loss in follow-on contract work. "The decision was made," in classic bureaucratic passive voice, to offer the part of the package that GSRC could build for the $3 million and to offer a detailed proposal for the remainder of the package. Management was aware that this was not strictly responsive to the RFP, but Kroger's argument was this: "It's time we talked some realism to these guys."

2. This change of scope meant that Paul Kroger suddenly had a massive repricing task, one he believed could not be reasonably turned over to the budgeting staff without his heavy participation. As a consequence, he was effectively crippled as the proposal manager, even though he worked almost impossible hours for the last two weeks of the proposal effort.

3. Merle Blake was finally released from work that had been occupying her and was, for the first time, able to devote all of her attention to the ATLAS proposal.

## Collapse of the Storyboard Effort

From this point on, the storyboard procedure collapsed. Because Kroger had to devote most of his attention to revising the cost proposal, Dr. Bob, Kroger's boss, asked that Merle Blake be given a major role. Blake is a physicist, and she had saved a number of proposals in the past, largely because she could quickly get a firm grasp of the technical concepts and is an excellent writer. Unfortunately, she had not been involved in the ATLAS effort from the start, when the storyboard approach was introduced. She was skeptical when she heard about it, and agreed to nothing more than to "work with it so long as it didn't get in her way."

Kroger gave Blake a copy of the outline and all text that had been written. She made major revisions to the outline and substantive changes in the text. HM urged Kroger to discuss the changes with the team members, but Kroger decided to rely on Blake's judgment because of the limitations on his own time. The proposal team reconvened to review Blake's edits. Kroger announced that Blake had taken over as editor. The new version no longer strictly conformed to the storyboard format; many sections now had several pages of text without the typical storyboard structure of text on the left page with a supporting illustration on the facing right page. Kroger defended the changes as responses to the change in technical approach.

Though no one disagreed with the changes at the meeting, many contributors to the technical proposal complained to HM about the new text organization and the collapse of the storyboard effort. HM expressed these concerns to Kroger; Kroger said he hated to go against any of Blake's plans, as she had a good track record and he was desperately busy with the recosting exercise.

## Proposal Post-Mortem

The effort we have described was not a success in some key ways: the proposal was rejected by the customer, and the proposal team was plagued by technical difficulties and office politics. The storyboarding, however, *was* a success. The engineers and managers who learned the technique of group brainstorming, planning, writing, and critiquing have strong positive feelings about its benefits. They note its usefulness as a group-writing management tool, and they feel that it is a particularly good way to make proposals persuasive documents as well as documents of technical description. The publications supervisor has since written a proposal for an alternate publications management plan for GSRC, one that would make storyboarding politically attractive as well as practically feasible.

## THEORETICAL CONSIDERATIONS

Recent ethnographic studies of writing in nonacademic settings have challenged some widely held conceptions about what writing is, what authors are, and how writers learn to perform competently. What we describe of the ATLAS proposal appears to confirm the following observations:

1. In contrast to much classroom writing, much writing in nonacademic settings is collaborative (see Selzer, 1983; Faigley and Miller, 1982). Further, much writing at work is unsigned by the writers who have contributed to it.

2. In contrast to what students learn in many essay-bound English composition classes, writers at work produce many kinds of written products, in a number of different styles, for varying audiences and purposes. In Faigley and Miller's words, "the types are so diverse that they challenge any definition of what we have been up to now calling 'writing' " (p. 566).

3. In contrast to the notion of "a" writing process, writers at work use a variety of processes for composing written products (see Faigley and Miller, 1982; Selzer, 1983; Broadhead and Freed, 1986).

4. In contrast to many students who, in Patricia Bizell's words, "can see little purpose for their own attempts ('essais') other than to get a grade" (1982, p. 232), writers at work often know that their work can have important consequences (see Odell, Goswami, Herrington, and Quick, 1983).

5. In contrast to students who often complain that they have nothing to say about a subject, writers at work rarely make that complaint. James A. Reither (1985) argues that when we teach students to look "heuristically into their own hearts, experiences, long-term memories, information- and idea-banks to discover what they have to say on the assigned or chosen subject" we send some problematic messages. One is that "composing can be learned and done outside of full participation in the discourse communities that motivate writing." Another is that "writers do not need to know what they are talking about: they can learn what they are talking about as they compose; they can write their way out of their ignorance" (p. 622).

6. In contrast to students, who are often permitted to choose their own subjects for writing and encouraged to seek their own truths and their own language, writers at work rarely choose their own subjects, their own truths, or their own language. Les Perelman (1986) notes that academics possess a relatively privileged position in our society in their ability to select the subjects of their discourse. Underlying the belief that students should be allowed to choose their own subjects and seek their own truth, says Perelman, may be the assumption that academic discourse is normative and all other types of discourse are debased aberrations. Broadhead and Freed's proposal writers "do not 'grow' into a sense of purpose, but begin with it" (1986, pp. 124–125). Their writing is a task-specific response assigned by the firm they work for, not self-initiated.

7. In contrast to students, who often have trouble getting started, writers at work must get started quickly and must write under the pressure of strict deadlines. "Those who cannot are in the wrong business," write Broadhead and Freed of the proposal writers in the management consulting firm they study (1986, p. 55).

8. In contrast to the idea of writing as the action of a private consciousness, studies of writing at work appear to affirm that writing is a social activity that does not begin with prewriting and end with revision. Some sort of human interaction may be important throughout the production of a text (Odell, 1985). Trimbur (1985) writes that the romantic image of the author as artist in a garret is deeply imprinted in the consciousness of English teachers; they picture writing as an inherently private, intensely individualistic activity. Brodkey too sees problems with the image of the solitary author in the garret as the "scene of writing": "To the extent that the scene of writing encourages the reification of one moment in writing *as* writing, the image itself is hegemonic" (1987, p. 400). Cooper (1986) calls attention to the growing awareness that language and texts are dependent on social structures and processes in their *constructive* as well as in their *interpretive* phases.

9. Closely related to item 8 above, activities that have not been thought of as "writing" appear to be crucial to writing: telephone conversations, face-to-face conversations, formal and informal meetings (see Selzer, 1983; Doheny-Farina,

1986). James Tracey contrasts the storyboard process to the conventional "scene of writing":

> During a storyboard reviewing session the proposal team flounders through a lot of debates and filibusters. The participants argue and mill around, and generally look like they are wasting time. Those who mistake composing on paper for writing worry about the schedule and wish the authors were away doing their writing, which is assumed to result in creativeness. This illusion about the source of creativeness is so strong that we often demand the production of a writing assignment while being resigned to throwing half of it away. [1983, p. 75]

10. Also related to item 8 above, organizational culture appears to be a major influence on writing. Paradis and Dobrin (1985) study writing at Exxon ITD. The kind of writing they observed "demanded that its practitioners develop a kind of social consciousness of the organizational environment" (p. 293). "An employee has to learn how to think within the framework of R&D objectives before he or she can write proposals or progress reports" (p. 299). A writer's goals at work are defined in terms of community goals.

11. Writers at work learn to write as they need to from a variety of signals. Paradis and Dobrin call the work environment "an effective training ground for R&D writing" (p. 287). Felker, Redish, and Peterson (1985) point out that the job setting provides constant reminders of "this is what we write" and a model of "what we write looks like this and sounds like this" (p. 49).

## IMPLICATIONS FOR TEACHING

The gap between traditional instruction in English and the needs of writers in the world of work is the subject of the essays in this volume. There is no obvious program for bridging that gap. We would say, with Broadhead and Freed (1986), that "we still know next to nothing about the composing and revising processes of writers in industry . . . next to nothing about how composing processes are affected by organizational traditions and practices or about how writing functions politically within and is affected politically by the organization itself" (p. 3). Joseph Williams's comments on this subject are trenchant:

> We know almost nothing about the way individuals judge the quality of writing in places like Sears and General Motors and Quaker Oats. What counts as good writing at Exxon? . . . We have felled entire forests to provide the paper on which to report how English teachers grade papers higher after their students have been exposed to transformational grammar or the lyrics of "Let's Do It in the Road," without knowing whether anything English teachers have to say about writing has much to do with what their students will be judged on several years hence. [1977, p. 13]

In the absence of "hard evidence"—whatever that might turn out to be—we would suggest that the following courses of action seem at least prudent:

1. Talk to composition students about the concept of discourse communities. Explain to them that their writing, too, takes place within a discourse community, and help them to assess the conventions of that community.

2. Show them what their writing is supposed to look like and supposed to sound like. In Patrick Winston's taxonomy of ways to learn in his book *Artificial Intelligence* (1977), "being told" and "seeing samples" are important steps on the way to the most difficult kind of learning, "learning by discovery" (pp. 42–43).

3. Teach students to write in more than one institutional role. Do not rely exclusively on assignments that privilege "innovation or individualistic problem definition, rather than communal problem definition. . . . the literary portion of the profession may need, in its own theories about writing, to overcome some provincialism that comes from especially privileging indeterminacy—privileging the individualistic and innovative in problem-definition and solution" (MacDonald, p. 329).

4. Offer experience in collaborative learning and writing, providing the kind of context in which students can "practice and master the normal discourse exercised in established knowledge communities in the academic world and in business, government, and the professions" (Bruffee, 1984, p. 644).* Help students to acquire the interpersonal skills that will enable them to function effectively in a dialogue or group discussion (see Odell, 1985; Doheny-Farina, 1986).

5. Help students to develop rhetorical awareness and sensitivity to style and tone. Such awareness is crucial in editing multiple-authored documents. At The Firm, for example, in Broadhead and Freed's study, writers often lift "boilerplate" passages from one document, their own or someone else's, to another. Less skilled writers who cannot detect stylistic and tonal differences often have difficulty in integrating passages that originally came from several documents (1986, p. 57).

6. Help students to become less ego-involved in their writing. Some of their work will be edited by editors like Merle Blake, whose loyalties were to her sense of a direction for the ATLAS proposal that was validated by management, rather than to the authors' sense of what was right. Some of their work will be unsigned. Dare we ask them to read Foucault?

Consequently, we can say that, in our culture, the

> name of an author is a variable that accompanies only certain texts to the exclusion of others: a private letter may have a signatory, but it does not have an author; a contract can have an underwriter, but not an author; and similarly, an anonymous poster attached to a wall may have a writer, but he cannot be an author. In this sense, the function of an author is to characterize the existence, circulation, and operation of certain discourses within a society. [1977, p. 124]

7. Help ourselves to become less ego-involved with our teaching and our students. If we do, in fact, create situations that allow students to act as though

---

*See also Trimbur (1985); Ede and Lunsford (1983); Arms (1983). For ways to teach the group-written industrial proposal, see Goodman (1986) and Zimmerman (1986).

they were colleagues in an academic enterprise (see Bartholomae, 1985, p. 144), we may need to rethink our authority as teachers. We may feel more like Bruffee's *metteur en scene:* facilitators, people who create a situation in which others can learn (1972, p. 470).

## EPILOGUE

In our continuing studies of the proposal writing processes at GSRC, we are focusing on several areas. For one, we are studying the kinds of revisions that the engineers suggest to each other in storyboard review (for example, "filtering" as the caption for an illustration is changed to "filtering is optimal in this advanced system"). Storyboarding does, indeed, appear to facilitate persuasive writing. For another, we are studying the formal and informal teaching of writing that goes on all through the proposal writing process. And for another, we are trying to plumb the meaning to "authors" of the anonymity that comes with collaborative writing. On that point, we give the last words to Foucault:

> We can easily imagine a culture where discourse would circulate without any need for an author. Discourses, whatever their status, form, or value, and regardless of our manner of handling them, would unfold in a pervasive anonymity. No longer the tiresome repetitions:
> "Who is the real author?"
> "Have we proof of his authenticity and originality?"
> "What has he revealed of his most profound self in his language?"
> New questions will be heard:
> "What are the modes of existence of this discourse?"
> "Where does it come from; how is it circulated; who controls it?"
> "What placements are determined for possible subjects?"
> "Who can fulfill these diverse functions of the subject?"
> Behind all these questions we would hear little more than the murmur of indifference:
> "What matter who's speaking?" [1977, p. 138]

## *Works Cited*

Arms, V. M. (1983). Collaborative writing on a word processor. *Proceedings of the IEEE Professional Communication Society.* New York: IEEE, 85–86.

Bartholomae, D. (1985). Inventing the university. In M. Rose (Ed.), *When a Writer Can't Write* (pp. 134–165). New York: Guilford Press.

Bizzell, P. (1982). Cognition, convention, and certainty: What we need to know about writing. *PRE/TEXT,* 3, 213–243.

Broadhead, G. J. & Freed, R. C. (1986). *The Variables of Composition: Process and Product in a Business Setting.* Carbondale, Ill.: Southern Illinois University Press.

Brodkey, L. (1987). Modernism and the scene(s) of writing. *College English,* 49, 396–418.

Bruffee, K. A. (1972). The way out. *College English,* xx, 457–470.

—— (1984). Collaborative learning and the "conversation of mankind." *College English*, 46, 635–652.

Cooper, M. M. (1986). The ecology of writing. *College English*, 48, 364–375.

Doheny-Farina, S. (1986). Writing in an emerging organization: an ethnographic study. *Written Communication*, 3, 158–185.

Ede, L., & Lunsford, A. (1983). Why write together? *Rhetoric Review*, 1, 151–157.

Faigley, L. (1985). Nonacademic writing: the social perspective. In L. Odell & D. Goswami (Eds.), *Writing in Nonacademic Settings* (p. 231–248). New York: Guilford.

——, & Miller, T. P. (1982). What we learn from writing on the job. *College English*, 44, 557–569.

Felker, D. B., Redish, J. C., & Peterson, J. (1985). Training authors of informative documents. In T.M. Duffy and R. Waller (Eds.), *Designing Usable Texts* (pp. 43–61). Orlando, Fla.: Academic Press.

Foucault, M. (1977). What is an author? In D. F. Bouchard (Ed.), *Language, Counter-Memory, Practice* (pp. 113–138). Ithaca, N.Y.: Cornell University Press.

Freed, R. C. (1987). A meditation on proposals and their backgrounds. *Journal of Technical Writing and Communication*, 17, 157–163.

Goodman, M. B. (1986). Winning with words: effective uses of storyboards for brainstorming and proposal management. *Proceedings of the IEEE Professional Communication Society*. New York: IEEE, 261–265.

Hill, J. W. (1985). How to work win strategies into your proposals. *Proceedings of the IEEE Professional Communication Society*, New York: IEEE, 175–179.

—— (1986). The proper structuring and use of strategies, outlines, and theme statements for technical proposals. *Proceedings of the IEEE Professional Communication Society*. New York: IEEE, 267–271.

Myers, G. (1985). The social construction of two biologists' proposals. *Written Communication*, 2, 219–245.

Norman, R., & Young, M. (1985). Using peer review to teach proposal writing. *The Technical Writing Teacher*, 12, 1–9.

Odell, L. (1985). Beyond the text: relations between writing and social context. In L. Odell and D. Goswami (Eds.), *Writing in Nonacademic Settings* (pp. 249–280). New York: Guilford.

——, Goswami, D., Herrington, A., & Quick, D. (1983). Studying writing in nonacademic settings. In P. V. Anderson, R. J. Brockmann, & C. R. Miller (Eds.), *New Essays in Technical and Scientific Communication* (pp. 17–40). Farmingdale, N.Y.: Baywood.

Paradis, J., Dobrin, D., & Miller, R. (1985). Writing at Exxon ITD: Notes on the writing environment of an R&D organization. In L. Odell & D. Goswami (Eds.), *Writing in Nonacademic Settings* (pp. 281–307). New York: Guilford.

Perelman, L. (1986). The context of classroom writing. *College English*, 48, 471–479.

Reither, J. A. (1985). Writing and knowing: toward redefining the writing process. *College English*, 47, 620–628.

Selzer, J. (1983). The composing processes of an engineer. *College Composition and Communication*, 34, 178–187.

Tracey, J. (1982). The practice of STOP. *Proceedings of the IEEE Professional Communication Society*. New York: IEEE, 10–13.

——. (1983). The theory and lessons of STOP discourse. *IEEE Transactions on Professional Communication*, PC-26, 68–78.

Trimbur, J. (1985). Collaborative learning and teaching writing. In B. W. McClelland &

T. R. Donovan (Eds.), *Perspectives on Research and Scholarship in Composition* (pp. 87–109). New York: Modern Language Association.

Weiss, E. H. (1982). *The Writing System for Engineers and Scientists.* Englewood Cliffs, N.J.: Prentice-Hall.

Williams, J. M. (1977). Linguistic responsibility. *College English,* 39, 8–17.

Winston, P. (1977). *Artificial Intelligence.* Reading, Mass.: Addison-Wesley.

Zimmerman, M. (1986). An added dimension: industry-university collaboration in the teaching of proposal writing. *Proceedings of the IEEE Professional Communication Society.* New York: IEEE, 135–138.

# WRITTEN COMMUNICATION: THE INDUSTRIAL CONTEXT

*J. C. Mathes*
University of Michigan

*J. C. Mathes, Ph.D., is Professor of Technical Communication, College of Engineering, University of Michigan, Ann Arbor, Michigan. He teaches courses primarily for senior and graduate engineering students, although students from other professional schools also enroll in the technical communication program courses. He also has been a communication consultant for such organizations as Chrysler, Dow Corning, and the Michigan Judicial Institute as well as several corporations in Japan and has led many seminars in his field.*

*He is the author of numerous articles, papers, and research reports in technical communication and social decision analysis as well as author or coauthor of eight books, including* Designing Technical Reports: Writing for Audiences in Organizations.

Written communication in industry depends to a considerable degree on the way a company is organized and managed. Most decisions professionals in industry have to make before they write are influenced by the way their department is organized and by company policies and procedures. That is, the same type of report, such as a test report or a progress report, varies from organization to organization and even from department to department within an organization. These reports—the selection and organization of information as well as the tone and format—cannot be analyzed effectively without accounting for this environment. In rhetorical or situational terms, a concern for the industrial context is a prerequisite to the teaching and mastery of technical-communication skills.

From the management perspective, the industrial context is analyzed and modeled in organizational literature. From the communication perspective, it is introduced in some technical-communication literature. At present, however, the two perspectives have not been combined in sufficient detail to explain how written communication varies according to the specific industrial context. An examination of this context should introduce second-order considerations for written communication by professionals.[1] It also should suggest directions for research to define these considerations so that practical applications can be developed.

Technical- and business-communication models[2-4] and audience-analysis techniques[5] directly introduce the industrial context, although rather generally. In technical communication, the seminal article on the corporate context is James Souther's "What to Report."[6] "The Manager's Job: Folklore and Fact," by Henry Mintzberg,[7] occasionally is referenced in technical-communication literature because it provides relevant background from the field of organizational theory.

Complementary approaches also explore the industrial context, such as analyses of discourse communities and corporate cultures. These studies have varying emphases: on differences among professionals themselves,[8] on differences between subcultures within a corporation,[9] on differences between corporations,[10] and on differences between national cultures.[11] Similarly, a process approach to technical communication, such as Selzer's "The Composing Processes of an Engineer,"[12] introduces the organizational context to shed new light on invention in technical writing. The technical-communication literature that provides an introduction to the organizational context is thoroughly reviewed in *Research in Technical Communication,* especially the chapters "Communication Theory and Technical Communication," "Audience Analysis and Adaptation," "Invention in Technical and Scientific Discourse," and "Technical Reports."[13]

An important feature of some of the literature is that it goes beyond generic models and approaches to technical and professional communication. Although generic models and approaches are necessary for the teaching of basic technical-communication skills, for persons to make the transition from the classroom to the professional arena they should be sensitive to the specific contexts they will encounter. A generic information-transfer or problem-solving communication model[2,3] is inadequate for the actual written-communication situations in any specific organization context—that is, in a department in Ingalls Shipbuilding, Dow Corning, IBM, Caterpillar, Chrysler, or Amoco.[14]

To refine current technical-communication models to approximate the industrial context more effectively, it is necessary to examine how this context varies. For the purpose of this analysis, therefore, I discuss how written communication in part depends on (1) the organizational context in general and then on specific aspects of this context; (2) the specific decision-making context of the organization, that is, on the way managers make decisions in a specific organization; (3) the nature of the organization, that is, on the type of industry; and (4) the location in the organization, that is, on the units involved in any specific communication, from R&D to engineering to manufacturing to service. Organizational literature provides details on these aspects of the industrial context. Thus, it is very useful to examine written communication from the perspective of the organizational context.

## THE ORGANIZATIONAL CONTEXT

An appropriate introduction to the organizational context, especially to the aspects that tend to be assumed in many technical-communication models, is Herbert A.

Simon's *Administrative Behavior*.[15] The subtitle of this pioneer study in organizational theory is: "A Study of Decision-Making Processes in Administrative Organizations." The close dependency of technical communication on the organizational context is clear:

> Decision making in organizations does not go on in isolated human heads. Instead, one member's outputs become the inputs of another. Because of this interrelatedness, supported by a rich network of partially formalized communications, decision making is an organized system of relations, and organizing is a problem in system design.[16]

Technical communication translates the "outputs" into "inputs" to facilitate decision making and effect changes.

The organizational context for the technical-communication process is introduced by Simon:

> Communication in organizations is a two-way process: it comprehends both the transmittal *to* a decisional center (i.e., an individual vested with the responsibility for making particular decisions) of orders, information, and advice; and the transmittal of the decisions reached *from* this center to other parts of the organization. Moreover, it is a process that takes place upward, downward, and laterally throughout the organization. The information and orders that flow downward through the formal channels of authority and the information that flows upward through these same channels are only a small part of the total network of communications in any actual organization.[17]

The typical technical-communication model generically defines the process but not the specific flows. To use our own model as an example (especially as I criticize it below), the flows must be determined for each communication.[18] That is, the communication is output to various audiences in the organization. Effective audience analysis specifies the paths that any specific communication takes throughout the organization.

The problems that the organizational context poses for written communication are defined by Simon: "There is nothing to guarantee that advice produced at one point in an organization will have any effect at another point in the organization unless the lines of communication are adequate to its transmission, and unless it is transmitted in such form as to be persuasive."[19] The typical technical and professional report in an organization essentially presents advice. This advice often is called "conclusions and recommendations" from the writer and his or her department to persons in other departments. It requires adequate lines of communication and must be persuasive.

The first problem for the writer is to establish adequate lines of transmission for a report. In terms of formal lines of authority, however, the lines of transmission for any report are quite inappropriate and inadequate.[20] Almost every memorandum or report is constrained by a formal organizational structure because the "advice" is put in writing. Writing formalizes it—for decision making, implementation, documentation, and the record. Therefore, a memo or report is disseminated by formal communication procedures, which often are standardized or follow certain protocols. The situation the writer addresses, however, is unique: it involves specific departments, many of them in a horizontal relationship (equal) with each other, which requires the lines of communication to cut across the formal organization structure, which is vertical (hierarchial). Only the most routine status and administrative reports might have lines of communication that generally correspond to lines on the organization chart, but these types of reports seldom are those of concern to the technical writing teacher and practitioner.

In a test facility of one automotive corporation where I have analyzed the report writing situations, a typical report addresses various engineering (design) departments—engineers are designing automobiles and the test facility tests the designs. The working relationships therefore are horizontal—between design engineers and test engineers, including their supervisors and managers, in two different departments in two separate locations (70 miles apart). Any specific test report has additional audiences—in service, quality control, manufacturing, for example—depending on its subject. A report on standardizing front-end sheet metal could involve engineers in manufacturing processes, quality control, and production in addition to those in engineering.

The lines of communication appropriate for these test reports go in several directions, most of them horizontal. Protocol, however, requires the actual lines of communication to follow the formal organizational structure. A test report goes from an engineer to his or her supervisor, then to his or her manager, then to the chief engineer of testing and development, then to the director—all persons within the test facility—then to the director of truck engineering, the chief engineer, a manager, a supervisor, and finally a design engineer—all persons within engineering—as well as on to several managers, supervisors, and engineers in manufacturing processes, quality control, and production. Protocol furthermore requires that the test engineer address the report to his or her manager in the test facility, who already has reviewed the report before it is distributed. In such a situation, the test engineer has actual lines of communication dictated by the formal lines of authority that are inconsistent with the lines of communication appropriate solely for the purpose of the report.

Standard technical communication models and guidelines introduce the organizational context. They usually do not, however, clearly introduce the necessary inconsistency between the formal organizational network and the appropriate communication paths. Our audience analysis procedure, for example, asks the writer to identify the audiences for a report, characterize them, and then prioritize (classify) them on an egocentric organization chart.[21] Our procedure does not clearly alert writers to the fact that this audience analysis results in communication paths that are inconsistent with the formal organization structure. The analysis might identify a primary reader or decision maker that the report should address but whom organizational protocol prevents the report from addressing directly. Or it might identify secondary readers that cannot be put on the distribution list by name. It might require the writer to send the report to a nominal reader who in turn should transmit the report to others. These are second-order complications for which there is no clear solution, although a heuristic could be developed to identify and cope with the two dissimilar audience situations (by preparing and contrasting normative and actual egocentric charts) for a report.

The second problem for the writer is make the report persuasive. This is a consideration that tends to be subordinated in information transfer models of communication[22] and in the design of certain types of communication systems, such as what are called MIS (Management Information Systems) and DSS (Decision Support Systems).[23,24] However, the organizational context suggests that routine information transfer is inappropriate and almost impossible. Simon observes that "no plague has produced a rate of mortality higher than the rate that customarily afflicts central-office communications between the time they leave the issuing office and the moment when they are assumed to be effected in the revised practice of the operative employees."[25] Although he refers to top-down memoranda, his observation applies to all memoranda and reports in an organization. Until actual organizational practices change, no communication has occurred. Routine transfer of information, however, does not always lead to action or to the appropriate action. To effect change usually requires persuasiveness.

The organizational context suggests many impediments to effective persuasion. Simon's book and other organizational literature explain these impediments. Simon mentions problems caused by vertical specialization and division of decision-making responsibilities, by coordination of disparate activities and functions, by subdivisions according to expertise, by administrative control and responsibility, by formal and informal lines of authority, by organizational and departmental loyalties, and by the criterion of efficiency, to start with.[26] Each of these presents barriers to communication effectiveness as well as to decision-making effectiveness. The Mintzberg article referenced above suggests role constraints—managers have limited time to read and focus their attention.[27]

Thus, effective persuasion is difficult because the premises for acceptance vary from writer to reader and among various readers. For any specific report there are no generic premises of persuasive appeal, although a rational model for technical communication usually assumes that there are. For example, many recommendations state a cost-savings premise as though that should be acceptable to everyone in the organization. Such premises, however, actually are relative to specific organizational departments and processes. Different departments have different functions and various persons have different roles. They respond to different appeals. Cost savings may be the most important premise to one manager, while quality control may be the most important to another. There may be no tradeoff that will satisfy both managers.

In a nuclear power plant engineering company whose reports I have analyzed, the lack of persuasive communication has been quite dramatic.[28] In part, this resulted from the different roles of writers and readers. Babcock and Wilcox (B&W), the company that designed the nuclear power plant at Three Mile Island, has two basic units in its nuclear power division: engineering, which designs nuclear plants, and nuclear services, which provides operational support for the utilities that have nuclear power plants designed by B&W. Over a year and a half before the accident at Three Mile Island, an engineer and a manager in engineering identified an operating problem in B&W nuclear plants and recommended changes in operating instructions and procedures. If their advice had been accepted and implemented, the accident at Three Mile Island probably would not have occurred: "the failure of B&W to provide guidance recommended by [the engineers] was primarily the result of a gross failure by several individuals, including [the engineers], to communicate effectively, and ineffective management practices that resulted in this issue not being adequately addressed."[29] From this perspective, the accident at Three Mile Island resulted from ineffective technical communication.

An engineer and then the manager of emergency core coolant system design wrote memos recommending changes in operating instructions. The manager pointed out the likelihood of "core uncovery and possible fuel damage" if the changes were not made (he actually forecast the scenario of Three Mile Island) and concluded, "I believe this is a very serious matter and deserves our prompt attention and correction." He wrote this on February 9, 1978; his recommended changes in operating instructions were issued on April 4, 1979—one week after the accident at Three Mile Island.[30]

Many of the organizational barriers introduced by Simon could be relevant in this situation, some of which are discussed below. Few engineering students in a technical writing course and even few engineers in industry can accept the fact that managers in B&W might not immediately act upon a recommendation to change operating instructions in order to avoid core uncovery and possible fuel damage. In terms of technical communication in an organizational context, however, the logical question to ask is, why should they? What will persuade them to accept the advice of an engineer or manager in another department?

Typical technical-communication guidelines—including ours—do not address some important implications of actual organizational behavior. Instead, they assume, as I have, Simon's observation "that human behavior in organizations is, if not wholly rational, at least in good part *intendedly* so." They then present models and guidelines that implement the assumption of rationality: given an organizational problem and goals, a report is designed to solve the problem in terms of the goals (to use our problem-solving approach). They ignore much of what Simon discusses as "the limits of rationality."[31] To introduce the organizational context completely is to introduce the constraints and limits of reasonable guidelines for report writing: "the fallacy here is equating the purposes or goals of organizations with the purposes and goals of individual members. The organization as a system has an output, a product or outcome, but this is not necessarily identical with the individual purposes of group members."[32] Effective written communication in an industrial context, or in any organizational context, requires that a rational approach to audience analysis, definition of purpose, and selection and arrangement of material account for the limits to rationality imposed by the organizational context.

The specific aspects of the organizational context that I discuss below introduce some of these limits. When these do not involve limits on rationality, they involve particularizations that are not implicit in generic technical communication models. Either way, when analyzed in terms of guidelines for technical communication, they would lead to somewhat different reports than might be written following generic technical communication guidelines. They could enable some lines of communication to be more appropriate and some reports to be more persuasive than these otherwise might be.

## THE DECISION-MAKING CONTEXT

Organizational literature is rich with discussions of alternative decision-making contexts. Examination of actual practices in organizations indicates that rational models of organizational behavior do not always provide the most convincing explanations of how human beings actually behave in organizations. At best, they provide normative guidelines that may or may not be easily implemented. "At its extreme, the rational tradition is completely unrealistic and there have been numerous criticisms of it in recent years. There is virtually no *descriptive* support whatsoever for its conception of decision making."[33] Consequently, other models of organizational behavior have been developed to explain how decision making actually occurs in various organizations. These models modify the rational model or offer an alternative to it. They have implications for technical communication that need to be examined.

The technical-communication implications are nicely illustrated by Barbara Mirel in her excellent study, *Text and Context: The Special Case of In-House Documentation*. She began her investigation with the purpose of developing guidelines for writing in-house computer user manuals, as current literature assumes "that documentation writing is situated only in commercial software corporations or that the methods that apply to commercial contexts readily translate to all writing situations."[34] For her case study, she analyzed the writing of a manual that would enable cashiers in the bursar's office of a university to implement a new, computerized student accounts system. The manual was a users manual for programs written by programmers in the systems department of the university. She found that current documentation theory was inadequate because it assumes a rational model of organizational behavior, with "no need to examine ways in which social and political factors might impinge on the production of a manual."[35] She analyzed how the "manual's development and use were influenced by interdepartmental conflict, organizational uncertainty about the implications of the new computer system, garbage-can decision practices, users' established patterns for accessing information, and the Bursar's supervisory style."[36] The manual itself had little or no utility for the users, who adopted other means of learning the system. However, it served other organizational purposes, and became "a force behind organizational change."[37] Thus, the manual became functional, but not as communication for the purpose it originally was intended.

To a large extent, I think most models of technical communication assume or explicitly describe an organizational environment that is primarily rational, or at least an environment in which rational problem solving heuristics can be applied. If these assumptions are not supported by the evidence presented in organizational literature, then we must reassess our prescriptions for technical communication. A quick survey of relevant organizational literature suggests some of the additional considerations that must be taken into account when teaching and doing technical writing. Organizational literature presents a spectrum of perspectives from a rational model to a political model, with various situational, process, or behavioral models in between. Many of these models assume some element of rationality. However, as with Simon's concept of "the limits of rationality," these models introduce considerations that are not consistent with subject-oriented, information-transfer, or rational problem-solving approaches to technical communication.[38]

A rational model of organizational behavior does not assume that all activities occur in a planned, systematic fashion. After all, an organization consists of people; it is not a machine. However, a rational model assumes that the organizational processes can be explained and controlled systematically, by calculation and planning if not by mathematical algorithms:

> At a minimum, then, organizational rationality involves three major component activities: (1) input activities, (2) technological activities, and (3) output activities. Since these are interdependent, organizational rationality requires that they be appropriately geared to one another. The inputs acquired must be within the scope of the technology, and it must be within the capacity of the organization to dispose of the technological production.[39]

Technical communication functions to modify organizational processes to achieve organizational goals. It is an important means by which the "activities" are "appropriately geared to one another." Ordering raw materials, maintaining equipment, inventory control, scheduling, instructions—typical subjects of technical reports—are means by which organizational processes are controlled.

For example, the manager in the nuclear services department of B&W who received the recommendation to change operating instructions did not accept the recommendation. Instead, he wrote a memorandum requesting another manager in engineering to "resolve the issue of how the HPI system should be used." He even quoted from the memorandum he received, which suggested "the possibility of uncovering the core [of the nuclear reactor in a power plant] if present HPI policy is continued."[40] In a rational organization, one would assume, such a serious request in a one-page memorandum would elicit a response by the manager in engineering. However, an analysis indicates that the memorandum had been poorly designed, with the important information coming at the end, had a poor subject line, and had an incomplete distribution list.[41] This could have been why the request was neglected and therefore failed to elicit a response. Based on a rational model of organizational behavior, technical communication texts explain how to design effective memoranda to attract a reader's attention to the important issue and information.

Even if it had been designed according to these principles of technical communication, however, the memorandum still might not have elicited a response. Other factors limit rational behavior in organizations. For example, the response might have depended in part on the attitude of a receiver toward the source of a communication. Simon observes that "an individual who does not have a recognized status, or who is not recognized by his associates as expert with respect to a certain kind of knowledge will have a more difficult time convincing his listeners that a recommendation is sound than one who possesses the credentials of 'expertness.' "[42] As Mr. Karrasch, the engineering manager, testified, he "glanced over" the memorandum from nuclear services very quickly and thought that it raised "rather routine questions from the Nuclear Service Department to the Engineering Department and that they could be answered in a routine fashion."[43] From Simon's perspective, it is interesting to review Mr. Karrasch's testimony and analyze his attitude toward the writer of the memorandum, Mr. Hallman, the Manager of Nuclear Services. Mr. Hallman failed to persuade Mr. Karrasch to act (which is not the same as persuading Mr. Karrasch to accept a point of view). Why did Mr. Karrasch take the memorandum too lightly and handle it in a routine manner? Why did he fail to respond even after Mr. Hallman had contacted him three or four times afterwards to resolve the issue? In his eyes, was Mr. Hallman, in charge of Nuclear Services, not an expert in engineering matters with respect to the technical issues raised in the memorandum? Even if the report had been effectively designed according to typical technical communication principles, therefore, it seems quite possible that Mr. Karrasch would not have responded to the memorandum.

A typical technical-communication approach usually does not introduce these types of concerns, which would require a persuasive rather than informative approach to writing a memorandum—but a rather different type of persuasive approach than a logical argument over an issue. A business communication model based on Berlo might indicate that often "people react more according to their attitude toward the *source* of facts than the facts themselves,"[44] but usually such a model provides few guidelines on how to take that into account when writing within an organizational context. Even a qualified rational approach to communication within organizations introduces considerations that have not yet been explored systematically from the perspective of technical communication. Other organizational models introduce considerations even more difficult to cope with.

To the extent that other organizational factors interfere with rational decision-making processes, we should explore alternative tactics for writing any technical report. Although a behavioral approach assumes that organizations attempt "to be rational," it introduces a context that poses considerable challenges for technical communication.

> Organizations, as we observe them, do not have a single, internally consistent goal at a particular point in time. Instead, they exist with considerable conflict and potential conflict. What they decide at one point in time is often apparently inconsistent with what they decide at another time. What is decided in one part of the system is often apparently inconsistent with what is decided in another part. Instead of a single overriding goal, organizations have a series of more or less independent goals.

> Instead of a single decision center, organizations have a number of decision centers, each dealing with some subset of the organizational goals.[45]

As Mr. Karrasch testified, he believed the issue was "not so much one of lack of communication" as "one of priorities."[46] Both he and Mr. Hallman had other things to do than to complete the communication process initiated by Mr. Hallman.

A rational model of technical communication might assume an integrating person or unit to coordinate or make tradeoffs among departments with different, independent goals. "Perhaps the most common solution to solving an integration problem among two or more subunits has been to have them report to the same supervisor, who would then see to it that their activities were properly integrated by facilitating communications, resolving conflicts, and the like."[47] However, technical communication usually goes between those departments, not to some mediating agent. For actual communication to occur requires more report design considerations than the typical informational or problem-solving communication model introduces. Some of these considerations might be entirely outside of even plausible extensions of these models. "Because of conflicting demands, imperfect information, contests for control, and the loose coupling between organizations and environments, rational actions and rational designs are by definition virtually impossible. Imbedded in all definitions of rationality is the idea of goal attainment, but if there are multiple and conflicting goals, how can we define rationality?"[48]

An organizational solution to such an interpretation of organizational behavior introduces technical-communication considerations that are inconsistent with much current teaching.

> An alternative model can be called an external model, a political model, a coalitional model, a ceremonial model, or a loosely coupled model of organizations, depending upon which particular features are singled out for attention. Basically, this alternative perspective on organizations holds that information is limited and serves largely to justify decisions or positions already taken; goals, preferences, and effectiveness criteria are problematic and conflicting; organizations are loosely linked to their social environments; the rationality of various designs and decisions is inferred after the fact to make sense out of things that have already happened; organizations are coalitions of various interests; organization designs are frequently unplanned and are basically responses to contests among interests for control over the organization; and organizations' designs are in part ceremonial.[49]

What are the functions of reports in this organizational world? Such an environment, for example, calls into question a rational concept of report purpose, at least as we discuss it.[50]

In regard to technical communication, one of the

> "most important design considerations" of the political model "is the distribution of information.... Secrecy is one of the practices used to institutionalize control, maintain power, and leave the organization with more discretion—at least on the surface.... In many ways, secrecy helps to maintain organizational control. Power

is easier to wield if few in the organization know exactly how it is exercised and if performance data or other indicators of problems are withheld."[51]

From this perspective, current technical-communication models are normative, not prescriptive, and clearly do not prepare professionals to write reports that will satisfy their managers on the job or to write reports that will both satisfy their managers and their own ethical requirements.

Henry Mintzberg presents an expanded political model of the organization which introduces "systems of influence" in terms of direct control, bureaucratic control, ideology or culture, expertise, and politics. The organization functions according to the distribution of power among these various systems, with the relative power of any manager dependent on his or her level in the line hierarchy. A senior executive has relatively more power than a first line supervisor but relies much more on bureaucratic control, for example, than expertise.

Within this model, Mintzberg then describes thirteen kinds of "games" by which influence and power are exercised.[52] The technical-communication implications are diverse, and few conform to rational guidelines. On the budgeting game, he observes that budgets often are distorted because "many projects involve technical information known only to the unit doing the proposing, not to the management higher up doing the approving." As an extreme example mentioned in another study, he quotes an assistant comptroller:

> Our top management likes to make all the major decisions. They think they do, but I've just seen one case where a division beat them.
> I received for editing a request from the division for a large chimney. I couldn't see what anyone could do with just a chimney, so I flew out for a visit. They've built and equipped a whole plant on plant expense orders. The chimney is the only indivisible item that exceeded the $50,000 limit we put on the expense orders.
> Apparently they learned informally that a new plant wouldn't be favorably received, so they built the damn thing. I don't know exactly what I'm going to say.[53]

Not only does the assistant comptroller have an interesting challenge in technical communication, it would seem that all of the communications between that division and headquarters would require techniques usually not introduced in technical communication courses.

This superficial introduction of organizational theory introduces second-order considerations for technical communication. It does not necessarily imply that what we teach at present is wrong; but it does suggest that what we teach might be limited and needs to be qualified so that professionals can communicate more effectively in their organizations.[54]

## THE NATURE OF THE ORGANIZATION

Regardless of their actual decision-making style, organizations differ significantly in function. These differences result in different approaches to report writing and in different report writing standards. Shipyards, for example, are organized to manufacture large, one-of-a-kind products in projects that take several years. Speciality chemical corporations have a diversity of products for both the consumer and other industries and require constant attention to applied research to keep ahead of their competitors. Professionals have to adapt their report-writing practices accordingly.

I have analyzed shipyard communication procedures in detail.[55] Except for various reports required for the government, technical communication functions to integrate design activities with construction activities over an extended period of time. There are few "conclusions and recommendations" reports of the type that require some management decision in the sense that those reports usually are described in textbooks on technical writing. There is almost no research and development (R&D) activity and there is no customer-oriented product development. In a shipyard, the important reports, which I label "problem-solving reports," are action-oriented. They formalize decision making for changes that cannot be made routinely and they implement changes in the design and construction of a specific hull. Although they must be persuasive, they usually are direct and to the point. Most working reports—and there are thousands associated with any one project—are one or two pages in length.

Many of the reports, especially a second category of reports that I label "administrative reports," appear quite routine on the surface. They concern design details and construction procedures and address a series of small, isolated problems rather than fundamental manufacturing and organizational decisions. Production in a shipyard is integrated and coordinated, so most of the professionals from design to production constantly interact with each other. The result is that considerable decision making is oral and considerable information is known to all parties. The reports package and transmit information through standard written-communication procedures and formats, even when considerable judgment and decision making is presented. Functionally, the reports keep the construction process moving efficiently along predetermined paths.

The problems the report writers have are problems with selectivity and arrangement of material and especially problems with clarity and discursiveness. Most students and many engineers on the job would tend to overwrite these reports considerably. In addition, my research was concerned with a specific problem with the relationship between oral and written communication, a problem that does not necessarily arise in complex, diverse organizations.[56] (No matter their size, shipyard organizations are functionally similar.) In general, to address these problems, report-writing guidelines can be quite stipulative. The introduction or purpose statement, for example, should be brief and direct or, often, embodied in the format rather than stated. It can be stipulated for each type of report. Similarly, the selectivity and arrangement can be stipulated to a considerable extent. In organizations such as shipyards, report-writing style standards and guidelines can be developed and used effectively.

Communication procedures in a speciality chemical products corporation, whose reports I am familiar with, differ significantly from those in a shipyard. The corporation thrives by keeping ahead of the market with new and improved products. These products vary considerably in kind and customer, and many are produced in small quantities. The corporation, therefore, is concerned with R&D and with the quality of its products, especially in regard to its competitors' products. Consequently, its reports lack the instrumental quality of shipyard reports. Many are quite informational, and most of the specimens I have examined consist of research reports, analytical laboratory reports, and progress reports. These reports usually have no immediate decision-making or action-oriented purpose. Occasional problem-solving reports occur related to production and quality control, but these are infrequent.

An uncertain purpose often poses problems for the writers of these reports. With no clear sense of utility for their reports, they have difficulty with selectivity and arrangement of information. They tend to present information as an end itself and to underestimate the need for analysis and judgment. The corporation has no standard written-communication procedures and practices beyond a two-page style standard for research reports (that seems optional for a writer to follow). Practices vary from department to department and from manager to manager. Report writing therefore requires considerable judgment, and it would be a mistake to be too stipulative beyond certain generic writing principles. In essence, the corporation depends on flexibility, creativity, and adaptiveness in order to meet constantly changing needs.

Its technical-communication procedures, therefore, should reflect these same characteristics. Introductions to reports can vary considerably, and the statement of communication purpose often cannot be formulated directly. Most of the characteristics of the reports cannot be stipulated; instead, heuristics or procedures have to be developed so that report writers can determine what to put in the introduction, what material to select, how to arrange the material, etc. In organizations such as these, company style standards and report-writing guidelines might not be too effective.

Technical-communication procedures in an automotive corporation differ from those in a shipyard as well as from those in a specialty chemical corporation. Although both a shipyard and an automobile company manufacture a transportation product, the organizations differ significantly. Cars and trucks come in many different models; designs are modified according to an annual cycle, and new designs are developed to production according to a ten-year cycle. Each model has many parts assembled from numerous vendors as well as diverse facilities within the automotive corporation itself. The mass-production process has many stages and problems, and quality and performance are constant concerns. Because of its mass-production processes, an automobile company differs from a specialty chemical company just as significantly as it does from a shipyard.

Consequently, technical-communication procedures in an automobile company differ. The complexity of communication tasks distinguishes an automobile company. Yet the manufacturing environment provides a functional context that enables communication procedures to be formalized and communication purposes to be delineated clearly. Writers must be able to define a purpose clearly because of the size and complexity of the organization. However, they must be able to distinguish among a number of different possible purposes, whereas in a shipyard they and their audiences rarely would have a concern or question over the purpose of a document. Unlike shipyard reports, many reports in an automobile company are decision-making reports requiring considerable judgment. Unlike specialty chemical company reports, therefore, the reports usually embody a persuasive approach. The writers must be able to select and arrange material both functionally and persuasively. Typical report-writing guidelines, such as our heuristic for the purpose statement, seem to apply to many of these reports more directly than they do to typical reports in some other types of organizations.

Differences in organizations are variables often discussed in organizational literature. The differences among various industries are characterized according to type of industry, as I have discussed above. In complex industries, the differences are explained in terms of various organizational functions (subsystems) within an industry itself (similar to my division of reports in shipyards into problem-solving and administrative categories). These vary according to the way an industry is organized. Differences between organizations also are defined in terms of organizational design variables, such as whether the organization is market-driven or resource-driven.

We all realize, of course, that organizations vary according to their products and activities.

> A large enterprise like the General Electric Company will apportion a sizable chunk of its resources to varous forms of research with respect to increasing basic knowledge in the physical sciences, applying such knowledge to the manufacture of new and improved products, and investigating the needs of the changing world which the company serves. . . . In contrast to General Electric, automobile companies deal with a single complex product which calls for little basic scientific research. They are, therefore, more concerned with the utilization of knowledge than with the development of new knowledge.[57]

The result is, or should be, differences in organizational structures:

> A fair amount of variation in both firms and industries is due to the type of work done in the organization—the technology. We are now fairly confident in recommending that if work is predictable and routine, the necessary arrangement for getting the work done can be highly structured, and one can use a good deal of bureaucratic theory in accomplishing this. If it is not predictable, if it is nonroutine and there is a good deal of uncertainty as to how to do a job, then one had better utilize the theories that emphasize autonomy, temporary groups, multiple lines of authority and communication, and so on.[58]

The structural differences result in differences in technical-communication procedures.

The function and form of technical communication are dependent variables that can be defined theoretically. For analytical purposes, Katz and Kahn divide organizations into five formal subsystems:

Production or technical subsystems
Supportive subsystems
Maintenance subsystems
Adaptive subsystems
Managerial subsystems

The implications for technical communication within each of these subsystems can be defined in terms of their functions. The production subsystem depends on status reports, quality control reports, specifications, etc.—the "nuts and bolts" reports that typify much shipyard reporting. Maintenance requires procedures, adaption requires trip reports, sales contact reports, recommendations, etc. Management requires policy statements, directives, and decision-making reports. Katz and Kahn then, in turn, "describe organizations as they assume a production, maintenance, adaptive, or managerial role in the society."[59]

This suggests that the same "type" of report can vary according to type of industry. For example, a progress report in a manufacturing industry often serves a maintenance function—sustaining the production processes and standard operating procedures. A progress report in a research-oriented industry, however, often is informational, serving an adaptive function; it has little immediate utilitarian function. Progress reports therefore vary in both content and form according to type of industry. In technical-communication terms, they vary according to their purposes. An analysis of an industry in terms of its function, then, provides the guidelines by which to teach and write progress reports. Such an analysis could be introduced in technical-communication discussions of "types of reports."

Organizations are analyzed from different perspectives as well. One analysis views organizations as "product-focused" or "process-focused."[60] In a product-focused organization, "communications and coordination across groups" are important. Written communication would seem to be a primary management tool. A process-focused organization, however, requires coordination and integration of functional responsibilities within a system. Written communication would seem to become secondary to informal or interpersonal communication-management approaches. Therefore, the relationships between written communication and other forms of communication are important report design considerations in some types of industry.[61]

Galbraith views organizational design from the point of view of uncertainty, and stresses the role of planning: "planning achieves integrated action and also eliminates the need for continuous communication among interdependent subunits as long as task performance stays within the planned task specifications, budget limits and within targeted completion dates."[62] Such organizations probably would rely more on status reports, for example, than on problem-solving or decision-making reports. Status reports are one means of formalizing information: "the cost of information processing resources can be minimized if the language is formalized."[63] A logical extension of this approach is to rely more heavily on visual than on verbal communication, which is just what status reports usually do.

As I mentioned above, technical communication is a dependent variable in organizational design. Consequently, all approaches to organizational design introduce considerations for the teaching and writing of technical communication. These approaches have differing implications for technical communication. I have introduced some of them above. Other approaches discuss, for example, the matrix organization, centralized versus decentralized organization, participatory management organization, and the evolution or maturity of the organization. Each of these approaches introduces additional report-writing considerations.[64]

## THE LOCATION IN THE ORGANIZATION

In addition to differences among organizations, organizational literature discusses differences within organizations. Organizations consist of multiple units with differing purposes, and these various units must be coordinated if the organization is to achieve its goals. Technical communication, of course, is a means of coordination. However, different units within an organization have different functions and needs; therefore, technical communication varies within organizations as well as among organizations.

The different functions of technical communication within an organization can be explained in terms of the product cycle: R&D produces new product ideas and concepts; engineering translates these into designs and manufacturing specifications; manufacturing develops procedures and actually produces the products, supported by purchasing and other support groups; marketing sells the products; service supports the customers' use of the products; and technical liaison with the customers provides feedback to R&D for new product development as well as to engineering for current product modification.

Therefore, just as report writing practices vary according to type of industry, they vary within an organization as well. Reports connect different types of units. The need for effective technical communication is nicely illustrated in organizational literature:

> For example, product design and product manufacture must be tightly coordinated in the CIM [computer-integrated manufacturing] facility. Yet the usual communication pattern between these units shows product engineers "throwing the design over the wall" to production managers, who complain bitterly about the "nonmanufacturability" of the design.[65]

Effective technical communication often requires report writers to bridge barriers rather than circulate among cooperating units.

The premise for technical communication, as an analysis of the product cycle indicates, is that organizations themselves are not homogeneous. "Any organization design has to permit differences between subunits. . . . The members of each unit must develop differential patterns of behavior and ways of thinking consistent with who they are and what tasks they must perform in dealing with their particular part of the environment." These differences mean "that members of each unit will see problems that involve them with other units primarily from their own point of view. It is not surprising, therefore, that differentiation produces conflict. The sales manager wants to move up scheduling an order from a big customer. The plant manager is opposed because such an interruption will lead to higher manufacturing costs."[66]

Such differences within an organization require various means of "achieving integration," that is, of coordinating diverse efforts to achieve organizational goals. Technical communication is one of the means by which these units are interconnected. The task is to design technical communication to promote coordination rather than conflict. The difficulty of this task is illustrated by the observation that each unit sees problems from its "own point of view." For technical communication that goes between units (as does almost any important type of technical communication deserving of attention in a technical communication course), how does a writer formulate what we call the "purpose statement"?[67] Whose point of view or what point of view on the problem is defined in the purpose statement?

R&D illustrates the unique features of a unit within an organization. An examination of R&D illustrates how the unique qualities of each type of unit in an organization need to be analyzed in order to determine the implications for technical communication. R&D is an organizational function that has received considerable attention in organizational literature (Katz and Kahn classify R&D as an adaptive subsystem). It has also received some attention in technical-communication literature. The following discussion in general applies to engineering, production, marketing, etc., as well to R&D. The problem is that these other areas have not received the attention that R&D has, so the technical-communication implications remain even considerably less clear for these other units.

R&D is described as a distinctive unit in an organization, with values, thinking, and priorities at odds with those of other units in an organization. One writer characterizes R&D from an outsider-insider point of view. From the outside, others in the organization consider R&D a luxury and those in R&D to consider themselves special and difficult to communicate with. "R&D managers often appear not to be result-oriented. They seem to stray from the key purposes of the enterprise and seem actually to avoid managing their operations. They seem to have less control over their employees than managers in other parts of the organization have over their employees." From the inside, R&D staff feel that R&D "must be supported on faith by the other parts of the organization." "Research cannot be planned," and the activities do not correspond with annual budget cycles. "Much of the financial planning that we are asked to do takes us away from meaningful and important work."[68]

The concept of R&D, furthermore, is a generic concept. Research and development have different functions, which can be operationalized by the fact that "one recruits Ph.D. scientists for research and . . . M.S. engineers for development."[69] The distinction between scientists and engineers has been the subject of considerable research, and has been characterized as "cosmopolitan" versus "local."[70] The engineer's goals and values typically are in harmony with those of the company, whereas the scientist's are in harmony with those of his or her profession or field. The result is that there are differences within R&D units as well as between R&D units and the rest of the organization.

Most of the literature, however, focuses on R&D as a distinct and even unique organizational unit. It is a type of unit whose communication tasks have also received considerable attention in organizational literature. Allen observes that "an overwhelming body of research evidence indicates that the most direct route to increasing research and development productivity is through developing good technical communication within the R&D organization itself."[71] He then goes on to propose improvements in information systems to improve R&D performance. "At present, most projects are coordinated, as they have been for years, by means of periodic review meetings and written status reports or memoranda. There is absolutely no reason why such devices cannot be put 'on line.' " He also proposes changes in organizational structure so that the "second layer of communication . . . insures that the technical staff of the project remain in close contact with developments in their technical specialties."[72]

Along with Allen, Tushman has investigated means of improving R&D communication. He proposes a "contingency" approach to managing communication because "projects with different work characteristics will require systematically different communication networks in order to deal with the problem-solving requirements of their work. There will, then, be no one best communication pattern." He divides communication patterns into three types—intraproject, intrafirm, and extrafirm—and proposes a communication design model. Unlike Allen, however, Tushman concentrates on verbal (i.e., oral) communication and prefers it because it "is a more efficient information medium than written or more formal media (e.g., management information systems)."[73] It remains a matter for research in technical communication to determine how written communication should complement "verbal" communication and a communication model such as Tushman proposes. It seems to me, at least, that not all of Tushman's communication tasks, especially for "extraproject communication," can be performed orally. The question is, can all of these tasks be relegated to information processing systems or should some of them be performed by written communication (on-line or hard copy) networks?

A central problem with R&D units is the "technology transfer" problem. Organizations need an effective means of transferring the technology developed in R&D to their operational units. This primarily is a communication problem: "managements have provided neither the organizations necessary to generate required information nor the procedures to effectively bring this information before the right people."[74] The role of technical communication seems central to the means proposed to develop and use information effectively. One of the problems, for example, is defined as follows: "Many marketing and market research groups do not have technically trained people who can communicate well enough with R&D either to understand the potential significance of R&D results or to specify market opportunities in technical terms researchers can appreciate." The converse also is true, as discussed below. R&D groups often cannot or will not communicate with other groups. The solutions to these various problems involve numerous organizational strategies in which the role of technical communication often is undefined.

The communication barriers between R&D and the rest of the organization are seen to be so rigid that Tushman proposes what he calls "boundary-spanning individuals," whom he also calls "gatekeepers."

> In order to more effectively accomplish the work required for any project, distinctive norms, values, and language schemes typically evolve. These local languages make communication across boundaries difficult and prone to bias and distortion. . . . Since communication across boundaries is difficult, and given that external information is vital to the project, one technique for attending to information from highly differentiated areas is through the use of boundary-spanning individuals. These individuals straddle several communication boundaries and serve as liaisons to external areas.[75]

It does not necessarily follow that technical-communication techniques do not provide satisfactory solutions or alternatives to such approaches as Tushman proposes. But the applicability of technical-communication solutions has yet to be explored.

The Paradis, Dobrin, and Miller study of "Writing at Exxon ITD: Notes on the Writing Environment of an R&D Organization" is an important study from the point of view of technical communication.[76] Although the authors do not define the organizational needs of R&D units in the same way that these have been defined in organizational literature, they propose that "written communication offers many advantages" over oral communication. Yet, as they observe in their case study and as illustrated in most of the organizational literature I have referenced, writing is not "widely recognized as a key work activity."

It seems to me that certain advantages would enable written communication to overcome barriers between R&D and other units in an organization. Progress reports, analytical reports, and various memoranda can be designed to communicate across unit boundaries—if the technical-communication procedures and practices are designed to facilitate "boundary-spanning." If one approaches technical communication as a problem-solving process, as Paradis et al. and we elsewhere define it, such design might be possible.[77] Our own analysis of certain types of documents in an industrial research organization, in particular progress reports and some analytical reports, indicates that this can be accomplished by training R&D staff to think in terms of the organizational functions or purposes of written communication. The point of view to be defined in the purpose statement is not that of the writer or of the primary audience but one which comprehends both the writer's (and unit's) purpose and that audience's (and unit's) needs. Such a definition, of course, is not easily formulated.

The differences among units in an organization is familiar to technical writing consultants who teach in-house courses in industry. Many of these courses are attended by persons from different departments, and they often have quite different concepts of technical communication and its purposes. Consequently, except for such common concerns as sentence editing and paragraphing, they have different needs. Unfortunately, the differing functions of technical communication among the various units have not been clearly defined except in terms of different types of reports, such as the research report, the progress report, the proposal, etc. What is needed is a model of the technical-communication processes within organizations that can account for the differences in these types of reports within the organization itself, such as differences in progress reports among departments.

The industrial context therefore introduces numerous independent variables into written-communication processes. These organizational factors influence the forms, the content, and the processes by which written communication actually functions in industry. The nature and extent of most of these influences, however, can be explored much further than they have been to date. The results of future research in these areas should considerably enrich the field of technical communication.

A final note on the organizational approach to technical communication. The organizational literature that I have briefly introduced has been both descriptive and normative. That is, some of the literature "models" organizational behavior. Other of the literature proposes means of improving organizational behavior.

The same distinction applies to its implications for written communication. I started this essay from a descriptive perspective, and introduced four components of the organizational context that influence how written communication actually occurs in organizations. These four components have normative implications as well. Because of this context, written communication procedures and practices in industry often should be changed in order to be more effective than they are at present. This is a challenge for technical communication.

In addition, written communication procedures and practices have to be designed to complement normative organizational approaches. In the multinational economic environment, strategies for organizational change and for managing innovation—for designing factories and enterprises of the future—are becoming increasingly important in the industrial world as well as in the academic world. Implementation of these strategies in part will depend on effective support systems such as those of written communication.

These technical-communication support systems have yet to be defined.

## Notes

1. Written communication by professionals. My discussion concerns the writing that various professionals—accountants, engineers, scientists, managers, etc.—have to do as part of their job or role in an organization. This primarily is written communication for persons elsewhere in the organization or in other organizations, not for the public or the private citizen. Although this can include written communication by professional technical writers, I usually do not have them in mind.

2. Models derived from *The Process of Communication,* David K. Berlo, New York: Holt, Rinehart and Winston, 1960, p. 72, define the "source" and "receiver" in organizational terms.
3. In *Designing Technical Reports,* New York: Macmillan, 1976, p. 7, Dwight W. Stevenson and I explicitly put the "report design process" in the context of the "organizational system." Although our model embodies some aspects of the Berlo model, it essentially adopts a problem-solving, systems approach. (A revised edition is forthcoming that addresses some of the issues I am discussing here.)
4. In *Effective Business Report Writing,* 4th ed., Englewood Cliffs, N.J.: Prentice-Hall, 1985, pp. 6–10, Leland Brown combines the communication process model with our organizational model.
5. Audience analysis within organizations is discussed by Kenneth W. Houp and Thomas E. Pearsall in *Reporting Technical Information,* 5th ed., New York: Macmillan, 1984, pp. 20–47, as well as in references 3 and 4.
6. James W. Souther, "What to Report," *IEEE Transactions on Professional Communication,* PC-28:3 (September 1985), pp. 5–8. This article originally appeared in 1962; it has been reprinted several times.
7. Henry Mintzberg, "The Manager's Job: Folklore and Fact," *Harvard Business Review* (July–August 1975): 49–61.
8. Robert L. Brown, Jr. and Carl G. Herndl, "An ethnographic study of corporate writing: job status as reflected in written text," in *Functional Approaches to Writing,* ed. Barbara Couture, Norwood, N.J.: Ablex, 1986, pp. 11–28.
9. Carol Lipson, "Technical Communication: The Cultural Context," *The Technical Writing Teacher,* XIII:3 (Fall 1986): 318–323. She also discusses differences between organizations.
10. Richard C. Freed and Glenn J. Broadhead, "Discourse Communities, Sacred Texts, and Institutional Norms," *College Composition and Communication,* 38:2 (May 1987): 154–165. Also, Teresa M. Harrison, "Frameworks for the Study of Writing in Organizational Contexts," *Written Communication,* 9:1 (January 1987): 3–23.
11. William V. Ruch, *Corporate Communications: A Comparison of Japanese and American Practices,* Westport, Conn.: Quorum Books, 1984. The need to supplement "technical information" with "social information" (e.g., cross-cultural) in multinational corporations is the theme of Vladimir Pucik and Jan Hack Katz in "Information, Control, and Human Resource Management in Multinational Firms," *Human Resource Management,* 25:1 (Spring 1986): 121–132.
12. Jack Selzer, "The Composing Processes of an Engineer," *College Composition and Communication,* 34:2 (May 1983): 178–187.
13. *Research in Technical Communication,* ed. Michael G. Moran and Debra Journet, Westport, Conn.: Greenwood Press, 1985. See also *Handbook of Organizational Communication,* ed. Fredric M. Jablin, Linda L. Putnam, Karlene H. Roberts, and Lyman W. Porter, Newbury Park, Calif.: Sage Publications, 1987, especially "Evolving Perspectives in Organization Theory: Communication Implications," "Organizational Culture: A Critical Assessment," "Formal Organization Structure," and "Power, Politics, and Influence."
14. My approach, at least, when doing research or teaching industry, is to particularize our generic problem-solving communication model so that it is seen to be appropriate for that specific organizational context. For teaching, when possible I generate a manual or workbook specifically for that industry rather than use a text or generic workbook. These field studies provide some of the information that I use in this analysis.

15. Herbert A. Simon, *Administrative Behavior*, 3rd ed., New York: The Free Press, 1976.
16. Simon, p. xxxvi.
17. Simon, pp. 154–155.
18. Mathes and Stevenson, *Designing Technical Reports*, pp. 14–23.
19. Simon, pp. 14–15.
20. This is evident when our audience analysis procedure [18] is applied to any report in industry and the results compared with the lines of authority (the organization chart) of the organization. The problem is mentioned by Simon: "Barnard's [one of the founders of organization theory] discussion of communications . . . suffers somewhat from his identification of communication channels with channels of authority" (p. 155). It also is mentioned in other organizational literature, such as in Jeffrey Pfeffer and Gerald R. Salancik, "Organization Design: The Case for a Coalitional Model of Organizations," *Introduction to Organizational Behavior*, L. L. Cummings and Randall B. Dunham, Homewood, Ill.: Irwin, 1980, p. 482: "The pattern of interactions, responsibilities, and communication flows invariably differs from the formally specified pattern."
21. Mathes and Stevenson, *Designing Technical Reports*, pp. 14–23.
22. Although Berlo [2] conceives of communication as persuasive, his model is often used as an information transfer model in which technical communication is discussed as expository with a purpose to present scientific and technical subject matter clearly and objectively. Although this is an important aspect of technical communication, it is not the primary purpose of much of the writing that professionals actually do on the job.
23. Management information systems (MIS) are information processing communication systems that are data-based, programmed "technical communication." "The system that monitors and retrieves data from the environment, captures data from transactions and operations within the firm, filters, organizes, and selects data and presents them as information to managers, and provides the means for managers to generate information as desired is called the management information system (MIS)": Robert G. Murdick, *MIS Concepts and Design*, 2nd ed., Englewood Cliffs, N.J.: Prentice Hall, 1986, p. 6.
24. Decision support systems (DSS) are computer-based problem-solving systems to help managers make decisions. MIS systems focus on providing information; DSS process information in a decision-making heuristic. An excellent introduction to DSS, especially relevant to this discussion, is Peter G. W. Keen and Michael S. Scott Morton, *Decision Support Systems: An Organizational Perspective*, Reading, Mass.: Addison-Wesley, 1978.
25. Simon, p. 15.
26. Simon, pp. 11–18.
27. Mintzberg, "The Manager's Job," pp. 50, 52.
28. My discussion is based on an analysis of the *Transcript of Proceedings*, President's Commission [the "Kemeny Commission"] on the Accident at Three Mile Island, Public Hearings, July 18, 1979, and July 19, 1979. The *Transcript* is available at the Public Document Room of the Nuclear Regulatory Commission, 1717 H St. NW, Washington, D.C. My analysis is presented in my unpublished monograph "Three Mile Island: The Management Communication Failure," and reference 30.
29. *Three Mile Island: A Report to the Commissioners and to the Public*, Nuclear Regulatory Commission Special Inquiry Group, Mitchell Rogovin, director, II:1, p. 161.
30. The quotes are from the memorandum written by Mr. B. M. Dunn, the manager of the Emergency Core Cooling System Analysis department of B&W; this and the other

memoranda discussed are included as "exhibits" in reference 28. I analyze this particular communication process in "Three Mile Island: The Management Communication Role," *Engineering Management International*, 3 (1968): pp. 261–268.
31. Simon, p. xxviii.
32. Daniel Katz and Robert L. Kahn, *The Social Psychology of Organizations*, 2nd ed., New York: Wiley, 1978, p. 19.
33. Keen and Morton, p. 65.
34. Barbara Mirel, *Text and Context: The Special Case of In-House Documentation*, a University of Michigan doctoral dissertation, p. 3.
35. Mirel, p. 3.
36. Mirel, p. 7.
37. Mirel, p. 9.
38. Organizational theories and models are classified in various ways. A brief but convenient introduction is provided in Keen and Morton [24], who divide decision-making literature into five categories: the rational manager view, the satisficing or process-oriented view, the organizational procedures view, the political view, and the individual differences perspective (pp. 62–63ff). An in-depth survey of organizational theory is provided by Jeffrey Pfeffer in "Organizations and Organization Theory," *Handbook of Social Psychology*, vol. 1, eds. Gardner Lindzey and Elliot Aronson, New York: Random House, 1985, pp. 379–440. He divides organization theory into three "perspectives on action": rational or boundedly rational, externally constrained or situationally determined, and process. The chapter then details numerous theories or models within these three broad perspectives [pp. 383–384ff]. Yet another convenient survey is presented by Dennis J. Palumbo in "Organization Theory and Political Science," *Micropolitical Theory*, vol. 2, eds. Fred I. Greenstein and Nelson W. Polsby, Reading, Mass.: Addison-Wesley, 1975, pp. 319–369.
39. James D. Thompson, *Organizations in Action*, New York: McGraw-Hill, 1967, p. 19.
40. Memorandum by D. F. Hallman, exhibit 5 in reference 28.
41. J. C. Mathes, "Technical Communication: The Persuasive Purpose," *English in Texas*, 11:4 (Summer 1980): 83.
42. Simon, p. 128.
43. Karrasch testimony, reference 28, pp. 240 and 241. Hallman actually was a Ph.D. and addressed by the committee as "Dr." This, of course, introduces another possible complication in the attitude of each toward the other. Within B&W, however, most persons seemed to have called each other by their first names.
44. Herta A. Murphy and Herbert W. Hildebrandt, *Effective Business Communications*, 4th ed., New York: McGraw-Hill, 1984, p. 28.
45. R. M. Cyert and J. G. March, "The Behavioral Theory of the Firm: A Behavioral Science—Economics Amalgam," *New Perspectives in Organization Research*, eds. W. W. Cooper, H. J. Leavitt, and M. W. Shelly, New York: Wiley, 1964, pp. 291–292.
46. Karrasch testimony, reference 28, p. 249.
47. John P. Kotter, Leonard A. Schlesinger, and Vijay Sathe, *Organization*, 2nd ed., Homewood, Ill.: Irwin, 1986, p. 131. The authors are describing, not endorsing, the practice.
48. Pfeffer and Salancik, p. 484.
49. Pfeffer and Salancik, p. 482.
50. Mathes and Stevenson, *Designing Technical Reports*, pp. 24–42.
51. Pfeffer and Salancik, p. 487.

52. Henry Mintzberg, *Power In and Around Organizations*, Englewood Cliffs, N.J.: Prentice-Hall, 1983, pp. 187–212.
53. Mintzberg, *Power in and Around Organizations*, p. 198.
54. Some considerations also clearly have ethical implications, but these are not easy to resolve. Any organizational model has ethical implications. Political considerations, for example, may seem unethical to some persons. However, if these are operative in the real organizational world, to what extent should they be considered in technical communication? And, when they are, what are the ethical implications of alternative communication strategies?
55. J. C. Mathes and Dwight W. Stevenson, *Writing Shipyard Reports*, 1988, a product of the Written Communication for U. S. Shipyard Professional Project, DTMA 91-82-C-20022, J. C. Mathes, Project Director, Program in Technical Communication, The University of Michigan, 1988.
56. The problem is discussed by Jone Rymer Goldstein in "The Interface of Oral and Written Communication: Margin of Excellence for the Beginning Engineer," *Proceedings of the North Central Section of the American Society for Engineering Education*, University of Toledo, Toledo, Ohio, April 13–14, 1978, Washington, D.C.: American Society for Engineering Education, pp. 102–107.
57. Katz and Kahn, p. 88.
58. Charles Perrow, "The Short and Glorious History of Organizational Theory," *Perspectives on Behavior in Organizations*, 2nd ed., eds. J. Richard Hackman, Edward E. Lawler, and Lyman W. Porter, New York: McGraw-Hill, 1983, p. 96.
59. Katz and Kahn, pp. 51–59, 83–84, 143–148.
60. Robert H. Hayes and Roger W. Schmenner, "How Should You Organize Manufacturing?" *Readings in the Management of Innovation*, eds. Michael L. Tushman and William M. Moore, Cambridge, Mass.: Ballinger, 1982, p. 456.
61. Thomas J. Peters and Robert H. Waterman, *In Search of Excellence*, New York: Harper & Row, 1982, pp. 218–223.
62. Jay R. Galbraith, "Organization Design: An Information Processing View," *Perspectives on Behavior in Organizations*, p. 433.
63. Galbraith, p. 435.
64. The implications for communication of the contingency approach to organizational design are discussed by James DeConinck and Dale Level, "An Analysis of Current Perspectives of the Influence of Communication in Successful Organizations," *The Bulletin of the Association for Business Communication*, L:1 (March 1987): 7–11.
65. David B. Roitman, Jeffrey K. Liker, and Ethel Roskies, "Birthing a Factory of the Future," *Corporate Transformation*, eds. Ralph H. Kilmann, Teresa M. Covin, and associates, San Francisco: Jossey-Bass, 1987, p. 209.
66. Jay W. Lorsch, "Organizational Design: A Situational Perspective," *Perspectives on Behavior in Organizations*, pp. 442, 444. The subsystems defined by Katz and Kahn [59] also demonstrate how organizations are not homogeneous.
67. Mathes and Stevenson, *Designing Technical Reports*, pp. 24–42.
68. Donald Britton Miller, *Managing Professionals in Research and Development*, San Francisco: Jossey-Bass, 1986, pp. 33, 35, 36.
69. Miller, pp. 42–43.
70. Richard Ritti, "Work Goals of Scientists and Engineers," *Readings in the Management of Innovation*, p. 364.
71. Thomas J. Allen, "Organizational Structure, Information Technology, and R&D Pro-

ductivity," *IEEE Transactions on Engineering Management,* EM-33:4 (November 1986): 212.
72. Allen, p. 216.
73. Michael L. Tushman, "Managing Communication Networks in R&D Laboratories," *Readings in the Management of Innovation,* pp. 355, 350.
74. James Brian Quinn and James A. Mueller, "Transferring Research Results to Operations," *Readings in the Management of Innovation,* pp. 63–64, 69.
75. Tushman, p. 357.
76. James Paradis, David Dobrin, and Richard Miller, "Writing at Exxon ITD," *Writing in Nonacademic Settings,* eds. Lee Odell and Dixie Goswami, New York: Guilford, 1985, pp. 289, 286.
77. Paradis, et al., p. 290, and Mathes and Stevenson, pp. 29–38.

# THE DISCOURSE COMMUNITIES AND GROUP WRITING PRACTICES OF MANAGEMENT STUDENTS

*Janis Forman*
*University of California at Los Angeles*

*Janis Forman designed and now directs the Management Communication Program of the Anderson Graduate School of Management at UCLA. After receiving her Ph.D. from Rutgers University, she was awarded a year-long National Endowment for the Humanities grant and a Fulbright Fellowship for her work in business writing, literature, and translation. She is currently completing a business writing textbook (Random House), conducting studies of computer-mediated group writing under a grant from IBM, and designing a course on organizational leadership that uses a "great books" approach. Her professional interests include group writing, program design, translation, literature, and the status of instructors in our profession. She has published widely in business writing, translation, and composition journals and consults for companies in the greater Los Angeles area.*

As writing instructors who teach in professional schools, we "transport" composition theory and practice to the teaching of writing in disciplines that represent discourse communities other than our own. Occasionally, our traditions are readily accepted.* This is true of the theory and practice of group writing. Management schools welcome our uses of group writing as the basis of writing instruction because group process is central to the education of managers. Upon graduating, management students (M.B.A.'s) enter work settings in which collaborative prob-

*This research has been funded by a grant from IBM. The author wants to thank Professors Jason Frand, Michael Granfield, Carol A. Scott, and Burt Swanson of the Anderson Graduate School of Management at UCLA for their support of this project.

lem solving and decision making are the rule, not the exception; this fact is reflected in the curricular emphasis on group work.

But, along with the welcome that group writing receives in management schools comes a challenge writing instructors must face: In order to assist management students with group writing, we need to familiarize ourselves with the kinds of discourse managers are expected to use. The most sophisticated is the discourse of management strategy.

The purpose of this article is to explore the discourse communities and group writing practices of M.B.A.'s engaged in writing strategic reports and to suggest how the instruction of M.B.A.'s may be improved. A specific kind of strategic report written by M.B.A. teams at the Anderson Graduate School of Management at UCLA serves as the basis of this analysis, but the analysis has implications for the education of M.B.A.'s at other schools.

To begin, let us look at what the writing task requires and what characterizes the language of management strategy. Then let us assess discourse errors and group writing problems of several representative M.B.A. teams. Finally, let us consider how the instruction of M.B.A.'s may be improved.

## THE WRITING TASK AND THE DISCOURSE OF MANAGEMENT STRATEGY

In their final year of the M.B.A. program and as the culmination of their course work, students are asked to form teams of three to five and to do a "real world" consulting project for a sponsoring organization under the guidance of a faculty adviser. The M.B.A.'s identify and solve a strategic business problem for the organization and present their analysis and recommendations in a strategic management report.

The term "strategic" is important here. The typical undergraduate business school project is not strategic. It requires students to use a discrete conceptual framework, such as marketing analysis, to address a problem. For instance, an undergraduate might investigate whether a company should revise its advertising campaign to increase sales of product X. By contrast, master's-level students doing strategic studies are expected to use several conceptual frameworks (e.g., economics, finance, human resources, and marketing) to address issues that go beyond one functional area, such as marketing, and influence the organization as a whole. The work of M.B.A.'s resembles the kind of thinking done by top management in a company. For instance, a team might investigate which product lines a company should buy or sell *given its long-range or strategic goals of steady growth in a few product lines.*

Strategic studies, then, use the other management disciplines[1] (e.g., economics, finance, human resources, marketing) as they help to elucidate a top-level problem faced by an organization. Each of these management disciplines has its own discourse—the language of economists, financial analysts, human resource managers, market researchers, etc.[2] The discourse of management strategy includes each of these discourses in addition to a language that refers to the long-range and top-level goals of an organization. As an example of strategic discourse, let us look at an excerpt from a well-written strategic report. In this section, the M.B.A.'s are summarizing the scope of their project for a private social club in Los Angeles. Notice how the team's strategic language incorporates the languages of several other management disciplines (e.g., "breakeven" of finance, "penetration" of marketing, and "traffic flow" of operations management) and a language referring to the long-range goals of the club (e.g., "overall plans and objectives"):

> While the profit picture has improved, the Nonesuch Club still has many problems in a variety of areas. This project focuses on the marketing, financial and operational aspects of the Nonesuch Club. The study provides the club's management and Board of Directors with several recommendations for *making the club a more profitable entity while maintaining its exclusive reputation and clientele* [emphasis added]. The club has agreed to view our recommendations and to implement those that will fit in with its *overall plans and objectives.* [author's emphasis]

Our study involved the following:

1. *Financial Analysis*
   -calculation of breakeven
   -analysis of fixed and variable costs
   -analysis of various financial statistics and operations (e.g., cash flow)
   -comparison to industry statistics and local club cost structures.
2. *Market Analysis*
   -identification of current market and its preferences
   -identification of potential new markets and penetration of existing ones
   -comparison of the club's marketing strategies to its competitors'
   -development of a marketing plan
3. *Operational Analysis*
   -analysis of traffic flow through club
   -analysis of membership usage of club facilities
   -analysis of operating procedures (bar, dining room, etc.)

As this writing sample demonstrates, the language of management strategy is both interdisciplinary and hierarchical. As an interdisciplinary language, strategic discourse involves synthesis and a kind of global thinking. As an hierarchical language, it subsumes the discourses of other management disciplines under a reigning language—one concerned with organizational objectives.

In order to undertake strategic studies, M.B.A.'s are encouraged to form teams representing diverse management disciplines. In effect, as the writing sample suggests, teams need to be interdisciplinary to do strategic analysis.

For many of the M.B.A.'s, the strategic study is the first assignment for which they are required to *think* as top-level managers, to work for a sustained amount of time in an interdisciplinary team, and to write a full-fledged strategic management report. As top-level managers, the students are expected to define problems and help make decisions that have implications for broad-based organizational policies and goals. The project and report are, then, an initiation into a new discourse community—the community of top-level managerial decision makers.

Successful M.B.A. teams learn the discourse of management strategy. And, since, as Mikhail Bakhtin points out, "all languages . . . are . . . forms for conceptualizing the world in words, specific world views, each characterized by its own objects, meanings, and values,"[3] the new discourse acquired by these M.B.A.'s involves mastery of a new lexicon and much more. The successful teams learn to use the interdisciplinary and hierarchical discourse of management strategy; their acquisition of the discourse suggests that they have shaped a new role for themselves as top-level managers and a new perspective for both analyzing business problems and presenting solutions to the management community. Like the specialists in the sciences whom Thomas A. Kuhn discusses in *The Structure of the Scientific Revolution*, the successful M.B.A.'s have learned the same technical literature and have drawn the same principles from it by the time they begin their consulting projects.[4] Again, like Kuhn's scientists at work in the lab or the field, the successful M.B.A.'s internalize ways of thinking used by top-level professionals and are further socialized into the professional community as they engage in group work with an organization and in report writing. For each team member, the end result of the strategic study is, then, the use of a new discourse in the fullest sense of the term.

Before beginning their strategic study, the M.B.A.'s worked in other discourse communities such as the management school, specialized disciplines, and work environments where they were doing everything *but* strategic studies. Students may have written papers in the disciplines, case write-ups, and business communications.

## DISCOURSE ERRORS

For some students, the job of figuring out the kind of discourse required of managers doing strategic studies becomes an impossible one. It is as though these students have entered what Kenneth Burke calls an "unending conversation"[5]—in this instance the unending conversation of managers who engage in strategic problem solving and discourse about businesses—and cannot "throw in their oar" or participate in the new discourse and contribute to it.

This inability to "enter the conversation" is the common error demonstrated in the following passages from four strategic reports:

1. What is Los Angeles? There is a physical city of 464 square miles and over 3 million people. But L.A. is not just an ordinary city! It has a distinctive spirit that is L.A.—a spirit that combines opulence, casualness, glamour, success, newness, humor and excitement. This spirit is so loved by so many people that L.A. is expected to be the largest city in the country by the year 2000.
2. X Laboratories manufactures containers of pencil-style cosmetics, perfumes, and deodorants. To manufacture the pencil-style cosmetics, workers use injection-mold techniques. The pencils are then imprinted with decorations, brand names,

color names, etc., using stamping machines. . . . The final step of the process is to manually insert the retracting mechanism and the product stick (eyeliner, perfume, solid deodorant) and package.
3. Consulting is a multimillion dollar industry in the United States. It ranges from small, one-man operations to firms with hundreds of professionals. Entry barriers are low, and a successful consultant starting his own company will often be able to bring over clients from his former employer. The smallest companies tend to offer specialized services while the larger firms offer general management advice.
4. Chung Yen is a scion of a rich Chinese clan in Hong Kong. The family's wealth primarily came from ownership of a tobacco company which had over five thousand subcontracted farmers scattered all over Southeast Asia. In 1980, Mr. Yen came to the United States in search of a computer system that would aid his family business in handling the large number of farmer accounts. He needed a multiuser microcomputer system that would allow several users to operate at the same time. Yen found no such system. He discussed this with one of his friends, Mr. Wu, a computer engineer. Wu said he could make one. Thus, Wu designed the computer; Yen financed the production and that was the beginning of a new company.

Each passage was intended to represent part of a strategic report. But, despite the common assignment, if we ask ourselves where each of these passages is likely to be found, my guess is that we would all agree that passage 1 is from an ad, 2 from a technical manual, 3 from a textbook, and 4 from a narrative, perhaps a biography or a company history. None of the passages belong in a strategic report.

Errors in the four writing samples are not random. Each sample represents a discourse belonging to a community the students in that group formerly or currently belong to. Sample 1, the ad, was written primarily by a student who worked in advertising before entering the M.B.A. program. Sample 2, the technical description of pencil-style cosmetics manufacturing, is the work of students with undergraduate technical degrees. Sample 3, the textbook, and sample 4, the narrative, each represent a form of management-school discourse. As students, M.B.A.'s read only textbooks and cases (narratives about companies in crisis). Not surprisingly, these students reverted to writing the dominant institutional discourse they have been reading in their two years at school. In sum, these M.B.A. groups have not caught the gist of the management strategy conversation and have fallen back on one or another of the discourses familiar to the team members in charge of writing the report. For these teams, language is polyphonic; it calls up authoritative voices from their past that account for the discourse problems.

## PROBLEMS IN GROUP WRITING

One might argue that the discourse errors revealed in the consulting reports of the four M.B.A. teams would show up whether students worked alone or in groups. What part, then, does the group aspect of this assignment play in the discourse errors? Our answer lies in looking at the group processes of poorly functioning teams.[6]

Several problems that characterize the work of poorly functioning groups may contribute to discourse errors: team selection, client management, leadership, group values, revision strategies, and criteria for evaluating writing. The first four appear early in the strategic study and can influence the entire process, the last two toward the end of the project as the report is being written.

Sample 2, the technical manual, epitomizes the problem with team selection. This team was composed of students with similar technical backgrounds. Despite the interdisciplinary nature of the assignment, these students chose to work together. Since they shared similar paradigms for analyzing problems, theirs was a closed interpretive community like that of the scientific specialists Kuhn describes. As a result, little internal debate occurred and a broad managerial perspective for addressing strategic problems did not emerge.

Like team selection, poor client management may arise early in a group project and may result in a poorly written report. Client management involves the relationship the team establishes with the sponsoring organization. As outside consultants, students need to skillfully negotiate their study with the sponsoring organization. But, in some instances, even though the team is required by the university to do a strategic study, the client may ask for a technical manual or some other narrowly defined communication. Perhaps because a team sees itself primarily as students meeting a university requirement rather than as professional consultants, the M.B.A.'s may give in to the client's demands and forfeit their own objectives. The team does the technical manual and not the strategic report.

A third difficulty, which also may arise early in the group project, is the selection of a leader. It may result in the wrong person taking charge of the report. In the case of sample 1, the ad copy, the student on the team with the background in advertising claimed ownership of the report, and his claim went uncontested. When questioned, other team members reported that their admiration for his rich vocabulary convinced them to let him to take the lead.

Group values may also interfere with a team's ability to turn out a successful consulting report. For example, the ad copy team valued conflict avoidance above all. As a result, even if team members disagreed with the advertising framework used by their group leader, they would most likely have chosen group harmony over conflict and given in to the one strong team member. Sometimes teams have pluralistic or democratic values. As a result, every group member has his or her say in the project, and the end product can resemble what one M.B.A. has called a "pot-luck supper." (He used the term to praise his team's group process.) The report is written in multiple voices—in as many frameworks, jargons, and styles as there are team members—and it lacks a strategic perspective that integrates these voices.

Two problems can surface toward the end of a project as the team writes its report: poor assumptions about how to evaluate writing and poor revision strategies. Team members may apply varying criteria for evaluating writing that are derived from earlier discourse communities the students have belonged to. Especially if they have worked before getting their M.B.A., good writing may mean to these students the way it is done at Proctor and Gamble, Xerox, or wherever else they have worked. At P&G, a manager needs to express his or her ideas in one page. At Xerox, a report should be a bare-bones outline.

Yet another difficulty involves teams having no sense of holistic revision. Even if teams have difficulties with other aspects of the group writing process, they might still produce a good strategic report if they understand holistic revision. Such knowledge serves as a check, prompting writers to ask what a document should do and to reconceptualize a study if necessary. With this knowledge, the teams that wrote the four samples would have known that the kinds of discourse they produced were inappropriate given the rhetorical situation. If these teams were unable to revise their reports, at least they could have sought the assistance of their faculty adviser to help them reconceptualize their study. But most M.B.A.'s view revision as sentence-level changes. It is a rare group that "gets behind" the framework of their analysis and discusses whether their report is achieving its purpose.

## IMPROVING THE INSTRUCTION OF M.B.A.'S

Given the discourse errors and group writing problems of M.B.A. teams, we need to find ways to help students with their group writing of strategic reports. In doing so, we also help them enter a new discourse community and collaborate successfully with one another as members of this community.

The discourse errors and group writing difficulties of the representative M.B.A. teams suggest that sequential group writing assignments would be useful to them. Students need to move through a *sequence* of increasingly more difficult group writing assignments to prepare for the strategic report, which is a complex interdisciplinary group project. For instance, early in their education, M.B.A.'s can work in groups, doing analyses of cases involving simple problems faced by organizations. The students can focus on the intricacies of group work without having to tackle the difficult conceptual work of an interdisciplinary project at the same time. Our management colleagues in organizational studies and small-group problem solving may be able to help us design group writing assignments that explicitly address the group problems experienced by M.B.A.'s: group selection, client management, leadership, and group values.

If we have learned something about the discourse communities of the professional schools where we work, our understanding of discourse can also lead us beyond our writing classrooms into those forums where management curriculum is discussed. As we have seen, the discourse errors of M.B.A. teams are not merely surface features that can be "patched up" by a quick course in report writing. Rather, these errors may indicate that students have not yet grasped how to think about business problems from a top-level perspective that takes into account several conceptual frameworks; the unsuccessful M.B.A. teams are not yet strategic thinkers. More symptoms than problems, the discourse errors that appear in strategic reports provide clues concerning gaps in the education of M.B.A.'s. At present, M.B.A.'s take only one required course in strategy before conducting their consulting projects. Perhaps a second course is needed. More importantly, whether or not a new course is offered, there should be room in the study of strategic analysis for students to learn how to talk about strategic discourse so that they can sort out the multiple frameworks they bring to the study of significant problems in organizations, resolve conflicts about the different frameworks of group members, and formulate a strategic perspective. Although writing instructors cannot teach strategy as would a management instructor, they can contribute to the students' acquisition of a vocabulary for talking and writing about the complex language of management strategy.

Instruction in group writing is an easy course of study to "sell" in management schools, but teaching it effectively requires that we immerse ourselves in the discourse communities of management schools and businesses. Without knowledge of the languages of these communities, we remain on the periphery of the curriculum serving as "grammarians in residence" involved in remediation. With knowledge, our insights about discourse and group writing may influence not only our writing classes but also the core of the management curriculum.

## Notes

1. Some of the other disciplines include real estate, insurance, computers and information systems, accounting, and operations management.
2. This is an oversimplification, since each of these disciplines can be divided into several discourse communities. But I use the oversimplification to illustrate the interdisciplinary nature of strategic discourse.
3. See M. M. Bakhtin, *The Dialogic Imagination: Four Essays,* edited by Michael Holquist and translated by Caryl Emerson and Michael Holquist (Austin, Texas: University of Texas Slavic Series, No. 1, 1981).
4. See Thomas S. Kuhn's *Structure of Scientific Revolutions,* ed. 2, enlarged (Chicago: University of Chicago Press, 1970), p. 177.
5. Kenneth Burke, *The Philosophy of Literary Form,* ed. 3 (Berkeley, Calif.: University of California Press, 1973), p. 110.
6. For a more complete discussion of common errors in group writing, see Forman and Katsky, "The Group Report: A Problem in Small Group or Writing Processes?" in *Journal of the Association for Business Communications,* 23:4 (Fall 1986): 23–35.

# PART FIVE

# WRITING IN THE WORLD OF JOURNALISM

# DON'T PROFESS: COACH
## *Donald M. Murray*

*Donald M. Murray, Professor Emeritus of English at the University of New Hampshire, is a* Boston Globe *columnist and writing coach for the* Providence Journal *and the* Boston Globe. *Murray, who won a Pulitzer Prize as an editorial writer, is the author of* Writing for Your Readers *(Globe Pequot, 1983), which grew out of material he wrote as a writing coach. His other books include* A Writer Teaches Writing, Learning by Teaching, Write to Learn, *and* Read to Write.

*Teach writing to newspaper writers?*
  Yes. That's one of the part-time jobs an English instructor can get.
  *But that's crazy. A newspaper writer publishes more articles in a week than most English teachers do in a career.*
  That's right.
  *Then why would they hire me?*
  First, because newspapers are beginning to learn what has been obvious to many people for years: that they do not deliver most news first and that they have to complete with television, radio, magazines, paperback books, and VCR tapes for the reader's attention.
  *So?*
  Traditional newspaper writing does a superb job of delivering news—information about events that have just happened. But today's readers have heard about most significant events on the car radio or the tube. They will buy newspapers that tell them not only what but also why and how: what stories mean—stories that predict and interpret and analyze and sum up and probe and expose.
  *Don't newspaper writers know how to do this?*
  Sort of. Some do it well, but most reporters and editors are bound by strict traditions based on that "first news first" orientation. Newspaper people, like the rest of us, have difficulty breaking rules that were taught as theology. You may be able to help them see how they can extend the forms of writing to tell the stories that do not fit the conventional patterns—stories that deliver information their readers need and want.
  *Don't editors do this?*
  Some try, but you'll be amazed at the daily task they perform. Each day they scan volumes of information pouring in from the wires and from reporters. They

select the significant from what is happening everywhere in the world, even in space. They cover national, regional, state, and local news. Crime and courts and labor and business and sports and fashion and life-style and health and science and the arts and . . .

*O.K. already. I don't see the connection with a writing coach.*

Fair enough. You've got to realize that most editors are obsessed with the great mouth of the next edition behind them—and, before them, the growing alp of information pouring in from all over the world that has to be selected, filled out, cut, shaped, or rejected.

*You make them sound like fast-food fry cooks.*

They are, in a sense; and to do this job they depend on traditions—stereotypes, clichés, and formulas—to process the information. They don't have the time, most of them, to think about other ways the stories might be written—or the stories that aren't told because they would demand a new form of writing. They don't have time to think beyond the daily deadline, and they don't have the time or the training to teach reporters to write.

*But reporters are writers.*

Smile when you say that.

*Why?*

Most journalists consider themselves reporters, not writers. Even though there are more and more women reporters and editors, the city room is often a place in which too much attention to writing is seen as unmanly, literary, slightly unprofessional. The payoff is for "hard" news (phallic language intended)—murder, politics, devastation—not for "soft" news—features, backgrounders, profiles. The focus is on getting the story, not writing it.

*But they do write it, don't they?*

Yes, and more and more reporters seem to understand that the writing is important. Reporters and readers are better educated than they ever have been, and the stories they have to tell are more sophisticated, far more complex than when I started on a paper. Newspapers reflect a complicated, interrelated society in which social customs, environmental issues, politics, business, international affairs, and scientific developments all affect each other.

*A trained reader who knows something about writing may be able to help.*

And "help" is the right word. You can't go into a city room and teach in the traditional way. They may expect you to; after all, the only teachers they have known have stood before them talking, talking, talking. You have to be a coach.

*What do you mean by coaching? My football coach kicked ass.*

"Writing coach" may not be the right term, but it is the one that is used. The intent is to describe the process used by a singing coach, a tennis or golf pro, a sympathetic and experienced person who stands beside you and helps you decide how you could do a better job.

*Does that mean correcting the grammar, spelling, mechanics, stuff like that? I see a lot of sloppiness in the papers I read.*

Some coaches focus on such errors, but I think it is a waste of everyone's time. The paper has a sequence of story and copy editors whose job it is to catch such errors. They don't catch them all, but a system is in place that is designed to do that job. One of the problems in the city rooms I visit is that everyone is looking for error, and the staff may get the idea—and they may be right—that there are great penalties for small errors and few rewards for large successes. I like to spot what has gone *right* under the enormous pressures of time and space and reinforce it positively.

*I'm not sure I know enough to help them.*

If you know that, you won't be in trouble. You can't teach them their business, but you can help them see new solutions to old problems. It's not like traditional teaching, where you can control the subject matter, establish the standards, tell your students what to do, and then decide if they have done it. In the city room, the standards are established and enforced by others.

*Don't you get in their way?*

I don't, not so far, but I'm very careful. First of all, I do *not* comment on city-room politics; they are vicious, but Disneyland compared to campus politics. *Do not get involved.* Next, I encourage writers and editors to come up with their own solutions and, finally, if I make suggestions, I try to make three or more so the writer has to choose one—or, better yet, come up with a different solution. I peddle possibility.

*How do you do that?*

Well, I might say, "I wonder what would happen if you moved that paragraph down here. Or you could move it up, next to the lead. It might even make a good ending." I'm trying to get the writer to see the story in a way it hasn't been seen before.

*But I don't know what's considered right and wrong in a newspaper.*

Exactly. But you *are* a reader, and newspaper writers, unlike academic writers, have to reach a broad spectrum of readers. You can play the role of reader. And besides that, you are a special reader, one who knows the language and knows how the best writers have solved their writing problems. You'll see. You'll have plenty to say—perhaps too much, a common teacher failing.

*But I think I need to know more about how newspaper stories are written and edited.*

Of course you do, and you'll learn it by watching, listening, and, most of all, questioning. People won't expect you to be an authority, but they will be flattered if you ask them how they did a particularly good job of writing or editing.

*Will they tell me?*

They'll tell you. More than that, they'll tell themselves. Writing and editing are crafts that can seem to be done instinctively. When writers and editors tell you how they have gone about a task, they learn by articulating it; then you can spread the word, telling others what they have done or sending other reporters and editors to ask the same questions. We've made this strategy central to the program at the *Providence Journal* for the past seven years.

*How do you do that?*

There's a writing contest judged by the last three winners. To get a small check, you have to write an account "How I Wrote the Story," and that, with the story, is distributed to the staff. Many of these accounts have been collected in *How I Wrote the Story: A Book for Writers by Writers about Writing*, which was edited by Christopher Scanlan. The second edition can be purchased from the Providence Journal Book Club, 75 Fountain Street, Providence, RI 02902.

*What other techniques beside individual conferences and written accounts do you use to coach newspaper writers?*

When I was coach at the *Boston Globe* years ago, I put out a newsletter in which I wrote about writing, suggesting various solutions to common writing problems and printing interviews with *Globe* writers and editors. Many of those pieces were reprinted in my book *Writing for Your Readers: Notes on the Writer's Craft from the Boston Globe,* which was published by The Globe Pequot Press, Old Chester Road, Chester, CT 06412 and is still in print. Now that I'm back with the *Globe* I'm starting a new series of newsletters for the staff.

*I've heard about something called "Winners and Sinners" that critiques the writing and editing in the paper. Is that what you do?*

Not I. That can be very helpful, and at most papers such a publication is put out as part of the normal editing process. Both the *Globe* and the *Journal* have such publications and they do a good job. There is some overlap, but I try to discuss why some stories work, share tricks of the trade, and publish counsel on writing from published writers as well as from staff members. I try to communicate the excitement I feel about the craft of writing and to give specific suggestions, writer to writer.

*You haven't mentioned classes.*

Please. No classes. Workshops. Seminars. Brown-baggers. Lunches. Dinners. Roundtables. I've tried all sorts of such meetings and have discovered some guidelines that work for me. You'll have to develop your own with the writers and editors you're working with. Each paper has its own climate, what works for one may not work for another.

*Okay, but what are some of your guidelines?*

- I like to have the top editor participate, entering into every activity with the other workshop members.
- I find twelve a maximum number, which usually grows to fifteen or sixteen counting myself, the top editor, and other editors or contacts who keep the program going when I'm not there.
- I like to have us sit around a square of tables, four on a side so we can have a working surface, can face each other, and can hear what everyone has to say.
- I want at least one writer in any editors' workshop, at least one editor in each writers' workshop.
- I often have an activity so that we all do what we're talking about—writing leads, editing a feature, organizing a piece of writing. I write in public and share what I do. Writing is a surprisingly private activity—even in a city room.
- For a day-long meeting I like to have at least 3 hours in the morning, with

lunch served where we are meeting, and then 1½ hours after lunch to discuss what we've done in the morning and to answer questions. I usually start the morning session by having everyone write down questions, on 3- by 5-inch cards, that I answer before the day is over. But I delay answering them until I have created a context for my answering. For half-day sessions, I find 2½ hours minimal. In both cases I have coffee and tea available, but no official coffee break. And it's important to find a place away from the city room where people will not be disturbed.

- I prefer that participants volunteer. The session should not be seen as remedial or as punishment. Yes, the best writers will volunteer first, but they are often the most ignored writers; they need attention, and they can make use of it. They can also create an excitement about the program that makes others want to participate.
- I usually submit a list of topics for seminars or workshops. I make the list out of what I want to explore and what writers and editors want me to explore. Topics usually include lively writing, organizing complicated stories, and writing profiles, interviews, leads, ends, and so forth. I usually make a brief but well-organized presentation on the topic, generally backed up with a handout. If possible, I have an activity first, so that we participate in the kind of writing or editing we are going to discuss before I begin my presentation. Sometimes I use examples of good writing from the paper or from other sources. I prefer not to use bad examples. It's easy to say why a piece of writing fails, but it is more difficult, and more helpful, to have people discuss how and why a piece of writing works.
- I try to remember that my job is to get the participants talking about writing. It's hard for a professor not to profess, but they do not need to hear a lecture from an outsider; they need to learn from each other and to discover how to talk constructively about writing.
- I try to identify someone, usually a writer, who is interested in writing and who can become my contact person. This individual will be recognized by management as the person who will attend all sessions, clarify what has happened in our meetings, provide a continual contact with me to plan future meetings, and suggest ways to extend and continue the writing-improvement program.

*Okay, tell me if they think it's worthwhile to bring in someone like yourself to tell them what to do.*

They pay me and they invite me back. Seriously, I don't promise miracles, and no miracles occur. But the managements I've worked with seem to feel that the program has placed a constructive emphasis on writing, caused editors and writers to talk more about writing, and given them a common language with which to do it. Journalists are a critical bunch, and they doubt, question, and disagree, as they should and as our students should but usually don't. It's not important to me that they buy what I have to say as much as that we have the opportunity to learn together how effective writing is made.

*About that matter of pay.*

I wondered when you were going to ask about that.

*Well?*

I make more money as a writing coach than I do as a columnist. The pay is good. I find it helpful to charge by the day. Time is really the only measurable factor we have in such an intangible business. But don't forget that the daily fee may not be quite as good as you think it is when you figure in the time you take for preparation and travel. The days are long and intense. You're relating to new people and, in addition to formal sessions, there are lunches, sometimes breakfasts and dinners, and all sorts of spontaneous conferences in the informal climate of the city room.

*How much should I charge?*

First you have to take yourself seriously as a professional, and then you have to find out what other consultants get. Ask around and find out how much people on your faculty receive when they consult with businesses, or even when they speak at professional organizations or run workshops in the schools. Find out what lawyers pay English teachers who testify about language in libel suits. Talk to some people in companies in your area and find out what they pay on a daily basis for consultants. You certainly won't be able to charge what top-flight lawyers get, or experts in computers, but you should be able to charge a satisfying fee, and management expects to pay well for consultants. You'll find they respect you more if you respect yourself enough to have a daily rate that is on a professional level. The daily rate of consultants I know in the newspaper business ranges from $500 to $1,500 a day.

*I like the sound of that, but are there any other benefits than money?*

There certainly are. First of all, you have the opportunity to learn how professional writers and editors work. They will teach you far more than you will teach them. And this contact with professionals can give you a greater sense of authority with your students. This authority is mostly internalized. You will speak with greater confidence. But you should also let your students, colleagues, and administrators know that professionals respect and pay for your expertise in writing. This may not make you loved, but it may make you respected, or at least steered clear of. It is no small gift to have your colleagues give you some space in which to do your own work in your own way.

*Do you have any final tips or counsel?*

Always.

- It's easy for academics to dump on journalism or to dismiss the realities of time and space to which journalists must attend. Writing a news story or editing a paper is not astrophysics, but it is an unusually demanding intellectual discipline. Journalists have to absorb, order, and understand an extraordinary amount of information and then make their understanding clear. There is plenty of intellectual challenge in that.
- Be prepared—carefully prepared. Read the paper. Newspapers will send you copies, and I find it's important to read at least six weeks of a paper before

I run a session at a new publication. When I have read only a week of papers, or two weeks, I've made some very shaky assumptions. If you're going to make a presentation on a topic, have specific suggestions that are concrete and practical. What you can do is provide alternatives and present them as possibilities, so that your listeners can see routine tasks in a new way.

- Your greatest skill will be the ability to listen. Let editors and reporters tell you what they do and how they do it. Invite them to tell you other ways it might be done. Don't come on with the kind of peacock display that is often encouraged in the academic world. Be a student of the city room, paying attention to what is and what isn't going on.
- Watch out if you begin to think of yourself as an authority on journalism. You are not, and nothing will destroy your credibility faster than talking as if you belonged to the club. You don't. You're an outsider. That's your virtue, and that's your position. It may be a good idea to do a few stories to see what it feels like, or even to work on a newspaper for a summer. But if you do this, do not behave as if you were a professional journalist. Such part-time work or freelancing can only give you a taste of the business. Don't talk about your stories as if they were literature; they were, at best, amateur efforts, no matter how thrilling it was for you to write them. The paper isn't hiring you for your talent as a writer but for your ability to stimulate and inspire.
- Enjoy the city room. It will be a great relief from the academic department. The city-room style is informal, even breezy: full of humor and deceptively casual. Pay attention to what is really being accomplished in every edition. Journalists are task-oriented; they have a demanding job to do, and they do it day after day with remarkable discipline and skill. Watch, listen, learn, and apply what is appropriate to your own writing and to the writing of your students.

# A WRITING TEACHER IN THE NEWSROOM

## Carolyn B. Matalene
### University of South Carolina

*Carolyn B. Matalene likes to teach writing, at home and abroad, in school and on the job. An associate professor at the University of South Carolina, she directed the freshman English program for four years and since then has taught in China and Liberia. Her on-campus teaching includes a variety of writing courses for undergraduates as well as courses in rhetorical theory and the teaching of composition for graduate students. For the past five years she has been the writing coach at* The State *newspaper in Columbia, South Carolina, and she has been on the faculty at The Poynter Institute for Media Studies in St. Petersburg, Florida. With Elisabeth Alford she developed and taught a writing course for public administrators in the government department. Her articles on teaching and on testing have appeared in* College English, Journal of Writing Program Administrators, *and* Journal of Teaching Writing.

> From the teacherlike gray-haired man at the newsstand I also bought a copy of *The New York Times*, the previous day's issue of which I had seen the previous day at Puerto Rico. I was interested in newspapers and knew this paper to be one of the foremost in the world. But to read a newspaper for the first time is like coming into a film that has been on for an hour. Newspapers are like serials. To understand them you have to take knowledge to them; the knowledge that serves best is the knowledge provided by the newspaper itself. It made me feel a stranger, that paper.
>
> V. S. Naipaul
> *The Enigma of Arrival*

Mary Catherine, a student in an advanced writing class, writes a note on her first paper: "I need to know if my writing is shallow or juvenile. My journalism classes, I feel, have taken away my depth in writing as well as my sensitivity. Journalism writing is so factual and simple. I don't want to write that way."

Her comment, however naive, reveals an understanding that she inhabits two different discourse communities. One she knows from her English courses, where she believes she was encouraged to cultivate "depth" and "sensitivity." Now, as she tries to gain entry into the world of professional journalism, she is required to concentrate on the facts, to select them according to principles of news gathering, and to write with them according to rigidly structured forms and in carefully neutral language. She does not seem happy about the conventions of her chosen field, and her feelings are echoed by many journalism majors as they vent their frustrations about newswriting to English teachers.

In fact, a steady stream of students makes its way from the school of journalism to the English department. We welcome them smugly, sympathizing with their complaints about the superficiality of journalism training, the shallowness of the writing instruction, the mindless formalisms their professors require of them. We are likely to ignore, however, the equally steady stream of students making its way from the English department to the school of journalism. Here students tell welcoming journalism professors that they are nervous about getting jobs, that they want real-world skills and practical training with which to market themselves.

We may easily dismiss both groups of renegades as innocents or dilettantes, but their perceptions of professional journalism as well as of literary studies come from somewhere, if only from an explanatory vacuum. And trying to understand the source of their misunderstanding may lead us to some useful comparisons about the nature of writing and writing instruction in two different discourse communities. On one level the students do know what they are doing as they shuffle back and forth; they are trying to choose between two polarities of producing texts. Their English teachers are trying to initiate them into the genres and processes of academic discourse, the presentation of new knowledge or the construction of more encompassing theories and interpretations for academic audiences; they are being asked to discover, analyze, interpret, and argue. As Kristin Woolever explains elsewhere in this volume, academic discourse is characterized by writers revealing their own processes of discovery. Students in advanced writing classes are writing in the same genre of problem solving, though their writing teachers may be encouraging them to write from their own knowledge and experience. Their journalism teachers, however, are trying to initiate them into the requirements and conventions of journalism, carefully researched and unbiased reports of newsworthy information for the general public. They are being asked to investigate, interview, structure, and report—to convey information without expressing a voice or an attitude or a process. And in their professional training, they will most likely spend much more time learning the techniques of reporting and the structures of newswriting than they will practicing the greater freedoms of feature writing.

To use traditional explanatory language, we might say that journalists are primarily concerned with producing texts that are informative; English professors are primarily concerned with reading and responding to texts that are expressive. Certainly, this seems to be the difference that Mary Catherine perceives. But such explanations are oversimplified and fail to account for how profoundly social context affects the entire process of writing. Organizations, such as English departments and journalism schools and newsrooms, constitute unique rhetorical contexts, imposing constraints on how and why texts are produced. Teresa M. Harrison says, "As rhetorical contexts, organizations may influence the production, comprehension, and evaluation of discourse. This is because organizations are 'culturelike' phenomena constituted both by systems of knowledge and by patterns of symbolic discourse that are related to actions undertaken by organizational members" (14–15). To explain this to Mary Catherine, one might say that a newspaper, an organization that delivers new information to readers through the media of print, both creates journalists and is created by them; similarly, the professional study of literature, in the context of academic discourse, both creates literary critics and is created by them.

When students switch communities, carrying with them the "systems of knowledge" or the "patterns of symbolic discourse" or the conventions of the previous one, they tend to get it wrong. Thus, they perceive only a great and puzzling gap between these two discourse communities. That is surely not surprising; the truth is that journalists and English teachers view each other with frigid indifference, only occasionally warming to mutual contempt. Although departments or schools of journalism and departments of English are the two academic disciplines primarily entrusted with the teaching of writing in American higher education, they seldom examine each other's conventions, let alone admit any common goals. In fact, they seldom even talk to each other and never, it seems, read each other's books. Such a gap is strange and sad, since both groups of professionals spend their lives trying to help their students master writing (and both commonly despair of succeeding). As Mary Catherine has also noted, she is judged in both places by her writing.

Recently, a few members of both communities have begun to question as well as to cross the barriers between departments of English and professional journalism.[1] And they have found the experience useful and enlightening. The exploration that follows here, a discussion of journalistic writing in writing-teacher terms, results from my own experience as a writing coach during the last five years. Unlike Don Murray, I had no experience in journalism when I started working with reporters and had to quickly learn the ways of this world of writing in order to help its practitioners. And like any traveler in a foreign country, I learned a great deal about my own as well. Hanging around the newsroom, working with reporters, going out with them on assignments, covering beats, sitting in on budget meetings, conducting seminars with editors and copy editors, staying until the presses ran, looking over shoulders on election night were all heady experiences—exhilarating and even romantic—for someone used to the isolation and the slowness of an English department. But the experience was very definitely "for real." Newspaper people are faced not only with the grim reality of daily deadlines but also with the endless consequences of producing public texts, and I gained tremendous respect for this work that never stops.

Along the way I discovered some of the ways in which writing teachers are uniquely qualified to contribute to the journalistic endeavor; I also realized how much writing teachers might gain if they understood and admitted the value of some of the basic premises of journalism. The analysis offered here is intended to explain some of the discourse conventions that inform journalism and their effects on producing texts and then to suggest how we might learn from each other. Writing teachers and journalists, it seems clear to me, have more to share than despair.

## THE ETHOS OF THE NEWSROOM

"But is it news?" the editor asks when the reporter returns from the city council meeting and explains what happened. That question informs the myriad decisions made daily in producing a newspaper; it is asked so frequently that it is simply understood, an internalized principle of selection. In the system of knowledge of the newsroom, *new* information is privileged above all, and heroic feats of newspaper staffs in providing their readers with breaking news—shuttle disasters and assassinations—constitute the touchstones of journalistic life. These front pages are then framed to hang in the hallways, reminders of the glorious communal intensity that may seize the newsroom at any time. Then, all the dreary days covering sewer disputes and school board meetings will be forgotten.

One of the mythic possibilities for a reporter, endlessly retold, is the story of Joe and Mabel, two ordinary readers, looking over the morning paper at breakfast. Suddenly Joe comes upon a story so startlingly unusual, so *newsworthy*, that he yells, "Holy shit, Mabel, listen to this!" That's what we're after, editors tell reporters, a response like that. That's what sells papers, wins prizes, and constitutes the big one for a journalist. A recent feature story about Bob Woodward, called by one of the sources, "the best reporter in the country," repeats the parable:

> "He wants every reporter to be like him," said one *Post* reporter who has worked under Woodward. "The Holy shit! stories—the ones that people will read and then say, you know, Oh, God!—those are the only ones he really cares about. He's not for the bread-and-butter stories. And reporters who can't produce those loud, attention-getting pieces, well, they are just devalued."

Valuing new and surprising information, of course, contrasts importantly with the usual procedures of academic discourse. As Doheny-Farina shows, the academic community, devoted though it is to the presentation of original ideas in radical or "abnormal" discourse, nevertheless requires writers to begin their explorations by paying elaborate attention to previous authorities. Those who have written about similar ideas must be noted and recognized and built upon. The writer of academic discourse wants the Joe-and-Mabel response only at the very end of the argument.

The privileging of new information, the essential fact of the enterprise of journalism, affects production at every level. From the design of the newspaper plant itself to the structuring of a lead, what is new is what matters. And from this ethos of new information follow the practices of production, the principles of structure, and even the philosophy of language that we have come to understand as common to journalism.

Perhaps the first and most lasting impression that a writing teacher receives in the newsroom is the size and scope of this collaborative writing task. Here is a great open space—do members of any other profession all work together in the same room?—in which reporters come and go, talk to their assigning editors, make calls, write stories, and then send their copy to editors. And the editors assign, confer, read the wires, edit, meet, plan, and send their reporters' edited stories to the copy editors, who send them to the composing room for layout and then photographing, and at the right instant the presses roll and the distribution hierarchy from trucks to paper carriers kicks in. That a newspaper gets published every day with all of its information—from headlines and breaking news to features and stock quotations and ads and Heloise—seems to an outsider a miracle of cooperation. But this great corporate and linguistic flowchart manages to put fat papers on thousands of doorsteps daily. The speed and the quantity of production is mind-boggling, especially to someone trained in an English department, where writing tasks are measured in years, not minutes, and where our favorite author took twenty years for each of his two novels.

Delivering this much new information this quickly requires that the gathering of information be privileged over the presentation of it. Yesterday's edition, however well written, is wrapping paper. Both journalists and journalism professors agree that Joe and Mabel's amazement results from the reporting, the new information that the reporter found—not from the writing, the way the reporter presented the news. That there can't be good writing without good reporting or good reporting without good writing are truisms often repeated when journalists talk about their craft outside the newsroom but mentioned much less frequently while they practice it. Actually, many journalists believe deep down that reporting is all there is. An explanation from a recent textbook entitled *Uncovering the News* tells students: "You will see that stories based on solid information tell the audience what it needs to know quickly and clearly and move crisply from one well-developed point to another. Stories based on flimsy information, on the other hand, are often a jumble of ideas that leaves the audience confused" (7). Having enough of the right information, by this account, will automatically produce a well-written story. As Don Murray notes, reporting is macho, news is "hard." That makes writing sort of wimpy. In fact, according to the prevailing myth of the newsroom, writing should not even take any time. Another favorite newspaper story tells of the seasoned reporter who has gotten all the facts together, ready to write the big one. "How long 'till deadline?" he asks. Twenty minutes, he is told. "Good, I've got time to eat."

In the rush of the news, writing becomes a transparent medium. Even though reporters and editors work with words all day and even though their only medium for reaching readers is writing, the very word "writing" is seldom used. Nor do newspaper people like to be reminded that what gets put on our doorsteps each morning is writing—just as philosophers did not like having Derrida tell them that writing was what they were producing. Even the name for the writers who write the news emphasizes their gathering rather than their structuring efforts; they are called reporters. And when they are promoted, they are called editors.

To a writing teacher, used to analyzing the effects of writing on readers, the whole journalistic profession seems to depend upon wilfully not paying attention to how the presentation of information affects responses to it. Journalists, it seems, to keep the presses rolling, need to be positivists, need to believe that the language they live by is a transparent medium for conveying information neutrally. In spite of numerous analyses and criticism of the packaging of the news—see, for example, *News: The Politics of Illusion*, by W. Lance Bennett—they manage to maintain a cheerful and antique positivism about the relationship of language to the world.[2] David Brinkley explained this philosophy very succinctly during a recent television interview with James Lehrer. "Journalism is very simple really. Reporters tell people what happened today and if they understand, they tell people what it means. That's all there is to it."

## THE ROLE OF THE WRITING COACH

In beginning work as a writing coach, it is tempting to explain that journalism is really not all that simple, that rhetoric is epistemic, that language is not transparent, that writers do not just transmit reality but also construct it, that selecting means emphasizing, and so on. But to learn the latest theories is not why newspaper editors hire writing coaches. Perhaps as a result of their determined positivism, journalists are singularly resistant to academic theorizing. They are also unresponsive if not aggressively negative to special terminology for analyzing discourse. Journalists really do not want to know the explanatory terms for their linguistic practices. Using words like "cohesion" and "coherence" or "topical structure" and "global plan" tends to inspire glassy stares if not snickers. So big words are out.

The essential role of the writing coach, the real reason papers hire us, is to make writing, that transparent medium, less transparent. Paradoxically, if writing is going to be transparent for readers—if stories are going to slide down their throats like cold beer—then it can never be transparent—that is, unexamined—for editors and writers. The writing coach then emphasizes by her presence that *writing* is what happens in the newsroom and that writing is important enough to hire a specialist for help. Writing, after all, is all that readers get. How the story is written matters to them as much as what it is about—all editors would agree. Editors in practice, however, do not always have the time to get the story right for readers, and more importantly, editors do not really read like readers. They cannot; they have been processing the news for too long. Their speciality is structuring the news for thorough coverage, accurate attribution, and efficient production. Such requirements may well cloud the transparency of the medium, may work against the ideal of a newspaper that is easy on its readers. Nor do most editors have the time to offer writers the attention and the assistance and the feedback that they need and want. The ethos of the writing teacher in the newsroom, then, must be to help the writer and to represent the reader—not the grammarian or the text linguist but good old Joe and Mabel.

In working with reporters in one-on-one weekly conferences (my preferred mode), I always begin with the reporter's own composing process. To make the writer more aware of what writing requires if it is to meet the needs of readers—as opposed to editors—is the goal. How does information, gathered as notes on a pad, get structured into a story for readers? For many reporters, especially novices, the process of structuring or planning is often unconscious to the point of not occurring at all. Instead, the reporter, back in the newsroom, skims pages of notes and decides on a lead. "What's the lead?" may be the only question the writer—or the editor—asks. The composing process that follows can all too frequently be described as "notebook dump." Such stories cause readers to give up and turn to the ads. Getting reporters to structure stories for readers rather than write up their notes and to have a plan rather than just a lead is, of course, no different from what writing teachers always do. What is different from academic writing is the religion of the lead. Academic writers, asking their readers to share in their discovery process, take delicious pleasure in withholding the lead, as long as possible, even to the last exquisite sentence. Journalists get fired for this.

## ALL THE NEWS AT THE TOP

What matters is news, what happened today, not what happened yesterday. And the information that is the newest must—according to the most honored rule of journalism—be what hits the reader first. This simple rule governs the structuring of front pages, headlines, wire stories, news stories, and leads. That the new information must appear first constitutes an internal principle of production. And it accounts for the much-argued, much-maligned, and much-depended-upon structure for newswriting: the inverted pyramid. The long top line of the inverted pyramid stands for the single sentence that explains the five parts of any event: who, what, where, why, when. What follows are paragraphs that explain in more detail each of the parts of the lead in descending order of importance. The inverted pyramid offers an extremely efficient structure for packaging information. As news breaks, the lead can be revised to emphasize the new information; the paragraphs—often separate blocks of information that do not lead into or follow from—can be rearranged, and the story can be cut from the bottom up. (Watching the compositors slice off paragraphs with their razor-tipped knives makes that tired old metaphor "cut the story" come alive.) The advantages of the inverted pyramid, however, all seem to have to do with producing texts efficiently, not with processing them easily. The form is convenient for editors, not for readers.

First, the structure itself is the least memorable one for readers. As Meyer showed in her study of the effect of coherence strategies on readers, the descriptive plan which "develops a topic by describing its component parts, for instance, by presenting attributes, specification, or settings" (38) is "the least effective when people read or listen to text for the purpose of remembering it" (41). The inverted pyramid, then, contains the seeds of its own forgetting because it seems to offer the least structure for readers to hang stories on.

An equally serious problem of this production format is that editors have a very different context from readers for deciding what is news. As events unfold and stories get rewritten, the editors and reporters become experts; having known the background and the details of a particular story for days, they have their own structures to plug the facts into. Readers do not. And pulling the new information to the top can yield an impenetrable lead. Like this one from a local news story:

> An ill-worded appeal has shielded Richland County Council from paying an NAACP lawyer's fees, but council members as individuals are subject to an earlier judgment ordering the payment, a federal judge in Anderson said Wednesday.

This story is of a county council quarrel that has gone on for some time; the new news here, however, is the "ill-worded appeal" that somehow let council off the hook. But unpacking this information to construct a meaningful context requires more effort than most readers will expend. Dan Rather never talks like this.

Reminding or explaining to editors and writers how difficult news stories can be for ordinary readers is perhaps the most important function of the writing teacher—the outsider—in the newsroom. Editors, confronted with miles of information scrolling past their eyes all day, lust for the new and tend to edit copy so that other editors will approve of it. That means that the story must have no holes and that all the information must be accurate, but it also means that all the news will be at the top.

All the news or new information at the top is, however, what makes many newspaper columns user-unfriendly. The principle seems to have a powerful influence on all journalistic writing and affects structure at many levels. At the sentence level, the practice of getting all of the important items in the lead yields some extremely long first sentences. And long first sentences, filled with new information, are hard on readers. Readers do not really want to know everything they do not know all at once; their brains become overtaxed. Short-term memory, after all, can only handle seven items; leads that overload our processing abilities lose us.

That a lead should be one sentence, not two or three, constitutes another time-honored rule of journalism, one that again seems to have more to do with editors than with readers. Talking reporters into two-sentence leads is tricky; even trickier is getting a two-sentence lead through the assigning editor and the copy editor. An invisible force seems to be at work, pulling everything to the top by embedding clauses, combining sentences, making single sentences function as paragraphs. Here is a first sentence from the front page of the *New York Times*, famous for long leads:

> Exasperated by the seemingly endless deaths, crime and corruption generated by the world's illicit drug trade, a growing number of public officials and scholars in recent weeks have begun to call for debate on what for years was politically unspeakable: making drugs legal.

This sentence of forty-three words, though well constructed, makes fairly heavy demands on readers. Why must it be one sentence?

The word length of an individual sentence, however, usually matters less than the strength of its structure. Readers have an easier time with sentences in which the agent, the action, and the goal are easy to find, not separated by numerous modifying clauses. And parallel structure and the special cases of parallelism like antithesis make long sentences readable. Explaining to editors and writers the power of parallel structure is worth the time; journalists, always worrying about the news, need reminding that structuring the news is the route to readers.

The principle of the news at the top, of course, accounts for the religion of the lead. Taking a great deal of time to compose the first sentence certainly makes sense; as all writers know, the first sentence limits all the others. But worrying about it exclusively often means that the structure of the rest of the story gets too little attention. Most journalism texts concentrate on leads and conclusions and offer little useful advice or information on overall structure. Jon Franklin, the author of *Writing for Story*, provides one of the few journalistic explanations of structure; his chosen pattern of complication/resolution for feature writing reverses the inverted pyramid of news stories. But the best-selling writer on writing in the newsroom, William Zinsser, does not go beyond the standard journalism-school message about structure: get a good lead, use transitions, end with an ending. In the middle, it seems, you are on your own. So are the readers.

Transforming pieces of new information into writing means creating structure. So explaining structure to writers, in language as simple as possible, is central to coaching. Many writers, in talking about how they got from notes to story, offer explanations that seem arbitrary; their structural decisions are based on association, almost "stream of consciousness." "Well, this seemed to relate to this." Like the students in our classes, they need to move from writer-based to reader-based texts; they need to provide structure for readers instead of notebook dump. Most writers do not know that structures are—not just in stories but in readers too. Readers come to stories with many plans already in their heads—comparison, cause-effect, problem-solution, and the like—and are thus quick to connect with structural clues. Thus, writers need to learn to connect that much polished lead with the story as a whole. The function of the lead is not to tell all the news in the first sentence but to structure what follows; as John McPhee says, to shine a light into the story. Leads then should tip off readers to the story's structure, like the forecasting statements in business or technical writing. As Meyer's research also showed, readers have an easier time if they know the plan at the beginning and can use it as they read. Here is a lead from the *Charlotte Observer*—with short sentences—that announces the cause-and-effect structure of the article:

> Aiken, S.C.—Assume there will never be a nuclear reactor meltdown.
> Assume that deadly radioactive wastes will never leak.
> Even if there is never an accident involving radiation, the government's Savan-

nah River Plant is still the greatest long-term potential threat to the safety of water supplies in South Carolina.

## STRUCTURING THE FLOW OF INFORMATION

One of the most powerful tools for writers—especially for writers whose primary task is to convey information—is the analysis of discourse provided by functional sentence perspective (see Vande Kopple). Journalists, I believe, could forestall the decline in the number of newspaper readers and help to prevent the failure of newspapers if they would learn and adopt this principle for regulating the flow of information. Unfortunately, terms like "theme-rheme" or "cohesive ties" or "equivalence chains" pretty much guarantee glassy eyes. But writers and editors can learn about these principles with words no harder than "old information" and "new information."

They need to be shown that readers experience writing as transparent, as "pure message," when the flow of information is carefully controlled by the writer. The secret is simple; the writer links new information to old information, always starting with old. Readers—at least those outside the newsroom—like to go from old to new. That is a startling idea to journalists, however, and absolutely contrary, as we have seen, to the basic premise of newswriting. Unlike editors, readers like old information as the subject; new information as the predicate. After the new information appears in the predicate, it is old and can then appear as the subject. So the chain of information can be expressed abstractly as A + B, B + C, C + D, or old plus new, which becomes old plus new and so on. Readers don't like new plus new plus new plus new—the hard-news lead. Nor do they like new plus old very often; that kind of sentence has to be turned inside out to be processed, like the *New York Times* lead quoted above.

Analyzing published stories in terms of the progression of old to new information and pointing out cohesive ties and then coherence strategies can be extremely useful to writers. The kind of analysis that Robin Bell Markels explains in *A New Perspective on Cohesion in Expository Paragraphs* or that Colomb and Williams outline in "Perceiving Structure in Professional Prose" can be performed on both readable and unreadable pieces of writing. Examples of clear, brief, but highly informative articles are common in the carefully edited stories of *Time* and *Newsweek*. Examples of hard-to-follow writing—those that ask the reader to work very hard—are plentiful. When you give up on reading a column of print in your newspaper, you have probably found one. In fact, an unreadable passage often makes the point most strongly. Here is an example I use that shows what happens when the old-plus-new rule is violated:

Gov. Bob Graham is planning to move out of the governor's mansion, but he's not ready to let it be sold at public auction.

A Manatee County man arrested on drug charges has filed a lien against the governor's mansion in an attempt to collect $3,000 he says the state owes him for a 1978 green Datsun pickup truck.

Those really are the first two sentences of a news story (in a famous paper). But they do something strange to our brains. Most readers think someone switched columns on them. Actually, they just got the new information in the old information position. Such an example vividly proves the point of Colomb and Williams, "For we ordinarily become conscious of the form of a text only when we are troubled by it. The phenomenology of reading is most strikingly captured in our disappearance into a text" (89). Again, the paradox: if writing is to be transparent for readers, writers need to be highly conscious of their structures. And they do need and can use the kind of analyses writing teachers offer. In fact, the professional writers, both academics and journalists, to whom I have explained the old-to-new principle tell me that when they are stuck, unsure of how to get to the next sentence, they fall back on the old-to-new rule. Copy editors especially, working with wire stories in which the news has repeatedly been pulled to the top, find it a useful technique for rewrites.

Being able to "write short" is a valuable talent in the newsroom, where assignments are often given in inches. "Give me twelve inches on the beach erosion bill." Yet much of the advice reporters hear in press association meetings—about going for the human interest and the background and the color—seems to require that writers write longer stories. Understanding the flow of information, how to present facts quickly but clearly, enables them to write shorter. That's good news for both editors and writers.

## SENTENCES AND STYLE

Writers also need to know that another preference of readers is variety. Readers like variety in what they read. They like variety in subject matter and structure and point of view; they like variety in language and in levels of abstraction; and they seem to like variety especially in the length of sentences. Sentence length ought to get more attention than it does from journalists; it is, after all, a primary index of readability. Too many sentences—and not just leads—in many news stories are too long. Too often sentences are so heavily embedded that they are made to function as paragraphs rather than sentences. The writing coach, as representative of the reader, does well to ask about and then to count the average number of words per sentence on the front page—or to ask an individual writer "What is your average number of words per sentence?" Though readers prefer sentences that average under twenty words, most of the writers I have worked with write sentences that on the average are longer than that. Young writers often mistake sentence length for stylistic maturity. They are wrong. Our waistlines and our sentences seem inevitably to get longer as we get older; both tendencies need to be fought. In the stories I have analyzed by John McPhee, the average sentence length is around sixteen words. That's one of the reasons we like to read him.

Readers, however, don't like sentences to be the average length. What they really like is variety, extraordinary variety. They are much happier to read a carefully structured sentence of fifty words followed by one of three words than four sentences of twenty words each. I don't know why this is so, but it seems to be. Any of the writers whom we consider great—from Samuel Taylor Coleridge to Virginia Woolf to John McPhee and Joan Didion and Tom Wolfe—write sentences of really extraordinarily varied length.

All that writing teachers know about style is of use to journalists—especially to feature writers and columnists, who are less governed by the ethos of the news, who want help in cultivating style and voice. These writers need to be reminded of the power of the concrete, the importance of specifics, the value of conveying atmosphere. Because of the pervasive emphasis on reporting and news and facts throughout the journalistic enterprise, stylistic concerns—as we think of style—are likely to get scant attention. Thus, reporters easily fall into the habit of thinking of stories in terms of words, especially the sentences their subjects utter. "Getting the quote" is next in importance to getting the lead. But words come out of mouths, attached to bodies, in concrete settings. And readers often want to see how people look as well as to hear what they say. Stories that feature only "talking heads" have very likely been written on the basis of facts gotten over the phone. Reporters, struggling to get the words down, often forget that readers want to know the color of the new banners on Main Street, or how tall the candidate is, or what the teacher of the year's classroom looks like. Moving down the abstraction ladder, searching for precise and colorful language, working for informative and evocative descriptions of people and places are, of course, common emphases of writing teachers, emphases that deserve some space in the newsroom.

In fact, according to a number of journalists and journalism professors—among them Don Murray, Norman Sims, Jon Franklin—contemporary journalism need not be governed exclusively by the ethos of the news. They believe that conveying new information is no longer the primary function of print journalism, given the prevalence and superiority of the electronic media in transmitting breaking news. We are now much more likely to *hear* the latest news than to *read* it. This means that journalists need to offer readers more than David Brinkley's, "this is what happened today." Thus, the whole movement called literary journalism came into being to offer readers not just information but understanding. Literary journalists, according to Sims, "attempt to penetrate the cultures that make institutions work" (3). In interviewing a number of the best practitioners, he concluded that the hallmarks of such writing are immersion, accuracy, voice, structure, and symbolism (4,8). The last three qualities, most English professors would claim, come from the province of literature and make our interest in journalism and our usefulness to journalists not untimely. And helping writers with structure and voice and style provides a quiet way of moving beyond positivist understandings of language; the stories they write don't just mirror the world, they also construct it.

Most daily papers, of course, cannot provide the resources to support the long and expensive writing projects of a Tracy Kidder or a Jane Kramer; but they can make it clear that they value good writing and want to help their own writers grow. And we can help.

## WORKING WITH WRITERS

For most writers, getting to talk with a personal tutor who concentrates exclusively on their own writing is a luxury—albeit initially a nervous-making one. The pressure of deadlines allows little time for writers and editors to talk about how yesterday's story got written; tomorrow's story always demands attention. So the attention they receive from the writing coach tells them that writers and writing matter—not just reporters and reporting. I usually work with four reporters individually over a period of six weeks. They give me a week's worth of unedited copy, and a few days later I meet with each of them for a conference. A great deal gets packed into those conferences: close reading; analyses of structure and style; discussions of new assignments and long-term projects; talk of favorite writers and favorite newspapers; questions and answers and encouragement; and, always, consideration of readers. For a writing teacher, talking with such serious, experienced, and motivated writers about what makes writing work, about voice and variety, story ideas and approaches, leads and conclusions proves immensely rewarding. (Not only are these students' papers never turned in late, their final drafts are delivered to my doorstep.)

Certainly, writing teachers in newsrooms must above all be tactful and circumspect, aware of all that they don't know about journalism, aware of the delicate relationships between editors and writers. In representing readers, it seems necessary to suggest some practices that seem diametrically opposed to traditional news structures. Among them are these: don't put all the news at the top; try for a shorter lead that structures the story; move from old to new information, not the other way around; and write shorter sentences. Suggestions like these may need to be introduced slowly, but they do need to be introduced. *U.S.A. Today*, though commonly sneered at by traditional newspaper people as "television in print," was supposed to fail but hasn't. In fact, its short sentences, color graphics, and brief, decontextualized stories make it understandable to travelers in any airport—unlike many local papers. (Naipaul would surely feel less a stranger reading it.)

Listening to editors talk about writers and writing reveals how often they disagree in their evaluations. Just like English teachers, journalists never seem to agree on the strengths or the weaknesses of a particular piece; in fact, to bring in a story and announce that it's "good" is guaranteed to start a fight. But to focus on what readers need is a way to work with both editors and writers toward some common values, values that are not idiosyncratic but the product of reading research.

## MUTUAL CONTRIBUTIONS

This discussion, intended primarily for writing teachers who may be interested in becoming writing coaches, has so far concentrated on how what we know about writing can be used to help practicing journalists. We do know about composing processes; we do know what readers need; we can help writers. At any rate, the editors and writers I work with ask me back.

But as I think about how being a writing coach has changed me, what I have learned seems to far outweigh what I have taught. Mary Catherine's comment now makes perfect sense to me; I can explain to her what is going on in the discourse communities of the journalism school and the English department and help her and all of my students to understand and negotiate between them. A writing coach becomes a better-informed and more confident writing teacher for all students.

And a writing teacher in the newsroom gains tremendous respect for the profession of journalism. Its practitioners work extremely hard, undergo constant pressure, and take their ethical responsibilities seriously indeed. Copy editors, for example, are surely the most conscientious wordsmiths in our culture: their knowledge of the conventions of the print code and their understanding of syntax is extraordinary; as headline writers, they work under constraints of line and word length unthinkable to all but poets. Those who criticize the press routinely, who accuse reporters of superficial coverage and slanted approaches, ought to try covering a beat and meeting deadlines for awhile. Discovering, investigating, researching, gathering, structuring, and presenting essential information accurately, fairly, and at tremendous speed is not "very simple really." Try it.

Writing teachers would, in fact, do well to admit the value of the essential process that informs journalism: *reporting*. If journalists tend to ignore and undervalue writing, writing teachers, conversely, tend to overlook and underemphasize the many activities that make up reporting. This may not be surprising, given our home in the department of English, given our years of literary training, given our postromantic mentality which values the imagined over the examined, the fiction over the fact, that labels writing stories and poetry "creative," and everything else *non*fiction. But such attitudes might now be susceptible to change.

We could begin by admitting, for instance, that the line between journalism and literature cannot be drawn. Many of our greatest writers have been journalists: Defoe, Swift, Addison, Steele, Smollett, Johnson, Goldsmith, Macaulay, Dickens, Ruskin, Carlyle, Twain, Crane, Lardner, Mencken, Orwell, Hemingway, and Faulkner, to name just a few. Many of our canonized texts first appeared in magazines and newspapers.

And next, we could encourage our students to become reporters, to examine rigorously a piece of the world they live in as a "prewriting strategy"—instead of looping or cubing or remembering what they did last summer. Many invention exercises from elementary school onward ask students to look inside their own heads for material, to tune in to their creative inner voices, or to imagine fantasy worlds and place themselves in fictitious situations. Surely, asking them to investigate their own social contexts, helping them to do so honestly and systematically, and letting them write with real-world purposes makes more sense as we strive to turn out genuinely literate young people.

Roy Peter Clark, a professional writing coach who also works with student writers in public schools, believes that "journalism holds the key to improved writing instruction in America." In his recent book *Free to Write*, he discusses the English teacher's traditional "bias against reportage" (14) and argues "that real-life writing is no less creative than fiction or fantasy" (7). Clark, a former English teacher, realizes that reporting is more complex than translating or mirroring the world; it is also an act of construction:

> ... journalism is more than a trade or a craft, it is a way of looking at the world. Reporters see the world as a storehouse of writing ideas. The ordinary person walks down the street and sees a bar, a wig shop, a grocery store, a pharmacy, and a shoe store. The journalist sees dozens of story ideas behind the facades of those businesses. He sees people and issues. He asks himself:
>
> - Who drinks in that bar at 9:00 in the morning?
> - What kind of market is there for those huge rainbow-colored wigs in the shop window?
> - Why are there small grocery stores downtown but no major supermarket?
> - Is there a difference in service between the old-style pharmacies and the newer large drugstore chains?
> - When so many businesses are struggling downtown, how has this shoe store managed to make it? [12–13]

Helping our students to think like reporters, showing them how to cultivate the first two hallmarks of literary journalism, immersion and accuracy, seems essential in preparing our students as citizens and writers. Many worthwhile bridges are waiting to be built between schools of journalism and writing programs, and writing teachers can initiate them. First, we must give up privileging literary texts and instead insist that all writing requires creative acts of selection and structuring. Then, we need to convince our journalist colleagues that along with their concentration on news-based forms, they might recognize the value of literary forms and techniques in conveying complex information in readable ways. *They* need to recognize that part of the process of a great story is writing; *we* need to recognize that part of the process of a great story is reporting.

## Notes

1. The "Writing Movement" in newspapers was initiated at The Poynter Institute for Media Studies, St. Petersburg, Florida. Roy Peter Clark and Don Fry, both former professors of English, conduct seminars for writers and editors at Poynter and also travel around the country as writing coaches. Most writing coaches, however, are in-house journalists; they are the subject of a dissertation study by Tina Lesher, Rutgers University. A quarterly newsletter, *The Coaches' Corner*, is edited by Paul Salsini of *The Milwaukee Journal* and Lucille deView, *Florida Today*.
2. See also J. David Kennamer, "News Values and the Vividness of Information," *Written Communication* 5 (1988): 108–123.

## Works Cited

Bennett, W. Lance. *News: The Politics of Illusion.* New York: Longman, 1983.
Clark, Roy Peter. *Free to Write: A Journalist Teaches Young Writers.* Portsmouth, N.H.: Heinemann, 1987.

Colomb, Gregory G., and Joseph M. Williams. "Perceiving Structure in Professional Prose: A Multiply Determined Experience." *Writing in Nonacademic Settings.* Ed. Lee Odell and Dixie Goswami. New York: Guilford, 1985, pp. 87–128.

Franklin, Jon. *Writing for Story.* New York: Mentor, 1986.

Harrison, Teresa M. "Frameworks for the Study of Writing in Organizational Contexts." *Written Communication* 9 (1987): 3–23.

Kennamer, J. David. "New Values and the Vividness of Information." *Written Communication.* 5 (1988): 108–123.

Kessler, Lauren, and Duncan McDonald. *Uncovering the News: A Journalists's Search for Information.* Belmont, Calif.: Wadsworth, 1987.

Markels, Robin Bell. *A New Perspective on Cohesion in Expository Paragraphs.* Carbondale, Ill.: Southern Illinois University Press, 1984.

Meyer, Bonnie J. F. "Reading Research and the Composition Teacher: The Importance of Plans." *College Composition and Communication.* 33 (1982): 37–49.

Sims, Norman, ed. *The Literary Journalists.* New York: Ballantine, 1984.

Vande Kopple, William J. "Functional Sentence Perspective, Composition, and Reading." *College Composition and Communication.* 33 (1982): 50–63.

Zinsser, William. *On Writing Well.* 3rd ed. New York: Harper & Row, 1985.

# PART SIX

## WRITING IN THE WORLD OF FINANCE

# TEACHING WRITING TO CPA'S—OR ANYONE ELSE FOR THAT MATTER

*Dan Dieterich*
*University of Wisconsin—Stevens Point*

*Dan Dieterich is a professor of English at the University of Wisconsin-Stevens Point, where he teaches business writing and also serves as a senior staff member of the Academic Achievement Center. In more than ten years of private practice as a writing consultant, he has provided numerous workshops for clients in various fields, including accounting, insurance, medicine, and finance. He is a cofounder and past president of the Association of Professional Writing Consultants.*

Imagine that you are a business writing consultant who has had no experience whatsoever with the writing of accountants. A large accounting firm in your community contacts you and asks you to conduct a writing training program for their C.P.A.'s. How do you respond?

If you are like most business writing consultants, you jump at the chance to conduct such a program. Admittedly, most writing consultants lack even the most rudimentary understanding of accounting; but we know a thing or two about writing, and we are willing to share that knowledge with just about anyone in the business community.

Okay, now that you have agreed to conduct the program, what are you going to teach these C.P.A.'s about writing? Some writing consultants would give not a moment's thought to this question; their content is the same no matter who is in the audience. But let us say that you want to adapt your material to meet the needs of your audience. How do you do it?

What do you know about the people you will be teaching? Well, you know that they are C.P.A.'s. And even if you know nothing else, you know that C.P.A.'s are number-people as opposed to word people. In other words, they are not like you and me.

You might assume that, being number people, your C.P.A.'s are reluctant to write, ignorant about what it takes to write well, and fearful about writing on the job. You might also assume that, after they compile their numbers, their main writing task is to convey the numbers they have compiled to someone else. In other words, they mainly write informative documents.

How should you go about teaching these people to write? Should you conduct a writing program for C.P.A.'s differently from the program you do for attorneys, engineers, or journalists? And, for that matter, should you conduct a program for one group of C.P.A.'s differently from one for the next?

You probably suspect that the answer is yes, but you may lack a means of determining either the personality types of the participants in your workshop or the instructional strategies best suited to those personality types. As a result, you may well decide to use the same instructional approach that you used in the last workshop you conducted . . . and the one before that.

Most of us who teach business writing spend much of our instructional time urging people to analyze their audiences before they write and to modify their writing accordingly. Yet we ourselves too seldom follow our own advice. We often know nothing about the specific individuals in our programs, the kinds of writing they do, their attitude toward writing, or even their views on their own writing needs. As a result, we cannot effectively shape what we teach and how we teach it.

So, getting back to those C.P.A.'s, let us find out a little bit more about them. For example, exactly what kinds of documents do they write? One way to find that out is to read a book or two about the accounting profession. Another is to talk with whoever is setting up the workshop. Yet another way is to talk with the participants themselves before conducting the program. A final way is to ask the participants to give you samples of typical things they write on the job.

If you read books on the accounting profession, you will probably read about audit reports. For both public accountants and internal auditors, such reports are an important feature of their profession. The American Institute of Certified Public Accountants has issued guidelines for the writing of these reports—guidelines which many C.P.A.'s follow religiously in order to avoid legal problems. Individual firms may supplement the AICPA guidelines with in-house models and guidelines as well.

If you are knowledgeable about these guidelines, you may be able to help participants in your program to write well within them. However if, in ignorance of these guidelines, you encourage individual participants in your program to take a more "creative" approach in their writing of audit reports, you may be in for a rude awakening.

The fact is, C.P.A.'s write a great deal more than just audit reports, and reading books about accounting is not the best way to learn what types of writing the participants in your workshop do on the job. You can get a far more accurate picture by talking to the participants themselves and then reading a sample of typical pieces of their writing.

When I began conducting writing programs for C.P.A.'s several years ago, I was surprised to discover that many of them spend the vast majority of their writing time producing directive or persuasive letters and memos. As they rise to the top of the chain of command in their firms, C.P.A.'s spend a large part of each working day telling other C.P.A.'s what to do and how to do it. However, even C.P.A.'s low in the pecking order make proposals and request action and information. And people who use the services of C.P.A.'s usually do so because they want advice, not just numbers.

From looking at writing samples, I got an idea of what kind of writing I should help the C.P.A.'s to do. But how do they feel about the writing they do on the job? Do they avoid it? Are they afraid to write? Knowing the answer to such questions can influence both what you teach and how you teach it.

Before one recent workshop, I asked the participants to complete a Business Writing Attitude Inventory which measured their anxiety levels about writing. I based this inventory on one described by John A. Daly and Michael D. Miller in an article in *Research in the Teaching of English.*

Eleven of the fifteen participating C.P.A.'s completed the inventory, scoring between 42 and 73 on an instrument which records anxiety scores as high as 110 and as low as 22. The participants' average anxiety score was a 55. I had used the same inventory for several years with students entering my writing classes at the University of Wisconsin—Stevens Point. They scored between 43 and 103, with an average score of 71. The C.P.A.'s appeared far less anxious about writing than did the university students.

And where were their attitudes about writing formed? According to the comments they made on the inventories, mainly at the workplace. Here are three of those comments:

> Most of my attitudes in this area have been shaped by my career, although my college background does provide some influence. The partners of the firm I work for have influenced me the most with regard to business writing. They encourage fresh, imaginative ideas that can provide assistance to our clients.

> I had one business writing class in Madison. . . . Otherwise, I feel my writing has been shaped by other professionals.

> My writing attitudes have been shaped both by education and my career (particularly my bosses). . . . My bosses emphasize getting to the point rather than hedging, being flamboyant, etc. As a result, I try to use that style also.

A C.P.A.'s firm has an enormous influence on that individual's views on writing, but the accounting profession as a whole is also influential. For that reason, the following comments from the accounting literature about the importance of writing skills are significant:

> Probably no other personal quality is more important [to the accountant] than having the ability to communicate well—both in writing and orally. [American Accounting Association, 156]

> As an accountant, you need to be able to write clearly. Most readers will be impressed with your accounting ability only to the extent they are able to understand you. [John, 50]

> It is scarcely an exaggeration to say that the problem of communication is the axial problem in accounting. [Goldberg, 348]

> [After conducting a study which reveals that practicing accountants rank written and oral English as the most important subject for the beginning public accountant:] To the CPA, the ability to express himself is more than the hallmark of an educated man. It is a professional necessity. [Roy and MacNeill, 218]

According to the Business Writing Attitude Inventory which I distributed, the writing anxiety levels of the participants in my workshop were lower than I might have expected. They did not seem to be afraid to write; they saw writing as a necessary and important part of their profession. But what specific concerns did they have about the writing they did on the job? In what areas did they feel the greatest need for help? To determine this, I distributed an eighteen-item Writing Concerns Checklist to the same fifteen C.P.A.'s. The responses were revealing.

The two items that tied for the highest ranking by the eleven respondents were "Clarity" and "Completeness." Given the nature of the accounting profession, I had expected this. However, I had not expected the five-way tie for the second highest ranking. Participants showed great concern about "Accuracy" and "Grammatical Correctness," but they showed equally great concern about "Conciseness," "Reader Sensitivity," and "Tone/Tact." Two participants also added written comments to their checklists, both indicating their desire to write quickly, without sacrificing the quality of their written products.

Their rankings and comments indicated to me that the C.P.A.'s in my program had a good understanding of the skills they needed to develop in order to become more effective business writers. I drew quite heavily on these rankings and comments in deciding what content to present in the writing program.

I also drew upon my analysis of writing samples they had sent me before the workshop. This analysis suggested that many of them took a common approach to writing. Perhaps because C.P.A.'s spend so much time working with numerical data, perhaps because they strive to convey an image of complete objectivity, the participants in my workshop tended to "let the numbers speak for themselves." This made their writing appear more objective, but it also caused several problems.

Many sentences were people-less. Take, for example, these two sentences: "In last year's suggestions for next year's audit, it was mentioned to be aware of possible rehab credit on your building." and "The current year's loss for tax purposes was carried back, and a refund was obtained." These passive constructions deprive both the individual C.P.A. and the firm of their rightful credit for helping the customer. In these passages, as in many others, the writers themselves are invisible.

Here is another example: "The selection you received earlier should be disposed of, and only the items from this new selection should be used." Note that here the author assigns no one the responsibility for doing the needed work.

The need to take credit for services rendered, the value of clearly requesting action from the reader, the benefits of using the active voice and of focusing on people rather than things or abstract concepts, the advantages of getting directly to the point, and the importance of drawing conclusions from the data which they had accumulated—these were among the topics that I felt should be reviewed in my program. The only question left was how best to do so.

To select an appropriate instructional approach, I wanted to know something about the people I would be dealing with. What kinds of people were they? How did their personalities, temperaments, or attitudes differ from those of other people? How did my personality differ from theirs? And what did all this mean in terms of how I should teach them and how they should go about improving their writing?

I had recently taken the Myers-Briggs Type Indicator (MBTI), the most widely used personality measure for nonpsychiatric populations. I was fascinated by what I learned from that experience. The MBTI is a psychometric questionnaire that measures four main areas of personality differences based on differences in the ways people prefer to use their minds. According to Carl Jung's theory of psychological types, each person favors:

- One of two orientations toward life: extraversion (E) or introversion (I)
- One of two ways of perceiving: sensing (S) or intuiting (N)
- One of two ways of judging: thinking (T) or feeling (F)

To Jung's three pairs of preferences, Katharine C. Briggs and her daughter Isabel Briggs Myers added a fourth pair:

- One of two attitudes toward the world: judging (J) or perceiving (P) [Myers, 8]

Thus, every individual can be classified into one of sixteen personality categories on the basis of her or his personal preferences for E/I, S/N, T/F, J/P. None of the sixteen may be said to be better than any of the others, but, according to Jung's theory of psychological types, each preference makes a contribution to each type:

| | |
|---|---|
| Extraverted: | Breadth of interests |
| Introverted: | Depth of concentration |
| Sensing: | Reliance on facts |
| Intuiting: | Grasp of possibilities |
| Thinking: | Logic and analysis |
| Feeling: | Warmth and sympathy |

Judging:                          Organization
Perceptive:                       Adaptability [Myers and McCaulley, 32]

If you would like to learn more about the theory and practical implications of personality differences, I suggest that you read Isabel Briggs Myers's *Gifts Differing*.

My own MBTI scores classified me as ENFJ. About the same time I learned this, I learned of a doctoral dissertation that dealt with the psychological types of C.P.A.'s in Michigan (Otte). This study too used the Myers-Briggs Type Inventory. It found that 52 percent of the 494 C.P.A.'s surveyed were introverted, 65 percent were sensing, 78 percent were thinking, and 74 percent were judging. Only 3 percent of the C.P.A.'s surveyed were in my ENFJ category, while 54 percent were categorized as both sensing and thinking (ST).

This describes the personality types of "them" (the 494 C.P.A.'s surveyed) but does not show how they compare with "you and me." Consulting an *Atlas of Type Tables*, I found a table that described the Myers-Briggs personality types of 2,282 university teachers. Of this sample, 54 percent were introverted, 36 percent were sensing, 53 percent were thinking, and 66 percent were judging. Over 8 percent of the university teachers surveyed were in my ENFJ category, and 22 percent were categorized as both sensing and thinking (ST) (Macdaid, McCaulley, and Kainz).

All of this confirmed my suspicion that the average C.P.A. surveyed was indeed "not like you and me" (i.e., had a personality type dissimilar to mine and that of the average university teacher). But were the C.P.A.'s in the workshop I was going to conduct the same personality types as those of the Michigan C.P.A.'s? To find out, I asked the fifteen prospective participants in my program to complete the Myers-Briggs Type Indicator, Form F (Briggs and Myers).

Once again, eleven of the fifteen responded. Of this number, 73 percent were extraverts, 64 percent were sensing, 82 percent were thinking, and 55 percent were judging. None was in my ENFJ category, but 64 percent were categorized as both sensing and thinking (ST).

As I designed and conducted the writing program for my C.P.A.'s, I found this information quite valuable. Drawing on material developed by Margaret K. Morgan, I attempted to employ instructional strategies most appropriate to the personality types of my participants.

For example, since 64 percent of the C.P.A.'s were sensing types (while I am an intuitive), I tried to modify my approach to meet their instructional needs. According to Morgan, sensors like direct experience, audiovisuals, and well-defined goals; they also need to know *why* before doing something.

To respond to these needs, I provided more writing exercises than I usually do in my programs. Since I already use a wide variety of visual aids, I did not change much in this area. However I did spend more time in establishing with the participants the goals of the writing program and the benefits they could derive from improving their writing.

I also found it useful to know who in the group had a tendency toward introversion. I realized that these individuals were probably not inclined to contribute as much to class discussion as the extraverts were, and that silence on their part might be an indication of thoughtfulness rather than boredom or disapproval. I made a more conscious effort to involve these individuals in the group discussions, since they might have worthwhile contributions to make and yet be reluctant to speak out.

For these and other reasons, I found it valuable to know the personality types of the participants as I designed and conducted the writing program. I thought it might also be valuable for each participant to know her or his own personality type and the implications that type might have for her or his writing on the job. Thus, I not only gave all participants a report on their Myers-Briggs Type Indicator scores and a pamphlet explaining the general significance of those scores, but I also discussed with them some possible relationships between personality types and writing.

In discussing these, I drew heavily on a presentation by John DiTiberio (now of St. Louis University) at the MBTI (Myers-Briggs Type Inventory) IV Conference in Palo Alto on June 30, 1981. In that presentation, DiTiberio described the work he had done in using the Myers-Briggs to help graduate students write their theses and dissertations.

DiTiberio theorized that sensors, for example, feel more comfortable when following a pattern that others before them have found to be useful. They excel at presenting factual information, but they may follow "rules" too rigidly. When the rule does not meet the demands of the present writing situation, they may become blocked. An overconcern about mechanics may also block the development of their thoughts. And they need to make clear the implications (conclusions) of the data they are presenting. When sensors write to intuitives, they may need to concentrate on beginning with the main point or idea and on not getting bogged down in the facts.

In my presentations on the writing process and on ways of improving reader sensitivity, I incorporated advice such as this regarding the eight personality preferences.

Doing all this did, of course, take a great deal of time—far more time than it would have taken me to present a "canned" writing program. But I would not be writing this article now if I did not believe that it was time well spent. I am confident that the C.P.A.'s participating in my program attended a better workshop than they would have had I not surveyed their writing needs, measured their levels of writing anxiety, and assessed their personality types.

Writing teachers and consultants have long preached the importance of tailoring communication to meet the needs of specific audiences. It is time we practiced what we preach. Computer programs can present the same content that a live teacher can, but they cannot modify that content and adapt instructional approaches to meet individual needs in the ways that we flesh-and-blood types can and should.

C.P.A.'s are indeed "different from you and me." And so are engineers, attorneys, journalists, and college students. In addition, each individual C.P.A., engineer, attorney, journalist, and college student is different from every other. By acknowledging these differences and altering our instructional content and method to meet the specific needs of the individuals in our various audiences, we increase the chances that people will learn what we are teaching.

I urge you to undertake this extra level of preparation when you conduct writing programs for C.P.A.'s—or anyone else for that matter.

## Works Cited

American Accounting Association. *A Guide to Accounting Instruction: Concepts and Practices.* Cincinnati: South-Western, 1968.

Briggs, Katharine C., and Isabel Briggs Myers. *Myers-Briggs Type Indicator—Form F.* Palo Alto, Calif.: Consulting Psychologists Press, 1976.

Daly, John A., and Michael D. Miller. "The Empirical Development of an Instrument to Measure Writing Apprehension." *Research in the Teaching of English* 9 (1975): 242–249.

DiTiberio, John. "Type Differences & Approaches to Writing," MBTI IV Conference, Palo Alto, Calif.: Stanford University, June 30, 1981.

Goldberg, Louis. *An Inquiry into the Nature of Accounting.* Evanston, Ill.: American Accounting Association, 1965.

John, Richard C. "Improve Your Technical Writing." *Management Accounting* (September 1976): 49–52.

Macdaid, Gerald P., Mary H. McCaulley, and Richard I. Kainz. *Myers-Briggs Type Indicator Atlas of Type Tables.* Gainesville, Fla.: Center for Applications of Psychological Type, 1986.

Morgan, Margaret K. "Relating Type to Instructional Strategies" MBTI II Conference. East Lansing: Michigan State University, 1977.

Myers, Isabel Briggs. *Gifts Differing.* Palo Alto, Calif.: Consulting Psychologists Press, 1980.

———, and McCaulley, Mary H. *Manual: A Guide to the Development and Use of the Myers-Briggs Type Indicator.* Palo Alto, Calif.: Consulting Psychologists Press, 1975.

Otte, Paul J. "Psychological Typology of the Local Firm-Certified Public Accountant." Doctoral dissertation. Western Michigan University, 1983.

Roy, Robert H., and James H. MacNeill. *Horizons for a Profession.* New York: American Institute of Certified Public Accountants, 1967.

# CONSULTING WITH "DISCURSIVE REGIMES": USING PERSONALITY THEORY TO ANALYZE AND INTERVENE IN BUSINESS COMMUNITIES

George H. Jensen
Georgia State University

*George H. Jensen is an assistant professor with the Division of Developmental Studies at Georgia State University. He has published articles in* College Composition and Communication *and* Journal of Basic Writing. *With John DiTiberio, he wrote* Personality and the Teaching of Composition, *which is to be published by Ablex. With C. L. Sills, he is currently editing* The Philosophy of Discourse, *which will be published by Boynton/Cook. Jensen has also worked as an adviser for the governor of Georgia's Task Force on Adult Literacy and consulted with several businesses, universities, and school districts.*

Composition specialists are all too familiar with power politics. They have learned the theory of realpolitik from the likes of Machiavelli, and they have experienced its praxis through the academic power plays of departmental elections, tenure decisions, and interdepartmental budget fights. They are not naive about the real world, but they also tend to be egalitarians in the classroom. Their pedagogy owes more to Freire, Elbow, and Fish than to Machiavelli. As teachers, they typically strive to create a rarefied environment, a discourse community (or perhaps "commune" is more apt) of collaborative writers and peer editors. Thus, when composition specialists first enter the business world, they may find their pedagogy and their well-wrought intervention as ill suited to corporate life as their casual clothes.

One of the more frequent laments of novice consultants is that their efforts have so little effect on the corporate structure. They feel that they design superior writing programs (at least by educational standards), and they observe that the writing of their "students" improves as they compose in a classroom within the corporation. But, after the consultants return to campus, they often learn that the writing "problem" that they were hired "to fix" is not only breathing and well but is often not even wounded.

In this chapter, I will argue that such failed interventions can often be avoided if consultants first analyze the corporation's political/discursive structure. As an example, I will describe how I used Foucault's theory of "discursive regimes" and Jung's theory of personality type to analyze the political/discursive structure of a large mortgage company before designing a program for its underwriters.

## FOUCAULT'S THEORY OF "DISCURSIVE REGIMES"

In the field of composition, the term "discourse community" is typically used to describe the context in which one writes. The term projects an image of writers working harmoniously in some quaint neighborhood of the academy. In contrast, Foucault used the term "discursive regime" because it is suggestive of the "effects of power peculiar to statements" (*Power/Knowledge*, p. 113). In other words, Foucault believed that power and truth cannot be separated, that the epistemology (or episteme) of those in power determines what is considered truth or what is considered the legitimate discourse for delivering truth. In a 1977 interview, Foucault explained:

> The important thing here, I believe, is that truth isn't outside power, or lacking in power: contrary to a myth whose history and functions would repay further study, truth isn't the reward of free spirits, the child of protracted solitude, nor the privilege of those who have succeeded in liberating themselves. Truth is a thing of this world: it is produced only by virtue of multiple forms of constraint. And it induces regular effects of power. Each society has its regime of truth, its "general politics" of truth: that is, the types of discourse which it accepts and makes function as true; the mechanisms and instances which enable one to distinguish true and false statements, the means by which each is sanctioned; the techniques and procedures accorded value in the acquisition of truth; the status of those who are charged with saying what counts as true. [*Power/Knowledge*, p. 131]

Foucault realized that, to understand discourse, one must also understand the function of power. One must understand the impact of broad social forces (politics, institutions, epistemology, ideology) on the nature of discourse, but one must also understand "the person occupying a specific position" whose status is linked "to the general functioning of an apparatus of truth" (*Power/Knowledge*, p. 132). It is this "person occupying a specific position" and his or her impact on the operation of discourse in a specific context that Jung's theory of personality can help us to understand.

## JUNG'S THEORY OF PERSONALITY TYPES

Carl Jung first became interested in developing a theory of individual differences shortly after his break with Freud and Adler. He believed that a more fundamental cause lay behind the split than quibbles over therapeutic issues or the import of symbols; the fundamental cause, Jung felt, was that he, Freud, and Adler differed in the basic psychological processes that they used to perceive and make decisions. During his "fallow period," from 1913 to about 1918, Jung developed a theory of personality type that he presented in *Psychological Types* (1921). Jung believed that differences among people could best be explained in terms of preferences for three sets of opposite psychological processes: Extraversion-Introversion, Sensing-Intuition, and Thinking-Feeling. In the 1940s, Katharine Briggs and her daughter, Isabel Myers, began to develop an instrument to assess Jungian personality type, which was eventually called the Myers-Briggs Type Indicator. To Jung's theory, they added a fourth dimension: Judging-Perceiving.

Thus, Jung's model of personality, as expanded by Briggs and Myers, has four bipolar dimensions, each of which reflects a set of equally valid yet opposing psychological processes:

Extraversion (E) . . . . . . . . . Introversion (I)
Sensing (S) . . . . . . . . . Intuition (N)
Thinking (T) . . . . . . . . . Feeling (F)
Judging (J) . . . . . . . . . Perceiving (P)

Even though we use all of these processes each day, we begin early in life to prefer one of each set of opposites over the other. Because we use our preferred processes more frequently, they develop more completely. These preferred processes, therefore, more accurately describe who we are and how we act as well as our strengths as individuals (we have developed them more fully).

Here is what the terms mean. Extraversion is dealing with outer experience; introversion is dealing with the inner experience of contemplation and reflection. Sensing is concrete perception through the senses; intuition is an abstract perception through the imagination. Thinking types strive to make decisions objectively; in order to be objective, they tend to base decisions on an objective criterion or a general principle. Feeling types are less concerned about objectivity and more concerned about the personal issues in making decisions; they are more likely to base a decision on the personal values of those involved or on how it might promote group harmony. Judging is approaching tasks with a primary concern for getting things done; perceiving is approaching tasks with a primary concern for doing them thoroughly.

Although Jung's model may sound static when presented so succinctly, it is actually a dynamic and complex approach to personality type. An individual's preferences on each of the four dimensions combine to create sixteen possible types. Even a combination of a few of the four preferences can explain complex behaviors, as I will suggest in the next section.

## JUNG'S PERSONALITY THEORY AND DISCOURSE

DiTiberio and I have observed that the expanded model of Jung's theory can account for many of the apparently random variations in how individuals approach their own writing and how they evaluate the writing of others ("Personality and Individual Writing Processes," 1984; *Personality and the Teaching of Composition,* in press). Here, I will only attempt to summarize how the interaction of two dimensions of Jung's model (Sensing-Intuition and Thinking-Feeling) can explain some of the features that distinguish one discursive regime from another. To illustrate cogently the distinct discourse of different personality types, I will quote how my students (when divided into type-alike groups of STs, SFs, NFs, and NTs) described the concept of time to a Martian.

Sensing-Thinking types (STs)—found in large numbers among engineers, business managers, and surgeons—tend to be concrete, analytical, and objective, as the following description of time written by a group of STs indicates:

1. Time is a measurement of duration.
2. Time is based on the position of the sun during the day.
3. A unit of time is a second.
    A. 60 seconds make a minute.
    B. 60 minutes make an hour.
    C. 24 hours make a day.
        (1) A day is a rotation of our planet earth.
    D. There are 365 days in a year.
        (1) A year is one revolution of our planet around the sun.

As writers, STs tend to focus on the content of their message, stating it objectively and concisely in a clearly organized (usually also a prescribed and widely accepted) format. They value discourse that is concise, factual, clear, and accurate. Since they tend to view writing as rule-driven, they also value texts that follow what they believe to be the "rules."

Sensing-Feeling types (SFs), found in large numbers in nursing and elementary education, tend to be concrete, personable, and people-oriented. In the following description of time, the SFs' desire to connect with their audience is apparent:

1. sun's movement
2. 5 bleep-bleeps Martian time equal 1 hour of our time.
3. explain hours and minutes
4. months in a year
5. seasons in a year, colors of trees indicate seasons
6. temperature indicates season
7. rotation
8. revolution
9. time zones
10. bellyaches indicate sleep time
11. drooping antennae indicate sleep time
12. alarm clock means to get up
13. shadows indicate changing times
14. movement of ocean indicates changing times

Like STs, the SFs are concrete (describing time in terms of sensations such as "bellyaches"), but they are far more personal, adding humor in an attempt to connect with their audience. They generally regard the objective discourse of STs as too dull. They value the discourse of personal experience.

Intuitive-Feeling types (NFs)—found in large numbers in counseling, all levels of education, the fine arts, and journalism—are as interested in people as the SFs, but in a more theoretical, abstract way. Their thought relies heavily on metaphor, as the following description of time indicates:

1. method of social organization
2. label marking changes so we can communicate
3. circle of cycles
4. sands of sea
5. the eternity of possibilities

The NFs, like the SFs, value discourse that establishes contact with their audience. Yet, because they are more speculative and holistic, they are often bored by discourse that is too factual and concrete.

Intuitive-Thinking types (NTs), found in large numbers in law, science, and higher education, tend to be the architects of theoretical models. The NTs described time thus:

1. Based on earth's rotation around the sun.
2. Time is used as a point of reference to synchronize our activities on earth.
3. Time is measured in years, which break down into seasons, months, weeks, days, hours, minutes, seconds (and nanoseconds).
4. Time is also measured through our life. When someone is born, how long they live, or when they die, and through life the development of the body from infancy to adulthood.
5. We would send a Martian to someone who knows astrological math to explain how to break time down.

Like that of STs, the discourse of NTs tends to be objective, but it is also highly abstract. They most highly value discourse that presents innovative ideas or new theoretical models.

These descriptions of time suggest one of the ways in which personality type and power can interact to affect the constitution of a discursive regime. If, for example, an engineering firm is heavily populated by STs (as they usually are), then that type holds—by sheer number—considerable power over the normative rules that regulate that discursive regime. In such an organization, the metaphorical discourse of NFs would not, in all probability, be warmly accepted. An NF, even if in a position of power, could hope to have little or no effect on how that firm wrote. But, when a context is not so heavily dominated by a particular type, then the personality type of those individuals with more power can greatly influence, for better or worse, the discursive operations of that context. In business corporations, as my consultation with a mortgage company will illustrate, the personality type of the individual in power is usually more significant than the modal personality type of the workers at large.

## USING PERSONALITY TYPE DURING CONSULTATIONS

Before the consultant can understand the interplay between personality type and power within a corporation, he or she must determine the types of the individuals who work there. Because the Myers-Briggs Type Indicator is frequently used by organizational development consultants (see *Using the Myers-Briggs Type Indicator in Organizations*, 1985), many corporations have type data available or are open to having consultants administer the instrument.

If data is not available or is unobtainable, the consultant can still use his or her knowledge of type theory to formulate operational assumptions about the types of individuals in key positions. To do so, the consultant should possess a thorough understanding of type theory (see *Gifts Differing*, 1980, and *Please Understand Me*, 1978), including a knowledge of the distribution of type within certain professions (see *Myers-Briggs Type Indicator: Atlas of Type Tables*, 1987). In the case example discussed below, I did not administer the Myers-Briggs Type Indicator, but I was able to develop some useful hunches about the individuals in key positions. Such hunches, however, should always be used with a great deal of caution, for even an expert in type theory can often be fooled. Although one's personality type is often related to his or her behavior, there is by no means a direct and invariable correlation.

Human beings are complex, far more complex than any personality theory can describe. Thus, any use of personality theory, even when data from the Myers-Briggs Type Indicator is available, should be regarded as assumptions rather than infallible conclusions.

## A CASE EXAMPLE

In September 1986, I was asked to develop a writing program for a large mortgage corporation that did not initiate mortgages directly with homeowners. Rather, the company purchased mortgages from a number of mortgage brokers. It first trained mortgage brokers to initiate loans that would meet its criteria of acceptability. If the brokers agreed to observe these criteria, the company would purchase mortgages from them in bulk and without any prepurchase review. To ensure that its criteria were being observed, the company's underwriters conducted spot reviews of the mortgages. If a particular broker initiated a mortgage that marginally violated a policy or two, the underwriter would send him or her what was known as an "educational letter," which typically contained two basic messages: (1) you initiated a weak loan and (2) if you do it again, we will ask you to repurchase the loan. If a broker initiated a mortgage that egregiously violated the company's criteria, the underwriter would send a "repurchase letter" to the broker. The broker would then have to come up with $100,000 (or whatever the amount of the loan) to buy it back.

Herein lay the problem that I was asked to solve. Brokers were obviously unhappy about receiving educational letters, which made them feel like they were being scolded. And they were especially unhappy about receiving repurchase letters, which could have serious repercussions for their company's cash flow. The mortgage company wanted me to teach their underwriters to compose letters that would deliver the "bad news" clearly but would do so without unduly offending the broker, with whom they wanted to maintain a functional business relationship.

I began by interviewing the two supervisors who were the immediate superiors of the underwriters. The supervisors explained the basic process of reviewing loans. The underwriters first read the loan file and evaluated whether or not it had met the company's criteria. If warranted, they drafted either an educational or repurchase letter. The letter was first reviewed by one of the two supervisors, who either made minor revisions or asked the underwriter to redraft the letter completely. Once approved by the supervisors, the letter was read by the manager, who again might make minor revisions or ask the underwriter for a complete revision. Eventually, the letter was read by the regional vice president, who could ask for even more revisions before he signed the letter.

The supervisors also showed me examples of educational and repurchase letters. The letters represented business correspondence at its worst. The underwriters wrote concisely (even at the expense of being blunt) and employed the standard formats of business correspondence (enumeration, bullet pointing, etc.) with little variation or attention to the unique characteristics of the rhetorical situation. They even employed the same set phrases in letter after letter, producing with much sweat and toil what amounted to little more than an institutionalized form letter. Most letters began as follows:

> We have completed our postpurchase review of this loan and have found several underwriting deficiencies:
> 1. The borrower was credited with $320 per month of child support income. The divorce decree indicated an award of only $130 per month. The file did not contain evidence that the borrower was receiving this additional amount.
> 2. The existence of funds needed for closing was not verified. The settlement statement showed that approximately $4,500 was needed from the borrower at closing.

The letters usually ended as bluntly and routinely as they began. For example:

> These items make this loan an unacceptable risk for our company. Please repurchase this loan in accordance with Chapter 3, Part 5, Sections 504, 504.01, and 504.02D of our manual.
> Should your review of the file provide information which would mitigate our findings, we would welcome your response for a reevaluation of our position.
> Sincerely,

After reviewing the sample letters, I felt that part of the problem was clearly rhetorical. The closing attempt to make a concession to the audience ("Should your review of the file provide information which would mitigate our findings") is particularly inept. The underwriters needed to explore some stylistic options that could soften their message. But I was also concerned about the homogeneity of the letters. The letters were almost invariably ST discourse: they focused on factual content, presented the information concisely in a highly structured format, and were completely objective. The correspondence reflected the strengths of ST discourse (clarity, conciseness, organization, objectivity), but it also reflected its greatest weakness: the message was delivered routinely without attention to how it might affect the audience.

At this point, I felt that the most likely explanations for the homogeneity of the discourse were that either the underwriters were predominantly STs or an ST in a powerful position was enforcing a set of ST normative rules to which the underwriters had to adapt. To develop a better understanding of the relation of power and discourse within the corporation, I asked to meet with all of the executives involved with reviewing the underwriters' letter, the manager, and the regional vice president.

The manager, the second level of management, appeared to be an ESTJ, the type most frequently found in middle management. She was highly respected for her knowledge of mortgage underwriting within the company and throughout the mortgage community in the region, but she had, typical of many ESTJs, a fairly rigid and rule-governed view of rhetoric. During my meeting with her, she gave me a copy of the company's *Secretarial Handbook,* which she felt would help me in designing a program for the underwriters. The handbook was full of dicta, such as, "Don't begin a paragraph at the end of the first page unless you have space for at least two lines." Her concerns about the discourse of the underwriters seemed to come from the kind of rules that one learns from reading grammar handbooks or manuals on business correspondence. She basically felt that the underwriters' letters were full of grammatical errors, wordy, unclear, etc. As I learned more about the manager after the writing program began, I realized that she served the role of dictator within this discursive regime. Keirsey and Bates say of the ESTJ type:

> ESTJs are outstanding at organizing orderly procedures and in detailing rules and regulations. They like to see things done correctly. They tend to be impatient with those who do not carry out procedures with sufficient attention to those details, prescribed by those with the most experience, that will get the job done right. [*Please Understand Me,* p. 190]

The manager felt that she knew how writing could be "done correctly," and she made sure that the underwriters got "the job done right." At one point, she was so exasperated about what she considered a misuse of "since" in subordinate clauses that she threatened to fire the next person who used "since" when he or she actually meant "because." ESTJs typically like power and they are not afraid to use it. Also, the underwriters told me that they habitually used certain set phrases because they had learned from experience that the manager would approve these. To alter phrasing or format in any way was to risk being asked to revise the letter completely.

The regional vice president, the highest level of management to read the underwriters' letters, appeared to be an INFJ. An English major in undergraduate school, he too was concerned about grammatical correctness. But his approach to grammar came less from a rigid conception of correctness than from concern about how grammatical errors reflected on the image of the corporation. He also seemed far more concerned about how the letters affected the people who read them, which is typical of feeling types. Indeed, he attributed his own rise within the corporation to his ability to write well and to adapt his writing style to the style of his superiors.

After analyzing the individuals in key positions of power, I felt that any attempt to soften the underwriters' correspondence, which essentially meant moving them toward the discourse of feeling types, would probably be negated by the revisions of the ESTJ manager. I felt that I had to instruct the underwriters directly, but I also realized that, if this intervention were to be successful, I would have to intervene in the discursive regime as well. In short, I would have to find some way of getting the softened discourse past the ESTJ manager to the INFJ vice president, who I felt would understand the new discourse and approve of it.

For the underwriters, I developed a five-week course. During the first session, I discussed some approaches to analyzing audience, a wide range of organizational formats, and approaches to softening "bad news" business correspondence. A handout developed from Laib's "Territoriality in Rhetoric" (see Figure 1) proved particularly useful in helping the underwriters to explore ways to soften their discourse. During subsequent meetings, the underwriters analyzed a sample loan and practiced applying the theory presented during the first session. Their letters were reviewed in a workshop setting.

After the program was finished, I compiled a notebook that was ostensibly meant to serve as a reference tool for the underwriters but was actually intended for the entire company. I included handouts from the program, copies of chapters from business writing textbooks, and a selection of some of the better letters written during the program. I hoped that the letters would serve as models of acceptable approaches to the rhetorical problems facing the underwriters. After delivering the notebook to the company, I set up a meeting with the manager and the vice president so that I could discuss the models and obtain approval for them. About a week later, one of the supervisors called me to cancel the meeting. She said that the manager had already "signed off" on the models.

Just as ESTJs rely on a position of authority to exert their own power, so too do they typically defer to their superiors. This is not to say that they are in any way weak managers. Quite the opposite. They simply respect an orderly structure of power, a sentiment that the average academic (usually NFs or NTs) finds foreign. As Keirsey and Bates wrote: "ESTJs are so in tune with the established, time-honored institutions and ways of behaving within those institutions that they cannot understand those who might wish to abandon or radically change those

Rhetoric can be described as a means of increasing one's control over occupied property, expanding one's boundaries, or making oneself secure. It defends property, whether it be an acre of land, an idea, a way of life, one's reputation, or one's power. Viewed in this light, rhetoric is an aggressive act.

### Territoriality and Stylistic Dichotomies

*More Aggressive*

COMPLAINING:
"My property has been infringed upon or damaged."

ADVISING:
"This is my property. I know the way. Follow me."

DEPRECATION:
"You do not have a strong hold on your property; your ideas, identity, and values are not worthy of promotion or attention."

ASSERTION:
"This property is mine; I am important; my ideas are valuable."

TAKING:
"What you have claimed as your property is in fact mine."

*Less Aggressive*

NEGOTIATION OR MEDIATION:
"We both have some legitimate claim to this property. Let us compromise, negotiate redress, or divide blame."

ASKING FOR HELP:
"This territory is unfamiliar to me. Help me find my way."

REASSURANCE:
"You do own this property; your ideas, identity, and values are important and significant."

EFFACEMENT:
"You can take this property if you like; I am not a threat."

SHARING:
"I have discovered new territory that I intend to share with you."

*Figure 1 Rhetoric based on territorial motives. From Nevin K. Laib, "Territoriality in Rhetoric." College English 47 (October 1985): 579–593. Copyright © 1985 by the National Council of Teachers of English. Reprinted by permission.*

institutions" (*Please Understand Me*, p. 191). Although this is only conjecture, I believe that the ESTJ manager signed off on the models because a consultant (one figure of authority) was about to pronounce them acceptable to the vice president (another authority figure).

Subsequent follow-up with both the supervisors and the vice president indicated that the intervention had been successful. The supervisors felt that the underwriters were more aware of the impact of their message on the audience and that they were able to use the Laib handout to soften their discourse. They also felt that the "approved" models in the notebook allowed them to push the softened discourse past the ESTJ manager to the INFJ vice president. If a letter were rejected by the manager, they could often point to the approved model that it emulated and have it reconsidered. The vice president stated that he noticed a profound change in the underwriters' letters.

## CONCLUSION

Foucault, who spent most of his career analyzing the connection between power and knowledge, offers an important message to academics who consult with business corporations: the nature of discourse and the distribution of power are inextricably fused. As a result, the employees with the least power in the corporation will usually be perceived as being the fundamental cause of communication problems. Consultants who work with the clerks, secretaries, and workers alone will not only be ineffective but will also run the risk of acting unethically. If I had not intervened in the entire power structure, the underwriters would probably have followed my advice and (at least in my opinion) have improved their letters, but they would also have produced a discourse that some levels of management were unprepared to accept. Even though they might have been more effective writers, they could have been chewed up in the corporation's discursive regime.

If consultants hope to be successful teachers within the corporate world, they must instruct *and* protect. They must analyze the relation between the corporation's power structure and the normative rules that regulate its discourse, which Jung's theory of personality type can facilitate. Then they will be prepared to do more than teach rhetoric in a rarefied environment; they will be prepared to intervene in a discursive regime.

## *Works Cited*

Foucault, Michel. *Power/Knowledge: Selected Interviews and Other Writings, 1972–1977*, ed. Colin Gordon. New York: Pantheon Books, 1980.

Hirsh, Sandra K. *Using the Myers-Briggs Type Indicator in Organizations: A Resource Book.* Palo Alto, Calif.: Consulting Psychologists Press, 1985.

Jensen, George H., and John K. DiTiberio. "Personality and Individual Writing Processes." *College Composition and Communication* 35 (October 1984): 285–300.

⸻ and ⸻. *Personality and the Teaching of Composition.* Norwood, N.J.: Ablex, in press.

Keirsey, David, and Marilyn Bates. *Please Understand Me.* Del Mar, Calif.: Prometheus Nemesis Books, 1978.

Macdaid, Gerald, Mary McCaulley, and Richard Kainz. *Myers-Briggs Type Indicator: Atlas of Type Table.* Gainesville, Fla.: Center for Applications of Psychological Type, 1987.

Myers, Isabel Briggs. *Gifts Differing.* Palo Alto, Calif.: Consulting Psychologists Press, 1980.

# HOW TO APPEAR RELIABLE WITHOUT BEING LIABLE: C.P.A. WRITING IN ITS RHETORICAL CONTEXT

*Aletha S. Hendrickson*
University of Maryland

*Aletha Hendrickson teaches technical writing, business writing (for accounting majors), and computer-assisted technical writing at the University of Maryland and is managing editor of* Literary Research: A Journal of Scholarly Method and Technique. *She is currently researching I.R.S. rhetoric.*

## INTRODUCTION

The bankruptcy of any company often creates havoc for its owners, creditors, and even seemingly uninvolved third parties such as certified public accountants (C.P.A.'s).* For example, the PDQ Construction Company engaged A. John Smith, C.P.A., to write a financial report. In due time, the report was furnished to all stockholders, who thereupon decided to invest more money in the company. But PDQ suffered a financial setback due to a regional recession beyond its control. Do the stockholders sit back quietly and lick their wounds? Recovering their losses from PDQ is impossible because the company is protected by bankruptcy laws. Instead, the stockholders retain an attorney who specializes in suing C.P.A.'s. And soon Mr. Smith finds himself on the receiving end of a third-party lawsuit accusing him of failing to furnish full disclosure of PDQ's financial status. But Mr. Smith protests that his numbers are accurate—which they are. Nonetheless, the stockholders sue, not the now defunct PDQ but the *auditor* to recoup their losses. How does an honest, hard-working C.P.A. like Mr. Smith find himself liable for stockholder losses when all he did was tell the truth?

---

*I am grateful to the Certified Public Accountants and businesspersons who provided me with access to actual Financial Reports for research purposes (client identities and financial data are masked to preserve confidentiality). I am especially indebted to Professor Michael J. Marcuse for his reading and suggestions. The paper's shortcomings remain my sole responsibility.

The hypothetical Mr. Smith and numerous real-life C.P.A. defendants are, of course, players in an event described by Lloyd F. Bitzer as a "rhetorical situation." The C.P.A. is the rhetor; PDQ and the out-of-pocket stockholders are the audience, and the financial report constitutes C.P.A. discourse, the subject of our discussion.

To begin with, I will examine the textual characteristics of C.P.A. discourse for evidence of writer purpose and audience accommodation. Then I will look at the writer's purpose and projection of *ethos*, which seem to be at odds, and I also will investigate the writer's complicated relationship to diverse audiences. Finally, I will discuss "key technical concepts [that] underlie the shape and effectiveness of specialized argument by serving as special topics" (Miller and Selzer, 314)—as well as the "three constituents of any rhetorical situation: the first is the *exiqence;* the second and third are elements of the complex, namely the *audience* to be constrained in decision and action, and the *constraints* which influence the rhetor and can be brought to bear upon the audience" (Bitzer, 6). I will conclude with some thoughts on further research and pedagogical implications.

In considering financial reports, questions to keep in mind include:

1. How does the C.P.A. provide reliable information yet at the same time avoid liability?
2. How can the C.P.A. straddle the line between self-interest and duty to his or her profession?
3. How does the C.P.A. incorporate complex financial data into a reader-based text?
4. How can the C.P.A. engage in ethos-building yet at the same time control the widespread and sometimes inappropriate credence placed in the reliability of financial reports?
5. In short, how do C.P.A.'s cope with a complex, conflictive rhetorical situation?

## C.P.A. TEXTS

Before I discuss the characteristics of C.P.A. texts, I should begin by explaining what financial reports are. Simply put, these annual reports measure and communicate financial data about the health of a client company.[1] The C.P.A. writes the report, and the client publishes it so that all interested parties can make financial decisions based on their assessment of the company—an assessment based on the information contained in the report. Such readers include bankers, who grant or deny loans to clients; insurance agents, who bond or refuse bonding to a company; vendors, who extend or withhold credit; and stockholders, who invest or divest in a corporation based on the Report.

The point that C.P.A.'s provide reliable financial information yet attempt to avoid liability centers on the three levels of financial reports that C.P.A.'s write.

In the lowest level of report, the compilation, the C.P.A. offers virtually no assurance of reliability to the readers because the client furnishes all financial data; the C.P.A. merely arranges the information in a report format. Thus, the C.P.A.'s contribution is that of *compiling* the company's information. A higher level of report is the review report, in which the C.P.A. offers negative assurance. The C.P.A., having made inquiries of company personnel and having applied analytic procedures to furnished financial data, is not aware of any material problem with the information provided by the client company; it is, in fact, a review report because the C.P.A. *reviews* the company's information. The highest level of report is the audit, in which the C.P.A. offers assurance of full disclosure; that is, the C.P.A. *certifies* by means of the audit that the report correctly asserts the true financial condition of a company. In performing an audit, the C.P.A. uses professional standards of accountancy established by the American Institute of Certified Public Accountants, the AICPA, which is the accountant's equivalent to the physician's American Medical Association.

If the three levels of assurance were to be compared to a physician's examination, the compilation would be like a diagnosis determined only by a patient's testimony; the review would be like a diagnosis written on the basis of a patient's testimony and some thumping and poking; and the audit would be like a diagnosis derived from testimony, thumping, an extensive battery of laboratory tests, a CAT scan—and exploratory surgery, just to be sure.

Of those who work with financial data, only C.P.A.'s are licensed by each of the fifty states to perform reviews and audits. My study is limited to the texts associated with the financial reports generated by C.P.A.'s rather than to interoffice memos and other C.P.A. communications (see Figure 1).[2] I will first discuss the standard pre- and postreport documents associated with compilation, review, and audit reports, which usually include the engagement letter, the representation letter, AICPA brochures, and the management letter, followed by the financial-report opinion letter—all texts that tend to control reader expectation.

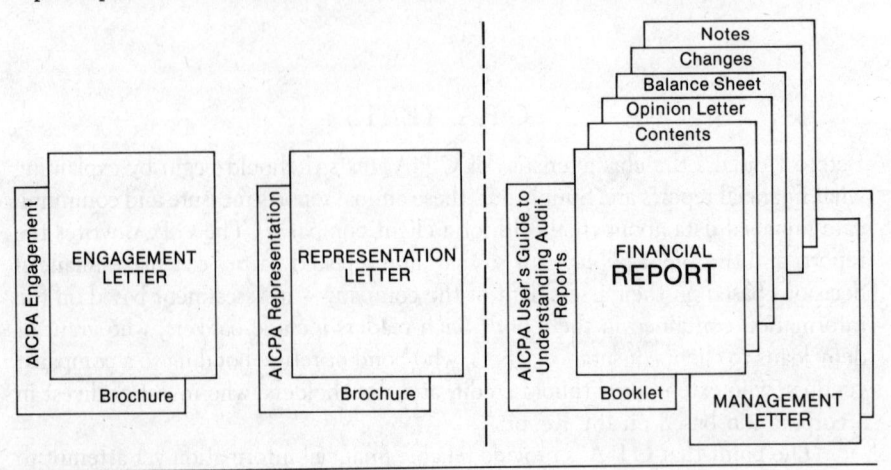

*Figure 1 Standard C.P.A. texts*

## The Engagement Letter

The prereport engagement letter is an agreement (written by the C.P.A.) between the C.P.A. and management (client) which defines the scope and limitations of the report and acknowledges mutual obligations. In containing the "type of engagement to be performed and the expectations they agree to fulfill" (AICPA, "Engagement"), Engagement letters establish the basis for C.P.A. compensation and define for the paying audience (client) the scope and limitations of the report—what it will and will not say. The engagement letter's primary purpose is to preclude litigation. It also sets up client-reader expectation by quoting the exact wording which will appear in the opinion letter covering the completed report.

## The Representation Letter

In another prereport document, the client representation letter, the client-audience becomes the client-writer in acknowledging that management "rather than the auditor—[has] primary responsibility for the financial statements..." (AICPA, "Representation"). Although the C.P.A. may draft the letter, the C.P.A. is technically its audience. The letter is signed by the client-audience, who promises that all relevant information (full financial disclosure) has been provided to the C.P.A., thus implying *client*, not C.P.A., liability.

To explain the functions of both engagement and representation letters, C.P.A.'s generally provide verbal and written instructions (AICPA brochures) which train the client-audience to read the report (see Figure 2). To further aid the client-audience in understanding the report, C.P.A.'s often personally deliver the report, discuss its meanings, and furnish a thirty-page AICPA booklet entitled *A User's Guide to Understanding Audits and Auditor's Reports* (Winters, 1982). Letters, brochures, and verbal explanations are also used to control legal liability arising from misinterpretations of financial reports. Although technically not a part of the actual report, the letters are widely used by C.P.A.'s to foster audience understanding of what the audit text does and does not say; they are highly recommended by the AICPA to preclude legal problems.

## The Management Letter

Generally furnished with the completed report, the management letter fulfills "a requirement that the auditor communicate to ... management ... material weaknesses in internal accounting control that came to [the auditor's] attention" during the audit procedure (AICPA, SAS). Although critiques of the client's internal controls are sometimes verbalized, a partner in a major regional Maryland/DC/Virginia firm contends that the letter is appropriate only in case of "serious deficiency." But a partner in a Maryland regional firm insists that such a postaudit letter should be written for all reviews and audits. Characteristics of the management letter text include the following:

1. More or less standardized language and format
2. Address to a definite audience—management
3. Acceptance of responsibility by management for the audit
4. Discussion of findings of the audit
5. A definition and justification for the scope of the audit
6. Definitions of the terms, compilation, review, and audit

Because the financial report itself is limited to a specific period in time, the management letter transcends that limitation by providing financial projections that the client can use in financial planning. In addition, the management letter discusses major and minor issues relevant to internal accounting procedures.

Both partners mentioned above feel that management letters accomplish an additional promotional purpose—giving the C.P.A. an opportunity to demonstrate expertise geared solely to the client's situation and to show concern for client interests. As a by-product of the audit function capable of promoting ethos, "[m]anagement letters can be a distinguishing characteristic of C.P.A. firms" (W. Wallace, 27). Those who favor the letters see them as "key communication devices" (27) which can attract and keep new clients. Like the audit report, however, "Management Letter contents can be evidence for or against the C.P.A. in case of litigation," according to a senior partner in a major regional firm. Therefore, the management letter is an example of C.P.A. discourse which positively contributes to ethos-building and to audience accommodation but is also a document which can be turned against its C.P.A. writer. Hence, some C.P.A.'s prefer to critique management's internal control procedures *orally* rather than to write still another document associated with financial reports for which the auditor can be held liable.

The aforementioned engagement letter, representation letter, AICPA brochures, and management letter constitute C.P.A. discourse designed to facilitate understanding of financial reports by C.P.A. audiences. These informative pre- and postreport texts point to the report and typify the accommodating nature of C.P.A. discourse. Since these instructive documents relate to the financial report from *without*, I refer to them in general as *extra* textual discourse—as opposed to *meta*-textual discourse, which occurs *within* the financial report.

## The Opinion Letter

The opinion letter is more than a cover or transmittal letter; it is an integral part of the financial report and is bound within its covers. Part of its function is to convey to report users what the report does and does not say by defining the level of report involved. In an audit report, for instance, the C.P.A. renders an *opinion* that the financial report is or is not "in conformity with generally accepted accounting principles" consistently applied (Figure 3). The C.P.A. cannot render an opinion one way or the other, however, in a review or compilation report, because sufficient auditing procedures to support such an opinion have not been carried out. A C.P.A. states, in the review report, that he or she "is not aware" of any problems with management's financial information. In a compilation report, the C.P.A. can only state that he or she has presented unverified (unaudited) information that is provided by management. To emphasize these distinctions, the C.P.A. employs the aforementioned extratextual documents and metatextual features within the opinion letter to claim or disclaim responsibility for the information contained in the financial reports.

## CHARACTERISTICS OF THE FINANCIAL REPORT

We turn now to the characteristics inherent in financial reports that typify C.P.A. discourse. Components of the report, which can run from a few pages to a hundred or more, usually include the following, in order:

1. The report covers
2. Table of contents
3. Opinion letter
4. Statement of financial position (balance sheet)
5. Statement of changes in retained earnings
6. Income statements
7. Statement of changes in financial position
8. Notes to financial statements
9. Footnotes (on individual report pages)

To approach rhetorically a study of writing in a discipline, Lester Faigley and Kristine Hansen observe that we "will have to explore . . . how the conventions of a discipline shape a text in that discipline, how individual writers represent themselves in a text, how a text is read and disseminated, and how one text influences subsequent texts" (149). Use of the aforementioned components of the financial report has evolved over time by the practitioners of accountancy, in response to accounting theory and to reader need—whether client, banker, insurance agent, vendor, or stockholder. I will return to the projection of ethos in C.P.A. discourse and to reader response to C.P.A. texts below. But first, we will consider textual characteristics of the financial report, including its referential properties, metatextual functions, standardized wording and formats, ambiguity, congruity, and readability.

### *Referential Properties*

A characteristic of C.P.A. discourse that limits liability and facilitates audience comprehension is the referent property of C.P.A. texts. Figure 2 shows how financial reports use referents within and without to aid audience understanding. Reading clockwise starting with the client/C.P.A. (a), the client engages the C.P.A. to perform a compilation, review, or audit. The C.P.A. explains to the client

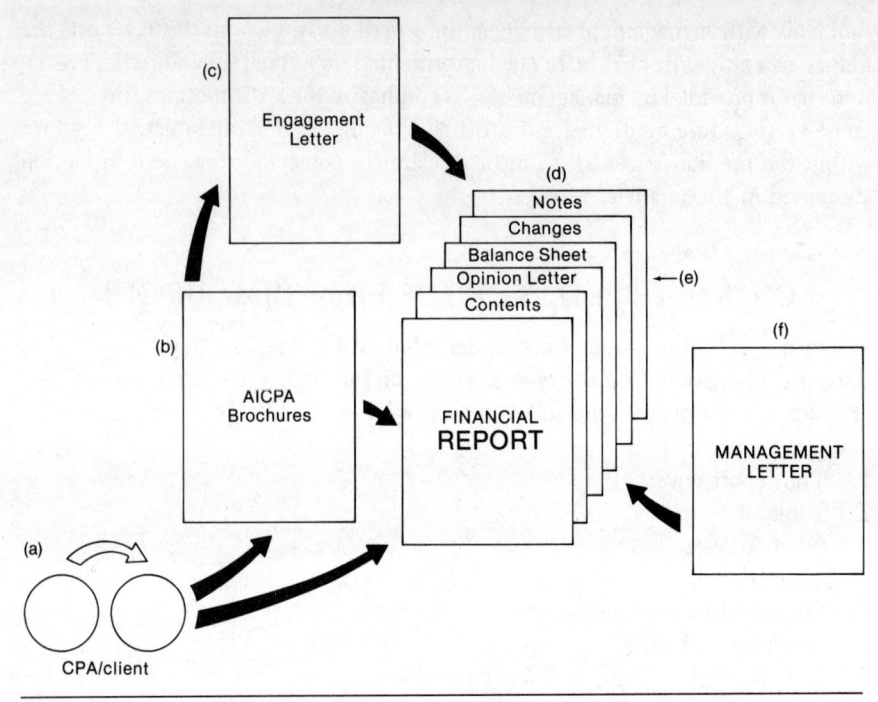

*Figure 2 Referential characteristics of C.P.A. texts*

(a), both orally and in writing via AICPA brochures (b), and the engagement letter (c), what the nature and scope of the report (d) will entail. As mentioned previously, the brochures and letters refer to the exact wording contained in the report opinion letter (e). After the report is completed and delivered, the C.P.A. furnishes the management letter (f), which restates what has already been said in the report and also critiques management's internal accounting controls. Such referents set up, control, fulfill, and reinforce reader expectation; hence, the C.P.A. employs these interrelated documents to eliminate legal consequences that may arise from reader misinterpretation of financial reports.

## Metatextual Functions

Because audiences fail to distinguish between various levels of financial reports, C.P.A.'s incorporate metadiscourse within their texts. To illustrate, Figure 3 shows wording from opinion letters covering the three levels of financial reports—the compilation, review, and audit. William J. Vande Kopple identifies seven kinds of metadiscourse (85), the first five of which appear in C.P.A. texts. In the first column I cite Vande Kopple's metadiscourse typology; I then quote appropriate sentences, phrases, and words from C.P.A. opinion letters attached to compilation, review, and audit reports.

### Compilation

We have compiled the accompanying balance sheet of XYZ Corp. as of January 31, 1985, and the related statements of income, retained earnings and changes in financial position for the year then ended, in accordance with standards established by the American Institute of Certified Public Accountants.

A compilation is limited to presenting information that is the representation of management in the form of financial statements. We have not audited or reviewed the accompanying financial statements and, accordingly, do not express an opinion or any other form of assurance on them.

Management has elected to omit substantially all of the disclosures required by generally accepted accounting principles. If the omitted disclosures were included in the financial statements, they might influence the user's conclusions about the Company's financial position, results of operations, and changes in financial position. Accordingly, these financial statements are not designed for those who are not informed about such matters.

### Review

We have reviewed the accompanying balance sheet of XYZ Corp. as of January 31, 1985, and the related statements of income and changes in the financial position for the year then ended. All information included in these financial statements is the representation of the owners of XYZ Corp.

A review consists principally of inquiries of company personnel and analytical procedures applied to financial data. It is substantially less in scope than an examination in accordance with generally accepted auditing standards, the objective of which is the expression of an opinion regarding the financial statements taken as a whole. Accordingly, we do not express such an opinion.

Based on our review we are not aware of any material modifications that should be made to the accompanying financial statements in order for them to be in conformity with generally accepted accounting principles.

### Audit

We have examined the accompanying balance sheet, income statement, and statement of changes in financial position of XYZ Corp. as of January 31, 1985. Our examination was made in accordance with generally accepted auditing standards and, accordingly, included such tests of the accounting records as we considered necessary in the circumstances.

In our opinion, the financial statements mentioned above present fairly the financial position of XYZ Corp. as at January 31, 1985, and the results of its operations, and the changes in its financial position for the year then ended, in conformity with generally accepted accounting principles applied on a basis consistent with the preceding year.

*Figure 3 Opinion letter text from compilation, review, and audit reports*

| Vande Kopple's metadiscourse types | Quotations from C.P.A. texts |
|---|---|
| 1. Text connectives | "See Accountant's Compilation/Review Report," written on every page of financial reports, refers to the opinion letter. "See Accountant's Report, Notes and accompanying supplemental data." |
| | [From audit report] |

Notice that the text connectives here employ a referent function similar to the engagement letter, management letter, AICPA brochures and audit guide previously discussed; that is, all refer to the text contained in the report opinion letter.

| | |
|---|---|
| 2. Code glosses | "A Review consists principally of inquiries of company personnel and analytical procedures applied to financial data." |
| | [From review report] |

This gloss or definition of a review (or a compilation or an audit) contained in the opinion letter is critical to reader interpretation of the report, and to legal liability. Knowledgeable readers understand the distinction between the three levels of report; such readers would not place undue reliance on lesser levels. The purpose of the report is stated in positive (in the audit) and in negative terms (in the compilation and review)—to specify what it does and does not say, and to define the scope of the report, thus limiting areas of consideration. For instance, financial reports—whether compilation, review, or audit—depict the financial health of a specific fiscal entity for a stated point in time (see Figure 4). This exact pinpointing

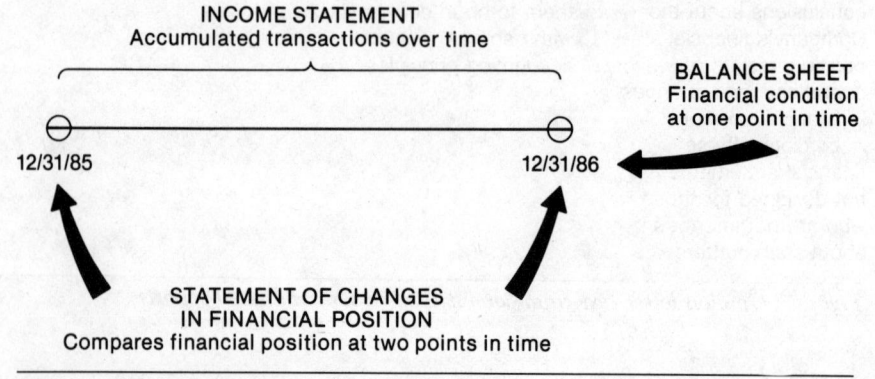

*Figure 4 Reference to time in the financial report*

in time limits the auditor's liability; that is, the C.P.A. provides assurance *only* for a specific point in time, and that point is precisely defined:

> In our opinion, the Financial Statements mentioned above present fairly the financial position of XYZ Corporation *as at* January 31, 1986. [italics mine, sentence from audit report]

The audience is also carefully defined; that is, those who are qualified to read the report are identified: "[t]hese financial statements are *not* designed for those who are *not* informed . . ." [italics mine]. I emphasize the double negative in this sentence from an opinion letter to highlight the curious syntactic complexity C.P.A.'s use as they grapple with liability—they tend to define negatively in compilations and reviews. Daniel M. Clements, plaintiff's attorney against C.P.A.'s, states that the C.P.A. "can't disclaim away responsibility, but can disclaim classes of people the report is not intended for" (1986). Alvin I. Frederick, who defends C.P.A.'s, says, "Cases are turning on points as to who should read the report" (1986).

Another kind of code gloss employed by report writers involves the sometimes voluminous footnotes in financial reports that explain, modify, and clarify information:

> XYZ Construction Company Inc. is engaged in the performance of construction contracts which usually last less than one year. The percentage of completion method of accounting is used to recognize income on contracts which are preformed during more than one accounting period.
>
> Income tax returns are prepared using the completed contract method of revenue recognition and accelerated depreciation methods. *Deferred income taxes reflect taxes recognized for report purposes* which are not currently payable under the tax return preparation methods used by the Company. [italics mine]

The phrase "deferred income taxes" in the actual report does not tell *why* taxes, which are ordinarily payable currently, are deferred. Therefore, the C.P.A. adds a footnote to clarify the rationale behind deferring taxes, thereby defining the term *deferred income taxes* for the purposes of the report.

3. Illocution markers            "In our opinion, the balance sheet mentioned above presents fairly the financial position of XYZ Corp. . . ."
                                 [From audit report]

Because the C.P.A. can make a claim only when the audit conditions permit full disclosure, illocution markers are found in audits but not in compilations or reviews.

4. Validity markers
a. Hedges

"If the omitted disclosures were included in the financial statements, they might influence the user's conclusions about the company's financial position . . ."
[From compilation report]

The "omitted disclosures" which might tip the reader to the true financial position of a company do not necessarily appear in a compilation; the C.P.A. may hedge, therefore, to indicate that full disclosure is not contained in this level of report. Even though such statements are not the brief kind of hedge described by Vande Kopple, such as "perhaps," "seem," and "to a certain extent" (84), I view them as pulling away from stated information, a giant hedge—which for want of a better term, I call a *mega* hedge.

b. Attributors

"Our examination was made in accordance with generally accepted auditing standards . . ."
[From audit report]
". . . in accordance with standards established by the AICPA."
[From compilation report]

Appeal is made here to authoritative Accounting Standards, as held by practitioners and by the prestigious AICPA. Mention of the AICPA in the opinion letter just cited adds to the credibility of the author, and implies that the auditor's findings bear the *imprimatur* of the official institution of accountancy.

5. Narrators

"Management has elected to omit substantially all of the disclosures required by generally accepted accounting principles."
[From compilation report]

Invocation of the management as narrator in a compilation is consistent with the C.P.A.'s assertion that all information was furnished by management and is therefore the legal responsibility of the client.

Two other metadiscourse types, attitude markers and commentary, will of course not be found in opinion letters. Attitude markers are inappropriate because the report constitutes only the C.P.A.'s findings; the C.P.A.'s *attitude* toward his or her findings would be the last thing one would expect to find in C.P.A. discourse—the C.P.A. must always maintain an independent point of view. Commentary involving second-person reference is also appropriately absent because the

C.P.A. is not interested in drawing readers "into an implicit dialogue" (85)—rather, the C.P.A. uses either the first person to claim or disclaim responsibility, *or* the C.P.A. refers to the third person when client representation of data is part of the evidence incorporated within the report.

Heavy use of metadiscourse facilitates the report reader's comprehension of complex financial data. Not surprisingly, the *less* the report is intended to say, the *greater* the use of metadiscourse. Consequently, one finds much more metadiscourse in compilations than in audits, resulting in an inverse ratio of words to full disclosure. In the opinion letter examples (Figure 3), notice that the compilation takes 151 words and three paragraphs to furnish *less* disclosure than an audit, which furnishes *full* disclosure with 111 words and two paragraphs. Use of instructive, often defensive metadiscourse also serves to protect the C.P.A. from legal attack. After all, a text which specifies its own interpretation, and a text which stipulates its very audience is unlikely to run into trouble in a court of law because the C.P.A. can prove *in writing* that the reader was fully informed as to the intent and meaning of his or her discourse. Through metadiscourse, then, the C.P.A. clearly claims (in audits) or disclaims (in compilations and reviews) responsibility for the report.

## Standardized Wording and Formats

To satisfy audience expectation, C.P.A.'s employ standard wording and formats, even though "specific findings . . . will depend on the audit approach and client setting." The profession has discovered that "a greater standardization [in opinion and management letters] ensure[s] a clearer communication link to clients . . . diverse [writing] practices prove detrimental to [one's] professional reputation, legal exposure and client base" (W. Wallace, 18). Reports maintain the same sequence; titles and headings such as "Assets," "Stockholder's Equity," and "Current Liabilities" are consistently used, and prescribed wording is standard (See Figure 3). Recommended wording has naturally evolved over the years in response to client needs, professional and industry standards, accounting principles, and legal liability. Yet, a 1987 AICPA "Exposure Draft" proposes the most comprehensive wording changes since 1948 in response to the need "to more clearly inform readers of the auditors' role and responsibility" (Kolins, 95). The proposed opinion letter incorporates more referents, definitions, specifications, hedges—in short, more metadiscourse—no doubt in an effort to preclude legal liability arising from reader misinterpretation of financial reports. Some analysts, however, question if these changes constitute "improvements in 'communication' between auditor and the user" or "alter the purpose of the report by adding new messages," thus *increasing* liability (Elliott and Jacobson, 72–73). One issue is whether reader education should be contained within the opinion letter (as it is now) or be moved to "more appropriate vehicle[s] for the message" (Elliott and Jacobson, 74). Criticism of the proposed wording centers around the audience's perception of the message in the following ways:

1. "... findings by researchers [indicate] that readers have difficulty understanding elements of the standard report's language."
2. "... the report does not, but should, educate users...."
3. The proposed wording would still be "capable of misleading" readers.
4. The new wording "would not promote user understanding of the audit function and could set it back."
5. A study on "shareholder's views of the auditor's report [reveals that the] subjects did not want more explanation in the report." (Elliott and Jacobson, 72, 75)

Whatever the reponse of practitioners to the current "Exposure Draft," I think it is inevitable that opinion letters will retain or even expand the use of metadiscourse. If the changes are adopted, it would follow that the proposed changes will necessitate more extratextual documents and that the proposed wording will become standard throughout the industry.

Before I discuss the format of financial reports, I should mention the "canned" or "boilerplate" aspect of reports. It is true, with the widespread use of word processors, that some C.P.A.'s grind out opinion letters by simply inserting pertinent information into form letters already on disk. However, two things distinguish the C.P.A.'s boilerplate letters from ordinary form letters: (1) The C.P.A. is responsible to third-party audiences for the content of the report; consequently, even boilerplate letters must be carefully chosen to suit the report's situation, and (2) form letters usually point to a generic or specific situation relevant to an audience. A look at the financial report's opinion letter, however, suggests that the text points to the report as it defines itself, as it specifies its readers, as it invokes authority, and as it assigns responsibility.

In discussing the wording of financial reports, I noted that C.P.A. discourse involves full disclosure or less than full disclosure of a company's financial condi-

| **Assets** | **Liabilities** |
|---|---|
| The order of currency (liquidity) is presented first—cash is most liquid. | The amounts currently due (accounts payable) are listed first. |
| ↓ | ↓ |
| Inventories are harder to convert into cash. | Notes payable are due within five years. |
| ↓ | ↓ |
| Goodwill is listed last because it is least liquid. | Long-term payables are listed last, such as stockholder's loans which have the least demand for payback. |

*Figure 5 Hierarchy of assets and liabilities*

```
                              XYZ CORPORATION
                    COMPARATIVE STATEMENT OF FINANCIAL POSITION
                         AS AT MARCH 31, 1986 AND 1985
                                                                    Increase
ASSETS                                    1986              1985    -Decrease
  Current Assets                        ----------       ----------  ----------
    Cash in Bank                     $   12,068.35    $    4,248.51  $  7,819.84
    Accounts Receivable                 113,852.29        76,643.91    37,208.38
    Inventory - Merchandise              39,000.00        37,581.18     1,418.82
    Inventory - Work in Process          32,734.00        36,950.00    -4,216.00
                                        ----------       ----------   ----------
    Total Current Assets                197,654.64       155,423.60    42,231.04
~~~~~~~~~~~~~~~~~~~~~~~~~~~~~~~~~~~~~~~~~~~~~~~~~~~~~~~~~~~~~~~~~~~~~~~~~~~~~~~~
  Goodwill                                3,597.44         3,597.44         0.00
                                        ----------       ----------   ----------
TOTAL ASSETS                         $  248,923.09    $  209,960.48  $  38,962.61
                                        ==========       ==========   ==========

LIABILITIES AND STOCKHOLDERS' EQUITY
  Current Liabilities
    Accounts Payable                 $   26,374.12    $   84,120.16  $ -57,746.04
    Accrued Payroll                       2,516.43             0.00     2,516.43
    Payroll and Sales Taxes               6,894.11         6,469.29       424.82
    Corporate Income Taxes                4,773.86             0.00     4,773.86
    Notes Payable - Current              20,701.36        15,140.36     5,561.00
                                        ----------       ----------   ----------
    Total Current Liabilities            61,259.88       105,729.81   -44,469.93
~~~~~~~~~~~~~~~~~~~~~~~~~~~~~~~~~~~~~~~~~~~~~~~~~~~~~~~~~~~~~~~~~~~~~~~~~~~~~~~~
  Stockholder Loans                      52,200.00        52,300.00      -100.00
                                        ----------       ----------   ----------
TOTAL LIABILITIES                       128,984.82       177,872.81   -48,887.99
                                        ----------       ----------   ----------
```

*Figure 6 Hierarchical arrangement in financial reports*

tion. If some readers are unfamiliar with the wording of opinion letters, most readers are at least familiar with the financial report format involving vertical columns of numbers. The arrangement of these numbers, plugged hierarchically into a column format, suggests a line of argument based on liquidity, which experienced readers learn to expect (Figures 5 and 6).

## Ambiguity

One feature of C.P.A. discourse that readers *do not* expect is ambiguity. C.P.A.'s are known for providing precise financial data—down to the penny. Most reports written for smaller to medium companies detail information in dollars *and* cents, contrary to the accounting theory of a famous ex-accountant, Bob Newhart, who quipped, "if you got within two or three bucks of it, [it was O.K.]" (Newhart). At any rate, many C.P.A.'s work long hours to chase down a nickel. Yet, despite the auditor's penchant for detail, accountants' opinion letters incorporate ambiguous language. Ambiguity in the opinion letter was one of the problems cited by a 1978 Commission on Auditor's Responsibilities (CAR), which called for "improved communications between auditors and readers of financial statements..." (Dillard and Jensen, 787). The CAR was formed to counter congressional investigation into the deficiencies of financial reports. The CAR concluded that "communication between the auditor and users of his work—especially through the auditor's standard report—is unsatisfactory" (787). Still, ambiguous phrases, such as "tests of the accounting records," "such other auditing procedures," "presents fairly . . . in conformity with generally accepted accounting principles" are employed in C.P.A. texts (see Figure 3). Perception of phrases as ambiguous, however, depends on the knowledge of the reader. An experienced banker or financial analyst knows what the phrases mean, but an inexperienced stockholder may not. Therefore, researchers conclude:

> . . . ambiguity may not be a problem at all. Auditors and users of audited financial statements may never be able to reach agreement on a completely explicit statement of the scope of audits and the responsibilities of auditors within the confines of the auditor's report. In such an environment, a document that reflects a consensus of views inevitably will be ambiguous. Moreover, the ambiguous document itself may contribute to the maintenance of the consensus. [Dillard and Jensen, 798]

Furthermore, ambiguity of language allows for variances in the C.P.A.'s purposes and appeals to a hierarchy of audiences. Accounting analysts Robert K. Elliott and Peter D. Jacobson, commenting on the latest "Exposure Draft," advocate keeping to the status quo in wording financial reports because of its proven adaptability to the fluctuating accountancy situation (78).

## Congruity

Additional hallmarks of the C.P.A.'s writing are conciseness and pertinence. In assessing the effectiveness or appropriateness in writing, I find H. Paul Grice's "four categories that govern the . . . exchange of information" helpful (Beach, 75–76):

1. *Quantity:* the rhetor should be as informative as required for purposes of the exchange but not more informative than required. (When composing an opinion letter, a Maryland sole practitioner reports that he states the bare essentials, "that, and no more.")
2. *Quality:* the rhetor should say only what he or she believes to be true and for which there is adequate evidence. (Auditing "consists of gathering and evaluating evidence . . . ." [AICPA "Guide"].)
3. *Relation:* the rhetor should make his or her contribution relevant, consistent with the writer's sense of purpose and how he or she assesses the audience's knowledge and need to know. (As previously mentioned, C.P.A.'s carefully define the scope of the financial report.)
4. *Manner:* the rhetor should be perspicuous and orderly, avoiding obscure expressions, ambiguity, and prolixity. (Although ambiguity occurs in the reports, C.P.A.'s employ definition to clarify unclear terms, especially those terms which, if misunderstood, could result in legal consequences.)

C.P.A. writing employs a plain style, consistent with Grice's maxims, to convey a message, to aid audience comprehension, and to lessen legal exposure.

## *Readability*

Previous analyses of C.P.A. texts which investigate audience misunderstanding of financial reports have concentrated on readability formulas (see listing below).[3] But we know that readability formulas alone cannot begin to account for communication gaps, however fascinating they may be to number-crunching analysts. Nevertheless, repeated attempts have been made since 1950 to analyze C.P.A. texts using readability formulas because "[p]reparers of annual reports who possess an interest in effective communication, need simple, quick and inexpensive yardstick techniques for predicting communication effectiveness *before* such reports are disseminated" (Courtis, 285). Readability studies have included:

1. Flesch (Pashalian and Crissy 1950, Soper and Dolphin 1964, Smith and Smith 1971, Pound 1981);
2. Lix (Bjornsson 1968);
3. Dale-Chall (Smith and Smith 1971, Worthington 1978);
4. Kwolek (Kwolek 1973);
5. The Fry Readability Graph (1977);
6. Cloze (Adelburg 1979);
7. Fog (Parker 1982);
8. An accounting syntactic complexity formula (Adelburg 1983);
9. WORDS computerized analysis technique applied to narrative data (Ingram and Frazier, 1983).

Readability researchers suggested in 1950 that "it is difficult to make the report both readable and understandable while also presenting sufficient technical data to comply with both legal requirements and the needs of financial experts" (Courtis, 287). Perhaps readability studies applied to C.P.A. texts over the years have not produced conclusive results because they "do not take account of the reader's interest level" (Lewis, 202); "It is also unlikely that readability measures account for the impact of reading speed which is a function of time required to assess issues in the text, breadth of the reader's previous knowledge and organization of material in the text being read" (Lewis, 202). Research suggests that "simplification alone does not automatically guarantee improved readability . . ." (Lewis, 202).

Readability formulas alone, then, do not account for lack of audience comprehension of C.P.A. texts. Other factors include the nature of the texts, the trust engendered by C.P.A.'s and their profession, and inappropriate reliance on the text by third parties.

The characteristics of C.P.A. discourse that include extratextual and metatextual functions, standardized wording and formats, ambiguity, congruity, and readability all suggest effective rhetorical strategies which contribute to reader comprehension. Why, then, are reports still misunderstood, and why are C.P.A.'s sometimes sued for their failure to communicate with their report readers? The answer lies partly in the C.P.A.'s purpose in providing reliable information while sidestepping liability, and partly in the C.P.A.'s projection of an ethos that encourages report audiences to place an often excessive and undiscriminating credence in the reliability of C.P.A. texts. This conflict involving a C.P.A.'s purpose, ethos, and audience contributes to the surprisingly complex dilemmas that I will discuss in the following pages.

## *Conflictive Purpose*

AICPA's "A Guide to Understanding and Using C.P.A. Services" neatly explains the uniqueness of C.P.A.s and their audit function:

> CPAs are professionals, distinguished from other accountants by stringent licensing requirements. They must have a college degree or its equivalent, pass a rigorous two-and-a-half day national examination and meet certain experience requirements to qualify for a state license. Many states also have continuing education requirements for CPAs to retain their license to practice.
>
> In addition to meeting the profession's technical requirements, CPAs are governed by a code of professional ethics which is among the most exacting of any profession.
>
> Auditing is a sophisticated process developed by the accounting profession for the examination of financial statements by CPAs. It consists of gathering and evaluating evidence to test the conformity of the statements with generally accepted accounting principles. An audit offers investors and creditors reasonable assurance that the statements present a company's financial position and results of operations in conformity with those principles. [AICPA, "Guide," 1–2]

Although the C.P.A.'s purpose is to provide *reliable* financial information, the C.P.A. also seeks to avoid *liability* for the accuracy of certain levels of reports—and flatly says so, as we have seen, in opinion letters. Thus, as a writer, the C.P.A.'s purpose is confused from the beginning (see Figure 7).

I have previously discussed the differences between compilation, review, and audit reports. On one hand, the compilation offers no assurance, and assumes no liability risk. The review, on the other hand, offers negative assurance and entails some liability exposure. And the audit, which requires extensive inside and outside verification, provides full assurance with an attendant assumption of responsibility and liability. If audits are so useful to the client and to third-party audiences in providing full disclosure, why are the lesser-level compilations and reviews often preferred by clients? The reasons are complex and somewhat beyond the scope of this discussion, but one of the most compelling answers is simply *cost.*

The verification required by the audit process can be expensive, which is why client companies often try to get by with less revealing—and less assuring— compilations and reviews. To translate that into dollars, consider the hypothetical XYZ Corporation, a small retail drugstore chain with fifteen stores, which grosses about $15 million per year. An annual audit report with no complications might

Drawing adapted and reprinted by permission of Grosset & Dunlap from *Cartooning the Head & Figure* by Jack Hamm, copyright © 1967 by Jack Hamm.

*Figure 7 C.P.A.'s write in a conflictive rhetorical situation.*

cost the company $20,000. A review would cost about 40 percent less or $12,000, and the least expensive compilation would cost only $5,000, or 75 percent less than an audit. Clearly, the prohibitive costs of an audit thwart the C.P.A.'s purpose in providing reliable information. Consequently, when the C.P.A. furnishes the often requested lesser levels of reports to clients, he or she makes every effort to disclaim responsibility for the accuracy of those reports.

Also frustrating to the C.P.A. as writer is the C.P.A.'s professional obligation to provide full disclosure for the paying audience who may or may not want it divulged to the public at large. The client who pays the bill is less than enchanted with an expensive but unfavorable report. Furthermore, the C.P.A.'s duty is not only to the paying client but also to the public readership who make important decisions based on these financial reports. The C.P.A.'s must furnish full disclosure about the wellness or illness of a company, commensurate with the level of report engagement, to these nonpaying readers. In addition, the C.P.A. *wants* to provide full disclosure to protect himself or herself from litigation; in fact, one practitioner told me that he exceeds what is required for each level of report, at his own expense, to preclude the possibility of litigation. Even so, the report is written first for a paying client whose interests do not necessarily coincide with those of the C.P.A. retained.

The current litigation crisis is forcing many C.P.A.'s, like other professionals, to reconsider their purpose; that is, some C.P.A. firms severely limit the audits they perform to minimize risk. In some firms, audits comprise less than 1 percent of total services performed. One recent professional article questions, did you "[e]xpect that clients and non-clients would be willing to sue you at the slightest provocation" (Wahl, 24)? In an effort to control the rhetorical situation in which they write, C.P.A.'s are advised to avoid their audience by evading what they alone are licensed to do. In "8 Steps to Avoid Liability," Edward P. Leibensperger (attorney/CPA) counsels, "Screen your clients . . . [d]on't take the high risk client . . ." (5). A Price Waterhouse counsel cautions that to "assure a long line of unemployed lawyers . . . avoid an environment in which trouble can develop" (Young, 14). In a recent AICPA Conference on C.P.A.'s Malpractice Prevention and Risk Management, practitioners were advised that declining engagements is "the CPA's first line of defense" (Collins, 54).

Certain types of clients add to audit risk because of the nature of their businesses. These include financial institutions, construction companies, grain elevators, and manufacturers. A sole practitioner whose practice is 80 percent construction companies claims, "One way I avoid litigation problems is to keep audits to a minimum and perform less risky Compilations and Reviews whenever possible." A litigious environment forces the C.P.A., whose licensed purpose is to report full financial disclosure, to accept work which allows less than full assurance, that is, compilations and reviews. In refusing audits, C.P.A.'s also shoot themselves in the financial foot by passing up the lucrative fees that audits command.

## Conflictive Ethos

Complicating the C.P.A.'s thwarted purpose is the fact that the C.P.A.'s projection of ethos stems from the potential contradiction between a cautious self-interest *and* an assertive professionalism. While trying to survive in a climate of increasing legal threat, professional and nonprofessional competition, and cost to practice, the C.P.A. as writer concentrates on projecting and protecting a competent, professional image. "C.P.A.s, who reportedly rank among the highest collective I.Q.s of all professions" (Wahl, 24), also enjoy a respected public image, even though "the profession needs to be better understood" (*CPA Letter,* 5). A Lou Harris attitudinal poll reveals that "CPAs emerged at the top or close to it" when compared to other professionals among categories of ethics and morality; performance; concern for public interest; attributes of honesty, competence, reliability, objectivity; education; and enforcement of professional ethics (*The CPA Letter,* 5; Wahl, 24). The Harris poll points to the audience comprehension problem that plagues C.P.A.'s: the suing audience consists of those who might be unfamiliar with the intricacies of accounting theory such as vendors, stockholders, and investors. Obviously, the successful efforts of C.P.A.'s to project ethos have backfired. The trust and expertise that C.P.A.'s engender have become their own undoing because some readers trust reports that were never intended by the writer to furnish full disclosure.

Consistent with the C.P.A.'s concern for image are the actions recommended in a 1986 marketing plan which was prepared by C.P.A.'s and graduate students for use by a regional C.P.A. firm:

1. Enhance the "physical environment [with] professionally appointed offices."
2. "Be aware of potential areas of service which can be promoted to benefit both client and accountant."

```
            FLOTSAM & JETSAM, Chartered
            CERTIFIED PUBLIC ACCOUNTANTS
                      1 Court Street
                 Taneytown, Maryland 21787

        MEMBER                                    (301) 555-1234
   AMERICAN INSTITUTE OF                          (301) 555-5678
 CERTIFIED PUBLIC ACCOUNTANTS
              —
    MARYLAND ASSOCIATION OF
  CERTIFIED PUBLIC ACCOUNTANTS
```

*Figure 8 Typical C.P.A. letterhead*

3. Evaluate "newsletters objectively . . . to verify that they project the firm image."
4. Communicate to a client that "you have the means to fulfill [client] need[s]."
5. Review "all written communication . . . to determine that it portrays the desired image of the firm." ["Plan," 1–5]

The C.P.A.'s concern for a professional ethos projects through financial statements whose cover to cover presentation includes (1) "attractive, well-bound, color-coordinated covers which exude quality . . . ," (2) "crisp typography," (3) error-free writing that enhances the reader's "perception of reliability" ("Plan" 2), (4) quality paper and letterhead, and (5) appeal to the prestigious AICPA, as illustrated in the typical CPA letterhead (Figure 8).

Projection of ethos is critical to the C.P.A.'s purpose in writing because "source credibility is an important determinant of message acceptance" (Bailey, 883). Studies involving reader response have shown that "an auditor's report conveys more information about his own credibility than about management's" (Bailey, 883), not only because of the competent ethos projected, but because of assumptions about C.P.A.'s, the accounting profession, and the levels of reports, that readers bring to the text.

Table 1 compares the presence of tacit assumptions, or hidden text, suggested by the terms "compilation," "review," and "audit"; promoted by *ethos* projection; and fostered by presentation of the report. Tacit assumptions tend to increase with full disclosure. The tacit assumptions that readers bring to financial reports can cause uneducated, inexperienced readers to make unwise financial decisions. But despite the legal consequences tacit assumptions can cause, those same assumptions—when employed by knowledgeable analysts—aid the client financially. Less costly compilations and reviews are accepted by bankers and other audiences who understand their true significance.

Unfortunately, report readers tend to respond to the ethos more than to the logos inherent in C.P.A. discourse, an ethos promoted by the C.P.A. in the report's presentation, by the AICPA, and by tacit assumptions—assumptions readers bring

Table 1. Tacit Assumptions Associated with Compilation, Review, and Audit Reports

| Assumption | Compilation | Review | Audit |
|---|---|---|---|
| The CPA is licensed to write this report. | yes | yes | yes |
| The auditor is independent of the management. | no | yes | yes |
| A third party may reliably accept this report. | sometimes | yes | yes |
| The auditor is trustworthy. | yes | yes | yes |
| The management is trustworthy. | no | sometimes | yes |
| The auditor has conducted an independent evaluation of the management. | no | yes | yes |
| The management has furnished full disclosure. | no | no | yes |
| The auditor has legal responsibility for the contents of this report. | no | yes | yes |

to the text. It seems to me that ethos has been overlooked by many accounting researchers as a factor in the C.P.A.'s difficulty in communicating with report readers.

## Conflictive Audience

We have seen that C.P.A. discourse arises from pressure to impart a complex message, and to project a professional ethos. Complicating C.P.A. purpose and ethos is an audience situation in which the C.P.A.-writer has to consider multiple, sometimes hostile audiences, but usually has a prereport relationship only with the client. Because third-party audiences rely on the report's information regarding the client, the C.P.A.-writer is responsible for any audience response to the report.

In analyzing the audiences for technical reports, J. C. Mathes and Dwight W. Stevenson list a number of false assumptions about audience that apply to C.P.A. reports: It is false to assume that (1) the person addressed is the audience, (2) the audience specializes in the writer's field, (3) the report has a finite period of use (10). Figure 9 shows that the audience of financial reports can be anyone who reads the report. Also the writing has an almost infinite life because the liability clock starts only when "the injured party learns of the error," according to Frank M. Bolen, provider of C.P.A. professional liability insurance (1986).

To help assess the relationship of writer to audience, Mathes and Stevenson plug "*horizontal, vertical,* and *external* audiences" into an organization chart to relate these audiences to the writer. But identifying such relationships is admittedly "not very helpful" because the chart "does not describe how the organization functions" (14–15).

Mathes and Stevenson instead recommend an Egocentric Organization Chart which "identifies specific individuals . . . [and] categorizes people in terms of their proximity to the report writer . . . ," that is, (1) audiences in the writer's group, (2) audiences in close proximity to the writer, (3) audiences elsewhere in the writer's organization, (4) audiences outside the organization (15). Such a model seems appropriate to analyze most audiences in relationship to the writer, but does not account for the unique relationship of the C.P.A.-writer to multiple audiences. Mathes and Stevenson advocate "assign[ing] priorities to . . . audiences . . . classify[ing] them in terms of how they will use [the] report" (21):

1. The primary audience—who make decisions on the basis of the report
2. The secondary audience—who is affected by the decisions and actions
3. The immediate audience—who route the report or transmit the information.

But C.P.A. audiences do not layer into such a hierarchy of audience segments. The client-audience can be simultaneously primary, secondary and immediate—*primary,* because they make financial decisions for their company based on the report; *secondary,* because they are affected by decisions of others such as bankers who grant or deny loans based on the report; *immediate,* because they transmit or publish the report. Third-party users can play simultaneous roles as well. The stockholder plays a primary role by investing or divesting in a company based on report information; the vendor is a secondary audience because he or she makes a sale only if enough investors provide capital for the vendor's goods; Dun & Bradstreet transmit the report to any of their members who request it, and thereby act as an intermediate audience. And as mentioned before, the third-party audience often has no relationship to the rhetor either before or after publication of the report. Therefore, in cases where *the audience has no knowledge of the writer,* either personally or by reputation, I offer a model that relates the audience to the report, rather than to the C.P.A.-writer (see Figure 9).

C.P.A.'s, then, write simultaneously for diverse but indeterminate audiences whose conflictive needs frustrate attempts to establish a hierarchy for audience accommodation and reader relationship. The audience can include any party interested in the client's financial condition:

1. The clients who resent paying for less than a favorable report
2. The bankers/investors/vendors/stockholders and others who make decisions based on reports, and who hold the C.P.A. financially responsible via third-party law suits
3. The C.P.A.'s colleagues who use the report, and who may march to a different beat theoretically and ethically
4. The attorneys who use reports as evidence for or against the writer
5. The AICPA and state C.P.A. societies, which set the standards for each level of report

Given these complications, do C.P.A.'s attempt to establish a hierarchy among audiences as they compose the report? The answer varies. One Maryland/Pennsylvania senior partner establishes this hierarchy:

- The client who pays our bill
- The banker who uses the information

[Figure: A diagram showing circles labeled Banker, Insurance Agent, CPA-Writer, Client on the left (Audiences familiar with the CPA) with arrows pointing to a Financial Report, and Stockholder, Vendor on the right (Audiences unfamiliar with the CPA) with arrows pointing to the Financial Report. An arrow labeled "THIRD PARTY LITIGATION" curves from the Financial Report area back toward the CPA-Writer.]

Audiences familiar with the CPA       Audiences unfamiliar with the CPA

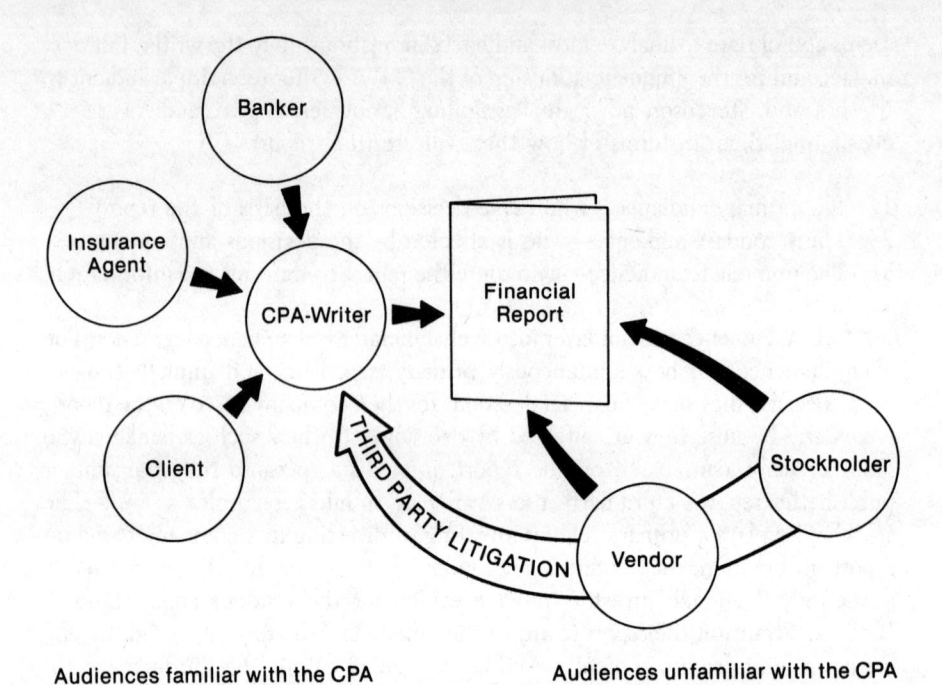

*Figure 9  The C.P.A.'s relationship to a hierarchy of audiences*

- The lawyer who is a double-bladed axe due to a problem with understanding [the Report]

Another District of Columbia sole practitioner makes no attempt to analyze audience, "I consider no audience whatsoever. I prefer to concentrate on my purpose." A partner in a Maryland regional firm concurs: "I don't think about my audience, only about the standards of my profession." A Maryland sole practitioner maintains that the client is the primary audience, but "after that, his audience depends on client need: the bonding company if the client requires bonding; stockholders for a publicly held corporation; bankers if financing is sought."

Whatever their conception of audience and its hierarchy, C.P.A.s respect the power of the audience to hurt them via lawsuits, which has changed the way C.P.A.s write their reports, resulting in more defensive opinion, engagement and representation letters. As one sole practitioner puts it, "I am trying to meet the needs of Report users who bite."

## RHETORICAL SITUATION OF C.P.A. TEXTS

### Special Topoi

We have looked closely at the characteristics of C.P.A. texts, at the C.P.A.'s conflictive roles as an independent verifier of information, and at the diverse audiences of C.P.A. discourse. In this last section, I concentrate on the C.P.A.'s rhetorical situation that includes the *line* of argument employed by C.P.A.'s and the unusual constraints under which it operates. Of particular help in understanding "special topics[,] patterns of thought deriving from specific genres, institutions, or disciplines—patterns that are material to gaining the assent of an audience within a particular discourse community," is the work on special *topoi* by Carolyn Miller and Jack Selzer (316).

The C.P.A., in attempting to gain the "assent" of a financial report audience, employs terms which send special signals to certain informed readers. These buzzwords appear throughout the report; following are quotations from the openings of opinion letters to the three levels of reports:

> *Compilation:* "We have *compiled* the accompanying balance sheet. . . ."
> *Review:* "We have *reviewed* the accompanying balance sheet. . . ."
> *Audit:* "We have *examined* the accompanying balance sheet. . . ." [italics mine]

(C.P.A.'s use the word "examined" instead of "audited" to reflect the investigatory nature of the audit process.)

The *special topoi* inherent in C.P.A. argument involve full disclosure or lack of full disclosure of a company's financial condition. If the C.P.A. did not employ the buzzwords in the opening lines of the opinion letters (as verbs) or as nouns elsewhere in the letters, in the report covers, and on the bottom of each page of the reports, a reader could not distinguish between a compilation, review, or audit report because the reports *sans* metadiscourse would appear identical. Consistent with the C.P.A.'s intent *to communicate* report findings, the significant buzzwords are not meant to send "secret" signals to certain readers—I have made the point repeatedly that all audiences *and* the writer would avoid financial disaster if the buzzwords denoting the scope of the examination were universally understood. To aid comprehension, the extratextual engagement letter, management letter, and AICPA brochures and guides discuss the meanings of the special terms.

## *Discipline-Specific Topoi*

Carolyn Miller argues that "Aristotelian *archai,* or key technical concepts, underlie the shape and effectiveness of specialized argument by serving as special topics" (314). Apparently, imparting *archai* of the discipline of accountancy to unknowledgeable audiences is an integral part of the profession, as a C.P.A. partner confirms, "Communication is critical to success as a C.P.A." Too often, though, the use of accountancy's "key technical concepts" renders the financial report incomprehensible to certain uninformed audiences.

Special *topoi* also have two roles in the theory of rhetoric according to Scott Consigny: "The topic is . . . construed as an essential *instrument* for discovery or invention"; it functions as "a *realm* in which the rhetor thinks and acts" (182). But special *topoi* do not necessarily compete with "the situation [in] determining the actions of the rhetor" (182)—obviously, the topic, *along with* the rhetorical situation, shapes C.P.A. discourse. Examining the relation of C.P.A. texts to Bitzer's exigence, audience, and constraints will illustrate my point.

## Exigence and Audience

Bitzer acknowledges that "a work of rhetoric is pragmatic; it comes into existence for the sake of something beyond itself . . ." (3). C.P.A.'s never instigate a financial report; rather, the client initiates one to obtain financing—the banker requires one to approve a construction loan; the insurance agent demands one to grant a performance bond. C.P.A. discourse, therefore, "can so constrain human decision or action as to bring about the significant modification of the exigence" (6)—that is, demand for assurance of a client's state of financial health. Bitzer sees the controlling exigence, the first constituent of a rhetorical situation, as specifying the audience (anyone interested in a client's finances) and the change to be effected (granting or denial of financial support).

The second constituent, audience, "consists of only those persons who are capable of being influenced by [the] discourse . . ." (8)—anyone with a financial interest in the client. C.P.A. discourse, however, can exert influence by means other than the bottom line of reports. We have seen previously how audiences place sometimes unwarranted and unwanted credence in C.P.A. reports. Of all C.P.A. audiences, perhaps the banker is most affected by what Aristotle called inartistic proofs—such as statements of witnesses and a rhetor's reputation. For example, a Maryland bank manager who reads over 200 financial reports per month assesses the reliability of reports by more than the actual numbers furnished. Because he claims that "C.P.A.s are sometimes reluctant to report the true financial condition of a client," the banker considers the reputation of the C.P.A. who writes the report when evaluating a company's financial health.

## Litigious Constraints

The last constituent of a rhetorical situation involves "a set of *constraints* made up of persons, events, objects, and relations" (8). Undoubtedly the strongest constraint affecting C.P.A. texts is an increasingly litigious atmosphere. C.P.A. writing as genre has evolved because of litigation; a C.P.A. text "is presumed to be premeditated . . . is its own witness, sufficient to convict," (H. Wallace, 8/1–2). For instance, in *Herzfeld v. Laventhol* (1976), the court concluded that the "opinion letter and the 'explanatory' footnote were as misleading as the figures in the financial statement" (8/2). Plaintiffs in *Oleck v. Fischer et al and Arthur Andersen & Co.* (1980) alleged "that financial statements certified by Andersen were 'seriously misleading in their presentation of the . . . transaction'" (8/3). Receivers in *Cambridge Credit Corp. v. Fell and Starkey* (1983)—on appeal from a $145 million award—allege that the C.P.A.'s failed to "qualify [a] 1971 audit" (*Accountant* 9). *Rosenblum, Inc. v. Adler* (1983) involved a statement in which the auditor furnished no limitation as to audience; therefore, he was held accountable to any audience who relied on the report (Frederick, 1986). Because these "claim[s] focused on words rather than numbers" (H. Wallace, 8/2–3), C.P.A.'s are being held liable for more than outright fraud and incompetence. And "accountants are occasionally innocent victims of the 'deep pocket' syndrome whereby they become the butt of litigation merely because they are thought able to pay compensation and costs" ("Litigation," 24). Consequently, "a plaintiff who has made a bad business decision that has nothing to do with the auditors' alleged negligence . . . will nonetheless look to them to recover his losses" (Rowan, 87). Obviously, a C.P.A. who accepts the audit responsibility accepts its litigious situation as well.

## POSSIBILITIES FOR RESEARCH

Miller and Selzer define "institutional special topics . . . products of the insiders perspective" (differentiated from the aforementioned discipline-specific *topoi*)—as being concerned "with . . . institutional purposes, methods, interests, and attitudes. . . ." (326). Investigation of C.P.A. communications within a "big eight" firm such as Price Waterhouse or a small to medium C.P.A. firm could provide another example detailing how the arguments of writers in the workplace are influenced by institutional considerations. Such a study could be compared with similar studies of legal, medical, and other "professional" institutions to identify respective institutional topics and also to note commonalities and differences germane to *professional* institutional activity. "Institutional and organizational topics [could] be discovered by surveying and comparing both the documents prepared by specific organizations and also the internal directives that accompany those documents," as Miller and Selzer suggest (327). It might be of particular interest to study and compare the roles of the American Institute of Certified Public Accountants, the American Bar Association, and the American Medical Association in institutional practices, and to investigate the seemingly circular influence of professionals on such organizations and vice versa.

## PEDAGOGICAL IMPLICATIONS

Focus by accounting researchers centers on readability, understandability, and confusion of C.P.A. texts—as well as message, auditor, and management credibility as perceived through the text. More appropriately, however, Odell and Goswami suggest that writing in the workplace be studied to learn "to what extent are nonacademic writers sensitive to rhetorical issues such as their relation to their audience or the *ethos* conveyed in their writing" (234). Studying C.P.A. texts in their rhetorical contexts, therefore, shows what constitutes a discourse community, and what is involved in coping with writing within that setting. The accounting literature's preoccupation with audience response to C.P.A. texts indicates that the rhetor must assume responsibility for the consequences of his or her discourse, a point that students on the verge of entering the workplace (and its various discourse communities) would do well to realize. Miller and Selzer find that discovering "how conventions work in the world and how they are transmitted" helps students to learn how "to write, reason and argue within their own disciplines" (310). Should we educators, then, formulate writing programs geared to specific professions? Not necessarily—for even though C.P.A. writing involves a conflictive situation and complex technical matter, rhetorical analysis demonstrates that "common rhetorical principles . . . underlie the design and development of all writing" (Tebeaux, 423).

Textual analysis of financial reports proves that heavy use of metadiscourse is critical to audience comprehension of the auditor's intended meaning. Vande Kopple sees an ethical dimension to metadiscourse; he advocates the wisdom of a teacher's effort:

> . . . getting students to consider how information taken to be true affects people, [helping] students . . . realize that they should comment accurately on the validity of their material so that readers do not act on the basis of that information . . . without proper justification. [92]

Analysis of writing by a rhetor in conflict—caught up in tensions between the demands of a profession, self-interest, clients, audiences, the Internal Revenue Service, and a mandate to convey a truthful message—demonstrates that C.P.A.'s employ generally successful rhetorical strategies, which include, by way of review:

1. The extratextual letters, brochures, and guides that educate report users about the three levels of assurance
2. The properties of C.P.A. texts that refer to the opinion letter
3. The text connectives, code glosses, illocution markers, hedges, attributors, and narrators that facilitate reader comprehension of complex financial data
4. The standardized wording and formats that maintain continuity from report to report—formats so standardized that levels of reports are indistinguishable without metadiscourse
5. The ambiguity of language that enables opinion letters to transcend individual business situations and evolving accounting principles
6. The congruity that tends to lessen legal exposure

A study of the strategies that C.P.A.'s employ to grapple with the diverse elements and constraints of their conflictive situations will enable future writers in the workplace "to make ethical rhetorical choices themselves" (Vande Kopple, 92)— to consider audiences as they write, and to assume responsibility for what they write. Thus, an analysis of C.P.A. discourse is one way of demonstrating the futility of attempting to divorce "reliable" from "liable" in today's litigious society.

## Notes

1. Because the audience for this discussion is primarily rhetoricians and teachers of composition, I describe accounting principles, terms, and publications briefly and simply. Fuller

explanations of the complexities of accountancy are beyond the scope of this paper and are certainly beyond the expertise of this writer.
2. My study is also limited to financial reports written by sole practitioners and partners of small to medium C.P.A. firms—these writers are more likely to make individual rhetorical choices than C.P.A.'s in "big eight" firms, who can tap the resources of large legal departments. Also, many "big eight" C.P.A.'s may work only on isolated segments of a financial report, and thus may lack an overall view of the rhetorical situation.
3. Laudable exceptions to the emphasis on readability formulas include John R. Jordan's 1979 in-house article "Financial Accounting and Communication" (*The Price Waterhouse Review*, vol. 14, no. 1, pp. 12–22). He refers to the 1962 work of Norton Bedford and Vahe Baladoune, "A Communication Theory Approach to Accountancy" (*Accounting Review*, Oct. 1962, 650–659). Jordan considers the entire communication environment: situation, subject, communicator, message, user, and feedback. He appropriately "suggests that the AICPA should direct considerably more research effort toward statement users and suggests that the participation of businessmen in the formulation of accounting principles to an increased extent is highly desirable" (20). If accounting researchers had devoted more attention to the elements of communication theory, their research would surely have gone beyond number crunching to more fruitful rhetorical analysis of financial reports.

## *Works Cited*

"Are You Being Sued? There's Less of It About." *The Accountant,* April 15, 1987; pp. 6–9.

Bailey, William T. "The Effects of Audit Reports on Chartered Financial Analysts' Perceptions of the Sources of Financial-Statement and Audit-Report Messages." *The Accounting Review* 56.4 (1981): 882–896.

Banker [assistant vice president, business development officer, branch manager]. Personal interview. June 2, 1987.

Beach, Richard. "The Pragmatics of Self-assessing." *Revising: New Essays for Teachers of Writing.* Ed. Ronald A. Sudol. Urbana: National Council of Teachers of English, 1982, pp. 71–83.

Bedford, Norton, and Vahe Baladoune. "A Communication Theory Approach to Accountancy." *Accounting Review,* October 1962, pp. 650–659.

Bitzer, Lloyd F. "The Rhetorical Situation." *Philosophy and Rhetoric* 7.1 (1968): 1–14.

Bolen, Frank M. "To Insure or Not to Insure—And If You Do, What's Available." Maryland Association of Certified Public Accountants Seminar: Protecting Your Practice and Personal Assets in a Litigious Environment. Jan. 12, 1987, Hunt Valley, Md.

Clements, Daniel M., Esq. "Why CPAs Are Sued—The Plaintiff's Attorney's View." Maryland Association of Certified Public Accountants Seminar: Protecting Your Practice and Personal Assets in a Litigious Environment. Jan. 12, 1987, Hunt Valley, Md.

Collins, Stephen H. "Malpractice Prevention and Risk Management." *Journal of Accountancy,* July 1986, pp. 52–58.

Consigny, Scott. "Rhetoric and Its Situations." *Philosophy and Rhetoric* 7.3 (1974): 175–186.

Courtis, J. K. "An Investigation into Annual Report Readability and Corporate Risk-Return Relationships." *Accounting and Business Research,* Autumn 1986, pp. 285–294.

C.P.A. [District of Columbia sole practitioner with 11 years experience in public accounting]. Personal Interview. Jan. 12, 1987.

C.P.A. [Maryland/Virginia sole practitioner with 25 years experience in public accounting]. Personal interviews. Jan. 2, 1987; June 1, 1987.
C.P.A. [Partner in Maryland regional CPA firm with 13 years experience in public accounting]. Personal interview. June 3, 1987.
C.P.A. [Senior partner in major Maryland/D.C./Virginia C.P.A. firm with 27 years experience in public accounting]. Telephone interview. June 3, 1987.
C.P.A. [Senior partner in Maryland/Pennsylvania regional C.P.A. firm with 24 years experience in public accounting]. Personal interview. Nov. 19, 1986.
"C.P.A.s Rate Highly in Public Survey." *The CPA Letter* 66.18 (1986): 5–6.
Dillard, Jesse F., and Daniel L. Jensen. "The Auditor's Report: An Analysis of Opinion." *The Accounting Review* 58.4 (1983): 787–798.
Elliott, Robert K., and Peter D. Jacobson. "The Auditor's Standard Report: The Last Word or in Need of Change?" *Journal of Accountancy*, Feb. 1987, pp. 72–78.
"The Engagement Letter: An Agreement Between the Client and the CPA." New York: AICPA, n.d. [Brochure]
Faigley, Lester, and Kristine Hansen. "Learning to Write in the Social Sciences." *College Composition and Communication* 36.2 (1985): 140–49.
Frederick, Alvin I., Esq. "How CPAs Are Defended—The Defense Attorney's View." Maryland Association of Certified Public Accountants Seminar: Protecting Your Practice and Personal Assets in a Litigious Environment. Jan. 12, 1987, Hunt Valley, Md.
*A Guide to Understanding and Using C.P.A. Services.* New York: C.P.A. Communications Council and AICPA, 1984.
Jordan, John R. "Financial Accounting and Communication." *The Price Waterhouse Review* XIV.1: 12–22.
Kolins, Wayne (ed.). "Accounting and Auditing Report." *The Practical Accountant* 20.6 (1987): 95–99.
Leibensperger, Edward P. "8 Steps to Avoid Liability." *CPA Statement* 22.6 (1987): 4–5.
Lewis, N. R., L. D. Parker, G. D. Pound, and P. Sutcliffe. "Accounting Report Readability: The Use of Readability Techniques." *Accounting and Business Research*, Summer 1986: 199–209.
"Litigation Aimed at Deep Pockets and Soft Bellies." *The Accountant*, May 6, 1987, pp. 24–25.
Mathes, J. C., and Dwight W. Stevenson. "Audience Analysis: The Problem and a Solution," in *Designing Technical Reports*. Indianapolis: Bobbs-Merrill, 1976, pp. 9–23.
Miller, Carolyn R., and Jack Selzer. "Special Topics of Argument in Engineering Reports." *Writing in Nonacademic Settings.* Ed. Lee Odell and Dixie Goswami. New York and London: Guilford Press, 1985, pp. 309–341.
Newhart, Bob. "Retirement Party." *The Best of Bob Newhart.* New York: Warner Bros. Records, Inc., n.d. [recording].
Odell, Lee, and Dixie Goswami. "Writing in a Nonacademic Setting." *Research in the Teaching of English* 16 (1982): 201–223. Reprinted in *New Directions in Composition Research.* Ed. Richard Beach and Lillian S. Bridwell. New York: Guilford, 1984, pp. 233–258.
"Plan of Action for [Flotsam and Jetsam, Chartered] to Implement a Marketing Plan." Report prepared by C.P.A.'s/graduate students in a "Management and Marketing" class, Frostburg State University, Dec. 1986, pp. 1–6.
*Proposed Statement on Auditing Standards: The Auditor's Standard Report.* New York: AICPA, 1987. [Exposure Draft]

"The Representation Letter: An Important Communication Between Management and the Independent Auditor." New York: AICPA, 1978. [Brochure]

"Required Communication of Material Weaknesses in Internal Accounting Control." *Statement on Auditing Standards* [SAS] 20 (1977): 1–12. [AICPA]

Rowan, Hugh (ed.). "Blaming the Auditors: Easier Tried Than Won." *CPA Magazine*, Aug. 1985, pp. 87–91.

Tebeaux, Elizabeth. "Redesigning Professional Writing Courses to Meet the Communication Needs of Writers in Business and Industry." *College Composition and Communication* 36.4 (1985): 419–428.

Vande Kopple, William J. "Some Exploratory Discourse on Metadiscourse." *College Composition and Communication* 36.1 (1985): 82–93.

Wahl, Roger W. "Are You Billing Enough to Survive in Public Accounting?" *The Practical Accountant*, Oct. 1986, p. 24.

Wallace, Harry. *Strengthening Writing Skills: Practical Skills for Accountants*, 2nd ed. N.p.: n.p., 1981.

Wallace, Wanda A. "More Effective Management Letters." *CPA Journal*, Dec. 1983, pp. 18–28.

Winters, Alan J. "A User's Guide to Understanding Audits and Auditors' Reports." New York: AICPA, 1982.

Young, Allen I. "The New Ten Commandments." *The Accountant's Digest*, Dec. 1986, pp. 9–14.

# PART SEVEN

# WRITING IN THE WORLD OF COMPUTERS

# BRIDGING THE GAP:
## IN WHICH THE AUTHOR, AN ENGLISH MAJOR, RECOUNTS HIS TRAVELS IN THE LAND OF THE TECHIES
### Edward Gold

*Edward Gold has taught numerous English courses, including business and technical writing, at the University of Maryland, and he frequently serves on the Technical Writing Institute faculty at Rensselaer Polytechnic. Currently, he is an independent writing consultant with extensive experience in writing and teaching writing in both government agencies and private corporations. He is also a prolific freelance writer—journalist, poet and scriptwriter.*

> *A computer product has to be so simple an English major could use it.*
>
> —A software developer

### WHAT THIS ARTICLE IS ABOUT

One of the biggest obstacles that nontechnical people encounter when first trying to use a computer isn't the computer. It's the written words that come with it—on the page and on the screen. Too often, manuals and on-line help reflect the assumptions of technical people about the audience. And these assumptions are so far off that the documentation misses us entirely.

I have seen powerful, easy computer products go belly up because people can't figure out the written words that teach you how to use them. Sometimes, the problem is a microproblem: words and sentences. But more often, the problem is a macroproblem: the book isn't designed and written with its audience in mind. Whatever the problems, the words don't bridge the gap between their world and ours.

The job of bridging the gap falls on the writer. For many of us old English majors, now working in the land of the techies, interfacing with these live-ware units presents some interesting challenges. We English majors want to use computers as tools without wasting time and energy struggling up a steep learning curve. The techies are developing products that they want us to buy, use, and recommend to others.

This article takes a look at the gap between the people who develop computer products and the people who buy and use computer products, particularly those consumers who don't know much about computers and don't want to learn. This article also suggests ways for writers to bridge the gap more effectively.

## SOME HORROR STORIES

In a writer's heaven, everyone's decisions lead inexorably to a clear, useful book that makes a computer product immediately useful to an English major. But other elements—like budgets and politics—often intrude to produce decisions that work directly against the reader's interests.

Here are some horror stories that I have encountered during my wanderings in the land of the techies.

### *Horror Story #1: The Dirty Dozen*

I was writing a user's guide for a new computer system that would soon be used by the employees of a water and sewage commission.

For most of these workers, the new system would be their first experience working with computers. Their old manual system hadn't changed in decades, and people were comfortable with it. Most of them recorded data in pencil, on file cards. Most were afraid of computers in general and the new system in particular.

First I studied the specs and began to figure out how people would use the manual. Then I broke down the tasks into groups and roughed out an outline, based on the way people would use the new system. I wrote informative, simple headings, checked against the specs to make sure I wasn't leaving out any function, and felt that I had done my job.

To my surprise, the "approval loop"—the reviewers with enough clout to demand changes—totally rejected my outline and my overall approach.

"We don't want a task-oriented manual," one of the techies explained. "We want a book with twelve chapters."

"Why twelve chapters?" I asked.

"Because twelve people built this system out of twelve subsystems, and we're proud of our work. We want twelve chapters."

I sprang to the defense of the reader. I pointed out that the manual was designed to help people perform certain tasks—not to be a blueprint of the system. I argued that most of the tasks required more than one subsystem, but, most important—the reader never needed to know that the twelve subsystems even existed.

"Thank you, Ed," I was told, "Now give us twelve chapters, one for each subsystem. Okay?"

Okay. They got the manual they wanted, but it wasn't the manual they needed. They needed a manual that helped nontechnical people use a computer system—people who were fearful about how their jobs were changing. Instead, they got a blueprint of the developer's architecture. It may have been very useful to another developer, but it certainly wasn't useful to the people who would use the computer system.

In the long run, developers often thwart themselves. A computer product can be well designed to meet people's needs, but if users can't figure out how to use it, they won't.

From my point of view, I wasn't permitted to bring as much value to the product as I could. I wasn't permitted to create a document that would have helped people do their jobs, that would have taught people without wasting their time, and that would have eased their fear of failure.

## *Horror Story #2: A Tale of Four Cursors*

Sometimes, self-protection overrides the other interests in the documentation process. I have seen developers use the documentation for a number of purposes that had nothing to do with making their product easy to use. Sometimes their purpose was to publicize their successes; sometimes they wanted to paper over their mistakes.

I witnessed the following in a review of a computer manual for a very large computer company:

"Ed, we need a section right up front about the four different ways to move the cursor," said one of the techies who had reviewed the draft.

"Very good," I said, "now tell me about the four ways. Which do I use when, what special function does each offer . . . ?"

"None of them offer anything special. They all move the cursor," he said.

"Well, are any of the four easier to use than the others?" I asked.

"Oh yeah," he said, "the easy way is just to press one key. The other ways take more keystrokes."

Now I was getting confused. "Well if you can move the cursor by pressing just one key, why bother the reader with other methods that don't offer any advantages and take more keystrokes? Readers don't like being burdened with information they don't need to know," I argued.

The answer was interesting. "Listen, Ed, as the project developed, we figured out better ways to move the cursor. Four people did the coding at different times, chewing up budget. If we only have one way to move the cursor in the book, then how do we justify those other budget lines? So we need a section on the four ways to move the cursor. Okay?"

Okay. This is an unfortunate example of the gap between our expectations as writers and the realities of the world of the techies. At times like this, it doesn't feel like a gap. It feels like a grim contest with a boa constrictor in which the enthusiasm is slowly squeezed out of the writer.

We writers represent the reader's interest in the process, but our work is approved by developers. When the interests of developers and readers clash, the reader is usually sacrificed.

## Horror Story #3: The Creature from the Bottom Line

Here's another example of how the developer's interests can work against creating a useful, clear document that helps people use the product. In this case, the compelling interest was economic survival.

I was working as an independent contractor for a small company on a project to develop software for the IBM Personal Computer. Financial pressure put a severe limit on the quality of the product, but I didn't realize how this would "impact on me," as the techies say.

I got nervous when I first looked at the schedules that my developer client proposed. My final draft was due the same day that the computer programmer would finish writing the code. It is a serious and expensive error to expect the book and the program to be ready on the same day.

I had already learned that the process of coding is creative and speculative. Often, the way to solve a problem isn't apparent until late in the game. The developer gives the writer a "best guess" about how the problem will be solved, how the product will ultimately look and work. Then the writer gets to work, trying to hit a moving target. Often, the solution that is finally worked out in March is different from the solution proposed in January. After all, the developer is trying to hit a moving target too.

I pointed out to my techie client that in order to ensure the book's accuracy, I would need time with the product to see for myself how it worked. Otherwise, I would be writing fiction, relying on the developer's clairvoyance.

"We can't afford to wait," my client told me. "We've spent so much money so far without a penny coming in. The quicker we can get on the market, the quicker we can start making money. It may be too late for us already."

"But that means the book has to be either inaccurate or incomplete," I said. "I either have to guess what the product's going to do, or I have to leave out the last functions that will be coded."

"That's right," he said. He thought for a minute.

"Let's go with incomplete," he said. "I'd rather get a manual that I can trust—even if it's limited—than a manual I can't trust at all."

Within the narrow parameters of damage control, he probably made the right decision. If the book is accurate as far as it goes, at least the reader can rely on what's there. A book that is generally inaccurate isn't useful at all.

These kinds of decisions are devastating to documentation, and usually to the product, too. And unfortunately it is not uncommon for the client to be overwhelmed by the difficulty of financing these kinds of projects. After all, computer products require the work of many specialists over a long period of time.

In the end, what can you, the writer, say about it? Nothing. It's not your business. You give your client or your boss your best advice, argue forcefully, and live to lobby the techies on behalf of the reader another day.

## WHAT'S GOING WRONG

### *They don't understand us*

Developers have misconceptions about who we writers are. They also have misconceptions about the audience—the people who will use the books and on-line help. Part of it comes from their different perspective; part of it comes from ignorance.

I often ask technical specialists and their managers for their concept of us writers. Who are we? What role do we play? What are our strengths and weaknesses?

Some view us as secretaries, dutifully recording their words and proofreading them. Some think we can be useful early in the process of designing a computer product, and others don't. Still others see us as saviors who can "fix it in the pubs" (publications) when the fledgling product doesn't function exactly as planned (usually at the last minute).

Too many technical people think of us as translators, whose role is merely to substitute everyday words for technical words and to untie any knots we find in the syntax.

Their definition of translating is too narrow. To truly translate, you need to study the audience, determine the reader's tasks, and understand what the reader knows and how well the reader reads. Then you need to organize the material to meet the specific needs of readers. For example, you take twelve subsystems and break them down into the tasks they let you perform. Then you organize the tasks relative to the needs of your reader. If the reader doesn't need to know that there are twelve subsystems, don't mention it.

Our job is to reach the audience for the computer product. The techies don't know their audience. One developer explained it to me this way, "I can't remember anymore what it was like before I learned all this. I don't remember anymore what I once didn't know," he said.

This is an important statement for writers. It tells us that the developers can no longer put themselves in the reader's shoes. Our job is to remember how it feels not yet to know how to use a computer or a particular computer product, how it feels to be an English major among techies.

I think that's where the gap really begins. We nontechnical folks are where he was "before he knew." And he can't remember what it's like not to know. It's our job to remember what it's like not to know how to use computer software and hardware.

Our job is to make contact between these two seemingly incompatible worlds. If we do our jobs well, nontechnical people can benefit from the value that technical people have built into the product. If we don't do our jobs well, the result is a terrible waste of talent and energy.

### *We Don't Understand Them*

And what is our perception of the techies? From our point of view, they seem almost as alien and baffling as the Laputans seemed to Gulliver.

The Laputans, you might remember, were scientists and musicians who lived on an island that floated in the sky. They served their food in geometric shapes: an equilateral triangle of mutton, a rhomboid of beef, a cycloid of pudding. Gulliver reported that "Their heads were all reclined either to the right or the left; one of their eyes turned inward, and the other directly up to the zenith."

The gap between our worlds is wide. Our training, skills, and language are very different. Developers have spent their careers developing their quantitative skills and learning their own unique jargon. As writers, most of us have spent more time developing our creative skills. We crave the freedom to reorganize, revise, and otherwise create based on our inner writer's clock—not on a schedule plotted out on a graph by a techie.

But underneath our various stereotypes of each other, there's an even more powerful difference—our interests. Much of the time, we share an interest in creating a useful, clear manual. But sometimes our interests are so different that writers and developers become adversaries instead of partners. And the reader usually suffers for it.

## *Our Interests Often Diverge*

A common thread that runs through the horror stories is that a number of interests express themselves in the process of creating a computer manual. Developers have their own interests in the process: political, financial, and professional. The writer's primary interest—producing a clear, useful document—doesn't always prevail. (And the writer's other primary interest—keeping the job or the client—might also be "negatively impacted.")

It is crucial to understand the other interests, particularly when deadlines are tight. The writer must successfully factor in X's desire for a promotion, Y's dissatisfaction with certain aspects of the product, and Z's need to cover up poor management.

The trick is to get a clear picture of where the interests converge and where they don't. Then you can pick your battles more carefully and spend your always limited bureaucratic capital more wisely.

## WHAT A WRITER CAN DO

### *Understand Your Many Roles*

The least difficult thing about writing a computer manual usually is writing it. Unfortunately, you have to be more than a writer. You also have to be a diplomat, a negotiator, a lobbyist, a teacher, and a guerrilla warrior on behalf of the reader.

Be an advocate for the reader. Determine as best you can who will be using the manual, how they will be using it; then design the book for them. If developers argue that the book should be a blueprint of their system or an argument for their promotion and advancement, fight the good fight for your readers in the battles that inevitably arise.

## *Understand the Developer's Problems*

Learn the various interests that are at work. Learn about the approval process—the perils and possibilities for the developers. Don't wait for the crisis. Try to stay a step or two ahead of the game.

It is important to know as quickly as possible where your relationship with the developers is adversarial. Then you can win what can be easily won and choose to fight or not to fight for what isn't easily won. Don't waste time and allies fighting for things you can't possibly win. Win the ones you're supposed to win; win a few that you're not supposed to win.

Also, learn more about the technical people themselves. Notice that they are usually careful, persistent, disciplined, systematic human beings. They use their quantitative skills all day.

(They think that we are systematic, too. They cannot conceive of the fact that we cannot conceive of the system they have been building for so long—or that the person who uses their products is probably not as systematic as they are.)

Be more patient with them. For creative, subjective writers, this isn't always easy.

## *Educate the Techie*

When technical people make decisions that hamper the writer's ability to communicate effectively, it's partly our fault. We may have done our writing job, but we haven't done our wider job: to best represent the reader's interests. We have failed to educate the techie about how we use manuals, how we English majors think.

Teach the technical people what we know as writers and readers: how people read, how people use manuals, and how people use computers, particularly people who don't have a technical background. Teach them what the research teaches us.

Your job is to make the decision makers aware of the trade-offs. Be as persuasive as you can.

## *Roll with the Punches*

After you've made your best argument, step back and see what the decision is. It's not your call. Sometimes you win; sometimes you lose. Don't take it personally when you lose. Don't take it too much to heart. You can still win other battles.

In writers' heaven, there are good books and bad books. You always either win or lose. In the real world, there are books and there are better books. You never entirely win, but each victory improves the reader's chances of success in using the product. Each victory adds a little more value to the product that the techies are working so hard to create.

It isn't easy to keep from taking things personally. By all the measures used by the techies, we often don't measure up. The impatient ones can't deal with us, and the patient ones work with us in a gathering exasperation. Gulliver felt it in Laputa. It's the feeling that you're not taken very seriously as a human being.

Here's how Gulliver put it, reflecting on his visit: "Although I cannot say that I was ill treated in this island, yet I must confess I thought myself too much neglected, not without some degree of contempt. For neither prince nor people appeared to be curious in any part of knowledge, except mathematics and music, wherein I was far their inferior, and upon that account very little regarded."

# WRITING FOR AN ON-LINE AGE: THE INFLUENCE OF ELECTRONIC TEXT ON WRITING

*Philip Rubens*
*Rensselaer Polytechnic Institute*

*Philip Rubens, associate professor of visual and technical communication, teaches in the graduate technical communication programs at Rensselaer Polytechnic Institute in Troy, New York. Before coming to RPI he directed technical communication programs at William Rainey Harper Community College and Michigan Technological University. With over a decade of commercial, corporate, and industrial publishing experience, he has also consulted with a variety of major corporations as a principal of TechWriting Affiliates, Inc., in Boston. At present his research and consulting interests are in electronic publishing, on-line information, the development of publication standards, and innovative communication technologies.*

The major premise underlying the concepts currently used to produce text is that people will continue to read and use texts in the same manner in which they have for many centuries. That is, we expect readers to be interested in the printed word presented on pieces of paper in some "booklike" form. For the most part this seems like a safe assumption. It is highly unlikely that we will abandon our alphabet, words, or grammatical structures, much less the technology we have developed for creating texts. But some writing communities have begun to consider new ways of presenting text, especially text that supports the performance of a task. The most common area in which these new text production techniques occur relates to a variety of computing interactions. In these discourse communities text appears solely on a computer display and supports interactive or ongoing tasks. In general, this kind of text can be defined as *on-line information*.

Like any other text, on-line information has some general characteristics as well as some unique ones. The most important distinguishing characteristic is that on-line information must be available for a reader only on a display screen. However, like any text or text presentation technique, on-line information has a variety of forms based on the capabilities of the host computer, the quality of the display device, the purpose of the text, and the abilities of the expected audience.

At the most basic level, on-line information offers little more than system messages, usually one or several words that provide the user with some indication of the status of their activities during an interactive process. In this basic form, the user is actively attempting to complete a task and the on-line information provides her with an indication of the progress of that task. For instance, in sending a file over the telephone lines with a telecommunication package, the program could display such messages as "File being transmitted" or "File successfully sent." Both of these messages tell the user that the invisible electronic processes controlling the file transfer have been successful. The first one informs the user that a task is ongoing; the second that the task has been completed. Similar results can be obtained by displaying a graphic, such as an indicator bar similar to a fuel gauge found in an automobile, that shows how much of an activity has been completed. Obviously, without these messages the user would have no way of knowing whether or not anything had occurred.

While these basic messages are very terse, they do provide information to support tasks. The next logical step beyond help messages is to provide a "help facility." This means that within the machine or its supporting software the manufacturer includes substantial texts to assist the user. Help facilities differ from help or system messages in that they are more discursive and textlike. Once again, the vitality of these messages depends on the system's or software's capabilities. In general, help facilities can be accessed concurrently from within a task. For example, if a machine operator—perhaps in a paper mill—is configuring a paper run to produce a particular finish or color and needs to know what programming code sequence will allow him to perform that task, he can access (or open) the help facility, usually with a single keystroke, find the appropriate information, and return to the task with that information. This contrasts with paper text-supporting tasks in which the user must leave his work to find supporting information. At the least, on-line information creates the illusion that tasks and supporting information are a coherent environment.

In addition to help messages and facilities, on-line information includes text on-line, reference information, data bases, and the like. One particularly interesting line of development that has considerable impact on the writing process in on-line information is a concept called *hypertext*. This is a rather fancy word for an elegant program that treats text as a large relational data base. That is, any text closely related in content or meaning will be accessed simultaneously as though the user were using a data base rather than a text-based help file.

By now it should be evident that the people who prepare on-line information operate in a totally new text-production environment. They must be able to write succinctly about hidden processes and electronic events; they must be able to understand both the uses of the language they create and the machine or product on which it operates; they must know something about the ways in which readers or users expect to interact with both texts and machines; and they must understand the capabilities and limitations of the medium.

For writers, this new medium presents a set of problems unlike any other. Text no longer appears on paper; text "feels" less permanent (since it disappears from the display as the reader proceeds through a series of screens); text must be more terse; text must be produced to support tasks and to work within the capabilities of the display device and the driving hardware and software. Obviously, these limitations require very different kinds of interactions and capabilities from authors. In the next two sections the unique demands of this new medium will be discussed. Following this discussion, several examples of the typical products of this discourse community will be offered. Finally, some implications for the teaching of writing will be outlined.

## TYPICAL DEVELOPMENT CYCLE AND INTERACTIONS

How do we develop texts? Aside from recent research into joint authorship, little has been done to examine the nature of group or corporate authorship. This lack of research is further confounded by the fact that much corporate authorship occurs electronically and is edited and otherwise scrutinized, usually for legal reasons, in the same manner. Thus, writing in a corporate setting, in a large measure, removes many aspects of the communication task from the individual author's control. For the most part, however, multiple authors in a corporate communication group come together to discuss their tasks, agree on the general shape of the text and the controlling corporate style sheets, and the review and approval responsibilities. In addition, they also generally identify subject-area specialists who will act as informants and screeners for technical details. Other versions of the same writing group may have the writers, editors, and graphic artists acting as part of a larger design team. In this scenario the text developers are included in a product-development team that operates as a steering committee throughout the development process (Grice, 1987). In contrast to the less integrated groups, these writers have direct contact and, sometimes, equal standing with the more technical production staff. Obviously, the range of interactions open to authors is as varied as the corporate identity under which they work. The position of the authoring group in relation to other aspects of product development is extremely important for on-line information to succeed.

What is so different about developing on-line information? The primary difference concerns the words and the ways in which the words become available to a reader. These two functions, although distinct, must be considered as a single element in both the development and implementation of on-line information. One could argue that this kind of thinking is completely foreign to writers who have had little to do with the actual printing of their publications. The fallacy in such an argument is that writers of paper texts still have a reasonable expectation that their final product will be a paper text of some sort. Such an assumption carries with it a large measure of cultural baggage. That is, authors of a paper text can expect the readers of that text to come to their task with a certain set of strategies and expectations. Since the characteristics of on-line information are so radically different, these strategies and expectations can be confounded by a purely electronic text. Since developing on-line information is so different in character, the authoring process and the interaction and display conventions, although closely integrated, have to be considered separately in the development phase. The development process described here has three elements: creation of an authoring tool, development of display and interaction techniques, and creating text and graphics.

Most corporations fail to produce adequate or useful on-line information because they neglect to create an authoring tool. Quite simply, this means that authors and those concerned with the display of on-line information need a writing tool that acts like a word processor that uses the screen rather than a piece of paper as its "printer." A few corporations have developed some very elegant authoring tools. In one instance the corporate on-line authoring tool is a natural extension of a current word processor with the addition of the "screen" as an output or printing device. Other versions allow the authors to send their text to a variety of printers, electronic transmission cables (to other sites, groups, or even typesetting machines), various storage devices (tapes, hard disks, compact disks, etc.), and a range of display devices. In the two examples cited, the power of the authoring tool resides in the range of capabilities provided for the authors. Since such tools allow the author to display text routinely, on-line information can be seen as a part of all electronically mediated writing activities.

Planning such tools, however, entails understanding the fundamentals of reader expectations and typical text usage as well as the ways in which people want to (or are willing to) deal with machines. As you read this text, you employ some well-known, perhaps culturally bound, abilities for dealing with texts. You also assume that the author and the printer have played fair with you and imposed known words arranged in predictable patterns on a sheet of paper. For the author to violate your expectations—except for the best of reasons—would be foolish.

Since we normally acquire information from print (despite the growing dominance of visual information in our culture), on-line information should continue to employ those print conventions we seem to use best. But to use these conventions we must provide some degree of booklike interaction and display for readers. Providing such capabilities can seem very difficult when one considers that on-line texts cannot be held or (generally) written on.

How do we expect readers to use on-line information? Before we can consider how to develop such information, we have to know something of the ways in which people typically interact with texts. For the most part, text usage patterns can be divided into three general classes of operations: biomechanical, conceptual, and mechanical.

Biomechanical patterns depend on the way in which the eye presents raw data to the brain and any associated filtering agents. We know, primarily from eye-motion studies, that the eye sees in specific wavelengths of light, that it has predictable movements and fixations, and that it can be attracted by such features as color or motion (Rubens, 1986; Krull and Rubens, 1986). For the most part we have very little control over what the eye apprehends. If we look in a particular direction, the eye takes in all of the detail in that visual field (with some sorting out of detail in the periphery). The only real filter we can impose on that field is the attention that we pay to specific areas of interest. Admittedly this is an oversimplification; I have not addressed the entire range of visual possibilities here simply because they are beyond the scope of this essay. Suffice it to say that biomechanical processes imprison our perceptions within any visual field. We cannot choose to ignore all of the stimuli in a visual field.

In addition, these same biomechanical processes limit or distort information. Color blindness, for instance, provides some individuals with erroneous data. Visual degradation, over both long- and short-term visual events, also creates problems. Readers with both excellent and corrected vision experience eye fatigue during reading. Readers also accidentally introduce confounding conditions, by ingesting caffeine or nicotine, that alter their vision for short periods of time. All of these biomechanical elements influence the reader's ability to apprehend the form of a visual stimulus and to interpret that stimulus accurately under ever-changing conditions.

In addition to biomechanical elements, there are also a number of mechanical elements associated with reading. We have a well-developed set of reading strategies for dealing with paper texts. We expect to read left to right and top to bottom; we expect a book to begin at page 1 and go to the end. We highlight texts, underline information, insert marginalia, fold down pages, talk to text, argue with the author, read specific span widths, look for information summaries, and understand that typographic variations have special purposes. These and many other strategies provide us with a potent repertoire of skills for discovering and preserving a critical information path through a text.

Finally, we possess a considerable number of conceptual capabilities. These reading and information-gathering strategies help us understand what texts mean and how to use that meaning to our best advantage to accomplish tasks. These are also the most highly sedimented and culturally derived of the three areas discussed here and, as such, are likely to be the most resistant to change. Given the vitality of typical interactions people employ to use paper texts, the developers of on-line information would be well advised to retain as many of these interactions as possible.

What does this mean for writers of on-line information? Basically, it means that they must be aware of these interactions and their potency as well as the ways in which the new media prevents them from using these interactions to their best advantage. In terms of biomechanical elements, for instance, providing color on a screen may not be useful even though it is attractive and easy to accomplish. Primarily, this is true because screen adjustments remain in the hands of the user. They can simply alter all or any of a screen's characteristics locally at whim. Thus, if color is used to attract their attention to specific details, that feature can be arbitrarily rejected by any user simply by turning the color feature off or altering the color. Even those characteristics of screen displays that developers control can present problems. Typical paper texts, for instance, provide an optimal contrast level of 85 percent because of the varying characteristics of the reflected wavelengths of light emanating from the paper and ink. Screens present information by employing "projected" light, which slightly distorts the images on the display through a phenomenon know as irradiation. Basically, this means that the large areas of light around the characters on a display subtract some detail from the characters and make them appear fuzzy and out of focus. You witness the same problem with white characters on dark backgrounds when watching the credits for most commercial films. But displays controlled by computers can also provide some novel techniques not available in books. For instance, the developers can control the display rate to make certain characters appear slower or can make characters move to attract attention. Neither of these capabilities are available in paper texts.

The mechanical elements of on-line information are those qualities that provide the greatest challenge for the developer of such material. If we want to use interactions like those found in books, we must allow readers of on-line information to turn pages, write in the texts, and browse through the material by relying on tables of contents, indices, headings, and the like. All of these can be accomplished but require the cooperation and understanding of the programming and/or product-development staff.

If on-line information that emulates a book can be developed, then those capabilities that allow us to use books should also allow us to use on-line information successfully. Thus, it is important for us to consider the kinds of strategies readers normally employ in using texts that allow them to extract meaning from those texts and to use that meaning to accomplish tasks. On-line information should be no different than any other information or text in this respect.

What do writers need to know to produce on-line information? There is still no substitute for good writing ability. In developing on-line information, a capable writer must bring to bear the ability to discern the central premise in any one piece of information and to present that information in as small a chunk as possible. Reducing the text to a useful length requires an understanding of word choice, sentence structure, punctuation, information mapping, and paragraph structure. All of these writing strategies are necessary for the production of useful texts. Several examples of these techniques are detailed in the following section on sample texts.

Writers must also know something about the programs controlling the devices that display their texts and the interactions possible on that equipment. To provide booklike interactions, the screen must be used to its best advantage. Typical industrial-grade monitors, for instance, limit the developer to 80 characters across the screen and 24 rows. This yields 1,920 characters. However, any good writer knows that using the entire available space on a sheet of paper to print text creates a very unreadable and unusable page. Typically, printed text occupies about 50 to 65 percent (the image area where type will be placed) of the available surface of a sheet of paper. If we use the same percentage range to establish an image area for developing on-line information, we would only be able to use 960 to 1,250 characters. As you may have already guessed, this is far fewer than can be printed on a similar sheet of paper with good legibility characteristics (Krull and Rubens, 1985). Of course, more sophisticated displays do allow more pagelike text. In fact, such machines are so versatile that they often display multiple pages or provide the reader with recordkeeping areas for noting their critical path through a text. These, however, are currently far from being industry standards and represent the exception rather than the rule.

In addition to display capabilities, on-line information is limited by the capabilities and sophistication of the driving hardware and the available software. To provide booklike interactions, we would want to make such possibilities as bookmarks, marginalia, highlighting, and the like possible. While these can be accomplished in a variety of ways, they all require machine memory and keystroke allocation. For instance, if we want to allow readers to keep track of their progress through a text, we can provide a facility that operates invisibly behind their search and that simply records screen numbers the reader can recall later in the session. The same process could work by allocating a section of the active screen, the one the reader is using to read information, and placing this record in view. In the first example, the advantage is a savings in screen space, but the disadvantage is that the record must be recalled to overwrite the active screen (all of the text must be removed before the record can be displayed) and a keystroke or combination of keystrokes must be reserved to recall the record. In the second example, the biggest disadvantage is the loss of screen space; it is also likely that there would be a limit to the length of any record that could be stored in this window. Thus, in planning for providing booklike interactions, a variety of trade-offs in the operational characteristics of the system must be considered. It is the writer with her knowledge of reading strategies who will help implement these booklike interactions.

Another major area of concern for the writer is the psychology of human-machine interaction. As I said earlier, the oddest aspect of using on-line information is that an electronic device mediates the reading event. This means that writers must be concerned with how people interact with machines as well as with texts. This is decidedly new territory for writers and one of the most difficult to both understand and employ. For instance, in the earlier example of electronic bookmarks, neither of the possibilities are actually booklike in character. When we add bookmarks—either slips of paper or dog-eared pages—they provide a sense of spatial relationship within the entire text. Thus, we can see that we have read a particular idea in several places in the same text and can consider the physical space that separates these ideas. This allows us to comprehend quickly that the author may have "framed" a text by repeating the same idea in an early, middle, and late chapter; or, it may provide the user with quick access to similar, or even additive, information necessary to complete a task. We can even employ the simple technique of flipping pages to compare information rapidly and repetitively. On-line information cannot currently emulate these simple yet powerful actions.

The more critical issue here, however, is that writers need to understand these kinds of limitations and discover ways of assisting the product developer to create techniques that minimize the presence and dominance of the machine. Most readers interact with books with very little thought given to the sophisticated techniques they employ. Layering another level of interaction, mandated by a device's limitations, onto the reading task will require the reader to manage both the reading and the interaction tasks simultaneously. While selective attention may assist the reader, it will not resolve all of the demands made by this situation. Writers will be the catalyst in helping product developers understand the ways in which people want to use texts.

Another major capability of on-line information developers is the ability to analyze tasks. Task analysis means that the writer can assess the ways in which people use both texts and products. The basic question here is: What do people want to do to successfully perform tasks? While that at first seems fairly straightforward, one must remember the nature of most machine-mediated tasks in which the operator cannot physically handle the product or process. This is true of virtually all computing tasks. In producing this manuscript, for instance, the initial text was typed into one machine, sent via a telecommunication program to another machine, formatted with a word processor, checked with a grammar checker, and printed. Each event was mediated by the machine and the author never saw anything on paper until the printing process. These tasks, however, could all have been completed by a single device or program in a different kind of environment. The important point is that different people will have radically different preferences or options for ways to complete tasks; it will be impossible to address all of these preferences, so product developers will create products that address the general needs of users.

In supporting these users with on-line information, the same kinds of concerns will be evident. For instance, when you are performing a task and want additional information—perhaps some reference material—how and where do you expect to be able to find that information? With an on-line information system, the expectation is that it will be available in the same environment that supports the task. But this support is also fraught with difficulties. The most typical one has to do with the ways in which people understand problems and seek solutions to these problems.

In performing any specific task, information can be assembled in a variety of ways. However, the most basic kinds of tasks can be seen as either simple— one-dimensional—or complex—multidimensional—tasks. That is, the resolution of the tasks depends on the hierarchy of possible responses needed to resolve the task. In a one-dimensional task only one piece of information is necessary to complete the task. For example, printing a file would require a simple PRINT command. In contrast, a multidimensional task is one that requires the user to assemble information from more than one location in a text (whether on-line or on paper) and assemble that information in a unique manner to resolve a problem. Thus, to print a portion of a file, the user might have to add a series of special characters to the basic PRINT command. For writers of on-line information and, indeed, most documentation, this means that some basic assumptions about problem setting, the formation of questions, must be analyzed.

Why is this so important? Basically, it is important because finding an answer in information does not always mean finding the right answer in the right location. Let me explain. If a user is searching for a command to save a file to a buffer for subsequent transmission to another device, that command *should* be found in a section dealing with telecommunication functions. However, a similar command could also be found in the word processing function of the same program. If the user discovers this location first and relies on it to resolve the problem, it may, indeed, work. However, it is not the correct answer to the problem. The deleterious aspect of such searches is that users are likely to search for subsequent responses in the same location—after all, it helped in the past—and they will likely fail to resolve all of their problems in that wrong location (Rubens and Rubens, 1988). Such failures may, predictably, cause the user to distrust their information source and lead to more and more frustration and anxiety. The problem is compounded in using on-line information, because the typical signals that help users return to specific text sections are missing. In addition, the path through the text, one that might have even overshot the correct location, will have to be remembered by the reader. This would require a considerable human memory overhead.

A characteristic of product developers and writers that exacerbates this dilemma is that the most common solution to a perceived or potential problem is to provide the user with more text to help them solve that problem. Early awareness of such problems really suggests that the product should be revised to eliminate the potential difficulty. There should be a definite distinction made between writing to be read—typically both fiction and nonfiction narratives—and writing to do work—terse, referential text amenable to on-line treatment. This is the primary dilemma of the writer of on-line information.

A final capability of on-line information developers should be an awareness of the totality of symbol systems and their potential applications for supporting tasks. Given the increasing international nature of audiences and the dominance of visual symbology in our everyday lives, on-line information should capitalize on their practical power to convey information (Marcel and Barnard, 1980). This is not to suggest that iconic or graphic interfaces have some inherently powerful capabilities that obviate against command-driven systems. Instead, it is important to understand that a picture of a product—perhaps a disk or other object—seems to be easily recognized and acted upon. The accompanying reduction in operating time makes it well worth incorporating iconic or symbol representations into the operating characteristics of any product.

In addition to an understanding of iconic representations, it is also important for the developer of on-line information to understand how to make decisions about basic screen layout. Most of these abilities have already been discussed.

On-line information, then, requires writers to write well, to have the ability to prepare terse texts that support tasks, and to be able to define the limits beyond which information will *not* help someone use a flawed product. It requires them to understand how people want to interact with both texts and machines as well as the power and limitations of machinery and supporting program. Writers must also be able to perform complex task analyses and address the ways in which people formulate and resolve problems. Finally, it requires them to be able to assess and implement the use of symbolic or iconic elements. While this is a considerable inventory of knowledge and abilities, it represents the range of demands placed on writers by this new medium. It does not, however, exhaust the range of possibilities. I have neglected, for instance, those more futuristic and atypical elements of on-line information such as color, sound, and motion. All of these are more cinematic and videographic than the booklike interactions I have concentrated on here. I have done so because most industrial situations do not admit of the use of these more advanced display and interaction techniques, though, at some point in the future, I expect they will become more commonplace and become part of the repertoire of the on-line information developer. To this point we have explored the basic characteristics of on-line information and the unique demands of the media. The following section will offer several examples of the kinds of on-line information development currently underway.

## CONTEMPORARY ON-LINE INFORMATION

A considerable number of corporations are in the process of defining or developing on-line information. Most of this activity is confined to system message; however, there is a growing community of sophisticated on-line information development. In this section, two systems will be described. The first operates on a large mainframe computer and supports a data base retrieval program that is publicly available. The second system supports a word processing program on a microcomputer. (While every effort has been made to obscure the identity of the authoring corporations, it is likely that these products will be recognized. It is not the intention of this discussion to assess or recommend any one product. The discussion will focus on the operational characteristics of the on-line information and not the program or activity it supports.) In addition to the detailed examination of these two programs, this section will conclude with a brief excursion into a number of other emerging or operational on-line information systems.

The first on-line information system to consider operates on a large mainframe and supports a public data base. In its earliest conception, this program began by offering an introductory screen (Figure 1) that supplied details about the structure of the data-base collection and something about its history. The bottom of this screen contained a rudimentary selection menu. Let's examine this screen from the standpoint of the user.

Two aspects of the screen immediately impress the user. First, the screen is filled with text. The image area, in fact, occupies nearly three quarters of the screen. Second, the text is "set solid"—without interline (leading) spacing—on very long lines (74 characters). Most readers find such text density too oppressive and refuse to read such texts. A more tangible language problem is the fact that the sentences lack variety or transitions and that the terms used in the menu are either redundant (search) or jargon (acquisitions and serials). The second screen (Figure 2) has only about half of its area devoted to image. Similar language ambiguities occur on this screen. For instance, why are the abbreviations for "by"

- The Library online system contains several components which represent
- most of the materials found in the library collections. The Online
- Catalog provides access to items added to the collection since 1974
- as well as to most of the pre-1974 holdings. The Serials Database
- contains information on journal titles. The Acquisitions Database
- identifies items on-order, as well as items received but not yet
- represented in the Online Catalog. The card catalog must be consulted
- for the following materials: new theses, phonograph records, art prints,
- cassettes and audio-visual items. Information on special subject
- bibliographies can be found in the subject card catalog. A HELP command
- will be available at any time once you begin to search a database.

- Please enter a number from the list below

   1 Search the Online Catalog
   2 Search the Acquisitions Database
   3 Search the Serials Database
   4 Send us a Message
   5 Stop

*Figure 1 Mainframe introductory screen*

"author" or "au," while all of the other abbreviations are shorter versions of the original term? What is an index name? However, the most significant problem on this screen is the lack of any indication about subsequent actions. The user arrived here by selecting the number 1 from the menu on the bottom of the first screen but has no idea how to continue.

For one year, the authoring corporation monitored the use of this on-line help with a system log that recorded all the search paths employed by users. From that log they were able to ascertain that the typical user searched for books, periodicals, and other media in that order. The log also revealed that the most typical mistakes were simple typing or syntax errors which the program ignored. Based on this usage study, the authoring agency revised the system to reflect its typical usage (Figure 3). The new initial screen uses less than 20 percent of its area to display image; the text has also been "opened" with additional leading. More importantly, how-

- The following indexes are available in the ONLINE CATALOG:

| Index Name | Alternate Names or ABBREVIATIONS | Index Name | Alternate Names or ABBREVIATIONS |
|---|---|---|---|
| by | author, au | ‖ publisher | pub, pu, p |
| title | ti, t | ‖ language | la, l |
| exact-title | e-t, et | ‖ date | |
| subject | su, s | ‖ number | nu |
| about | | ‖ material | ma |
| call-number | call, cn | ‖ collection | coll |

- After each system prompt, you will be given a list of commands that you can use.
- If you don't know how to use these commands, try HELP.

*Figure 2 Mainframe secondary help screen*

```
┌─────────────────────────────────────────────────────────┐
│                                                         │
│   Folsom Library Catalog: Main Menu                     │
│                                                         │
│   Which collection do you want to search?               │
│       1 Books                                           │
│       2 Periodicals                                     │
│       3 Other media                                     │
│                                                         │
│   Type a number and press ENTER.                        │
│                                                         │
│   ─────────▶                                            │
│                                                         │
│   HELP = PF1      Main Menu = PF2     Expert = PF5      │
│   Back = PF3      Forward = PF4                         │
│                                                         │
└─────────────────────────────────────────────────────────┘
```

*Figure 3 Interrogation screen revision*

ever, the screen reflects something of the ways in which one would expect someone to try to resolve a problem. It posits a question, provides some alternatives, and gives directions for continued action. In addition, a running head places the reader in the same way that similar typographic techniques are used in books, and a static secondary menu at the bottom of the screen lists other options for interacting with both the program and its supporting on-line information.

For instance, a new user approaching this screen can elect to press the PF5 (programmable function key number 5) and register as an expert user. This action clears the screen, with the exception of the prompt line (where the arrow appears) and the static secondary menu. In effect, the user enters "terse" mode and can interact with the database in much the same manner as the original version. That is, the expert user must know all of the commands that appeared on the original second screen (Figure 2) or know how to access HELP with PF1 to learn about these commands. This was the most typical path used by professional searchers.

A new, casual, or occasional user could either select a number or press one of the programmable function keys listed on the secondary menu. The most common action was to select 1 from the main menu. However, PF1 was always available to provide on-line information. For instance, a new user who did not know what the terms on the first screen meant could press PF1 and another screen (Figure 4) would appear that offered a definition of each term. Similar screens are also available to assist users in refining their searches in a variety of ways.

One type of innovation that is difficult to demonstrate in a written explanation of on-line information involves the ways in which the revised program tries to address the problem of keystroke errors. If a product developer supplies paper documentation to support a product, the most typical interaction when trying to resolve a problem requires that the user leave the task and refer to that text. In most work situations the user is trying to accomplish a task and might be working

```
┌─────────────────────────────────────────────────────────────┐
│                                                             │
│   Folsom Library Catalog: Help                              │
│                                                             │
│   These collections contain:                                │
│       1   Books—items added since 1974, as well as most pre-1974 holdings. │
│       2   Periodicals—magazines and journals, both loose and hard-bound issues. │
│       3   Other media—theses, recordings, and audiovisual materials. │
│                                                             │
│   Type a number and press ENTER to begin your search.       │
│                                                             │
│   ─────────> 1                                              │
│                                                             │
│                                                             │
│                         Main Menu = PF2                     │
│       Back = PF3        Forward = PF4                       │
│                                                             │
└─────────────────────────────────────────────────────────────┘
```

*Figure 4 Layered information screen*

under less than optimal conditions. For instance, his desk might be cluttered; he might be balancing the documentation on his knee; or he might have to refer to several texts. Typically, the user leaves the task, enters this information gathering routine, locates an answer, and either types the action directly into the machine or writes the response on paper for later typing. In contrast to this scenario, the on-line information system under consideration offers the user an electronic scratchpad that she can carry around with her while she searches and reads through the on-line information. In most instances, she can even construct a possible resolution for her questions, check that response, and have the program act directly on her final version. This is generally referred to as a "passback" routine and is one fairly simple method for resolving keystroke errors.

This, then, illustrates an instance in which task analysis revealed that the basic operating characteristics of the program were flawed and that more information would not help improve user performance. Instead of producing additional text, the on-line information developers reduced the amount of text, focused certain portions of the text on direct assistance, provided additional information and interaction techniques, and gave the user some control over interaction style.

The second system is cited to provide some sense of the kinds of writing strategies one must use to prepare on-line information. In this instance, the product developers provide paper and on-line information to support the same tasks found on a common microcomputer. Let us consider first the screen and then the text.

In Figure 5 we see a "help" screen that overwrites the task. That is, the activity remains active behind the help screen; this serves as a reminder for the user of the purpose for the on-line information search. The top of the help screen acts as a running head and provides a reference (p33) to the location in the text where further explanation can be found. Finally, a series of "soft" but-

```
  File   Edit   Search   Format   Font   Document   Window
┌─────────────────────────────────────────────────────────┐
│                       Untitled1                         │
├─────────────────────────────────────────────────────────┤
│         ▓▓▓▓▓▓▓▓▓▓▓▓ Help ▓▓▓▓▓▓▓▓▓▓▓▓                  │
│      Copying Character or Paragraph Formats     p33     │
│    ┌─────────────────────────────────────────────┐      │
│    │ (Full menus) To copy formats, select the   ▲│      │
│    │ source, press ⌘-Option-V, then select the  ▓│      │
│    │ destination. Complete by pressing Return.   │      │
│    │ To copy character formats, select          │      │
│    │ characters as the source. To copy paragraph │      │
│    │ formats, select a paragraph as the source  │      │
│    │ by double-clicking in the selection bar    │      │
│    │ next to the paragraph with the format you   │      │
│    │ want to copy.                               │      │
│    │                                             │      │
│    │ If the destination is just the insertion    │      │
│    │ point, simply press ⌘-Option-V, then select │      │
│    │ the source and complete by pressing Return. │      │
│    │                                             │      │
│    │ You can cancel this command by pressing ⌘-.│      │
│    │                                            ▼│      │
│    └─────────────────────────────────────────────┘      │
│                                                         │
│      [ Topics ]  [ Next ]  [ Previous ]  [ Cancel ]     │
│                                                         │
└─────────────────────────────────────────────────────────┘
```

*Figure 5  On-line help screen*

tons on the bottom of the screen allow the user to move around in the on-line information, and an "elevator" bar on the right margin lets the user scroll through the current help screen. All of these features are similar to those found on the mainframe system and allow some booklike interactions. Despite these elegant interaction techniques, the user is restricted to only one interaction style (there is no expert option) and users must rely on memory to carry any information back into their task (lacks a passback feature). In most instances, then, this on-line information system is not as useful as the rather simple one operating on the large mainframe.

The text treatment in moving from paper copy to on-line information reveals the strategies writers must employ in creating this type of information. In Figure 5, there are six sentences. Four sentences are fairly short (8 words in average length); the remaining two sentences average 23 words in length. There is also considerable redundancy in these sentences. Three of the sentences begin with "To copy" and contain the terms "formats" and "select." Many technical writing textbooks would suggest that the writers consider providing a table for this information rather than text. In addition, it is obvious that the operating details of this procedure are not particularly straightforward. They seem to require significantly different actions on the user's part. The first requires a select, some keystrokes, and another selection. The second only requires a selection, and the third asks the user to make a selection and then perform some keystrokes in a particular screen area. The remaining cause-consequent sentence and the escape sequence do not clearly apply to all of the commands; one could easily infer that they apply only to the last command—paragraph formats. Thus, the text is not at all helpful on the screen. Let's compare this text with the manual version (p33 as cited in the running head of the on-line information):

### Copying character or paragraph formats (Full Menus)

1. To copy character formats, select a character or word with the format(s) you want to copy.
   To copy paragraph formats, double-click in the selection bar to select the paragraph with the format(s) you want to copy.
2. Press Command-Option-V.
3. Select the text you want to format.
   The selection is shown with a dotted underline.
4. Press Enter or Return.

To cancel this procedure, press Command-. (period before pressing Enter or Return).

You can also quickly copy formats while you type. At the insertion point, press Command-Option-V, and then select the text you want to copy formats from. When you press Enter or Return, Warp copies the selected formats to the insertion point; new text you type will have those formats. If characters or paragraphs in the selection have different formats, Warp copies the formats from the first character or paragraph.

When you press Command-Option-V, Warp prompts you for the next action with a message in the lower-left corner of the window. The message says "Format to" when you have selected formats to copy and "Format from" when you still need to select the formats to copy.

| For information on | See |
| --- | --- |
| Moving text | Cut Command |
| | Moving Text |
| | Paste Command |

This text has thirteen sentences. About half are short (average of 7 words) and seven are long (average of 20 words). It is immediately apparent that, while the paper documentation has more total words, the sentences are, on the average, shorter. Another immediate reaction is that the paper text seems structured in a manner that makes information more retrievable; the reader can see, at a glance, that this operation requires four basic steps. The same information is buried in the on-line information. In addition, the concluding paper copy provides some vital information for the user to be able to understand the changes that will occur on the screen as the task is in progress ("Format to" and "Format from"). This information is absent from the on-line information. Finally, the paper text points users to similar topics in the event that this section does not solve their problems.

Thus, we can see that simply providing on-line information does not ensure that such information will help users perform tasks. In this instance, a useful set of interaction techniques have been developed—the screen interactions and navigational capabilities that they provide—and the text displayed using these techniques has been neglected. In addition, the interaction techniques themselves remain somewhat restricted. Users must employ the interaction methods provided by the program. It lacks a fast path for experts and does not allow the user to pass back information from the on-line information to the task. Even the rudimentary on-line information discussed in the previous example allowed fairly sophisticated interactions.

I would be remiss if I did not at least refer to some useful on-line techniques that have emerged from a variety of corporations. I am not going either to offer illustrations of these systems or to discuss all of their operating characteristics in detail. That would be time-consuming and would serve only to reveal the blemishes that most of these systems still have. Instead, I will point out the best features of each of these systems and offer some remarks on their importance for those who will be or are already developing on-line information.

The biggest single obstacle to developing useful on-line information is storage and manipulation. Words simply require a great deal of memory, and the display techniques have to become part of the operating characteristics of the computer or product they are intended to support. One encouraging technological development that shows some promise for resolving this problem is the compact disk. Several companies now use this new medium and a specially designed reading device (much like a compact disk player found in the home) to tap its incredible storage potential, which typically ranges from 50,000 to 100,000 text pages per disk. While this medium is currently restricted to read-only (or write-once-read-many, known as WORM), this presents no obstacle to using it to display large amounts of information. In fact, several professional journals and reference books have already been "published" in this media, and several companies have begun preparing their documentation with it as well.

Another innovation involves the creative use of screen space and development of truly sophisticated interaction techniques. In this instance, large displays, usually twice as large as a piece of paper (17" × 11"), are employed to provide areas capable of displaying text, other areas occupied by tasks, other areas with tracking and bookkeeping information, and still other areas with operational information. These systems also often employ the hypertext concept mentioned earlier. While such innovations are intriguing, their current costs make them rare in the workplace.

As you can see, the development of on-line information has already presented a set of interesting problems for writers. The writer must not only be concerned with writing text but must also be able to perform a range of tasks, tasks that are ever-changing and challenging. The final section will examine what these challenges mean for the teaching of writing.

## IMPLICATIONS FOR THE TEACHING OF WRITING

In most written communication tasks, we have learned to expect a certain level of capability and a specific range of knowledge for writers to produce useful information. On-line information, however, has introduced a new variety of problems into their work. Writers have long enjoyed having a "clay tablet" that has supposedly unlimited space available. They have been limited in industrial settings only by their employer's unwillingness to produce high-page-count documents (many pages cost more to run through presses). This reluctance, based on cost, is somewhat offset by the writers' opinion that people need more information to perform tasks and by the need to document product features that do not work very well.

On-line information is usually designed to operate in environments similar to those generally supported by paper information. Thus, the writer must be significantly more judicious about the kinds of decisions previously made about paper information. How much support is really necessary to help a reader perform a task successfully and when should a product be revised to alleviate difficult operating procedures rather than document them? Writers must, then, begin to take the concept of audience seriously. We have talked a great deal about audience for years in writing courses, but we have rarely been able to state exactly what it is we expect a writer to know about an audience. This lack of guidelines is exacerbated by the concomitant need for an understanding of the process the audience will be involved in while the text is being addressed. The purpose for the text is to support a task, nothing more or less. Thus, the characteristics of the person performing the task are important considerations. For instance, in searching a data base for car insurance information, is it likely that the agent will perform this task or a data entry clerk? What are the differences in the backgrounds of these two groups? Does one read better than the other? Does one have more education? Is one group more likely to want to make decisions rather than gather data? Which group should make searches based on costs per search?

Notice that in answering such questions we arrive at a more accurate picture of the use of both the product and the text. If we decide that certain tasks will fall to particular personnel, then we should plan our text accordingly. This, of course, means that the text could have a very different character depending on the likely audience for any one task. There is nothing wrong with such an approach; indeed, it is addressed in the data base discussion in the previous section.

We also need to teach writers that people change over both long and short time spans. As people become more familiar with products, they make guesses about more advanced operations and ignore supporting text. As they succeed in any one product they work faster and make more leaps of understanding. At the same time, they also become tired, their physiological reactions to light change, their eyes become strained, and so on. Thus, we need to teach writers something about the limits of the human machine.

Writers also need to consider the reductive writing techniques necessary for writing on-line information *and* their implications, especially ethical. It is likely that such writing will have an impact on language behaviors in general. In addition, writers must learn to distinguish between writing to be read and writing to support tasks. As demonstrated by the examples in the previous section, the answer to addressing users' problems is *not* always to provide more information; in some instances, the product must be revised to work better. However, the ability to make such distinctions requires the writer to understand how people want to perform tasks and how they conceive of questions that support tasks.

Developing on-line information is not a trivial task. It is not simply massaging paper text into another format with an eye to reducing page counts and their associated costs. On-line information is a new area of discourse. It is a community made up of user/readers who find themselves in an alien environment in which they must deal with invisible processes. Often the sole contact with those processes is offered by messages, helps, and fully developed texts that are unlike any text we have used before. They have an air of impermanence; we feel lost in them as they disappear from view. The challenge in providing useful on-line information is in addressing the anxiety of these users and in providing useful information.

## Works Cited

Grice, Roger A. "The Structure of Documentation Development Groups: An Industry Study." Unpublished dissertation. Rensselaer Polytechnic Institute, Troy, N.Y., 1987.

Krull, Robert, and Rubens, Philip. "Application of Research on Document Design to Online Displays." *Technical Communication*, 4th Quarter (1985): 29–34.

Marcel, Tony, and Barnard, Philip. "Paragraphs of pictographs: the use of non-verbal instructions for equipment," in *Processings of Visible Language*, vol. 2. Paul Kolers et al., eds. New York: Plenum Press, 1980.

Rubens, Philip. "Online Information, Traditional Page Design, and Reader Expectation." *IEEE Transactions on Professional Communication* PC-29, 4 (December 1986): 75–80.

———, and Krull, Robert. "Effects of Color Highlighting on User Performance with Online Information." *Technical Communication*, 4th Quarter (1986): 268–269.

———, and Rubens, Brenda K. "Question Type and User Performance," in *Usability Principles in Document Design*. Steve Doheny-Farina, ed. Cambridge, Mass.: MIT, 1988.

# PART EIGHT

## WRITING IN THE WORLD OF LAW

# IN THE LAW THE TEXT IS KING

*Teresa Godwin Phelps*
University of Notre Dame

*Teresa Godwin Phelps is associate professor of law at the University of Notre Dame Law School. She holds a Ph.D. in English and is presently on sabbatical pursuing a master's of science in law degree at Yale Law School. She is the author of a legal writing textbook as well as numerous articles on legal writing, legal interpretation, and law and literature. She also conducts writing seminars for law firms, banks, and accounting firms.*

Language is the heart and spirit of the legal system in the United States. When Thomas Paine wrote "In America the law is king" (Paine, 1776; 29) he meant that a text, the Constitution, assumed the symbolic role of ruler, the role held by the monarch in England. "What was proposed, and perhaps achieved in America, was nothing less than the self-conscious reconstitution of language and community to achieve new possibilities for life." (White, 1984; 231) The notion of the "writtenness" of the law, though commonplace to us now, was novel and crucial to the thinking of the early practitioners and interpreters of the new government. In 1803 John Marshall, in his renowned *Marbury v. Madison* opinion, eulogized the writtenness of the Constitution, establishing the text as the unalterable supreme rule of the country. He, additionally, perceived and noted a dichotomy between written and unwritten law: "Those who controvert the principle that the constitution is to be considered in court, as a paramount law, are reduced to the necessity of maintaining that courts must close their eyes on the constitution, and see only the law. This doctrine would subvert the very foundation of all written constitutions. . . . [i]t thus reduces to nothing what we have deemed the greatest improvement on political institutions, a written constitution."[1]

Language in the legal discourse community, therefore, has a reality and an efficacy beyond that of its certainly estimable power in other discourse communities. It is itself the subject matter of the community, and although "contemporary scholars in a surprising diverse range of fields now recognize language as central to human experience," (Ede and Lunsford, 1986; 78) in few fields does language possess the nearly magical and incantatory power that it does in the law. Independence is "declared"; defendants are "pronounced" guilty; "I promise" has legal contractual significance. And the legal discourse community is not closed or self-contained: it encompasses and affects everyone who comes under the power of the state, citizens and noncitizens. Some scholars, in fact, argue that language can and does corrupt the system and disguise its reality; language is an instrument of oppression.[2] Others argue that it has the potentiality to transform the legal system.[3]

That debate, however fascinating, is not my focus in this chapter. My purpose is to discuss the ways in which texts are produced, used, and valued within the legal discourse community. I hope to answer these questions: Why does a lawyer write something? Under what conditions and in answer to what questions? What is the legal writer's relationship with his or her audience? In order to do this, I will discuss and offer as specific examples four typical legal documents: office memoranda, opinion letters, briefs, and judicial opinions. I then turn from the analysis of the nature of legal discourse to pedagogical concerns. What strengths do students bring from a traditional composition course and what skills do they lack? And, how can we bridge the gap between traditional composition skills and the skills needed for legal discourse?

## THE NATURE OF LEGAL DISCOURSE

Students entering law school and the public at large harbor many misconceptions about what it means to be a lawyer, and not least among those misconceptions is that concerning the amount of writing lawyers do. Most lawyers spend at least 50 percent of their time writing, and those in their first five years of practice can expect to spend at least 75 percent of their time writing. To be a lawyer means to be a professional writer, and lawyers write a variety of documents, each with its particular rhetorical situation.

Legal writing can best be classified generally with reference to its purpose or aim.[4] Legal writing is either referential or persuasive; although at its best it has literary qualities and serves its writer well, these concerns are secondary. A practicing lawyer writes objective and persuasive documents such as office memoranda, letters, pleadings, wills, contracts, and briefs.[5] Judges primarily write judicial opinions. For each of these documents, a discussion of purpose, audience, and constraints can reveal why each document is written and how it is used and valued.

In the following subsections I analyze the rhetorical situation of several common legal documents to establish when and how texts are produced in the legal discourse community. As I proceed through this analysis, it will become clear how any legal text involves and incorporates other texts. In the law, language interacts with language in an almost endless chain. In fact, in a given case all the legal documents answer the same basic question of how the law affects a specific set of facts, and the documents provide a written record of the case, with the lawyer's role and the audience changing in each instance. The examples that follow demonstrate how this record evolves.

## *Office Memoranda*

An office memorandum (also called a memorandum of law) is often the first formal written record of a case. In general, all office memoranda answer this question: What is the nature of the client's case and what can we do for him? To write an office memorandum, a lawyer uses the facts as the client has related them and numerous other texts: any relevant texts that the client has provided, such as contracts or wills; any codified law that applies (statutes, regulations, constitutions); and appellate opinions.[6] The document answers a specific question, the legal *issue* that the interaction of facts and law generates. Each issue is specific to a particular case as it involves both law and the client's own factual situation.

The audience for an office memorandum is another lawyer, generally one in a superior position in the firm. The purpose of the memorandum is to relate the relevant facts, to state the legal issue, to analyze the facts and the applicable law, to conclude how the client's case should come out, and to recommend an appropriate course of action. The lawyer for whom it is written will use it to make decisions about the case, to write an opinion letter to the client, and to write the many subsequent documents that will result as the case progresses. Thus, the office memorandum not only depends greatly upon other texts but it, in turn, generates further texts.

The memorandum writer's role is that of objective legal thinker. His analysis must be a legal analysis—that is, how the law applies to facts. Other kinds of analysis—emotional, sociological, economic, political—may be tangential but never central to the memorandum. The writer is also constrained by form; some law offices have rigid memorandum formats.

## *Letters*

Although lawyers write many kinds of letters, the formal letter written to clients in which the lawyer gives advice is known as an opinion letter. This letter takes the analysis, conclusions, and recommendations from the office memorandum and translates them for the client. It answers the same general and specific questions as the office memorandum—what can the lawyer do for the client and what is the legal answer to the issue involved—but the audience is dramatically different, and thus the rhetorical situation differs significantly.

The audience for an opinion letter is both professional and personal. A client goes to a lawyer for legal advice, but many clients also look to their lawyers for reassurance and consolation: hence the dual appellations and roles of attorney *and* counselor. The legal writer must effectively control the tone of her letters to achieve this dual and somewhat contradictory role. The legal matter, which was stated succinctly and objectively in the office memorandum, must be stated in terms that the client can both understand and accept.

## Briefs

The term "brief" is used for a variety of documents, but it means generically an argument concerning a case written by an attorney who is trying to persuade a judge how a case (or part of a case, such as a motion) should be decided. Like an office memorandum and an opinion letter, a brief is a written explanation of how the law applies to a particular factual situation. But, and this distinction is crucial, a brief is not an objective document; it is an advocacy document. The subject matter of the office memorandum and the opinion letter is translated once more for a different audience and for a different purpose, and legal language enters the adversarial world of the law.

The audience for a brief is a judge, who will read it and decide the issue in the case. Since the judge will also read a brief from the opposing side which will offer different answers to the legal issues involved, the good brief writer must incorporate counterarguments in her brief. The judge will synthesize the arguments and applicable law and make a decision.

Brief writers encounter multiple constraints. First, the argument must be a legal argument based mainly on codified law and precedent.[7] Second, courts have inflexible rules concerning format and length that a writer violates at great risk to her client. Third, the writer in an advocacy document does not write for herself but in another's stead. Nonetheless, paradoxically enough, the text should reveal the writer's own voice in conversation with the court.

## Judicial Opinions

With this document, not only audience and purpose change but also the professional role of the writer. Judicial opinions are written by judges, usually concerning cases on appeal.[8] A judge reads legal briefs submitted by both sides to a controversy, reads and analyzes the applicable law, may hear oral argument from both sides, and writes her written decision in the case, supported by reasons.[9] Judges on the same panel who agree with the decision may (but need not) write concurring opinions, and those judges who disagree with the decision may write dissenting opinions. These opinions are published, become part of the body of law known as the *common law,* and can be used as authority in other cases.

We have thus come full circle in the written record of a particular case. Below are two charts: Figure 1 depicts the legal process and highlights where discourse arises; Figure 2 depicts the interaction of legal texts and shows the circle of interactive texts described above. We can now delineate six characteristics of legal discourse:

1. Language itself is the subject matter of the discourse community.
2. The writer may assume different roles in writing documents; a legal writer has many different "voices."
3. Different legal documents have dramatically different audiences.

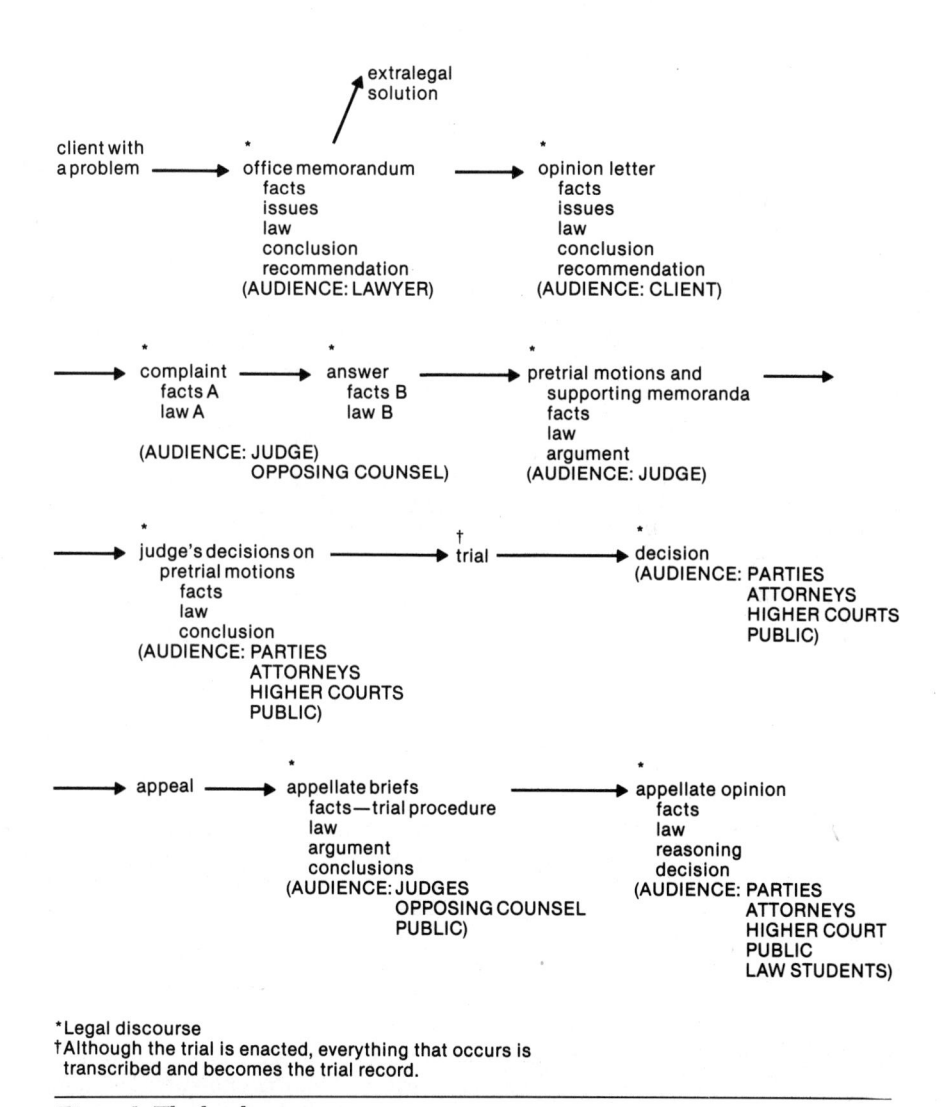

```
                                    extralegal
                                  ↗ solution
                          *                          *
   client with
   a problem    ──▶  office memorandum  ──▶  opinion letter
                       facts                    facts
                       issues                   issues
                       law                      law
                       conclusion               conclusion
                       recommendation           recommendation
                       (AUDIENCE: LAWYER)       (AUDIENCE: CLIENT)


              *              *                *
          ──▶ complaint ──▶ answer  ──▶ pretrial motions and  ──▶
               facts A      facts B       supporting memoranda
               law A        law B         facts
                                          law
              (AUDIENCE: JUDGE)           argument
                           OPPOSING COUNSEL)  (AUDIENCE: JUDGE)


              *                        †              *
          ──▶ judge's decisions on ──▶ trial  ──▶ decision
               pretrial motions                    (AUDIENCE: PARTIES
               facts                                        ATTORNEYS
               law                                          HIGHER COURTS
               conclusion                                   PUBLIC)
              (AUDIENCE: PARTIES
                         ATTORNEYS
                         HIGHER COURTS
                         PUBLIC)


                             *                         *
          ──▶ appeal  ──▶ appellate briefs  ──▶ appellate opinion
                           facts—trial procedure    facts
                           law                      law
                           argument                 reasoning
                           conclusions              decision
                          (AUDIENCE: JUDGES        (AUDIENCE: PARTIES
                                     OPPOSING COUNSEL          ATTORNEYS
                                     PUBLIC)                   HIGHER COURT
                                                               PUBLIC
                                                               LAW STUDENTS)
```

*Legal discourse
†Although the trial is enacted, everything that occurs is transcribed and becomes the trial record.

*Figure 1  The legal process*

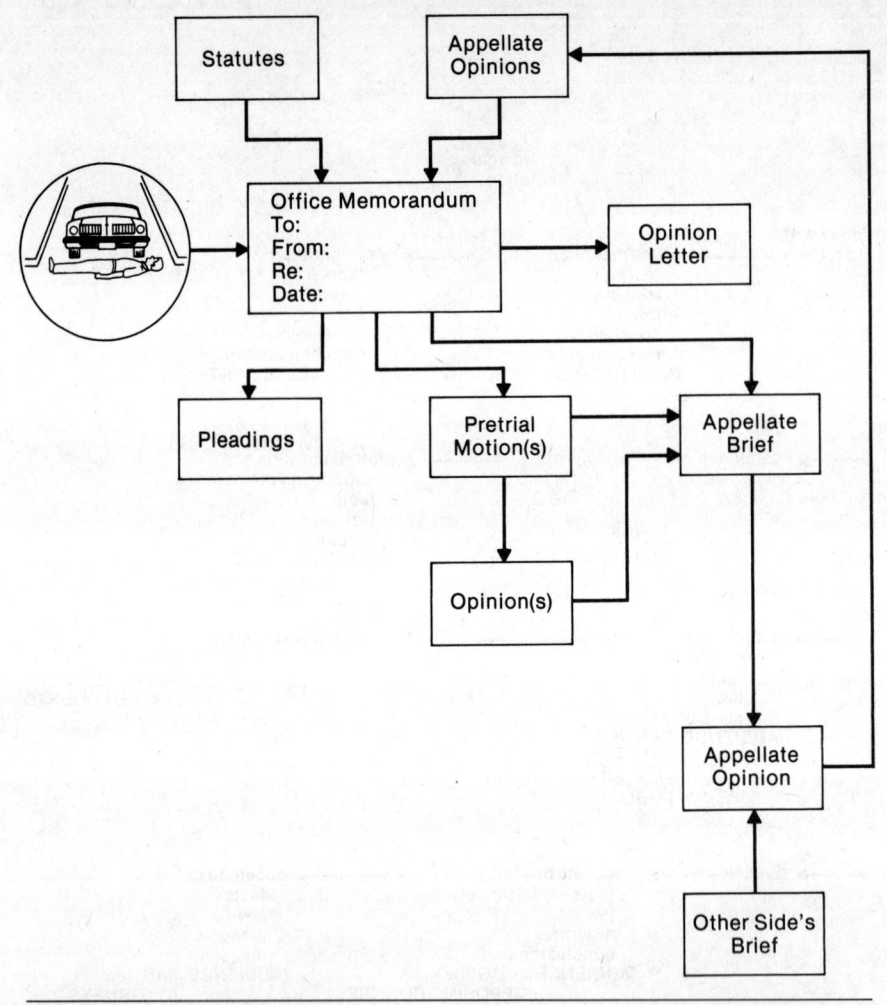

*Figure 2 No text is an island*

4. Legal texts depend upon and generate other legal texts; no legal text is an island.
5. A legal writer sometimes writes in someone else's place.
6. Legal discourse is not confined to the legal discourse community; any legal document will almost certainly have some impact on people outside the community.

Traditional writing instruction in the university (freshman composition, for the most part) does not prepare students for the world of legal discourse. With their nearly exclusive concentration on academic discourse, these courses leave the students inadequately prepared and perhaps even with some misconceptions about their writing experience and ability. What is "good" writing in academic discourse may not necessarily be "good" legal writing. In fact, what is appropriate for one kind of legal writing may not, as we have seen, be appropriate for another kind.

Maxine Hairston has accurately described the kind of writer who enters the legal discourse community:

> [Advanced writers] are not easy to teach. Most of them come into the course at a level of proficiency that has earned them good marks in previous writing courses, a level that may even be getting them A's on papers they write for other college courses. They have reached that level because they write standard English easily and because they have mastered formulas that enable them to spin out smooth, well-organized papers quickly. [1984; 196]

Hairston goes on to describe the characteristics of these students' writing: wordy, overly nominalized, impersonal, unrealistically ambitious, long on generalizations and short on specifics, and lacking a sense of audience. "They display what Paula Johnson calls a 'flat competence'; what they do not have is what Wayne Booth calls 'the rhetorical stance.' That is they reveal no sense of audience for their writing, they show no sense of purpose except to fill a requirement, and they have no persona or 'voice'" (1984; 198–199).

By returning to the six characteristics of legal discourse, we can see how these problems can afflict the production of competent legal writing, and we can ascertain what applicable skills students bring to a legal writing course and what skills they are likely to lack.

*Language is the subject matter.* Some students who have majored in certain areas of the humanities will be accustomed to paying close attention to texts. Literature and theology, for example, share with the law the characteristic centrality of texts to the discipline. Such students have been trained to read well, and reading well is the first crucial step in producing effective legal discourse.[10] The relationship of literature to criticism and of scripture to commentary is somewhat analogous to the relationships among legal texts.

Nothing, however, prepares students for the unavoidable difference between the law and all other disciplines: the "bottom line."[11] The interpretation of legal texts, their incorporation into other texts, and their application to people's lives require care and responsibility in that the texts' influence goes far beyond the legal discourse community. Choosing one word, one syntax, over another—even the presence or absence of a comma—*matters* in the law. Most students are unaccustomed to their writing mattering to anyone but themselves and their teachers.

*A legal writer has different voices.* As Hairston has pointed out, few undergraduate writers have developed even a single voice, let alone the various voices—analyst, counselor, advocate—required of a lawyer. Shifting roles means changing tone: choosing different words and different structures for different rhetorical situations.

Even good undergraduate writers are rarely in control of tone enough to vary their voice when their roles change.

*Legal documents have different audiences.* Likewise, few undergraduate writers have experience analyzing audience and are thus unable to tailor a document for a particular audience. Most novice legal writers are not cognizant of the subtle distinctions among documents dealing with the same legal matter that are commonplace in legal discourse and thus cannot change language and structure for a new audience.

*Legal texts depend upon and generate other legal texts.* If students have come directly from undergraduate school, they have no experience with their writing being used by another person to make a decision or to write a different document. They have written primarily for teachers and to get grades. This has taught them to produce well-organized, error-free academic discourse. Their skills are valuable and applicable to legal writing but limited. If a student writes something that fails to communicate successfully, the teacher may note this failure and the student's grade may suffer; but the student has probably not been required to stick with the document, revising substantially, until it becomes successful.

*A legal writer sometimes writes in someone else's place.* A well-taught traditional English composition course should make students feel accountable for their work. They do not, however, experience the kind of accountability that results when what they write will make a significant difference to someone else's life. To be an advocate means to plead for someone else; an advocacy document, such as a memorandum in support of a motion or an appellate brief, is that plea in writing. An effective legal writer needs to speak with two voices: her own and her client's.

*Legal discourse is not confined to the legal discourse community.* Everyone inhabits the culture of the law; everyone is a member of the legal discourse community in one way or another. Those who produce legal discourse, then, are writing and interpreting our laws and influencing the way we live. Some skills that may be appropriate to other kinds of discourse may even be appropriate to *some* kinds of legal discourse (such as the use of jargon and technical language), but they can be alienating and oppressive in legal writing. Typical composition courses do not enable students to see when their writing must be accessible to all who read and do not teach them to control language in such a way that they can do so.

It should now be clear that there is more than a gap, rather a chasm, between traditional English instruction and the needs of legal writers. The chasm can begin to be bridged by better instruction in undergraduate composition courses, instruction that introduces students to audience analysis and the concept of rhetorical situations. It is difficult to circumvent, however, the fact that undergraduates for the most part learn to write academic discourse, and legal discourse differs significantly from academic discourse.

A deeper problem, as far as I am concerned, is that law schools either renege on the task of introducing students to legal discourse or they do it poorly. Few lawyers, law professors, or law school deans would deny that the ability to write effective legal discourse (although they probably would not put it that way) is crucial to the practice of law. Yet they allow legal writing to be taught by inexperienced teachers in courses that change as the part-time teachers revolve through the door.[12] In the next section, I put forth what I see as the basic goals of a legal writing course and offer some suggestions as to how these goals can be met.

## BRIDGING THE CHASM

I have written extensively elsewhere (Phelps, 1986; 1987) about how legal writing should be taught. Here, I synthesize my earlier opinions with the six characteristics of legal discourse that I have set forth in this chapter and offer a double-pronged suggestion.

To understand how a discourse community operates and to become a full-fledged member of that community requires two things: practice and guidance. To facilitate law students' entry into the new discourse community, writing teachers must provide an environment in which the students can practice writing the documents that they will have to write as lawyers. But, more importantly, the students need active teacher and peer intervention in the writing process as they begin to acquire the necessary skills. An effective legal writing course should create classroom situations that approximate typical legal rhetorical situations, *and* teachers with knowledge of contemporary writing pedagogy should work with the students throughout the planning, drafting, and revising stages of the writing process.

Here is one possible scenario. Students, in workshops of no more than twenty students, form two "law firms" of ten associates each. They are given either a simulated live client interview or some basic documents, such as notes from a client interview and depositions. From these "facts" and from the applicable law (which can be provided for them in a "closed" situation or for which they can search in the library in an "open" situation), they each write an office memorandum for the "senior partner" (the teacher), each "firm" taking one side (plaintiff or defendant for a civil case, prosecution or defense for a criminal case).

The teacher provides instructions as to format; the students discuss approaches among themselves and comment on each other's work. The "audience" (the teacher) can respond and make suggestions along the way.

When the students have completed office memoranda, they can write pleadings and opinion letters, using their own or other students' memoranda. Throughout the semester they can progress through the legal process as depicted in Figure 1 (skipping some stages, of course), learning how an attorney's role varies and learning how to vary their own writing as role, purpose, and audience change. The students can experience the ongoing conversation of the law and can acquire their professional voices within the legal discourse community. Law, for these students, will be seen as a rhetorical activity, "as something we do with our minds, with language, and with each other" (White, 1985; x). If rhetoric can be seen as "enlightened cooperation" and as "an instrument for understanding and improving human relations" (Ede and Lunsford, 1984; 83), this way of teaching legal writing can achieve even more than the crucial task of teaching law students to write effective legal discourse. In a workshop atmosphere, their writing cannot be impersonal and solipsistic. The students see others interpreting and using what they have written. They become cognizant of the social and political dimensions of their work.

This suggestion is not perfect, of course. The workshop is still a simulation; real lives are not at stake. The cavalier student can remain careless without ramifications other than a low grade. But the constant peer and teacher presence and intervention is still likely to raise such a student's consciousness about her writing mattering to others.

This particular pedagogy (or variations on it) requires a commitment on the part of law schools to provide qualified teachers and academic credit: money and time. This may be the biggest obstacle of all.

The world of legal discourse is a wonderful one in which to work. It is a lush and lively world of language and power. One's words rarely fall on deaf ears; they almost certainly are heard and acted upon. With this verbal power comes immense responsibility. Students entering the legal discourse community should not be expected to become a functioning member of that community merely by relying on skills they bring from academic discourse. Legal language (legal writing) should be reinstilled with the reverence afforded it by the founders.

## Notes

1. *Marbury v. Madison* 5 U.S. (1 Cranch) 137, 178 (1803).
2. See, for example, the classic George Orwell article, "Politics and the English Language." Richard Weisberg makes a similar argument in *The Failure of the Word* as does James Raymond in "Legal Writing: An Obstruction to Justice."
3. James Boyd White (1984) argues that there is

    a set of possibilities implicit in the [legal] institution and its practices, to define the kind of aim that the lawyer can have for himself. And these possibilities and aims are remarkable. The "case arising" can be seen as a place for cultural definition, testing, and change; as a way of assuring continued congruence between our languages of justice and expediency; as a means for complicating clichés and first attitudes into deeper understanding and for extending imaginative sympathy to those differently situated from ourselves; and, finally as a way of making a place of coherence in a process of cultural change. Even more: the case establishes an essential equality between people making this value real; and it proceeds by a method of argument and conversation that both recognizes the individual's view of his own situation and complicates that view by forcing him to recognize the claims of another. It is like dialectic in that it is refutational, and it is a kind of friendship in its insistence on the reality and validity of others. It proceeds by a conversation in which each speaker is invited to present an ideal version of himself, speaking to an ideal audience.

4. I have discussed the application of Kinneavy's theory of discourse and of the communication triangle to legal discourse in my article "The New Legal Rhetoric" (1986).
5. Not all lawyers write all kinds of legal documents; lawyers specialize in their writing as in their practice. An appellate attorney, for example, may never write pleadings, contracts, or wills and may write only appellate briefs.
6. Appellate opinions apply to a case because legal decisions are made using a principle known as *stare decisis*. This means that where a court has laid down a legal principle as applying to a certain set of facts, courts will adhere to that principle and apply it to factually similar cases. Like cases are decided alike.
7. There are, of course, other arguments acceptable in a brief—a policy argument, for example, that contends that a particular course of action is in the public interest and will further the common good or, as is becoming the vogue, an economic argument: a cost-benefit analysis. Nonetheless, these kinds of arguments still are constrained in that the writer must be fairly certain that her audience will find these "nonlegal" arguments acceptable.
8. Although most jurisdictions do not require written trial opinions, trial court judges are more and more frequently writing them if the issues are complex, if an appeal is likely, or if an unpopular decision is rendered.
9. I must raise the point that some, myself included, believe that judges frequently invert this order. That is, they come to a conclusion (intuitive or political) and then concoct reasons. Nonetheless, we continue to operate under the legal fiction that the written reasoning really led to the decision.
10. George Gopen argues this point eloquently in "Rhyme and Reason: Why the Study of Poetry Is the Best Preparation for the Study of Law."
11. See, for example, Richard A. Posner, "Law and Literature: A Relation Reargued" and Thomas C. Grey, "The Constitution As Scripture."
12. For some speculation on why law schools persist in this practice, see George Gopen's "A Question of Cash and Credit: Writing Programs at the Law Schools" and Philip Kissam's "Thinking (By Writing) About Legal Writing."

## *Works Cited*

Ede, Lisa, and Andrea Lunsford. 1986. "Classical Rhetoric, Modern Rhetoric, and Contemporary Discourse Studies," 1:1 *Written Communication* 78–92.

Gopen, George D. 1977. "A Question of Cash and Credit: Writing Programs at the Law Schools." 3 *J. Contemp. Law* 191.

———. 1984. "Rhyme and Reason: Why the Study of Poetry Is the Best Preparation for the Study of Law." 46:4 *College English* 333.

Grey, Thomas C. 1984. "The Constitution As Scripture." 37:1 *Stanford L. Rev.* 1.

Hairston, Maxine. 1984. "Working with Advanced Writers. 35:2 *Coll. Comp. & Comm.* 196.

Kissam, Philip C. 1987. "Thinking (By Writing) About Legal Writing." 40 *Vand. L. Rev.* 135.

Paine, Thomas. 1776. *Common Sense*, Philip S. Foner, ed. *The Complete Writings of Thomas Paine*. New York: Citadel Press, 1945.

Phelps, Teresa Godwin. 1986. "The New Legal Rhetoric." 40:4 *Southwestern Law Journal*, 1089–1102.

———. 1987. "The Case File Method of Teaching Legal Writing." 1 *Journal of Legal Writing*.

Posner, Richard A. 1986. "Law and Literature: A Relation Reargued." 72:8 *Virginia L. Rev.* 1351.

Raymond, James C. 1978. "Legal Writing: An Obstruction to Justice." 30 *Ala. L. Rev.* 1.

White, James Boyd. 1985. *Heracles' Bow: Essays on the Rhetoric and Poetics of the Law.* Milwaukee: University of Wisconsin Press.

———. 1984. *When Words Lose Their Meaning: Constitutions and Reconstitutions of Language, Character, and Community.* Chicago: University of Chicago Press.

# TO ENGLISH PROFESSORS: ON WHAT TO DO WITH A LAWYER

*John Warnock*
University of Wyoming

*After graduate work in English at Oxford University, John Warnock took a J. D. degree at New York University School of Law, then clerked for a year in the U.S. Court of Appeals for the Ninth Circuit. In 1970, he joined the Department of English at the University of Wyoming, where he has directed the composition program and the Writing Center and now directs the Wyoming Writing Project. For almost ten years, he has been giving lectures and conducting workshops for judges and lawyers in practice in the United States and Canada. He has written widely on rhetoric and composition. His recent book* Representing Reality *(St. Martins Press, 1989), is an introduction to literary nonfiction.*

"The first thing we do, let's kill all the lawyers." We hear it often, uttered usually with an air of righteous indignation. It is the sort of thing that gets printed on T-shirts.

As is common when Shakespeare is quoted, we are not given the context of the quotation. It is provided in this case by 2 Henry VI. The recommendation to kill all the lawyers is made by Dick the Butcher who, together with a group of other utopian thinkers abroad in the troubled world of this play, will a few lines later condemn a clerk to death because he knows how to write. Dick also speaks the words with an air of righteous indignation. But by the time the clerk is hauled offstage to meet his fate, the play's audience is unlikely to take Dick's recommendation on the same terms that Dick does. We are more likely to see Dick's hostility to lawyers as part of his general hostility to literacy and its consequences.

Now we do not very often see it claimed that the first thing we should do is kill all the English professors. This is not, I think, because of any great love borne English professors as a class, nor is it because people believe that English professors are crucial to the well-being of the polity in a way that lawyers are not. Rather it is, I would guess, that we are thought to be harmless, even quaint. A revolutionary might not think it worth the sweat to kill us. Not at first, at least, though it did not take Dick and his colleagues long to get around to the clerk. Once you think about it, the connection is certainly there: If "they" do kill all the lawyers, can the English professors be far behind?

I would be in danger on both counts. I have a law degree, though I decided not to practice law, and I am an English professor. Furthermore, I have in the last ten years taught writing in a law school and have worked a good deal with judges and lawyers on their writing. I suspect it would not help me much with Dick the Butcher and his colleagues to argue that I do not practice law and that I am only marginally an English professor in the eyes of many of my colleagues in English, since my "areas" are rhetoric, literary nonfiction, and writing. I could hardly deny knowing what the clerk knew—how to write his name—and that would be enough for "them."

In any case, I could not deny that I think a telling relationship does exist between what lawyers do in discourse and what makers of literature do ("makers of literature" is a very different conception from "English professor," I know—more like "poet" than "professor"—but we will ignore the differences for a moment). This telling relationship exists, I believe, despite the fact that the practice of the law schools denies it, and the practice of teaching "English" ignores it, and governing notions of "the practice of law" and "the profession of literature" do nothing to encourage us to recognize the relationship.[1] Very likely I have been brought to perceive this relationship by the numerous apparent tensions in my own position—as a professor of rhetoric and writing in a literature department; an English professor in a law school and a law professor in an English department; a professor of English and law working with judges and lawyers, many of whom do not wish to see themselves only as "legal" writers; and last but not at all least, as a writer whose writing has rarely inclined toward the established models of "research" in either English or law. But that's all right: If my proposals are but strategies for encompassing a situation,[2] they are no different in that respect from anyone else's proposals. The question is whether we are appealed to by what these strategies might do for us, as English professors, in the situations in which we find ourselves.

## LAW SCHOOL AS AN ENVIRONMENT FOR WRITING

Law school: The place where nonlawyers start to become lawyers, and a machine for mystifying writing if ever there was one.

The aim of law school, professors of law often say, is to teach students to "think like a lawyer." This means, among other things, learning better than to

---

[1] The validity of this claim has not been affected much, if at all yet, by recent exchanges by legal and literary theorists on the relation between legal and literary interpretation. See, e.g., Ronald Dworkin, "Law as Interpretation" and responses to it in *Critical Inquiry*, 9:1, September 1982, an issue on The Politics of Interpretation.

[2] The term is Kenneth Burke's. Burke's influence can be noticed elsewhere too.

think that you get to be a lawyer by memorizing rules. But what does law school tend to say to law students about the role of writing in what they will do when they practice law? Or, to enlarge the question further, how does the law school's version of "thinking like a lawyer" relate to "thinking like a writer?"[3]

Lawyers used to learn to be lawyers the way other artisans learned their trades—in an apprenticeship. Apprenticeship has now been replaced by the experience of law school. Does law school produce better lawyers than the apprenticeship system did? It is possible that law schools teach *more* law than it was possible to learn under the apprenticeship system. It is certain that law schools allow the production of more *lawyers* than the apprenticeship system did. It is also certain that the law schools do a worse job of teaching matters of "practice" than the apprenticeships did.

The law schools' failure to teach "practice" is pointed out again and again in examinations of the schools' performance. Some schools have acted upon these criticisms, but not in a big way. By and large, practice continues to be relegated to secondary status in law schools. Unless students have had a summer clerkship with a firm or some other "useful" experience, they are likely not even to know how to write or file an affidavit. When a situation militates so persistently against the interests of the group it nominally serves, we probably should examine the politics of the institution, specifically at how those within the institution get on within it. Teaching practice is not how one gets on in law school, any more than it is in English departments.

Writing is, of course, a matter of practice.[4] When it comes to writing, outcome for law students may well be worse than it is with respect to other matters of practice. Recent graduates from law school will not deny that they do not yet know much about legal practice, and they may be concerned about this. They are not nearly as likely to be concerned about what they do not know about writing. And worse, what they do "know" about writing from their experiences in law school may well put them in a worse position as writers than would simple ignorance.

Writing is not directly addressed in most law schools in any forum beyond a short course taught the first year which also teaches how to find things in the library. With respect to writing, the course teaches how to cite authorities and produce legal memoranda and briefs in the proper form, but if it gets very far beyond that—to consider the writing process, or the rhetoric of brief writing, for example—it does so only glancingly.

The real writing that is done in law school—the writing that really counts—is exam writing, for exams that are given once at the end of the course. This kind of writing provides the worst kind of model for the writing that lawyers actually

---

[3] I will be using "writer" and "poet" interchangeably in this essay. It may be inferred, then, that I intend to extend the conception of writer beyond that of "transcriber of thoughts" or "communicater," and I intend not to restrict the conception of poet to one who writes in rhyme. We could use the terms "maker" or "composer," if they did not seem so idiosyncratic.

[4] This is not to say that it is merely a matter of "skill" as this term is usually understood.

do. Typically, the exams describe a fact situation and ask students to set out the rights and duties of the parties. The aim in such writing is coverage. Students learn that professors will not infrequently tick off the "issues" that a student mentions in her writing, and add up the ticks for a grade. Students believe that in this situation more is better, even if that more cannot be convincingly or coherently related to the situation presented. In most cases, they are right, in the context of the law school, though not in the practice of law.

Practicing lawyers will write memoranda and briefs, all right, but if they write them well, it will not be primarily because they know how to cite cases in the proper form. And memoranda and briefs will be but a small part of what most lawyers will write. Neither in these memoranda and briefs nor in the other things they write will more necessarily be better. Often it will be worse.

In law school, students have little interest, however, in how lawyers actually write, and still less interest in any argument that lawyers are writers in the way that poets are writers. They will think about that sort of thing, they tell themselves, after they have passed the Big One—the bar exam—if indeed they will have to give much thought at all after that to the business of writing—after all, when they are lawyers, they will have secretaries. There is not much—usually nothing—in law school that would challenge such assumptions, not much—usually nothing—that is intended to let students discover what is at stake for them as writers in the practice of law.

The students who do well on their exams may be allowed another kind of writing experience—the experience of writing pieces for the journal known as *The Law Review*. While this kind of writing is very much like the writing that law professors do, it bears scant relation to what most lawyers do. Law review articles typically "cover" an area of the law, and criticize the reasoning of judges. Unlike exams, law review articles may make an authentic argumentative point—concerning legislation that ought to be proposed, for example. But this kind of writing distances itself from particular situations and actual clients. The principal readership for law review writing is other law professors, not other lawyers, not clients, and not judges needing to decide a case. Students with law review experience writing their first memoranda as clerks in a law office will frequently have to "unlearn" their impulse to "cover" a point of law. Writing for the law review does expand the writerly horizon of the ordinary law student. But as an experience of writing, the law review does little to let students in on what lawyers do as writers, and what, as writers, they might do.

Given the kind of environment for writing that most law schools provide, it is not surprising that many beginning lawyers believe that writing is reducible to a formalism. How far this assumption can go is illustrated by the true story of the young lawyer who asked the experienced general practitioner if he had a form for the facts. The experienced lawyer's response offers an elegant critique: He told the young lawyer to sit down and write her mother (whom he assumed the young lawyer probably owed a letter to anyway) and tell her what the facts of the case were. That, he said, will give you the form.

## PROFESSIONALIZING DISCOURSE

I have been hard here on law school concerning what it teaches about writing. But if law school is a machine for mystifying writing, it may not be worse in this respect than many other educational settings that are designed to professionalize students, including English departments.

The language suggests a tension between being a "professional" and being a "poet." To call someone a professional is ordinarily a term of praise. To call a poet a "professional poet," however, would be to suggest that the person in question presents the appearance of being a poet without really being one—wearing puffy-sleeved shirts open at the throat and haunting the moors, that sort of thing. It seems just a bit much to write "poet" in the blank on the loan application that calls for one's occupation. There is no such problem with writing "lawyer" there, though "attorney" might be preferred as conferring a more refined quality, the difference here, linguistically speaking, being the difference between "cow" and "beef" (the one from Germanic and the other from Latinate roots).

So the language suggests that to become a professional may be to deny poetry, or at any rate to run a risk of doing so. Let us explore some of the ways this tension gets worked out for lawyers.

Whatever else it might mean to become a member of such a profession, it means at least that one has "acquired" a special language. It is very nearly a commonplace that acquiring a language in this way is not just to acquire a "tool," if we think of a tool as something we simply use for our own independent purposes. It is now commonly acknowledged that we acquire our purposes, to no negligible extent, from our language, even though we may continue to act as if our language were simply the servant of our autonomous intentions.

Law students are in the process of acquiring this special language. Their naive use of legal terminology can be endearing to those who can remember growing into this language; it makes them tedious in the extreme to people who do not have this sympathy. They will use legal terminology in any company, as if the meanings should be obvious to all, in the hope (and it is not a vain one) that if they use the expressions enough, their meanings will become clearer to themselves. Outsiders—that is, other kinds of students—are usually spared this apparent rudeness: Law students associate mostly with other law students. They are not just learning "terminology," of course; they are learning to think of themselves as different from others. This is not a perversity in them: law schools take measures to separate themselves from the rest of the university. Their buildings are usually separated from the main campus, and law schools usually have separate mailing addresses, even when there is no reason for one.

George Bernard Shaw seems to have thought of the professions as social evils. He called all professions "conspiracies against the laity."[5] There is a little of Dick Butcher in this claim. If we considered this assertion a theory of what causes our

---

[5] It is not Shaw but the character Sir Patrick Cullen, a doctor, who says so in the *Doctor's Dilemma*, Act I. But this is a character we are entitled to identify more closely with Shaw than most.

problems with legal writing (and writing by other professionals, including English professors), we would have to conclude that our problems arise because lawyers are consciously trying to make trouble for us.

I would not want to deny that some of the problems nonlawyers have with legal writing, and with other kinds of professional writing, may be attributable to conspiracy, to intentional efforts to mystify readers. But my experience with lawyers and judges convinces me that, just as with our students, the larger proportion of our difficulties comes not from the fact the writer herself is a mystifier so much as that she is mystified. This assumption produces a different idea of what to do with a lawyer. Mystifiers (and conspirators) need to be convinced, not just with reasoned argument but with threats and punishments perhaps, that they should not do that sort of thing. Those who are mystified present a different kind of problem. When the problem is mystification in the writer, it is not evil intentions that must be dealt with. Nor is the problem simple ignorance. Was it Will Rogers who said that most of the time the problem is not what we don't know, but what we do know that ain't so? On the first day of my job as a clerk in the U.S. Court of Appeals for the Ninth Circuit, Judge Chambers, my boss, introduced me to another judge as follows: "This is John Warnock. He's been in school for the last twenty-one years. He's got a lot to unlearn." Those who are mystified do not need fixed; they need freed.

But when the lawyers are free of mystification, can we expect that the language of the law will appear in "plain" English? Dick Butcher would insist on it, but I think this is not possible, not if we grant that lawyers know something that the rest of us do not, or know what they know in a way that the rest of us do not. We grant this to poets; we do not assume that poetry can be made plain to everyone everywhere all the time. We need to grant this to lawyers too.

"Fee simple" is an expression that means something to a lawyer that it does not mean to someone who is not a lawyer. So is the term "burglary," even though, unlike "fee simple," it is a word in common use. A claim that there has been a burglary raises questions in a lawyer's mind about whether a place was actually broken into, whether it was a dwelling place, whether the break-in took place at night. The difference in the meaning such a term has for lawyers and for nonlawyers is not the sort of thing that can be eliminated by the non-lawyer looking up the expression in Black's dictionary of legal terms. The words "fee simple" carry with them a history of extended conversations to which the lawyer has gained at least some access. These conversations raise questions and may introduce other expressions, like "a cloud on the title" and "the rule against perpetuities." No advocate of plain English should assume that such expressions can be rendered perfectly transparent to everyone, though it is of course fair enough to ask a lawyer to realize this too, and to respond appropriately in the situations in which she is using such expressions.

Surely, we can get rid of the "legalisms," however. We might define a "legalism" as an obscure use of legal terminology that performs only the function of announcing itself as legal terminology. Even so, legalisms may not be dispensable. "Why," a lawyer was once asked, "do you write 'Last Will and Testament'?

Don't 'will' and 'testament' mean the same thing?" "I don't know why," was the reply. "But I'm damn sure not going to change it. If I do, something is sure to go wrong."[6]

The lawyer's point is a point of practical rhetoric; it is not invalidated by pointing out that the expression "Will and Testament" is one of those yokings of the Anglo-Saxon and the French that run through the common law because Norman French became the language of the law courts in England after the Norman Conquest. I have had lawyers defend language to me that they knew was not as clear and economical and nonlegalistic as it might be on the grounds that the other lawyers working on this complex deal were used to it and if they changed it, those other lawyers would want to know why, and the deal might not go down. We should note that, in their eyes, they were not just serving other lawyers by not improving the language; they were serving their client.

It is not just lawyers who insist on "difficult" legal language. We the readers sometimes demand it. We want all the magic that might attach to the ritual incantation. We want the "whereas's" and the "comes now's" and the "fee simple's." Now that's language worth paying for. And some mystified readers do think that more language is better because it is more: I have met lawyers who think some judges weigh arguments by the pound. A story is told that the famous jurist Elihu Root was asked to explain a $1,000 bill for a one-page will. "Happy to oblige," he replied. The explanation read as follows: "For Writing Will—$100. For Knowing What to Write—$900." The story carries an unwelcome suggestion that knowing and writing are two entirely separate undertakings, but it does remind us not just that brevity may require more time, but that sometimes one must dare to be brief.

## FICTION IN THE DISCOURSE OF LAW AND POETRY

Perhaps, then, legal language cannot in the last analysis be made "plain." But this is far from saying that the lack of plainness we find in legal language is what gives it its kinship to poetry. To discover that kinship, we need to shift perspective and look at legal language in terms of its relationship to discourse communities.

The forging of group identity as against those not part of the group comes with any process of professionalization, whether in boot camp or medical school or in a Ph.D. program in English. Group identity may well pose a threat to poetry; it is certainly the case that poetry poses a kind of threat to group identity. Or rather, it threatens the aspect of group identity that is given, conventional, if we think of poetry as that which escapes from the conventional through the exercise of a vital principle. Poetry invites new identifications.

This reflection points to a danger in identifying good writing with meeting the requirements of particular discourse communities. The notion of discourse community may be useful in that it allows us to criticize writing in law schools in

[6]This is a story I have from Jim Raymond who told it at a seminar on judgment writing we and others were teaching. The seminar was sponsored by the Canadian Institute for the Administration of Justice.

terms of its relation to writing outside law schools. It could also be useful in criticizing the world of English studies in relation to other worlds of writing. But "discourse community" is also a notion that could lead us into a pedagogical mistake, if it is writing we are after.

When we analyze the world into different discourse communities, we can argue that to get along in a particular discourse community (say "college," or "law school," or "the corporate world," or even "the pop world"), you need to know the conventions of the particular community. Observing these conventions is what allows us to belong to a community, and to perform appropriately in it.

We see it argued that much nonwriting, particularly as we see it in the work of our students, is a result of their ignorance of established conventions. But what do we imagine is the status of these conventions? Do we wish to suggest that they are naturally given, or if not that, that they are established in such a way that we may treat them as brute facts? It seems to me that much of the nonwriting I see in the academy and in the world of the law can be blamed on taking one or another convention as a brute fact rather than as a cultural and rhetorical artifact. To our long-suffering freshmen we may say "No, you do not always have to avoid 'I' in your writing; No, you do not have to begin your final paragraph with 'In conclusion'; No, you do not have to summarize your paper in your conclusion . . . etc." This seems less a matter of acquainting students with the conventions of good writing than of clearing away what they have been taught to think of as conventional. The experience does not encourage one to assume that there exists somewhere a set of conventions that would be the "right" one and that would permit students to do writing in the situations in which they will find themselves.

For a number of reasons, first-year law students are entirely sold on the idea that writing is "just" a matter of learning the conventions. I have discovered that it is next to impossible, in the context of law school, to unsell them on this idea. This is also true, I have found, of the kinds of students who are placed in honors programs. In both cases, it is likely that the students are under such pressure to "succeed" that they need for it to be true that writing is just a matter of learning the conventions. If this were true, then they would be able to "master" writing. They are good at learning conventions; that is what got them where they are.

None of what has just been said entitles us to doubt that it is sometimes helpful to view language as a conventional system. It is no doubt true that in the academy, as in the schools the students came from, and in the outside world, there are people who will demand this or that conventional formalism out of a sense that it amounts to writing, or perhaps that they are serving their students because such formalisms are "what you'll be asked for later." The five-paragraph theme is the obvious and all-too-easy example here; "the expository essay" might also be adduced.

I think we place our students in a better position to deal with such situations not by teaching the conventions as if they could suffice, but by teaching students to ask the kinds of questions that will allow them to recognize particular practices as "merely" conventional, a recognition that will put them in a better position to write for meaning in the situations in which they find themselves. Students who would write must learn to criticize their situations in this way, not merely accommodate to them.

The same point must be made with respect to lawyers and judges. Most judges these days have "learned" that they should begin an opinion with an extended statement of the facts, even though they can be made to understand immediately that in the usual case neither the reader nor the judge herself can know what facts need to be recited and why until the issue in the case is specified. Lawyers will begin a letter to a bereaved wife with "Enclosed you will find the following documents . . ." rather than "Your late husband's will should allow us to distribute his estate with little delay. As part of the process, we would like you to sign the documents I have enclosed." The problem in this instance is not a problem of style, and it is not a problem of not following conventions that have to be learned before they can be followed. It is a failure of rhetorical imagination, a failure to remember that the reader of this letter is a worried widow, and a failure to ask what you would want her to read first. It is when the imagination fails in this way that letters become conventional exercises, rather than a matter of someone saying something to someone.

Still less does a knowledge of the conventions of a discourse community or of psycholinguistic principles governing style seem adequate to account for the graceful moments, as when the student revises the description of a teacher from "tough but fair" to "tough and fair."[7]

Notions of "discourse community" and "convention" can, if we let them, purport to place us *outside* the world of writing, in the position of the analyst, making us "the one who knows," rather than the one who, like one's students, *writes*. But here an aspiring consultant might want to ask: If the English professor is not "the one who knows," who is going to want to ask one to be a consultant? I suppose we could say that the English professor we are discussing here, the writer who teaches writing, is one who knows that he or she knows not. I have to admit that that is not much of a selling point, though I regard it as a crucial criterion of a good writing consultant.

It is not that as a writing consultant you know *nothing,* of course. There is a lot that we ought to know or ought to know how to figure out—how to form the plural of "testatrix," for example. We should know the psycholinguistic research on readability. If we are to deal with lawyers, we should know the scheme of arrangement of a classical oration, since variations (and perversions) of that scheme lie behind a good many of the conventions that one finds operating in legal argument. We should know the usefulness of certain questions, like: Who's going to read this? What do they need here? We should know the research into the composing process that confirms the fact that writing is not merely a means of communication, but a uniquely powerful means of thought, and we should know how to help writers get rid of impediments to that power. But first of all we should

---

[7]This is an example I have from William Coles. See his extraordinary essay on writing, "Writing as Literacy: An Alternative to Losing" in *The Plural I—And After*, Portsmouth, N.H.: Boynton/Cook-Heinemann, 1988.

know the status of any such knowledge when it comes to writing, that it does not really count as knowledge of how to write.

Law firms, like many others, including our students, frequently think that what they want when it come to writing is "one who knows." They do not know that if they got what they wanted, they would not want it. The point is not that our various schemes for containing writing are necessarily harmful to writing. We must hope that these schemes are not necessarily harmful, since they are unavoidable. We are bound to develop such schemes when we, even as readers of our own writing, attempt to come to terms with our discourses. The point is that if we want to write, these schemes must be kept from defining writing for us. To a writer, they can have no status other than as one of the resources we have available to us, a kind of scaffolding we might use to get a temporary purchase on something that is quite beyond the reach of any of these schemes.

## FICTION AND THE DISCOURSE OF THE LAW

I agree with those who argue that the world within which law is practiced is to an extraordinary extent a fiction. This is not to trivialize the world in which law is practiced, not to say that it is *just* a fiction. It is to emphasize that it is a *made* world, one that has been created, that is maintained, and that may be changed, by human action in discourse.

The same is of course true of the world of literature. We do not have to go as far as some *littérateurs* have and claim that the world *is* literature. For our purposes, it is enough to say that the world *of* literature is fictional in the same way that the world of the law is fictional. We are not proposing that these worlds are identical—only that they share this fictional nature.

Discourse takes place in a world, a culture. Discourse does not simply flow *from* culture, however; it also flows *into* it. If discourse is determined by culture, it is also true that culture is constituted by discourse. If Shakespeare's plays were determined by the culture in which they were produced, it is also true that his culture, and ours, was to some extent created by virtue of his plays. This point about the status of discourse is not new, but it is frequently lost sight of in worlds, including the academic world, where we facilely divide utterance into the "objective" and the "subjective," the "expository" and the "personal" or "creative," where we assume that *langue* is given and *parole* entirely derivative from it.[8]

Lawyers and poets both do discourse that does not take, that cannot take, its discourse community as given. Neither operates just *within* particular communities. Lawyers come into play—and this is part of what accounts for the animosity nonlawyers tend to have toward them—when particular discourse communities (from marriages to nations) prove inadequate to situations. I do not think we stretch the comparison too far when we recognize that lawyers and poets both

---

[8]The distinctions are from Ferdinand de Saussure, *Course in General Linguistics*, ed. Charles Bally and Albert Sechehaye in collab. with Albert Riedlinger, trans. Wade Baskin, New York: McGraw-Hill, 1966.

make, or remake, community in situations where communities have been found not to perform adequately in the terms the culture provides. The truth of this claim is quite clear in some cases: when a lawyer draws a contract or a will, she constitutes a relationship between parties that alters their previous relationship, and to some extent creates a specific future for the parties in relation to each other. It is a future the parties did not have before the lawyer wrote, and before they assented to what the lawyer wrote. This is true whether the document is a contract to buy a television set on the installment plan, or the Constitution of the United States.

We are arguing that poets and lawyers remake discourse communities or the world. But poets are called needlessly difficult, and lawyers are often blamed for sowing the seeds of discord. Poets seem to thrive on extremity; discord is what makes money for lawyers. Without denying that some lawyers do try to create strife for their own benefit in spite of professional ethics, it seems clear that blaming lawyers for discord is like blaming messengers for the bad news. The lawyer suing someone on behalf of a client who has been injured in an accident may ask in the initiatory pleadings that his client be "made whole" with an award of damages. The agon begins in a situation where wholeness has already been found lacking. The agon of the trial does not create strife where none was before; it stands in the place of other struggles that might take place in the absence of this kind of recourse, with someone who "suffered an injustice" deciding to "take the law into her own hands." Trials are offered as an option more likely to produce wholeness.

After the trial, it is not likely that everyone will be happy. Lawyers are the first to acknowledge that probably *no* one will be happy, except perhaps the winning lawyer and the judge. But happiness is not the aim in a trial, any more than it is the aim of poetry. A new order is the aim. Not perfection, but something that will suffice. Not heaven on earth, but a strategy satisfactory for encompassing a situation.

Lawyers, then, like poets, need an approach to discourse that recognizes the need to depart from discourse that has proved inadequate to encompass particular situations. From this point of departure, lawyers must make a new discourse that will suffice, using whatever resources they may have. Furthermore, for lawyers and poets, it is not enough, finally, if this discourse suffices among fellow specialists. It must suffice both in terms of the ways lawyers and poets talk among themselves, and in terms of the ways lawyers and poets talk to those who are not lawyers and poets.

The position of the lawyer as a maker in a fictional world is excellently developed in several works by James Boyd White.[9] In *The Legal Imagination*, White uses examples from texts as diverse as Shakespeare's *Troilus and Cressida* and the U.S. Army's sniper's manual, demonstrating that the discourse of lawyers creates worlds within which "to practice law" acquires one or another meaning.

---

[9] *The Legal Imagination*, Little Brown, 1973, abbreviated edition by the University of Chicago Press, 1986; *Heracles' Bow: Essays on the Rhetoric and Poetics of Law*, University of Wisconsin Press, 1985; *When Words Lose Their Meaning: Constitutions and Re-constitutions of Language, Character, and Community*, University of Chicago Press, 1985.

Lawyers are not completely free in their discourse to make the law in any way at all, of course, any more than poets are completely free to make their fictions in any way at all. But in the language they choose, lawyers, like poets, to a significant extent make the worlds within which their actions have meaning. In the law, then, as in poetry, and perhaps even in criticism, we need to ask not just whether the point is clear but: What is the world that is made in this discourse? What is it made in the name of?

In consulting to lawyers, I do not speak to them in the terms I have used here. Nor would one in the ordinary case expect to talk to a poet in this way. Lawyers and poets are both too deeply involved in making, usually, to take much interest in such talk. But I have found it important and sometimes deeply consoling to the judges and lawyers I have worked with to begin by telling them that, as I see it, they are not just technicians when it comes to writing, and that I do not intend to deal with them as if what they were lacking is simple linguistic or rhetorical know-how. The fact is, I tell them, that judges and lawyers are writers, real writers—or might be.

This is good news and bad news, I may go on briefly to tell them. It is good news because it says that in your writing you can expect the rewards that can come to writers, intrinsically, from the work they do. And it is the intrinsic rewards, we should realize, that keep writers writing. Writers know that the extrinsic rewards—wealth, fame, winning the case—are no sure thing, no matter how good the writing. Because of this, we should beware of the definitions of writing that beg the question: Writing is "communication," writing is "persuasion." To a writer, there will be little pleasure in communicating foolishness. The best argument does not always persuade the judge, or the appellate judge: Lawyers know this full well. We do have reason to hope that taking care with writing will make us more communicative or persuasive. But the real payoff is not in that coin. As a Canadian judge I have worked with put it in a speech to his colleagues on the bench: "What it means is, you'll be *right* more often." He may have been saying simply that you will be reversed less frequently on appeal, but his voice said that this was not the most important criterion. He was claiming that something even more important than this was at stake.

The bad news, if it is that, is that a writer is only what you and I might become, never what we are. We will not learn to write in the sense I mean by learning anyone's set of rules for writing. Neither will we learn to write by mastering the conventions of any discourse community. We will come to write only by deciding to use everything we can in the effort to write, and by refusing to accept the substitutes for writing that the world is ever asking us to accept in the place of writing.

The language of a specialized group in a culture will necessarily pose problems to members of the culture not in the group. Indeed, many specialized groups come to be viewed as such *because* their language is special. The special quality may amount to no more than self-serving mystification, but it may also be this special quality that justifies the special status of the group.

We do not think of poets as constituting a group in the way that "the bar" does, but it is not just the existence of groups that accounts for our difficulties in understanding. Acts of language will pose difficulties for people to the extent that they are referrable to an unshared history. This is true even as we contemplate our own drafts, since the words we write are not only ours. In discourse, this unshared history trembles on a high wire: Is an act of language merely individual and idiosyncratic, or is it one of those acts of language that helps reconstitute the ways in which we all may live in relation to each other? At the point of utterance, we do not know. Neither do we know at the point of reception. What we know is the struggle—the struggle toward meaning.

No consultant from "English" will be hired to tell lawyers just how they should be remaking the fictional world of the law. But before writers can remake a world well, they must at least realize that remaking is what they are doing. Consultants from English can, and should, remind lawyers of their kinship to the poets, and remind them also that in world-making, what is at stake is the world.

# RHETORIC AS BRICOLAGE: THEORY AND ITS LIMITS IN LEGAL AND OTHER SORTS OF DISCOURSE

*James C. Raymond*
University of Alabama

*James C. Raymond is the author of* Writing (Is an Unnatural Act) *(Harper & Row), coauthor, with Ronald L. Goldfarb, of* Clear Understandings: A Guide to Legal Writing *(Random House), and editor of* Literacy as a Human Problem *(University of Alabama Press). He is currently professor of English at the University of Alabama, director of the Freshman English Program, and editor of* College English. *He has conducted numerous seminars on legal writing for judges and attorneys in the United States and Canada.*

Among composition teachers, the relationship between theory and practice is a sensitive issue. On the one hand, composition teachers are useless if they are not practitioners. On the other, they can be conduits of misinformation if they fail to examine the assumptions that govern their practice. In addition, composition teachers generally cannot earn tenure in places that require research unless they publish work that makes a gesture toward at least one of the various definitions of theory that have gained tacit acceptance in the academy.

Hence the ambivalence toward theory: composition teachers feel entitled to claim the vast tradition of rhetorical theory from the pre-Socratic rhetoricians to Kenneth Burke as part of their discipline or to borrow models and methods from quasi-scientific fields; and they feel equally entitled to criticize models for their reductiveness and theoreticians for indulging in an abstruse discourse with little apparent connection to pedagogy.

"Theory," of course, has no standard definition. Etymologically it is a metaphor that, over the centuries, has ceased to seem metaphorical. The Greek *theoria* refers to the view of the spectator, the theater patron, the outsider, the onlooker. One would imagine that being an observer of the action rather than a participant in it would be advantageous in some ways, disadvantageous in others. Eventually, however, theory became paired with praxis as its opposite, rather than with participation; and it became not just an alternative perspective but the preferred perspective. In the sixth century A.D., when Lady Philosophy appears to Boethius in *The Consolation of Philosophy* (130–131), the two Greek letters on her gown—theta (for *theoria*), pi (for praxis)—need no explanation. Nor does the significance of their relative positions: the theta at the top, the pi near the hemline.

In the recent past, theory in literature has meant the quest for explanatory models—with Northrop Frye in Canada and the structuralists elsewhere attempting in various ways to make literary criticism a respectable science by devising models within which diversity could be explained and disagreement resolved. These attempts eventually yielded to their own antithesis, the discovery that literature resists theory. We have long known that every grammar—every attempt to treat language as a logical code—leaks. Rhetoric and criticism, a fortiori, are porous beyond patching. Paradoxically, the cure for our professional obsession with theory seems to be in those discussions currently associated with the term "critical theory." Theory, it seems, has been its own antidote.

What follows is neither an attack on theory nor a defense of it. It is an exploration and application of the metaphor Claude Lévi-Strauss used in *The Savage Mind* to distinguish what might be called systematic knowledge from what might be called mythical knowledge—the knowledge of the engineer as compared with the less orderly and more subtle art of the *bricoleur*, the fixit person, the Jack or Jill of all trades who gets the job done with whatever odds and ends are at hand. The image is Lévi-Strauss's; but it is Derrida who makes bricolage respectable, using the term to correct Lévi-Strauss for his tendency to reduce myth to system—to invent the "engineering" of mythology—when in fact bricolage would provide the better metaphor for scholarship in the human sciences ("Structure," 255–256).

I will begin by conceding that all theoretical models of the universe of discourse—that is to say, all models and methods from antiquity to the present—are in some way defective. They all achieve whatever explanatory power they have at the expense of exclusions—the sort of "blindness" de Man describes as the price of insight. These defects, however, are scandalous only if one believes in the possibility of a theoretical model without limitations. If we accept rhetoric as bricolage—if we regard it as a collection of perspectives that yield useful insights in this situation or that, but always partial insights, never the whole truth—if we assume, as Derrida seems to assume, that language and literature and writing of all kinds are packed with their own resistance to theory, then perhaps we can begin to assemble and test likely tools, learning their limitations instead of resenting them, abandoning the theory envy that motivates much of our research and makes it inevitably vulnerable to counterexamples and logical subterfuge.

Instead of arguing for rhetoric as bricolage (an unwinnable argument in any case), I will illustrate what I mean with examples drawn from my involvement in another field resistant to theory: law. The rhetorical bricolage I will describe below is effective, I think, in working with the particular sort of student I have taught in a particular discourse situation—that in which judges write decisions. But it is also useful as a critique of the relationship between theory, pedagogy, and research within the academy.

## I. BRICOLAGE IN LEGAL WRITING: RHETORIC I

By Rhetoric I, I mean old-style rhetoric—practical writing lessons that presume a traditional, commonsense theory of language (language as container into which ideas are packed by one person and unpacked by another). Although the concept of bricolage is born of something I will call Rhetoric II, even Rhetoric I works better if bricolage is its dominant metaphor. (Rhetoric II will be discussed under III, below.)

One durable bit of bricolage is that fragment of the once current and traditional rhetoric, the familiar four modes of discourse generally attributed to Alexander Bain. Everyone knows that the modes—description, narration, exposition, and persuasion—are theoretically bankrupt. They rarely if ever exist in pure form. It is hard to imagine narration without descriptive elements; and while there might be description without narration, description rarely exists for its own sake, innocent of some persuasive or explanatory purpose. As categories, the modes overlap. As genres, they are artificial. They have been analyzed by Andrea Lunsford, historicized by Robert Connors, and dismissed by Cy Knoblauch and Lil Brannon. As a theoretical model they are beyond defense. And like all grand rhetorical schemes, they are questionable as pedagogical tools, but only if we assume that rhetorical theory can and ought to achieve the conceptual economy of physics or engineering.

Still they are valuable as pedagogical bricolage. Judges need to be taught narration and description—each for a different reason: narration, because every judgment contains a narrative section that judges find surprisingly difficult to organize; description, because it requires a principle of selection that judges tend to overlook.

Every decision has to tell a story, usually near the beginning: somebody did something wrong (or allegedly did something allegedly wrong) either to someone else or to society at large. No reader unfamiliar with the case will be able to understand the court's decision unless it is presented in the context of this elemental story. For many judges, organizing narrative is a formidable chore. When they write, they jot down whatever events surface in the record and in their memories, the relevant and irrelevant alike, arranged in whatever sequence that happens to emerge rather than in the actual order of occurrence. The result is an artless stream of consciousness, meandering back and forth in time without the shifts in tense and mood that would make the story coherent. It is a problem that has an easy solution: arrange the passage chronologically.

Here, for example, is a passage written by a state supreme court judge who had been given a set of facts as an exercise:

> The Court decided that it had authority to issue the writ. The parents of Julie Necaise asked the Court to issue a writ of habeas corpus ordering the Church of the

Moon to bring forth their daughter so that they could determine whether she was being restrained by psychological coercion. A hearing was held to determine whether the writ shall be issued. The Court refused to issue the writ because the Necaises had not established that the Church of the Moon was restraining their daughter by psychological means. Evidence was heard as to whether the Court had jurisdiction in the matter. The Court decided that it did have jurisdiction.

Diagnosing the major problem in this paragraph is easy enough: instead of arranging the events in chronological order, the judge has jumbled them. The first event in the series is mentioned in the second sentence, the second event in the third sentence, the third event in the fifth sentence, the fourth event in two sentences, the first and the sixth, and the last event in the fourth sentence. Revising the paragraph, then, is simply a matter of eliminating the repetition, arranging the sentences in chronological order, and correcting the modality ("should" for "shall"):

The parents of Julie Necaise asked the Court to issue a writ of habeas corpus ordering the Church of the Moon to bring forth their daughter so that they could determine whether she was being restrained by psychological coercion. A hearing was held to determine whether the writ should be issued. Evidence was heard as to whether the court had jurisdiction in the matter. The court decided that it did have jurisdiction. It refused to issue the writ because the Necaises had not established that the Church of the Moon was restraining their daughter by psychological means.

To teach narrative as chronological arrangement is, of course, to suggest a model that can account for only a small part of published narrative, and not well. Even the least experimental writers stray from past, to present, to future, to an ahistorical, eternal present ("Lovers always discover . . ."), to a hypothetical past ("If only he had . . .") with an easy and unnoticed grace. Here, for example, is a passage from "Gift of the Magi," selected because O. Henry, as far as I know, has never been accused of dabbling in experimental forms:

Della finished her cry and attended to her cheeks with the powder rag. She stood by the window and looked out dully at a gray cat walking a gray fence in a gray backyard. Tomorrow would be Christmas Day and she had only $1.87 with which to buy Jim a present. She had been saving every penny she could for months, with this result. Twenty dollars a week doesn't go far. Expenses had been greater than she had calculated. They always are. Only $1.87 to buy a present for Jim. Her Jim. Many a happy hour she had spent planning for something nice for him. Something fine and rare and sterling—something just a little bit near to being worthy of the honor of being owned by Jim. [14]

The first two sentences are in simple past tense, arranged in chronological order. The third leaps to the future ("Tomorrow") in the first clause, and back to the simple past ("she had") in the second. The fourth sentence ("She had been saving") moves back to a remote past; the fifth to an eternal present ("Twenty dollars . . . doesn't go very far"); the sixth to the remote past ("Expenses had been"); the seventh to an eternal present ("They always are"); the eighth and ninth are verbless but seem to be associated with Della's state of consciousness in a simple past; the tenth refers to a remote past; the eleventh and twelfth are verbless and could be as easily associated with Della's consciousness in the remote past, when she had been planning, as with the simple past, in which her plans are apparently frustrated.

If ordinary narrative is so complex, how can we justify telling judges (or other students) that narrative is best arranged in chronological order? One justification would be that ordinary narrative is not really ordinary. It just looks that way. Narrative as ostensibly straightforward as O. Henry's requires, among other things, a command of verbal modalities and sequences of tenses that is beyond the reach of ordinary writers, even those who are well educated and for the most part well above average in intelligence. When judges attempt narrative of this sort, they run afoul of a bewildering set of conventions that grammarians may know by rule and gifted writers by ear. Judges, being neither grammarians nor, for the most part, gifted as writers are best served by learning to cast their narratives in chronological order, in which the simple past and the indicative mode will generally suffice and their intuitions will likely guide them to whatever nonindicative modes the story may require.

Organization, oddly enough, is not a problem for judges when they attempt to write description. In fact, organization is rarely a problem for any writers, even college students, when they describe—unless we, as teachers and critics, impose upon them the a priori assumption that descriptive passages need to be logically ordered. Most descriptive passages in literature are not logically ordered; they are arranged randomly, or associatively, or in some sequence calculated to have a particular rhetorical effect quite apart from the perception of coherence. They do not proceed from top to bottom or left to right or outside to inside or in any logical arrangement. Of course, it is possible to find examples of orderly description in literary writing, but like chronological order in narrative, these are the exceptions rather than the rule. The rule is to accumulate descriptive details that enable readers to make whatever judgment the writer wants the reader to make, and to arrange these details in any order that suits the writer's purpose—logical, spatial, climatic, anticlimactic, arbitrary, associative, or even entirely random.

Here is the scene O. Henry describes in "The Furnished Room." The author's purpose, apparently, is to portray the room as a place that in current parlance would be called tacky. He achieves this effect by describing one item in the room after another with frequent cues to indicate that each is beneath the writer's good taste, and presumably the reader's as well.

> The mantel's chastely severe outline was ingloriously veiled behind some pert drapery drawn rakishly askew like the sashes of the Amazonian ballet. Upon it was some desolate flotsam cast aside by the room's marooned when a lucky sail had borne them to a fresh port—a trifling vase or two, pictures of actresses, a medicine bottle, some stray cards out of a deck. Upon the gay-papered wall were those pictures that pursue the homeless one from house to house—The Huguenot Lovers, The First

Quarrel, The Wedding Breakfast, Psyche at the Fountain. A polychromatic rug like some brilliant-flowered rectangular, tropical islet lay surrounded by a billowy sea of soiled matting.

With one exception, the sentences in this paragraph would seem equally coherent in any sequence; the one exception is the sentence beginning "Upon it," which must follow the sentence in which the referent for "it" occurs. Otherwise, any order will do.[1] The passage is perceived as coherent because of a convention that allows writers to describe things in random order. Neither artificial order nor transitional words and connectives are required by this convention (though, of course, they could and often do occur). The convention may be related to the fact that things—the stuff of description—exist synchronically (rather than in sequence) in the world as we perceive it; and because we are accustomed to perceiving items and various parts of items as synchronic phenomena, we do not require them to be ordered on paper.

The major focus of attention in teaching description to judges is not organization but selection. The need for a descriptive passage arises when a judgment on some particular issue depends upon physical or psychological details that can be conveyed in sensible imagery—when, for example, the judge assigns custody of a child to an agency rather than to abusive parents; or when the environment in which a crime is committed would alter the psychological state of the assailant in ways that would make the act seem either more reprehensible or less; or when the issue is whether an arresting officer could have identified contraband without trespassing, warrantless, on the defendant's private property. The purpose of descriptive passages in judgment writing is always the same: to enable readers to reach the same conclusion that the judge has reached after seeing or imagining a particular set of physical or psychological details. With this purpose in mind, judges have a definite and practical criterion for evaluating the passage. Does it convey the details that lead to the conclusion the judge has reached? Does it describe the welts and cuts and bruises that justify separating a child from parents to whom it is bound by deep, if irrational, affection? Does it convey the sense of terror that the defendant might have felt in the dark and deserted parking lot where she fired upon three men who later claimed they were only playing a joke? Does it enable the reader to see that the marijuana was growing within three feet of property to which the arresting officer had been legally invited? The details will seem coherent in virtually any sequence (though, of course, some sequences may be more effective than others for reasons other than coherence).

The rhetoric of bricolage does not mean rejecting models or methods outright; it does mean turning a blind eye, deliberately, to whatever a particular model does not adequately account for in general in order to exploit what it does account for in a given situation. It means taking advantage of bits and pieces of rhetorical lore whenever they seem to work, even though they invariably lack the elegance and universality of theory. It means borrowing from any theoretical model—Aristotle's, Bain's, Burke's, Kinneavey's, Moffett's, Flower and Hayes's—whatever the model can explain, *but not ignoring its limitations, not imagining that is a universal theory, a model without holes.*

The last two modes, persuasion and exposition, are not part of my bricolage for teaching judges because in judgment writing the distinction between the two has little to do with the structure or substance of the text and everything to do with the relative positions of writer and reader, neither of which can be altered by the judge. In forensic writing, the difference between these two modes is a matter of perspective. For the litigants, the trial court's decision is an explanation; for appellate court, an argument. Logic in judgments always takes the same form—the derivation of a conclusion from a particular set of facts (the minor premise) viewed in the context of a controlling law or principle (the major premise). The same syllogism, the same text has to operate in both modes at once. This is not to say that the distinction between these two modes is always irrelevant. It would be useful, for example, in teaching attorneys who write ostensibly persuasive documents, such as briefs and motions. But in the practice of the law there is this paradox to contend with: persuasion is best achieved when arguments are made to seem explanations rather than arguments.

## II. CAUSES AND CONSEQUENCES

The dissolution of distinctions traditionally presumed to be "objective" is precisely what makes the perfection of theory impossible. In fact, the difference between subject and object is itself among the distinctions dissolved in the evolution of structuralism (the quest for models) into poststructuralism (which accepts as a given that perfect models, at least in what the French call *les sciences humaines,* are unattainable).

Despite rumors to the contrary, deconstruction does not replace objectivity with subjectivity; it questions the dichotomy itself. What we once imagined as a clear and distinct polarity between the two turns out to be neither clear nor distinct. The dichotomy is still useful as a model, a metaphor, but only in the way that other theoretical models are useful—explanatory in some situations, obfuscatory in others. Other metaphors might work just as well to describe the relationship between perception and whatever lies beyond it, though these metaphors, too, would have their limitations. We might well, in fact, develop multiple metaphors—like the physicist's models for light, particle, and wave—contradictory, but each necessary to account for aspects of a phenomenon that is not quite either and not quite both.

In rhetoric, the merging of subject and object means that the reader (who may also be the writer) is inseparable from the text. The text conceived of as an object completely independent of readers, writers, contexts, and other texts is only the shadow of a text, featureless and unintelligible. With the recognition that subject and object are inseparable, that subjects have no way of perceiving things directly as they are, the possibility of text as pure object disappears—and with it the possibility of a universally persuasive model for constructing or interpreting texts.

Also altered in this scheme of things is the traditional distinction between words and ideas—the notion that language is a container for shipping ideas from one person to another. This container metaphor is not rendered useless: it just becomes, like all other metaphors in a collection of bricolage, a tool that sometimes works rather than a model of the way things are. We can still ask students (and judges and our colleagues, for that matter) what they *mean* by a passage we find unintelligible, and they, indeed, may find this a useful question. But we can no longer ask this question unaware, at least tacitly, that it presupposes a metaphor for language which, like all models, is both enabling and disabling. The disabling side is what it conceals: that there can be no ideas without language (or some other set of signs) and that ideas are therefore subject to the conditions of language.

The implications of this last observation are unsettling. Words have proved themselves capable of resisting all rational control. They always trail meanings of which we are unaware or that we perhaps do not intend even if we know them. If ideas are subject to the conditions of language and if language refuses to behave itself as an orderly system, what does this do to the assumption that everyone has access to some fundamental set of universal ideas on the basis of which we can reason our way to the resolution of all disagreements?

Finally, the distinction mentioned in the first paragraph of this essay, between theory and practice, turns out to be a rational construct, a metaphor like all others, useful only sometimes. It is still a useful distinction in certain circumstances; it still describes, however crudely, what we experience as two different enterprises; but as with all other distinctions of this sort, the boundary is imaginary. Practice, even for unthinking practitioners, always has a theory built into it; and theories—models—always arise from and return to practice, where they are susceptible to confirmation or disconfirmation.

The metaphor of bricolage does not explain the relationship between theory and practice; it is an alternative metaphor. It is certainly not the only possible alternative to the challenge deconstruction poses for theory; other possibilities range from sheer skepticism to sheer denial. As a metaphor, bricolage appeals to me not because it is perfect but because it fits my own experience as a practitioner who dabbles in theory and finds it always unsatisfactory and often useful anyway. My preference for this metaphor is itself the sort of choice a *bricoleur* would make, not an engineer.

## III. RHETORIC II

Rhetoric I might be called practical rhetoric or commonsense rhetoric. It presumes, among other things, the following:

1. That language is a collection of words, each independent of the other, and each with its proper meaning
2. That distinctions at the base of philosophy (subject/object, theory/practice, word/meaning) are real distinctions, not just rational or symbolic constructs

3. That all true knowledge is the result of sound logic proceeding from solid first principles
4. That all disputes can be resolved by applying logic to locate formal or material fallacies in an argument

Rhetoric II is based on a different set of assumptions. It presumes, among other things, the following:

1. That language is not a collection of independent signs but a system of differences in which each sign is susceptible to a multitude of interpretations
2. That the distinctions upon which philosophy is based are metaphors, symbolic constructs whose relationship to reality is imperfect or, in any event, not completely knowable
3. That all knowledge, even scientific knowledge, is based, ultimately, upon assumptions that cannot be proven
4. That because our knowledge is based upon assumptions and because language is an inherently ambiguous system, logic is often insufficient for resolving disputes

Rhetoric I and Rhetoric II also differ in the model of human consciousness (or personality) each presupposes. Rhetoric I operates as if human consciousness were independent of language; Rhetoric II presumes that consciousness is itself constructed by language, so that each individual is defined by his or her participation in the range of thoughts and values provided by a particular language in a particular environment. For Rhetoric II, even individuality is in large part a social construct, a system of differences.

No one can "prove" that Rhetoric II is superior to Rhetoric I. We can, of course, adduce contexts in which one rhetoric or the other will seem more acceptable, but we can never prove that either is intrinsically superior. In fact, one postulate of Rhetoric II is that things of this sort are beyond proof. We subscribe to one rhetoric or the other for reasons that cannot be entirely rational. One or the other strikes us as a plausible description of the way things work, and there's an end on it.

The *bricoleur* is happy to exploit either or both whenever they work. The law, for example, is built on a fiction based in Rhetoric I. As a society, we agree to pretend that within each human being is a rational, independent consciousness, not a social construct; without that presumption, we could never bring ourselves to punish people who violate the law. We also agree to pretend that judges can determine the true meaning of texts that any number of readers and even the writer might interpret differently; we agree to pretend that judges can glean the true facts from a glut of conflicting testimony. As long as we are working within this fiction (which turns out to be reasonable and necessary for any sort of social order), it makes sense to discuss judgment writing within the boundaries of Rhetoric I.

But Rhetoric I is a dangerous construct if we ever forget that it is a fiction.

It breeds a sense of certitude that brooks no opposition, an intolerance that views dissent as either ignorant or evil. It is, as Barthes might say, a "repressive discourse" ("Écrivains," 14), a discourse that achieves that appearance of balance, objectivity, and closure by concealing bias, unprovable assumptions, contrary or uncertain data.

The genius of the Anglo-American judicial system is that it projects an illusion of determinacy, reaching closure even on unanswerable questions so we can get on with our lives, while as a system it remains perpetually indeterminate. It gives the appearance of certitude, though in fact it operates from an inexhaustible reserve of inconclusiveness. Every decision is provisional. Each court can be overruled by a higher court. And even the highest court can, if it chooses, overrule itself (though, for the sake of civil order, it may take pains to disguise its inconsistency). Individual courts operate within Rhetoric I; the system as a whole is an institutionalization of Rhetoric II. Though it may be small comfort for individuals whose lives or fortunes may be ruined while the ideologues are in control of the courts, in the long run the courts themselves can recover from periods of control by ideologues.

## IV. CONCLUSION

Heady stuff, this untheory, this nonmethod we call bricolage—not necessarily difficult to understand, but difficult to accept because it radically alters the presuppositions we thought we needed for responsible teaching and research. Still less responsible, though, would be to teach without examining assumptions or to conduct research without recognizing the limits of theory. Much of it boils down to a couple of questions about every model or method, whether elaborated as a theory or implicit in our practice: What does this model (or method) overlook in order to achieve its elegance? And under what circumstances would it be useful anyway?

Bricolage does not mean ignoring empirical data. On the contrary, it means testing every generality against whatever data are available, not in the hope that one day a model or method will be achieved that perfectly matches or manipulates the data but in the expectation that despite inevitable mismatches, models can be useful if we know their blind spots. And unlike classical empiricism, bricolage respects subjective data on the theory that perception is no less real than whatever hides behind it (though the possibility of purely subjective data has disappeared along with the possibility of pure objectivity).

The *rhetoric* of bricolage—the practice of simultaneously exploiting and resisting generalizations—has implications for research and pedagogy. It resists the desire for panaceas (heuristics, sentence-combining, journals, free writing, collaborative learning, computerized instruction, diagrams of *the* writing process) and exploits home remedies (heuristics, sentence-combining, journals, free writing, collaborative learning, computerized instruction, diagrams of *a* writing process) whenever they work, knowing full well that they will be useless at times and even harmful in the wrong circumstances. Invention, for example, is not a problem for all writers. Judges do not need invention; they need a heuristic thresher to winnow the necessary from the irrelevant. Invention is a problem for students because students are forced to write even if they have no problem that only writing can solve, no ideas that cannot be expressed more easily by speaking, and no absent audience they particularly want to reach. When other adults find themselves in this situation, they do not turn to heuristics. They just do not write.

Rhetoric as bricolage means making peace with the fact that virtually every assertion we might make about writing can be true only in some circumstances and from certain perspectives. It also means that every assertion about virtually anything can be true only in some circumstances and from certain perspectives.

Some readers will regard the indeterminacy of this sort of rhetoric as a step toward nihilism. Others will regard it as the beginning of a cure for misunderstanding. It is nihilistic only in the sense that science itself is nihilistic—not a collection of established truths but a collection of hypotheses awaiting disconfirmation. "[T]he engineer and the scientist," as Derrida observes, "are also *bricoleurs*" ("Structure," 256). Progress in science is the discovery of blind spots in prevailing theories. In Rhetoric II, the cure for disagreement is precisely the same: discovering blind spots in the theories that govern us and our opponents. In some instances we may be required to amend our own theories; in others, to find acceptable data or shared assumptions that will lead our opponents to amend theirs. Often neither resolution is possible. For this reason, theories and political systems work best if, like the courts, they remain capable of subverting themselves.

The academy, of course, resists bricolage. Like the cultural and political systems that support it, the university is committed to the supposition that the goal of academic inquiry is objectivity. Bricolage seems like a return to mythology, an abandonment of science.

Specifically, if we abandon the belief in or even the quest for universally compelling theories, how would we tell the good bricoleurs from the bad ones? If we admit that good writing and bad are always, to some extent, consequences of circumstance, how can we claim to distinguish good writers from bad, or good writing teachers from bad ones?

In exactly the same way we tell good novels, good paintings, good houses, good people, good governments from bad ones. Where there are no compelling models, there is always room and necessity for debate. It is ironic that within the academy we sometimes accept the compulsion for objectivity (in evaluating the quality of writing programs, for example), whereas in analogous enterprises outside the academy (evaluating the quality of publishing houses or journals, for example), we comfortably resist the supposition of a theoretical model by which they might be judged. The fact that there are no objective criteria is not nearly as frightening as the possibility that someday people would pretend to know what the models are, thereby closing off the conversation that keeps art and culture alive and prevents disciplines from substituting orthodoxy for inquiry. Bricolage does, in fact, abandon the Platonic and scholastic concepts of truth as the correspondence of ideas with realities. In its place, "truth" is regarded as a process rather than a state, a continuous testing of concepts against phenomena.

It is in this context that Roland Barthes (18) makes sense when he recommends a style of teaching that is content to "confuse the Law" *("désorienter la Loi")*. The purpose of a teaching is not to convey final theory but to examine, constantly and communally, whatever theories are at the root of our judgments.

## Notes

1. In point of fact, the example in the text above is not presented as it occurs in O. Henry's text—the hope being that even resisting readers will admit that they found the revised version sufficiently coherent, not suspecting the revision. The original sequence, which appears below, may be preferred for any number of esthetic or rhetorical reasons; but it is neither less nor more coherent than the revised sequence.

    A polychromatic rug like some brilliant-flowered rectangular, tropical islet lay surrounded by a billowy sea of soiled matting. Upon the gay-papered wall were those pictures that pursue the homeless one from house to house—The Huguenot Lovers, The First Quarrel, The Wedding Breakfast, Psyche at the Fountain. The mantel's chastely severe outline was ingloriously veiled behind some pert drapery drawn rakishly askew like the sashes of the Amazonian ballet. Upon it was some desolate flotsam cast aside by the room's marooned when a lucky sail had born them to a fresh port—a trifling vase or two, pictures of actresses, a medicine bottle, some stray cards out of a deck. [21]

## Works Cited

Barthes, Roland. *"Écrivains, Intellectuels, Professeurs." Tel Quel* 47 (Fall 1971): 3–18.
Boethius, *The Theological Tractates; The Consolation of Philosophy*. Trans. H. F. Stewart and E. K. Rand. Cambridge, Mass.: Harvard University Press, 1968.
Connors, Robert. "The Rise and Fall of the Modes of Discourse." *CCC* 32 (1981): 444–463.
deMan, Paul. *Blindness and Insight: Essays in the Rhetoric of Contemporary Criticism*. 2nd ed., rev. Minneapolis: University of Minnesota Press, 1983.
Derrida, Jacques. "Structure, Sign, and Play in the Discourse of the Human Sciences." In *The Languages of Criticism and the Sciences of Man; The Structuralist Controversy*. Ed. Richard Macksey and Eugenio Donato. Baltimore: Johns Hopkins Press, 1970. pp. 247–265.
Knoblauch, C. H., and Lil Brannon. *Rhetorical Traditions and the Teaching of Writing*. Upper Montclair, N.J.: Boynton, 1984.
Lévi-Strauss, Claude. *The Savage Mind*. Chicago: University of Chicago Press, 1966.
Lunsford, Andrea A. "Alexander Bain's Contributions to Discourse Theory." *College English* 44 (1982): 290–300.
Porter, William Sydney (O. Henry). "The Furnished Room." In *Surprises: 20 Stories by O. Henry*. Richard Corbin and Ned E. Hoops, eds. New York: Dell, 1966. pp. 19–25.
———. "The Gift of the Magi." In *Surprises: 20 Stories by O. Henry*. Richard Corbin and Ned E. Hoops, eds. New York: Dell, 1966. pp. 13–18.

## DATE DUE

| 11:1816050 6/10/89 | | | |
|---|---|---|---|
| | | | |
| | | | |
| | | | |
| | | | |
| | | | |
| | | | |
| | | | |
| | | | |
| | | | |
| | | | |
| | | | |
| | | | |
| | | | |
| | | | |

The Library Store #47-0103